ASIAN ICONOGRAPHY SERIES III

# Sādhanamālā: Avalokiteśvara Section

## Sanskrit and Tibetan Texts

**Ruriko Sakuma**

ADROIT PUBLISHERS
Delhi-110 053

*Published by*
ADROIT PUBLISHERS
C-8/2, Yamuna Vihar, Delhi-110 053
Phone: 3266030, 3242552

*Distributors*
AKHIL BOOK DISTRIBUTORS
4675/21, Ganpati Bhawan, Ansari Road,
Darya Ganj, New Delhi-110 002
Phones : 3266030, 3242552
e-mail: akhilbooks@yahoo.com



ISBN : 81-87392-37-1

*Printed in India on behalf of M/s Adroit Publishers by*
Arpit Printographers, B-7, Saraswati Complex,
Subhash Chowk, Laxmi Nagar, Delhi-110 092

# Table of Contents

# Preface

The *Sādhanamālā* (*SM*) is one of the most important materials for the study of visualization of Tantric Buddhist deities. B. Bhattacharyya edited the *SM* in 1925 (Vol. I) and 1928 (Vol. II). Since then, his edition has been regarded as the standard edition of the *SM*. Although there are about forty manuscripts of the *SM* around the world, the edition is based on the only eight which were available in those days. The present work aims at providing a critical edition of the *SM* by using manuscripts not employed in the Bhattacharyya edition.

This volume, Asian Iconography Series III, includes the *sādhana*s of Avalokiteśvara. *Sādhana* is a religious practice of visualizing a deity. Bodhisattva Avalokiteśvara is one of the most popular Buddhist deities in Asian countries, such as India, Tibet, Nepal, China and Japan. The Bodhisattva has been worshipped as a symbol of compassion by non-Tantric and Tantric Buddhists from laymen to educated monks.

Tibetan translations of the *SM* have been regarded as the authoritative *sādhana* collections in Tibetan Buddhism. For example, the Sakya pa chapter of the *Grub mtha' śel gyi me loṅ* (*A Crystal Mirror of Systematic Doctrines*), which was written by Thu'u bkwan Blo bzaṅ chos kyi ñi ma (A.D.1737-1802), refers to one of the translations of the *SM*: *sGrub thabs rgya mtsho*. This Tibetan translation is mentioned as one of the basic instructions of the Sakya sect. We should not overlook that a study of the *SM* also has great importance to Tibetan Buddhism.

This work is part of my doctoral dissertation submitted to Nagoya University, Japan. I am grateful to have been awarded Grant-in-Aid for Encouragement of Young Scientists: no. 09710014, 1997-1998 (The Ministry of Education, Science, Sports and Culture, Japan) for a study on the Avalokiteśvara section of the *SM*. My special thanks are due to Prof. Junsho Kato (Nagoya University, Japan), Prof. Toshihiro Wada (Nagoya University, Japan) and Prof. Musashi Tachikawa (National Museum of Ethnology, Japan), who have encouraged me to accomplish my dissertation. I also wish to express my gratitude to Dr. Fujio Taniguchi (Nagoya Women's University) and Prof. Gudrun Bühnemann (Wisconsin University, U.S.A.) for helpful suggestions.

Nagoya
2001

Ruriko Sakuma

# I Introduction

The *Sādhanamālā* (*SM*)(*Sādhanasamuccaya, Sādhanamālātantra* or *Sādhanatantra)*[1] is a compilation of sādhanas which were individually written not later than circa the twelfth century A.D. As the *SM* has been revised again and again, we can find various versions of it today. Although each version has a different number of sādhanas and a different way of arranging them, theSM has been dealt with as a compilation on the whole.

Over the past decades, scholars have studied the *SM* by using the Bhattacharyya edition of Gaėkwad's Oriental Series,[2] but it would be difficult to say that a critical edition of the SM has been fully made. Some manuscripts which were not used in the Bhattacharyya edition have become available in recent years. Now, we have succeeded in locating thirty-eight manuscripts around the world.

This volume furnishes a critical edition of the Avalokiteśvara section, by utilizing ten Sanskrit manuscripts. Among them, nine were not used in the Bhattacharyya edition.[3] Although all the manuscripts have many scribal mistakes, we provide correct, different or alternative renderings in comparison with the Bhattacharyya edition. Furthermore, this volume also furnishes Tibetan translations. These translations are mainly based on the Peking edition and the Ningma edition of the sDe dge. Additionally, the Taipei edition has been used.

The above mentioned thirty-eight Sanskrit manuscripts may be listed in the following 14 groups:

(1) 8 manuscripts used in the Bhattacharyya edition.
(2) 4 manuscripts preserved at Tokyo University.
(3) 5 manuscripts preserved at Kyoto University.
(4) 8 manuscripts preserved at the National Archives of Nepal (Two of them used in the Bhattacharyya edition).
(5) 3 manuscripts recorded in A Microfilm Catalogue of the Buddhist Manuscripts in Nepal.
(6) 2 manuscripts preserved at the National Library, Paris.
(7) 3 manuscripts preserved at the University of Cambridge (Two of them used in the Bhattacharyya edition).
(8) A manuscript introduced by L. Finot.
(9) 2 manuscripts preserved at the Asiatic Society, Bombay
(10) 3 manuscripts preserved at the old Bir Library, Kathmandu (Two of them can be found in the National Archives of Nepal).
(11) A manuscript preserved at the China Library of Nationalities, Beijing.

---

1 Manuscripts (2-3) and (3-5) are titled *Sādhanasamuccaya*. Manuscripts (1-8), (2-1), (2-2), (2-3), (2-4), (3-4), (3-5), (4-2), (5-3), (7-1) and (12-2) are titled *Sādhanasamuccaya* in catalogues and so on. Manuscripts (1-2), (1-3) and (14) are titled *Sādhanamālātantra.* One manuscript, (3-3), is titled *Sādhanatantra* in catalogues. there are two titles, *Sādhanamālā* and *Sādhanamālā-pañjikāsahitā* in one manuscript, (4-1). One manuscript, (4-4), is titled *Sādhanamālā-tathā-dhāraṇī.* One manuscript, (10-1), is titled *Sādhanamālā-prathamakaṇḍa.*

2 [Thomas 1903], [Foucher 1905: 22-39], [Finot 1934], [Mallmann 1964: 187-241], [Koetsuka 1967], [Shimizu 1977], [Yoshizaki 1979], [Shimoizumi 1981], [Meisezahl 1980: 125-173], [Nihom 1992], [Mori 1992], [[Bühnemann 1994], [Sakuma 1990a; 1990b; 1991; 1993; 1995; 1996; 1998; 1999; 2001b], [Yamaguchi 1997], [Okuyama 1998]. Researches of the *Sādhanamālā* are summarized by Tsukamoto, Matsunaga, Isoda [1989: 382-485].

3 See list of the manuscripts (pp. 15-19).

(12) 2 manuscripts preserved at the Institute of Advanced Studies of World Religion, New York.
(13) A manuscript preserved at the Melville Memorial Library, the State University of New York.
(14) A manuscript preserved at the Bodleian Library, Oxford University.

We shall now look concisely at some of the characteristics of the Sanskrit manuscripts in the above groups.[1]

(1) (1-1) ~ (1-8) are based on the introduction of the Bhattacharyya edition [Bhattacharyya 1968b: preface XI-XV], *Catalogue of the Buddhist Sanskrit Manuscripts in the University Library, Cambridge [Bendall 1883], A Catalogue of Palm leaf and Selected Paper MSS belonging to the Durbar Library, Nepal, Vol. II [Hara Prasad Śāstri 1915], A Descriptive Catalogue of Sanskrit Manuscripts in the Government Collection Under the Care of the Asiatic Society of Bengal, Vol*. I [Hara Prasad Shāstri 1917] and references of Bühnemann [1994]. (Codes from A to Nb are used in the Bhattacharyya edition.)

(1-1) <A> This is preserved at the Asiatic Society, Calcutta. It is recorded as no. 74 and titled *Sādhanamālā* in the Hara Prasad Shāstri catalogue [1917: 114]. It is made of modern Nepalese paper. It has 342 folios. Complete.

(1-2) <B> This is preserved at the University of Cambridge. It is recorded as Add. no. 1686 and titled *Sādhanamālātantra* in the Bendall catalogue [1883: 174]. As the manuscript lacks a colophon, we cannot know the title. It is reconstructed as *Sādhanaśatapañcāśat*[2] by Thomas [1903: 2] on the basis of the Tibetan title: *sGrubs thabs brgya daṅ lṅa bcu.*[3] It is made of palm leaf. The date of the manuscript is Nepal Saṃvat 285 (A.D. 1165).[4] It was reprinted by Bühnemann [1994: 61-69].

(1-3) <C> This is preserved at the University of Cambridge. It is recorded as no. 1593 and titled *Sādhanamālātantra* in the Bendall catalogue [1883]. There is a title *Sādhanamālā* in the colophon. It is made of paper. The date of the manuscript is Nepal Saṃvat 939 (A.D. 1819).

(1-4) <N> This is preserved at the Asiatic Society, Calcutta. It is recorded as III. 387 in the Hara Prasad Śāstri catalogue [1915: 83], and titled *Sādhanamālā*. It is made of palm leaf. Judging from the scripts, the date of the manuscript is considered to be late thirteenth century A.D.

(1-5) <Ab> This is preserved at the Asiatic Society, Calcutta. It is recorded as no. 111 in the Hara Prasad Shāstri catalogue [1917]. It is made of palm leaf. Judging from the scripts, the date seems to be about the twelfth century A.D.

(1-6) <Ba> This is recorded as no. 112 in the Hara Prasad Shāstri catalogue [1917]. There are letters sā and mā on the margin of every page. The letters suggest the title *Sādhanamālā*.

---

1 For further information, see "Sanskrit Manuscripts of the *Sādhanamālā* "[Sakuma 2001a].

2 Bühnemann [1994: 18-19] suggests that this is a *sādhana* collection which is different from the *Sādhananmālā.*

3 The Tibetan title is actually *sGrub thabs brgya rtsa* which suggests the Sanskrit title *Sādhanaśataka.* However, the Tanjur index confirms that this *sādhana* collection includes about 150 *sādhanas.* Accordingly, Thomas assumes that the Tibetan title is more correctly *sGrubs thabs brgya daṅ lṅa bcu.*

4 The date is Nepal Saṃvat 287 (1167 A.D.) according to Bendall [1883: 174]. But Bhattacharyya [1968b: 93 (note 6)] corrects it as Nepal Saṃvat 285.

*The* date of the manuscript is Nepal Saṃvat 224 (A.D. 1104), but it seems to have been copied about 300 years ago.

(1-7) <Na> This was preserved at the old Durbar Library, Kathmandu. It is recorded as no. 603 in the old Durbar Library. There is a title *Sādhanamālā* in the colophon. It is made of paper. There are 150 sādhanas. The date of the manuscript is A.D. 1958.

(1-8) <Nb> This is recorded as III. 324 B in the Hara Prasad Śāstri catalogue [1915: 200-206]. It was preserved at the old Durbar Library. The title *Sādhanasamuccaya* is found in the colophon of every sādhana. There are 118 folios and 166 sādhanas.

(2) Four manuscripts are recorded as nos. 451-454 in *A Catalogue of the Sanskrit Manuscripts in Tokyo University Library* [Matsunami 1965: 161-162, 265-274]. (2-1) ~ (2-4) are based on the Matsunami catalogue [1965]. Yoshizaki [1979: 15-31] clarified the correlation between the four manuscripts and three kinds of Tibetan translations.

(2-1) No. 451 (old no. 318) is titled *Sādhanasamuccaya.* It is made of paper, and has 237 folios.

(2-2) No. 452 (old no. 332) is titled *Sādhanasamuccaya,* but another title *Sādhanamālā* is written in fol. 1a. It is made of paper, and has 168 folios.

(2-3) No. 453 (old no. 443) is titled *Sādhanasamuccaya.* It is made of paper, and has 237 folios. The date of the manuscript is Nepal Saṃvat 752 (A.D. 1632).

(2-4) No. 454 (old no. 569) is titled *Sādhanasamuccaya.* It is made of paper, and has 23 folios.

(3) Five manuscripts are recorded as nos. 117-121 in *A Succinct Catalogue of the Sanskrit Manuscripts in the possession of the Faculty of Letters, Kyoto University* [Goshima and Noguchi 1983: 35, 40-51]. (3-1) ~ (3-5) are based on Goshima and Noguchi [1983] and Shimoizumi [1981: 136-137].

(3-1) No. 117 is titled *Sādhanamālā.* It is made of paper, and has 126 folios and 201 sādhanas.

(3-2) No. 118 is titled *Sādhanamālā.* It is made of paper, and has 67 folios and 129 sādhanas.

(3-3) No. 119 is titled *Sādhanatantra.* It is made of paper. It has 354 folios and 301 sādhanas. Complete. The date of the manuscript is Nepal Saṃvat 862 (A.D. 1742).

(3-4) No. 120 is titled *Sādhanasamuccaya.* It is made of paper, and has 210 folios and 168 sādhanas.

(3-5) No. 121 is titled *Sādhanasamuccaya.* It is made of paper, and has 154 folios and about 100 sādhanas.

(4) Eight manuscripts are preserved at the National Archives of Nepal. They are recorded as III. 387 and III. 324 B in the Hara Prasad Śāstri catalogue [1915: 83-84, 200-206], as nos. 3-387, 4-603, 4-338 and 3-324 in *Nepālarājakīya-Vīrapustakālayasthapustakānāṃ Saṃkṣiptasūcīpatram* [*Pūrṇaratnavajrācārya Sāhityaśāstriṇā 1964*], as nos. 3-387 and 3-324 in *Nepālarājakīya-Vīrapustakālayasthapustakānāṃ Bṛhatsūcīpatram* [*Pūrṇa-ratnavajrācārya Sāhityaśāstriṇā 1967*], as no. pra 1697 kha 2 vi 169, no. tṛ 324, no. tṛ 387, no. tṛ 397-1,[1] no. tṛ 603, no. tṛ 693, no. pan 250 and no. C 396 in *A Catalogue of the Buddhist Tantric Manuscripts in the National Archives of Nepal and Kesar Library* [Moriguchi 1989: 134], and as III. 324 B and III. 3871 in A Concordance of H. P. Śāstri's Catalogue of the Durbar Library and the Microfilms of the Nepal-German Manuscript Preservation Project [Grünendahl 1989: CIII, LXXXV] .

---

1 Moriguchi [1989: 134] lists this no. as the manuscript of reel no. B24/11, but part of no. 3-387 is recorded on reel no. B24/11.

(4-1) No. 3-387 is titled *Sādhanamālā* or *Sādhanamālāpañjikāsahitā.* It is made of palm leaf. This is used in the Bhattacharyya edition: (1-4), but different renderings are sometimes found in comparison with the Bhattacharyya edition. According to the Hara Prasad Śāstri catalogue [1915: 83-84, 264-271], there are 258 folios and 256 sādhanas. The manuscript is recorded on microfilm on reel number (B 24/11), according to the Nepal-German manuscript preservation project [Grünendahl 1989: LXXXV] .

(4-1-1) Microfilm reel no. A936/15. *Sādhanamālā* with pañjikā. There are 112 folios.

(4-1-2) Microfilm reel no. 24/12. *Sādhanamālā-pañjikāsahitā.* There are 102 folios.

(4-1-3) Microfilm reel no. 24/11. *Sādhanamālā.* There are 151 folios and 147 sādhanas.

(4-2) No. 3-324 (no. 3-324 B) is titled *Sādhanamasuccaya.* This is identical to (1-8).

(4-3) No. 3-603 (Microfilm reel no. A129/2) is titled *Sādhanamālā.* It is made of paper. There are 258 folios.

(4-4) No. 4-338 (Microfilm reel no. B107/22) is titled *Sādhanamālā, Sādhanamālā-tathā-dhāraṇī or Sādhanamālā-tathā-dhāraṇī-saṃgraha* [Moriguchi 1989: 134]. It is made of paper. There are 116 folios (97 folios [Moriguchi 1989]). Incomplete.

(4-5) No. pra 1697 kha 2 vi 169 is titled *Sādhanamālā or Sādhanasamuccaya.* It is made of palm leaf. There are 5 folios. Incomplete.

(4-6) No. tṛ 693 (Microfilm reel nos. A59/22, A60/1) is titled *Sādhanamālā* or *Sādhanasamuccaya.* It is made of palm leaf. There are 109 folios.

(4-7) No. pan 250 (Microfilm reel no. B105/9) is titled *Sādhanamālā* or *Sādhanasamuccaya.* It is made of paper. There are 133 folios.

(4-8) No. c 396 (Microfilm reel no. C42/8) is titled *Sādhanamālā* or *Sādhanasamuccaya.* It is made of paper. There are 357 folios.

(5) Three manuscripts, KA 30, CA 26 and DH 201, are recorded in *A Microfilm Catalogue of the Buddhist Manuscripts in Nepal* [Takaoka 1981].

(5-1) KA 30 (Microfilm reel no. R-KA3) is titled *Sādhanamālā.*[1] It is made of paper. There are 299 folios and 300 sādhanas. Complete.

(5-2) CA26 (Microfilm reel no. R-CA3) is titled *Sādhanamālā.* It is made of paper. There are 192 folios. Complete.

(5-3) DH 201 (Microfilm reel no. R-DH5) is titled *Sādhanasamuccaya.* It is made of paper. There are 186 folios and 168 sādhanas. Complete.

(6) Two manuscripts are preserved at the National Library, Paris. Mallmann [1964: 13, 187-215] edited sādhanas of the Mañjuśrī section using them. (6-1) and (6-2) are based on *Catalogue du Fonds Sanscrit,* Fascicule I [Filliozat 1941: 91-92].

(6-1) Sanskrit 151 is titled *Sādhanamālā.* It is made of paper. There are 173 folios. The date of the manuscript is Nepal Saṃvat 956 (=A.D. 1836).

(6-2) Sanskrit 152 is titled *Sādhanamālā.* It is identified with the manuscript Dev(anāgarī) 123, referred to by Foucher [1905: 6-7]. It is made of paper. There are 193 folios. The date of the manuscript is the nineteenth century A.D.

(7) Three manuscripts are preserved at the University of Cambridge. Two of them, (1-2) and (1-3), are used in the Bhattacharyya edition.

---

1 This title is written in the manuscript, but the letters following it are illegible.

(7-1) Add. 1648 is titled *Sādhanasamuccaya.* It is made of palm leaf. There are 228 folios.The date of the manuscript is the year 336, in the reign of King Alimalladeva (A.D. 1216).[1] Foucher [1905: 16-100] edited and translated the iconographical descriptions of the sādhanas by using the three manuscripts and (6-2).

(8) Finot [1934: 1-86] edited and translated a manuscript in "Manuscrits Sanscrits de Sādhanas retrouvés en Chine." *Journal Asiatique* 225. The manuscript was found by H. Maspero in a Chinese temple, P'ou-ngan sseu . It is made of palm leaf, and includes nos. 217, 252 and 253 of the Bhattacharyya edition [Yamada 1959: 206][Koetsuka 1967: 72].

(9) Two manuscripts are preserved at the Asiatic Society, Bombay [Bhattacharyya 1968b: preface XIV]. (9-1) and (9-2) are based on references of Bühnemann [1994: 19] and our research.

(9-1) Buddhist MSS-16 BI 203 is titled *Sādhanamālā.* It is made of paper. There are 44 folios. Complete. The date of the manuscript is Nepal Saṃvat 993 (A.D. 1873).

(9-2) Buddhist MSS-17 BI 207 is titled *Sādhanamālā.* It is made of paper. There are 44 folios. Complete. The date of the manuscript is Nepal Saṃvat 993 (A.D. 1873).

(10) Three manuscripts were preserved at the old Bir Library, Kathmandu. The manuscripts are recorded as no. 209 in The Buddhist Manuscripts of the Bir Library [Sanskrit Seminar of Taisho University 1955: 75]. Two of them, (4-2) and (4-6), are found in the National Archives of Nepal.

(10-1) The other manuscript apart from (4-2) and (4-6) is titled *Sādhanamālā-prathamakhaṇḍa.* It is made of paper. There are 177 folios.

(11) A manuscript is preserved at the China Library of Nationalities, Beijing. It is recorded as Manuscript 140. Bühnemann [1994: 37-58] reprinted this manuscript. As it lacks a colophon, we cannot know the title. Bühnemann [1994: 31] recontructs it as *Sādhanaśataka,*[2] which is attested to by Bu ston, the Blue Annals and the later Tibetan tradition. It is made of palm leaf. There are 40 folios and 90 sādhanas.

(12) 2 manuscripts are preserved at the Institute of Advanced Studies of World Religion, New York [Bühnemann 1994: 21]. They are recorded as MBB-I-123 and MBB-II-43 in *Buddhist Sanskrit Manuscripts: A Title List of the Microfilm Collection of the Institute of Advanced Studies of World Religion,* 1975. (12-1) and (12-2) are based on research of the Microfilm Project of the Institute of Advanced Studies of World Religion.

(12-1) MBB-I-123 is titled *Sādhanamālā.* It is made of paper. The manuscript was copied in Nepal Saṃvat 757 (A.D. 1637). There are 310 folios and 38 sādhanas. Complete.

(12-2) MBB-II-43 is titled *Sādhanasamuccaya.* It is made of paper. There are 186 folios.

(13) A manuscript is preserved at the Melville Memorial Library, the State University of New York. Meisezahl [1980: 136-157] edited and translated two sādhanas using this manuscript. The date is Nepal Saṃvat 747 (=A.D. 1627).

(14) A manuscript is preserved at the Bodleian Library, Oxford University [Bühnemann 1994: 21]. It is recorded as no. 1455-Ms. Sansk. c. 16 (R) in *the Catalogue of Sanskrit Manuscripts in the Bodleian Library,* Vol. II, begun by M. Winternitz, continued and completed by A.B. Keith, Oxford, 1905. The manuscript is titled *Sādhanamālātantra.* It is made of palm leaf. Incomplete.

---

1 The date of the manuscript is verified by the calendar [Petech 1984: 81]. Bendall [1883: 154-155] reads the date as 336, but points out a possibility of 226 as well. Foucher [1905: 6] reads 336 as 226.

2 Bühnemann [1994: 18-19] suggests that this is a sādhana collection which is different from the *Sādhanamālā.*

# Sanskrit Texts

## List of Manuscripts

In editing the texts, we utilize ten Sanskrit manuscripts. All except one (N1) are not used in the Bhattacharyya edition.

Meisezahl edited the Sanskrit texts on the list, 3, 7.2, 14, by using five manuscripts. These are the four preserved at Tokyo University, nos. 451-454, and the one preserved at the Melville Memorial Library (the State University of New York).

In order to denote the above-mentioned manuscripts and editions, the following abbreviations are used in the list and the footnotes of the texts.

B: Bhattacharyya edition
TO1: Manuscript preserved at Tokyo University, [Matsunami 1965: no. 451]. See (2-1) in the introduction.
TO2: Ditto, [Matsunami 1965: no. 452]. See (2-2) in the introduction.
TO3: Ditto, [Matsunami 1965: no. 453]. See (2-3) in the introduction.
TO4: Ditto, [Matsunami 1965: no. 454]. See (2-4) in the introduction.
K1: Manuscript preserved at Kyoto University, [Goshima and Noguchi 1983: no. 119]. See (3-3) in the introduction.
K2: Ditto, [Goshima and Noguchi 1983: no. 120]. See (3-4) in the introduction.
N1: Manuscript preserved at the National Archives of Nepal, [Moriguchi 1989: no. 3-387 (Reel no. B24/11)]. See (4-1-3) in the introduction.
N2: Ditto, [Moriguchi 1989: no. 3-603]. See (4-3) in the introduction. There are many lacunas in the manuscript, but it is important as it includes sādhana 10.3, which is not found in the Bhattacharyya edition. The manuscript is only used for this sādhana 10.3.
BL1: Manuscript recorded in *A Microfilm Catalogue of the Buddhist Manuscripts in Nepal,* [Takaoka 1981: DH 201]. See (5-3) in the introduction.
BL2: Ditto, [Takaoka 1981: KA30]. See (5-1) in the introduction.
M: [Meisezahl 1980: 136-157].

The following list shows the folio-numbers corresponding to the Sanskrit texts. The arrangement of the sādhanas on the list is different from that of the Bhattacharyya edition.

A dotted line indicates the absence of the corresponding sādhana. An underlining means that the corresponding sādhana is not used.

1 Lokanāthasādhana

| no. | B no. | TO1 | TO2 | TO3 | TO4 |
|---|---|---|---|---|---|
| 1.1 | 8 | 13b4-14a1 | 10a5-7 | 13b4-14a1 | 9a4-7 |
| 1.2 | 18 | 19b1-6 | 14a5-7 | 19b2-20a1 | 13a1-8 |
| 1.3 | 19 | 19b6-20a2 | 14a7-9 | 20a1-2 | 13a8-10 |

| no. | B no. | K1 | K2 | N1 | BL1 | BL2 |
|---|---|---|---|---|---|---|
| 1.1 | 8 | 24b2-6 | --- | 15b6-16a3 | ---- | 16a3-7 |
| 1.2 | 18 | 34b5-35b1 | ---- | 23a1-4 | ---- | 22b6-23a6 |
| 1.3 | 19 | 35b1-4 | ---- | 23a4-6 | ---- | 23a6-b1 |

2 Khasarpaṇalokeśvarasādhana

| no. | B no. | TO1 | TO2 | TO3 | TO4 |
|---|---|---|---|---|---|
| 2.1 | 13 | 15a5-b3 | 11a7-b3 | 15a5-b3 | 10a5-11 |
| 2.2 | 14 | 15b3-17a5 | 11b3-12b6 | 15b3-17a5 | 10a11-11b1 |
| 2.3 | 15 | 17a5-18b4 | 12b6-13b3 | 17b5-18b3 | 11b1-12a11 |
| 2.4 | 16 | - - - - | - - - - | - - - - | - - - - |
| 2.5 | 24 | 21a4-24b1 | 15a2-17a7 | 21a4-24b1 | 14a3-26a8 |
| 2.6 | 26 | 25a3-b5 | 17b7-18a6 | 25a3-b5 | 26b7-27a5 |

| no. | B no. | K1 | K2 | N1 | BL1 | BL2 |
|---|---|---|---|---|---|---|
| 2.1 | 13 | 27a4-b6 | - - - - | 17b5-18a4 | - - - - | 17b7-18a6 |
| 2.2 | 14 | 27b6-30b3 | 163b4-165b8 | 18a4-20a3 | 144b7-146b8 | 18a6-20a4 |
| 2.3 | 15 | 30b3-33a3 | - - - - | 20a3-21b6 | - - - - | 20a4-21b6 |
| 2.4 | 16 | - - - - | 161b5-162a6 | - - - - | 143a3-b3 | - - - - |
| 2.5 | 24 | 37b2-43a6 | - - - - | - - - - | - - - - | 24a5-28b2 |
| 2.6 | 26 | 44b3-45b5 | - - - - | 25b1-26a5 | - - - - | 29a7-30a3 |

3 Vajradharmasya sādhanopāyikā

| no. | B no. | TO1 | TO2 | TO3 | TO4 |
|---|---|---|---|---|---|
| 3 | 10 | 14a4-b2 | 10b3-6 | 14a5-b2 | 9a12-b5 |

| no. | B no. | K1 | K2 | N1 | BL1 | BL2 |
|---|---|---|---|---|---|---|
| 3 | 10 | 25b1-26a1 | - - - - | 16b2-6 | - - - - | 16b5-17a3 |

4 Ṣaḍakṣarīlokeśvarasādhana

| no. | B no. | TO1 | TO2 | TO3 | TO4 |
|---|---|---|---|---|---|
| 4.1 | 6 | 11b5-12b3 | 8b6-9a8 | 11b5-12b2 | 7b9-8a10 |
| 4.2 | 7 | 12b3-13b4 | 9a8-10a4 | 12b3-13b4 | 8a10-9a4 |
| 4.3 | 11 | 14b2-15a3 | 10b7-11a5 | 14b2-15a3 | 9b5-10a2 |
| 4.4 | 12 | 15a3-5 | 11a5-7 | 15a3-5 | 10a2-4 |

| no. | B no. | K1 | K2 | N1 | BL1 | BL2 |
|---|---|---|---|---|---|---|
| 4.1 | 6 | 21a1-22b1 | 159a1-160a4 | 13b1-14b1 | 13b6-14b5 | 13b6-14b5 |
| 4.2 | 7 | 22b1-24b2 | - - - - | 14b1-15b6 | - - - - | 14b5-16a3 |
| 4.3 | 11 | 26a1-27a1 | - - - - | 16b6-17b2 | - - - - | 17a3-b4 |
| 4.4 | 12 | 27a1-4 | - - - - | 17b2-5 | - - - - | 17b5-7 |

5 Siṃhanādalokeśvarasādhana and Siṃhanādadhāraṇī

| no. | B no. | TO1 | TO2 | TO3 | TO4 |
|---|---|---|---|---|---|
| 5.1 | 17 | 18b4-19b1 | 13b3-14a4 | 18b3-19b1 | 12a11-13a1 |
| 5.2 | 20 | 20a2-6 | 14a9-b3 | 20a2-6 | 13a10-b3 |
| 5.3 | 21 | 20a6-b3 | 14b3-5 | 20a6-b3 | 13b3-6 |
| 5.4 | 22,23 | 20b3-21a4 | 14b5-15a1 | 20b3-21a4 | 13b6-14a3 |
| 5.5 | 25 | 24b1-25a3 | 17a7-b7 | 24b1-25a3 | 16a8-b7 |

| no. | B no. | K1 | K2 | N1 | BL1 | BL2 |
|---|---|---|---|---|---|---|
| 5.1 | 17 | 33a4-34b5 | - - - - | 21b6-23a1 | - - - - | 21b6-22b5 |
| 5.2 | 20 | 35b4-36a5 | - - - - | 23a6-b5 | - - - - | 23b1-6 |
| 5.3 | 21 | 36a5-b4 | - - - - | 23b5-24a2 | - - - - | 23b6-24a3 |
| 5.4 | 22,23 | 36b4-37b2 | 166a9-167a6 | 24a2-b4 | 147a8-148a5 | 24a3-b5 |
| 5.5 | 25 | 43b1-44b3 | - - - - | 24b4-25b1 | - - - - | 28b2-29a7 |

6 Nīlakaṇṭhāryāvalokiteśvarasādhana

| no. | B no. | TO1 | TO2 | TO3 | TO4 |
|---|---|---|---|---|---|
| 6 | 39 | 31a1-b1 | 22a3-9 | 31a1-b1 | 20a11-b7 |

| no. | B no. | K1 | K2 | N1 | BL1 | BL2 |
|---|---|---|---|---|---|---|
| 6 | 39 | 55a6-56a4 | - - - - | 32b3-33a4 | - - - - | 36a6-b7 |

7 Hālāhalalokeśvarasādhana

| no. | B no. | TO1 | TO2 | TO3 | TO4 |
|---|---|---|---|---|---|
| 7.1 | 9 | 14a1-4 | 10a7-b3 | 14a1-5 | 9a7-12 |
| 7.2 | 27 | 25b5-26a3 | 18a6-b2 | 25b5-26a3 | 17a5-10 |
| 7.3 | 28 | - - - - | - - - - | - - - - | - - - - |
| 7.4 | 29 | 26a3-27a4 | 18b2-19a7 | 26a3-27a4 | 17a10-18a3 |

7 Hālāhalalokeśvarasādhana

| no. | B no. | K1 | K2 | N1 | BL1 | BL2 |
|---|---|---|---|---|---|---|
| 7.1 | 9 | 24b6-25b1 | - - - - | 16a3-b2 | - - - - | 16a7-b5 |
| 7.2 | 27 | 45b5-46b1 | - - - - | 26a5-b4 | - - - - | 30a3-b2 |
| 7.3 | 28 | - - - - | 155a8-159a1 | - - - - | 136b5-140a8 | - - - - |
| 7.4 | 29 | 46b1-48b1 | 160a4-161b5 | 26b4-28a3 | 141b3-143a2 | 30b2-31b6 |

8 Padmanarteśvaralokanāthasādhana

| no. | B no. | TO1 | TO2 | TO3 | TO4 |
|---|---|---|---|---|---|
| 8.1 | 30 | 27a4-b4 | 19a7-b3 | 27a4-b4 | 18a3-a9 |
| 8.2 | 31 | - - - - | 19b6-8 | - - - - | - - - - |
| 8.3 | 32 | 27b4-6 | 19b3-6 | 27b4-6 | 18a9-12 |

| no. | B no. | K1 | K2 | N1 | BL1 | BL2 |
|---|---|---|---|---|---|---|
| 8.1 | 30 | 48b2-49a6 | - - - - | 28a3-b3 | - - - - | 31b7-32a7 |
| 8.2 | 31 | - - - - | - - - - | - - - - | - - - - | - - - - |
| 8.3 | 32 | 49a6-b5 | - - - - | 28b3-6 | - - - - | 32a7-b4 |

9 Hariharihariväahanodbhavalokeśvarasādhana

| no. | B no. | TO1 | TO2 | TO3 | TO4 |
|---|---|---|---|---|---|
| 9.1 | 33 | 27b6-28a3 | 19b9-20a2 | 27b6-28a2 | 18a12-b3 |
| 9.2 | 34 | 28a3-b5 | 20a2-b2 | 28a3-b5 | 18b3-19a1 |

| no. | B no. | K1 | K2 | N1 | BL1 | BL2 |
|---|---|---|---|---|---|---|
| 9.1 | 33 | 49b5-50a3 | ---- | 38b6-39a3 | ---- | 32b4-7 |
| 9.2 | 34 | 50a4-51a6 | ---- | 29a3-30a1 | ---- | 32b7-33b4 |

10 Trailokyavaśaṅkaralokeśvarasādhana

| no. | B no. | TO1 | TO2 | TO3 | TO4 |
|---|---|---|---|---|---|
| 10.1 | 35 | 28b5-29a6 | 20b2-21a1 | 28b5-29a6 | 19a2-11 |
| 10.2 | 36 | 29a6-30a5 | 21a1-b3 | 29a6-30a5 | 19a11-20a1 |
| 10.3 | ---- | ---- | ---- | ---- | ---- |

| no. | B no. | K1 | K2 | N1 | N2 |
|---|---|---|---|---|---|
| 10.1 | 35 | 51b1-52b3 | ---- | 30a1-b4 | ---- |
| 10.2 | 36 | 52b3-54a3 | 162a6-163b4 | 30b4-31b5 | ---- |
| 10.3 | ---- | 349a6-352b4 | ---- | ---- | 252b4-255a3 |

| no. | B no. | BL1 | BL2 |
|---|---|---|---|
| 10.1 | 35 | ---- | 33b5-34b1 |
| 10.2 | 36 | 143b3-144b6 | 34b1-35b2 |
| 10.3 | ---- | ---- | 295a4-298b2 |

11 Raktalokeśvarasādhana

| no. | B no. | TO1 | TO2 | TO3 | TO4 |
|---|---|---|---|---|---|
| 11 | 37 | 30a5-b3 | 21b3-8 | 30a5-b3 | 20a1-6 |

| no. | B no. | K1 | K2 | N1 | BL1 | BL2 |
|---|---|---|---|---|---|---|
| 11 | 37 | 54a3-b4 | 165b9-166a8 | 31b5-32a4 | 147a1-8 | 35b2-7 |

12 Lokeśvarasya vaśyādhikāravidhi

| no. | B no. | TO1 | TO2 | TO3 | TO4 |
|---|---|---|---|---|---|
| 12 | 38 | 30b3-31a1 | 21b8-22a3 | 30b3-31a1 | 20a6-11 |

| no. | B no. | K1 | K2 | N1 | BL1 | BL2 |
|---|---|---|---|---|---|---|
| 12 | 38 | 54b4-55a6 | ---- | 32a4-b3 | ---- | 35b7-36a6 |

| no. | B no. | TO1 | TO2 | TO3 | TO4 |
|---|---|---|---|---|---|
| 13 | 40 | 31b1-5 | 22a9-b5 | 31b1-5 | 20b7-12 |

| no. | B no. | K1 | K2 | N1 | BL1 | BL2 |
|---|---|---|---|---|---|---|
| 13 | 40 | 56a5-b6 | ---- | 33a5-b4 | ---- | 36b7-37a6 |

14 Sopacāramāṣamukhadhāraṇī

| no. | B no. | TO1 | TO2 | TO3 | TO4 | |
|---|---|---|---|---|---|---|
| 14 | 41 | 31b5-32a5 | 22b5-23a2 | 31b5-32a5 | 20b12-21a8 | |
| no. | B no. | K1 | K2 | N1 | BL1 | BL2 |
| 14 | 41 | 56b6-57b4 | ---- | 33b4-34a5 | ---- | 37a6-38a1 |

15 Sugatisandarśanalokeśvarasādhana and 16 Pretasantarpitalokeśvarasādhana are not found in the manuscripts.

17 Sukhāvatīlokeśvarasādhana

| no. | B no. | TO1 | TO2 | TO3 | TO4 | |
|---|---|---|---|---|---|---|
| 17 | ---- | ---- | ---- | ---- | ---- | |
| no. | B no. | K1 | K2 | N1 | BL1 | BL2 |
| 17 | ---- | 57b4-58a4 | ---- | ---- | ---- | 37b* |

*This sādhana is written in the margin of the manuscript.

## Orthography of the Manuscripts

Our manuscripts, which are written in the Newālī script, have the following orthographic characteristics:

1. *anusvāra* replaces all class nasals (ṅ, ñ, ṇ, n, m).
2. loss of *avagraha.*
3. vowels: "u" for "ū", and "ū" for "u".
4. duplication of the consonant immediately after an "r" (e.g. *dharmmaḥ*).
5. "v" of the script indicates "b" as well.
6. consonants: "ś" for "s", and "s" for "ś".
7. consonants: "ṣ" for "s", and "s" for "ṣ".
8. loss of "t": "satva" for "sattva".
9. "animitta-" is erroneously written as "animirtta-".
10. "kuryāt" is erroneously written as "kuyāt".
11. "vajra" is erroneously written as "vaja".
12. In order to indicate a "bīja", adjoining vowels are divided by a hyphen (e.g. *śukla-akāra*).
13. The manuscripts (K1, BL2) have a central dot (•).
14. The manuscripts (TO1, K2, BL1) have a colon (:).
15. Arbitrary punctuations with a central dot have been annotated as follows:
    य•देव : yad•eva
    लक्षयेदित्ये•व : lakṣayed ity•eva
    शुधता•मामुखीकृत्य : śuddhatām•āmukhīkṛtya

*To simplify the reading of the manuscripts, we have not annotated every occurrence of the features listed in points 1-11 above.

## 1.1 Lokanāthasādhana (Bhatt. no. 8)

(1) pūrvavidhānena candramaṇḍalaṃ[1] saptatṛtīyakaṃ bījaṃ[2] trayodaśākrāntaṃ[3] indubinduvibhūṣitaṃ[4]

(2) tenaiva niṣpannaṃ[5] śrīmallokanāthaṃ[6] jaṭāmakuṭadharaṃ[7] śāntaṃ candrāṃśum[8] iva nirmalaṃ[9] sarvālaṅkārabhūṣitaṃ[10] vāmena[11] padmadharaṃ[12] dakṣiṇe[13] varadaṃ[14] padmacandrāsanasthaṃ[15] bhāvayet/[16]

(3) hastadvayena[17] muṣṭiṃ[18] kṛtvā[19] madhyamapadmasaṃkocam[20] iva[21] anayā mudrayā[22] mudrayet/[23]

(4) tato jāpaṃ kuryāt//[24] oṃ maṇipadme hūṃ/[25] akṣaralakṣeṇa[26] vigatakalmaṣo[27] bhavati/[28] dvitīye[29] tṛtīye[30] svapnāni paśyati/[31] pañcānantaryakāriṇo[32] 'pi[33] koṭijāpena[34] sidhyati/[35] //śrīmallokanāthasādhanaṃ[36] samāptam//[37]

---

1 K1 and BL2 add. a central dot.
2 N1, BL2 bīja.
3 TO2 trayodaśākrānta; K1 and BL2 add. a central dot.
4 TO2, TO3, TO4, K1, N1 and BL2 add. /.
5 TO2 niṣpanna; K1 and BL2 add. a central dot.
6 TO4 and N1 add. /. K1 and BL2 add. a central dot.
7 TO1 -dhara; K1 and BL2 add. a central dot. N1 jaṭāmukuṭa-.
8 TO3 candrāṃśun; K1 candrāśum.
9 TO2 nirmitaṃ/; TO4 and N1 add. /. K1 and BL2 add. a central dot.
10 TO4 -kora-; K1 add. a central dot. BL2 sarvvālaṃkālabhūṣitaṃ.
11 TO4 vāme.
12 TO2, TO3, TO4, K1, N1 and BL2 add. /.
13 TO1, TO3, TO4, K1, BL2 dakṣiṇena; TO2 dakṣiṇena padmaṃ.
14 TO4 varada.
15 TO1 padmaṃ candrāsanasthaṃ.
16 TO1, TO3, K1, BL2 //.
17 TO1 hastadvayana.
18 TO4 muṣṭiṅ.
19 TO2 kṛ; K1 and BL2 add. a central dot.
20 TO1 madhyamapadmaṃ saṃkocam.
21 TO1, TO2, TO3, TO4 and N1 add. /. K1 and BL2 add. //.
22 BL2 om.
23 TO1, TO3, K1, BL2 //; TO2 om. /.
24 B om. //. TO4, N1 /.
25 TO1, TO2, TO3, TO4, K1, N1 //; BL2 // //.
26 TO1, K1 akṣararakṣeṇa; TO2 akṣaralakṣaṇa; TO4 akṣaralaṇa; BL2 akṣararakṣaṇa.
27 TO2 vigatakalmaso; K1, BL2 vigataṃ kalmako.
28 B om. / and add. a comma. TO1 bhavanti/; K1, BL2 //.
29 TO1 dvitī; TO2, TO3, K1, BL2 dvitīya.
30 TO1, K1, BL2 tṛtīya.
31 B om. / and add. a comma. K1, BL2 //.
32 TO1 pañcānaryakāriṇo.
33 TO1 pa.
34 TO2 koṭijāpeṇa.
35 TO1, TO3, K1, BL2 //; TO2, TO4 and N1 om. /.
36 BL2 -sādhana.
37 TO1 -taḥ//.

## 1.2 Lokanāthasādhana (Bhatt. no. 18)

(0) [(1-]namo lokanāthāya//[-1)]

(1) pūrvavatkramayogena[2] lokanātham[3] śaśiprabham/[4] hrīḥkārākṣarasaṃbhūtaṃ[5]
jaṭāmukuṭamaṇḍitam//[6] vajradharmajaṭāntaḥsthaṃ[7] aśeṣaroganāśanam/[8]
varadaṃ[9] dakṣiṇe haste[10] vāme padmadharaṃ[11] tathā//[12] lalitākṣepasaṃsthaṃ[13] tu
mahāsaumyaṃ[14] prabhāsvaram/

(2.1) varadotpalakarā[15] saumyā tārā dakṣiṇataḥ[16] sthitā//[17]

(2.2) vandanādaṇḍahastas[18] tu[19] hayagrīvo 'tha vāmataḥ/
raktavarṇo mahāraudro[20] vyāghracarmāmbarapriyaḥ//[21]

(3.0) [(22-]tadbāhyāṣṭadale[23] padme[24] maitreyādiṃ[25] vinyaset/[26]

(3.1) maitreyaḥ[27] pītavarṇaś[28] ca[29] nāgapuṣpavarapradaḥ/[30]

(3.2) kṣitigarbhaḥ[31] śyāmavarṇaḥ kalaśaṃ[32] cābhayaṃ tathā//[33]

---

1 B om.; TO4 namo lokanāya//.
2 BL2 add. a central dot.
3 K1 lokanātha; BL2 lokanātha•.
4 TO1 śaśiprabha.
5 TO1 hrīkārākṣasaṃbhūtaṃ; TO2 hrīkārabījasaṃbhūtaṃ; TO3 hrīkārākṣasaṃbhūtaṃ; TO4 -saṃbhūta; K1 hrīkārākṣarasaṃbhūtaṃ; BL2 hrīkārākṣarasaṃbhūtaṃ•.
6 TO2, TO4 jaṭāmakuṭamaṇḍitam/; K1, BL2 jaṭāmakuṭa-; N1 /.
7 TO1 vajadharmajatāntasthaṃ; TO2, TO3 vajadharmmajaṭāntasthaṃ; K1, N1 vajradharmmajaṭāntasthaṃ; TO4 vajradharmajaṭāntasthaṃ; BL2 vajadharmajaṭāntasthaṃ•.
8 TO1 aśeṣaroganāśane; TO2 aśeṣaroganāsanam/; TO3 om. /. TO4 //.
9 B baradaṃ; TO1 varada.
10 BL2 add. a central dot.
11 TO1 -ran; TO2 -ras.
12 TO2, K1, BL2 /.
13 TO1 lalitākṣepasasthan; TO2, TO3, K1, N1, BL2 lalitākṣepasaṃsthan; TO4 -saṃstha.
14 TO1 -ya; TO3 -yan; K1, BL2 mahāsaumya.
15 TO1 valadotpalākārā; TO3 valadotpalāṃkārā; TO4 varadotpalāṃkārā; K1 varadotparāṃkalā; BL2 varadotparāṃkalā•.
16 TO1 dakṣiṇata; TO3 illegible after dakṣiṇa-. TO4 dakṣiṇatā//; BL2 dakṣiṇata.
17 TO1 sthitāḥ; TO3 illegible; TO4 om.; K1, BL2 sthitāḥ/; N1 /.
18 K1 candanādaṇḍahastaṃ; BL2 candanā-.
19 K1 and BL2 add. a central dot.
20 K1 mahāraudre; BL2 mahāraudre•.
21 TO2 /; BL2 om. //.
22 TO2, N1 om. The sign "-22)" is found in the next page.
23 B tadvaraṭakāṣṭadale; TO4 tadvākoṣṭadala.
24 K1 and BL2 add. a central dot.
25 B add. [ca]. TO1 illegible before -treyādi. TO3 maitreyādi; TO4 metrayādi; K1, BL2 maitrīyādi.
26 TO4 //; K1, BL2 vinyaśet//.
27 TO1, TO3 -ya; TO4 metreya; K1, BL2 maitrīya.
28 TO1, TO3, TO4, K1, BL2 pītavarṇaḥ.
29 TO1, TO3, TO4, K1, BL2 om.
30 TO1, TO3, K1 and BL2 om. /. TO4 //.
31 TO1 kṣitigabbha; TO3, K1, BL2 kṣitigabha; TO4 kṣitigarbho.
32 TO4 kalaśañ vā.
33 TO1, TO3, TO4, K1, BL2 /.

(3.3) vajrapāṇiś[1] ca[2] śuklābho[3] vajrahasto[4] varapradaḥ/[5]
(3.4) khagarbho nabhaḥśyāmābho[6] cintāmaṇivarapradaḥ//[7]
(3.5) mañjughoṣaḥ[8] kanakābhaḥ[9] khaḍgapustakadhāraṇaḥ/[10]
(3.6) gaganagañjo[11] raktavarṇo[12] nīlotpalavarapradaḥ//[13]
(3.7) viṣkambhī[14] tu kṣāravarṇo[15] ratnottamavarapradaḥ/[16]
(3.8) samantabhadraḥ[17] pītābho[18] ratnotpalavarapradaḥ//[19]
(4) dhūpādicaturdevī[20] ca[21] vajrāṅkuśādidvāragāḥ/[22]
varṇāyudhe[23] yathā pūrvamaṇḍalasyānusārataḥ//[24-22)]
(5) evaṃ vidhaiḥ[25] samāyuktaṃ[26] lokanāthaṃ[27] prabhāvayet/[28] sarvakleśamalātīto[29] bhavet pūrṇamanorathaḥ//[30]
(6) atra mantraḥ//[31] oṃ hrīḥ[32] svāhā/[33]
// iti lokanāthasādhanaṃ[34] samāptam//[35]

---

1 TO1, TO3, BL2 vajapāṇi; TO4, K1 vajrapāṇi.
2 TO1, TO3, TO4, K1, BL2 om.
3 TO1, TO3, TO4, K1 śuklābhaṃ; BL2 śuklābhaṃ•.
4 TO1 vajābja; TO3 vajrābja?; TO4 vajrābja; K1, BL2 vajrābje.
5 TO1, TO3 -daṃ/; TO4 varaprada//; K1 varadaprabhaṃ/; BL2 varaprabhaṃ/.
6 TO1, TO3, K1 naśyāmābho; TO4 nabhaśyāmābho; BL2 naśyāmābho•.
7 TO1 cintāmaṇivalapradaḥ/; TO4 cintāmanivacapradaḥ//.
8 TO1, TO3, K1, BL2 mañjughoṣo; TO4 mañjughoṣa.
9 TO1, TO3, TO4, K1 -bhaṃ; BL2 -bhaṃ•.
10 B -dhārakaḥ(riṇaḥ)/; TO1 om./., TO3, K1, BL2 -dhāriṇaḥ/; TO4 -dhāriṇaḥ//.
11 TO1, TO3 gagaṇagañjā; TO4 gaganagajo.
12 TO1, TO3, TO4, K1, BL2 raktavarṇaḥ.
13 TO1 and TO3 om. //. TO4 nīlotpalavacapradaḥ//; BL2 nīlotpara-.
14 TO4, K1, BL2 viskambhī.
15 TO1, TO3, TO4 khāravarṇaḥ; K1 illegible before -navarṇaṃ. BL2 sāravarṇa.
16 TO1 om. /. TO4 //.
17 TO1, TO3, TO4, K1, BL2 -dra.
18 TO1, TO3, TO4 pītābhaḥ; K1 pītābhaṃ; BL2 pītābhaṃ•.
19 TO1 om. //. TO3 /; K1, BL2 ratnotparavarapradaḥ/.
20 TO3 -catudevī.
21 TO4 om.; K1 and BL2 add. a central dot.
22 B vajrāṅkuśyādidvāragāḥ/; TO1 vajākuśādidvāragāḥ; TO3 and K1 om. /. TO4 //.
23 TO1, TO3, TO4, BL2 -dha; K1 -dhaṃ.
24 B, K1 yathāpūrvvaṃ maṇḍalasyānusārataḥ//; TO1 yathāpūrvvamaṇḍaraśyānusārataḥ; TO4 yathāpūrvaṃ maṇḍalasyānusārataḥ//; BL2 yathāpūrvvaṃ •maṇḍalasyānusārataḥ//.
25 TO1 vidhya; TO2 vidhā; TO3, TO4, K1 vidhe; N1 vidhi; BL2 vidheḥ.
26 TO2 samāptaṃ; K1 and BL2 add. a central dot.
27 TO1 lokanātha.
28 TO4 prabhāvegret/; K1, BL2 //.
29 TO1 -kleśamarātīto; TO4 -kleśamalābhīto.
30 TO3 /; N1 pūrṇaṃ manorathaḥ//.
31 B om. //. TO1 mantra//; TO2, TO3 /.
32 BL2 hrī.
33 TO1, TO3 //; TO2, TO4, K1, N1 and BL2 om. /.
34 K1 and BL2 add. //.
35 K1, BL2 om.

## 1.3 Lokanāthasādhana (Bhatt. no. 19)

(1) loṃbījāt[1] sarvaṃ[2] pūrvavad vidhāya[3] śuddhiparyantaṃ[4]

(2) tato[5] loṃ pariṇamya[6] lokanāthaṃ[7] candraprabhaṃ[8] sarvābharaṇojjvalaṃ[9] jaṭāmukuṭinaṃ[10] padmacandropari paryaṅkiṇaṃ[11] vāme padmadharaṃ[12] dakṣiṇe varadaṃ cintayet//[13]

(3) samayamudrā/[14] muṣṭidvayaṃ baddhvā[15] madhyāṅgulyau padmasaṃkocākāreṇa[16] yojayet//[17]

(4) oṃ maṇipadme hūṃ[18] mantraṃ[19] japet/[20]

(21-//iti lokanāthasādhanaṃ//-21)

---

1 K1, BL2 lābījot.
2 TO1, TO2, K1 sarvva.
3 BL2 add. a central dot.
4 TO1, TO2, TO3, K1, N1 and BL2 add. /. TO4 -ta.
5 TO4 tatro.
6 TO2 parināmya.
7 TO2 lokanātha; BL2 add. a central dot.
8 K1 and BL2 add. a central dot.
9 TO1, TO2, TO3, TO4 and K1 add. /. BL2 -bharaṇojvalaṃ/.
10 TO1, TO2, K1 jaṭāmakuṭinaṃ; TO4 jaṭāmakuṭinaṃ/; N1 add. /. BL2 jaṭāmakuṭinaṃ•.
11 B paryyaṅkinaṃ/; TO1, TO3 paryaṅkinaṃ/; TO2, TO4 and N1 add. /. K1 paryyaṃkinaṃ; BL2 paryyaṃkinaṃ/.
12 K1 and BL2 add. a central dot.
13 B, TO2, TO4, N1 /.
14 TO1, TO2, TO3, K1, BL2 //.
15 K1 and BL2 add. a central dot.
16 TO4 -kāraiṇa; N1 add. /.
17 B /.
18 TO1, TO2, TO3, K1, N1 and BL2 add. //. TO4 add. /.
19 TO2, TO4 mantra; K1, BL2 ayaṃ mantraḥ//.
20 TO1, TO3 //; TO2, TO4 and N1 om. /. K1, BL2 om.
21 B, TO1, TO2, TO3, TO4 //lokeśvarasādhanaṃ samāptam//; N1 // lokeśvarasādhanaṃ sāmāptam//.

## 2.1 Khasarpaṇalokeśvarasādhana (Bhatt. no. 13)

(0) namaḥ khasarpaṇāya//[1]

(1) prathamaṃ[2] tāvan[3] mantrī sukhāsanopaviṣṭaḥ[4] kṛtamukhaśaucādikaḥ[5]

(2.1.1) śucāv[6] avakāśe[7] svahṛdi akāreṇa[8] candramaṇḍalaṃ vibhāvya[9] tadupari sitahrīḥkāraṃ[10]

(2.1.2) tadraśmibhir[11] ākṛṣyāgrato[12] 'mbare gurubuddhabodhisattvādīn[13] ānīya[14] hṛdbījaraśmisambhavapūjāmeghaiḥ[15] sampūjya[16] pāpadeśanādikaṃ[17] kṛtvā caturbrahmavihārabhāvanāṃ[18] ca/[19]

(2.1.3) tataḥ[20] śūnyatāṃ[21] bhāvayet/[22] oṃ śūnyatājñānavajrasvabhāvātmako[23] 'ham iti cādhitiṣṭhet/[24]

(2.2) tadanu[25] pūrvavad[26] hrīḥkāraṃ vibhāvya[27] gaganakuhare[28] saṃsphārya[29] saṃhṛtya[30] tadudbhūtaṃ[31] lokeśvaram ātmānaṃ[32] bhāvayet//[33]

---

1 B /; TO2, TO3, TO4 khasarppanāya//.
2 TO1, TO3, N1, BL2 prathaman; TO4 prathama.
3 TO1, TO2, BL2 tāvat.
4 TO2 add. //. N1 add. /.
5 TO1, TO3 -kaṃ/; TO2 mukhaṃ saucādikaṃ; TO4 -kaṃ//; K1 kṛtamukhaḥ śaucādikaṃ•; BL2 -kaṃ•.
6 TO1 śucav.
7 TO1 avakāśe/; TO3 and N1 add. /. TO4 avakāśo; K1 akāśe/; BL2 akāśe.
8 TO1 ākāreṇa.
9 K1, BL2 -yaḥ//; TO1 and TO3 add. / .
10 K1 and BL2 add. a central dot.
11 TO2 tadraśmir; TO1 tadraśmibhi/; TO3 tadraśmibhi.
12 TO3 add. /.
13 TO1, TO3 -sattvādin; K1, BL2 -satvādīnām.
14 K1 and BL2 add. a central dot.
15 TO1 -bijaraśmisabhava-; K1 svahṛdbījaraśmi-; N1 -pujana- .
16 TO1 sapūjya/; K1 and BL2 add. a central dot. N1 add. /.
17 TO1 -ka.
18 TO1 catubrahmavihārībhāvaṇāñ; TO2 -vihārībhā-; TO3 -vihārībhāvanāñ; TO4 caturbrahmavībhāvāñ; K1, N1 caturbrahmavihārībhāvanāñ; BL2 -vihārībhānāñ.
19 B and TO1 om. /.
20 TO1 tata.
21 TO1 śūnyatā.
22 B om. /. TO1 bhāvayat/.
23 TO3, K1, BL2 śūnyatāṃ jñā-.
24 TO1 //; TO3 cādhitiṣṭhitiṣṭhet//; TO4 cādhitiṣṭhiti cādhiṣṭhitiṣṭhat/.
25 TO4 add. cādhiṣṭitiṣṭat.
26 The rendering follows the Sandhi rule. B, TO1, TO2, TO3, TO4, K1, N1, BL2 -vat.
27 K1 and BL2 add. /.
28 TO1 gagakuhare; TO3, TO4 gagaṇakuhare; K1, BL2 gagaṇakuhara.
29 TO4 saṃsparya; K1 add. a central dot. BL2 saṃsthāyya•.
30 TO2 sahṛtya; K1, BL2 svahṛtya; TO3 and N1 add. ca.
31 TO1 ca tadhṛtaṃ; TO2, N1 ca tadudbhūtaṃ; TO3 tadbhūtaṃ; K1 cayated būtaṃ•; BL2 add. a central dot.
32 TO1 atmānam.
33 B om. //. TO2, TO4 and N1 add. /.

śītāṃśukoṭiprabhaṃ[1] jaṭāmakuṭinaṃ[2] amitābhakṛtaśekharaṃ[3] sarvālaṃkāravibhūṣitaṃ[4] ekamukhaṃ[5] ardhaparyaṅkena[6] padmacandrāsanasthaṃ[7] dakṣiṇena[8] varadaṃ[9] vāmena[10] padmadharam/[11]

(2.3) dakṣiṇapārśve āryatārāsudhanakumārau[12] vāmapārśve bhṛkuṭīhayagrīvau/[13]

(2.4) tataḥ śirasi oṃkāraṃ[14] kaṇṭhe[15] āḥkāraṃ[16] hṛdi hūṃkāram iti sañcintya[17] khedaparyantaṃ[18] yāvat tiṣṭhet/[19]

(3) khede[20] tu mantraṃ japet/[21] (22-tatrāyam[23] mantraḥ//[24] oṃ hrīḥ svāhā/[25] // ity āryakhasarpaṇalokeśvarasādhanam//[26-22)]

---

1 TO1, TO3, TO4, N1 and BL2 add. /. K1 add. a central dot.
2 TO2, K1 and BL2 add. /. TO4 jaṭāmukuṭinaṃ; N1 jaṭāmukuṭinaṃ/.
3 TO1, K1, BL2 amitābhaśeṣaraṃ•; TO2 amitābhasekharaṃ; TO3 amitābhaseṣaraṃ/.
4 TO1 sarvvālakārabhūṣitaṃ; TO2, TO3, TO4 -kārabhūṣitam; K1, N1 -kārabhūṣitam/; BL2 add. /.
5 B, TO1, TO3 smeramukhaṃ; TO2 add. /. TO4, N1 smeramukhaṃ/; K1 bhūsamukhaṃ•; BL2 sūsamukhaṃ•.
6 TO1 -paryaṅkeno; TO2 illegible between a- and -paryyaṃkiṇa. TO3 -paryyaṅkano; TO4 -paryyakena/; K1 -paryaṃkanā; N1 -paryaṅkeṇa; BL2 add. /.
7 TO1, TO2, TO4 and N1 add. /. K1 and BL2 add. a central dot.
8 TO1, TO3, K1, BL2 dakṣiṇe.
9 TO4 add. //. N1 add. /.
10 K1 vāmane.
11 TO1, TO3, TO4, K1, BL2 padmaṃ/.
12 TO1 āya-; TO3, TO4 ārya-; TO1 and TO3 add. //. TO2, TO4 and N1 add. /. K1 and BL2 add. a central dot.
13 TO1, TO2, TO3 //. TO4 and K1 om. /. BL2 a central dot.
14 B add. a comma.
15 K1 kaṇṭha.
16 B add. a comma. TO1, TO3, K1, BL2 ākāraṃ.
17 TO4 sacintyā; K1 and BL2 add. a central dot. N1 add. /.
18 TO2 khede paryantaṃ; K1 khedaryyantaṃ•; BL2 add. a central dot.
19 BL2 //.
20 TO2 kheda.
21 K1, BL2 //.
22 K1 om.
23 TO4 -ya.
24 B om. //. TO2 maṃtraṃ//.
25 TO1, TO2, TO3, TO4 and N1 om. /. BL2 //.
26 TO1, TO3, -khasarppaloke-; TO4 āyaṃkhasarppalokeśvarasādhanaṃ//; K1 om.; BL2 -khasarpalokeśvara-.

## 2.2 Khasarpaṇalokeśvarasādhana (Bhatt. no. 14)

(0) oṃ[1] namaḥ[2] khasarpaṇāya//[3]

(1) abhimataphaladānodbhāsikalpadrumaśrīḥ[4]
sugatanayamahādhvakṣemakṛtsārthavāhaḥ/[5]
bhavaśamasamabhāvaḥ[6] sarvabhāvasvabhāvaḥ[7]
śamayatu[8] jagadaṃhaḥ[9] (10-so 'yam-10) ambhojapāṇiḥ//[11]

(2) prātar[12] mukhādisaṃśuddhiṃ[13] vidhāya vijanālaye/[14]
hṛccandrabījakiraṇair[15] mṛduviṣṭarasaṃsthitaḥ//[16]

(3.1) svabījaṃ[17] hṛdaye[18] dhyātvā[19] pūrṇenduparibhāsvaram/[20]

(3.2) saṃcodya[21] tatkiraṇair[22] agre[23] samānīya[24] (25-nabho'ṅgaṇe//[26]
śrīmatkhasarpaṇaṃ[27] nāthaṃ[28] gurubuddhaughasatsutān/[29]

---

1 B, TO1, TO2, TO3, TO4, K1, N1, BL2 om.
2 K1 om.
3 B /; TO2 khasappaṇāya//; TO4 khasarppanāya//; K1 om.; K2, BL1 khasarpaṇāyaḥ//.
4 TO1 -nodbhāsikalpadrumaśrī; TO2 -nobhāsikalpadrumāṇimaśrī; TO3 -nobhāsikalpadrumaśrī; TO4 -nohāsikalpadrumaḥ śrī; K1 tatrānohāsikalpadrutaḥ; K2 -nodbhasila-; BL2 -nohāsikalpadrutaḥ śrī•.
5 TO1 sugatatanayamanāḥkṣepakṛtsārthavāhaḥ; TO2 -mahādhvakṣepakṛtsārthavāhaḥ/; TO3 sugatatanayamahāḥkṣemakṛtsārthavāhaḥ/; K1 śrīsugatanayamahāḥkṣepakṛtsārthavāhaḥ/; K2 -mahāthakṣamakṛtsārthavāha//; TO4 -mahādhvakṣepakṛtsārthavāhaḥ//; BL1 -mahāthakṣamakṛtasārthavāhaḥ; BL2 sugatatanayamanāḥkṣepakṛtsārthavāhaḥ/.
6 B, TO3, K1, BL2 bhavasamasamabhāvaḥ; K2 bhavasamasamabhāva; BL1 bhavasamasamabhāvaṃ.
7 TO2 sarvvabhāvasvabhāva/; TO3 sarvabhāvasvabhāva; K2 sarvabhāvaḥ; BL1 sarvabhāva.
8 TO2 śamayabhra; TO4 śamayabhu; K1, BL1, BL2 samayatu; K2 samayabhu.
9 TO1, TO3 jagadaṃha; TO2 jaganta; TO4, K1 jagadaṃbha; K2 jagadeha; BL1 jagadehaḥ; BL2 gajadaṃbha•.
10 K2 sauyam; BL1 śauyaṃ.
11 K2 -pāṇe•; BL1 om. //.
12 K2, BL1 prāta.
13 TO2 sukhādisauvādisaṃ; K1 add. a central dot. K2 mukhādisamuddhri; BL1 mukhādisamuddhi; BL2 add. a central dot.
14 TO2 vijanālaya; TO1, TO3 and TO4 om. /. K2 vijaṇolaya•; BL1 vijanolayaḥ//.
15 B -bījakiraṇaiḥ; TO1 hṛcandrabījakiraṇai; TO2 -ṇer; TO4, N1 -ṇai; K1, BL2 -ṇai •; K2 hṛcandrabījakiraṇai; BL1 hṛcandrabījakiraṇai.
16 TO1, TO2, TO3 -vistarasaṃsthitaḥ/; K1 -vistara-; K2 mṛduvīstarasaṃsthita//; N1 /; BL1 mṛduvistarasaṃsthitaḥ; BL2 mmṛduvista-.
17 TO2, K2, BL1 svabīja.
18 TO1, TO2, BL1 hṛdaya; K2, N1 hṛdayaṃ.
19 K1 and BL2 add. a central dot.
20 TO1 and TO3 om. /. K2 pūrṇenduparī •bhāsvaram•; N1 -svarāṃ; BL1 add. a central dot.
21 TO1 sacodya; TO4 sañcodya; N1 sancodya; BL2 saṃcodyaṃ.
22 B, TO4, K2, BL1 tatkarair; TO1, TO3 tatkaraṇair; TO2 tat karar.
23 TO1,TO3, K2, N1, BL1, BL2 agra.
24 TO3 samanīca; K1, BL2 samānīnaya; BL1 samāniya.
25 K2 om.
26 K1 bhāṃgane//; BL1 om. //. BL2 bhoṃgane//.
27 TO1, TO3, TO4 -khasarppaṇan; TO2 -khasarppaṇa; K1, N1, BL2 -khasarpaṇan.
28 BL2 add. a central dot.
29 TO1, TO2, TO3, TO4, N1 gurubuddhaughatatsutān/; K1 gurubuddhaughanan sutān//; BL1 om. /. BL2 gurubuddhaughanatsutān//.

pūjayed[1] vividhaiḥ[2] pūjāmeghais[3] tadbījasambhavaiḥ/[4]
(3.3.0) tato 'bhivandya[5] kurvīta[6] pāpasya[7] deśanādikam//[8]
(3.3.1) yad[-25)] anādim[9] iti[10] saṃsāre[11] saṃsaratā[12] mayā kṛtam akuśalaṃ[13] kāritaṃ[14] vā kriyamāṇaṃ[15] vā pareṇābhyanumoditaṃ[16] tat sarvam[17] bhagavatām[18] agrato[19] deśayāmi/[20]
(3.3.2) saṃbuddhabuddhaputrair[21] āryair[22] anyaiś[23] ca yat kṛtaṃ[24] kuśalam/[25]
anumodya tadavaśeṣaṃ[26] samyak[27] pariṇāmayāmi[28] sambodhau//[29]
(3.3.3) buddhaṃ[30] gacchāmi śaraṇaṃ[31] karuṇāmayam uttamam/[32]
dharmaṃ[33] ca sarvadharmaikarasarūpaṃ[34] nirañjanam//[35]

---

1 TO2, BL1 pūjayad.
2 TO4 -dheḥ; K1 -dhai; BL1 vidhibhir; BL2 -dhair.
3 K1 pūjā•meghaiḥ; BL1 -ghās; BL2 pūjā•meghais.
4 TO1 -bija-; TO2 //; TO4 tadbījasabhavaiḥ//; K1 -vaiḥ; N1 om. /. BL1 tabījasambhavaḥ.
5 TO4 abhivakṣya; BL2 -vadyaṃ.
6 TO2 kuvita•; TO4 kuvīta; K1 kurvvīt/; BL2 add. a central dot.
7 TO4 pāpasyā; BL1 pāpaśe.
8 TO1, TO2, TO3, TO4 /; K1, N1 a central dot. BL1 om. //. BL2 deśinādikam/.
9 K2 nādim.
10 TO2, TO3, TO4, K1, K2 ati.
11 TO1 sasasāre; TO2, TO3, TO4 sasaṃsāre; K1 and BL2 add. a central dot.
12 TO4 sasaṃsāratā.
13 TO1 -śaraṃ; TO2, BL1 -śala; K1, N1 and BL2 add. a central dot. K2 aṅkuśala.
14 TO1, TO4, K2, N1 kāritam.
15 TO1, BL1 -mānam; TO2 -mānaṃ; TO4, N1 -māṇam; K1 kṛyamāṇam; K2 -mānan.
16 TO4 pareṇātyanu-; K2 add. //. N1, BL1 and BL2 add. a central dot.
17 TO1, TO2, K1 sarvva; TO4 sarvam; BL2 sarva.
18 TO4 -tom; K1 -to me; BL2 -to•me.
19 K1, BL2 'grato; K2 add. a central dot.
20 TO1, TO3, K1 deśayā/; TO4 deśayā//; K2 and BL1 om. /. N1 //.
21 TO4 sambuddha-; BL1 -putrain.
22 TO1 āyer; TO4 āryair; K1 āryya; K2 ānyer ?; BL1, BL2 āryar.
23 K1 vanyaiś; K2 anyanyaiś.
24 TO1 kṛta.
25 TO4 //; K2 and BL1 om. /.
26 TO1 tavaśeṣaṃ; TO2 tadśeṣam; K1 tatavasyeṣa•; K2 tatadaśeṣaṃ; BL1 tadaśpaṣa; BL2 add. a central dot.
27 K2 samyaka.
28 TO2 āriṇāmayāmi; K2 parīṇāmayāmī.
29 TO1 sabodhau/; K2 and BL1 om. //.
30 TO1 buddha.
31 K1 and BL2 add. a central dot.
32 TO4 //; K2 has a colon and //. BL1 a central dot.
33 TO1, K1, N1, BL2 dharmmañ; TO2, TO4 dharmañ; K2, BL1 dharmaś.
34 B sarvvadharmeṇa rasarūpaṃ; TO1 sarvvadharmmarasarūpaṃ; TO2, N1 sarvvadharmmekarasarūpaṃ; TO3 sarvvadharmmerasarūpaṃ; TO4 sarvadharmarasarūpaṃ; K1, BL2 sarvadharmerasarūpaṃ; N1 -rasarūpan; BL2 -rasarūpa.
35 TO1 and K2 have a central dot. BL1, TO3, K1, BL2 /.

(3.3.4) muditādibhūpraviṣṭaṃ[1] ca[2] bodhisattvagaṇaṃ[3] tathā[4] nivṛttiṃ[5] ca kartukāmān[6] buddhān[7] parahitavidhānāya[8] cirasthitaye[9] yācayāmi//[10]

(3.3.5) sarvāvaraṇavimūlanahetubhūtāyāṃ[11] bodhau[12] cittam utpādayāmi[13]

(3.3.6) sasutasugataikamārgaṃ[14] ca āśayaviśuddhyā[15] samāśrito[16] 'smi/[17]

(3.4) (18-tata ekān-18) ekaviyogād[19] etat[20] sakalam[21] eva calācalaṃ[22] (23-jagac chūnyam-23) iti vicintya//[24] oṃ śūnyatājñānavajrasvabhāvātmako[25] 'ham[26] iti[27] śūnyatām[28] adhitiṣṭhet/[29]

---

1 TO1, TO3 muditādibhūpraviṣṭa; TO2, TO4, N1 muditādibhūpraviṣṭañ; K1 muditādibhūpraviṣṭa•; K2, BL1 muditādin praviṣṭaś; BL2 -praviṣṭa•.
2 TO1, TO3, K1, BL2 om.
3 TO1, TO3, TO4 -satvaga; BL2 bodhisattvaga.
4 K1 and BL2 add. a central dot. K2, BL1 om.
5 TO1, TO2, TO3, TO4, N1 nivṛtiñ; K1 nirvṛtiṃ; K2, BL1 nirvṛttiś; BL2 nivṛttitiñ.
6 TO1, TO2 kartukāman; TO4 kakartukāmān; K1 kartukāmāna•; K2, BL1 karkakāmāna; BL2 karttukāmāna•.
7 TO3 buddhādhān; BL1 buddhāna.
8 TO1 paraṃhitavidhāya; TO3 paraṃhitavidhānāya; TO4 parihitavidhānāya; K1, BL2 parahitaṃ• vidhānāya; K2 parahitavidhāyanāya.
9 K1, K2, BL1, BL2 -ya.
10 B, TO1, TO3, TO4, K1, K2, BL1 and BL2 om. //.
11 TO1, TO3, TO4 -lahetubhū-; TO2 -lahebhū-; K1 -lahetubhūtāsāṃ; K2 -lanahetubhutāyā; BL1 -bhūtāyā; BL2 -lahetubhūtāsāṃ.
12 TO1 bodhi; TO2 bodhe.
13 TO2, TO4 and N1 add. /. K1 and BL2 add. a central dot. BL1 utpādayādayāmi.
14 TO1 sasugatamārgañ; TO2 sasutasugatamārgaṃ; TO3 sasugatasugatamārgañ; TO4 sasugatamārgañ; K1 sasugatasugatamārgañ; K2 sakārālaṅkāradharasasutasutaikamārggaś; N1 sasutasugatamārgañ; BL1 illegible between sakāra- and -sasutasutaikamārgaś. BL2 sasugatasugatamārgañ.
15 TO2, K2, BL1 āsaya-; TO4 āśraya-.
16 K2, BL1 samāsito.
17 TO1, TO2, TO3, TO4, K1, BL2 //; K2 has a colon. BL1 has a central dot.
18 TO2, K1 tataḥ ekān; TO4 tata ekār; BL2 tata ekāne•.
19 BL2 kavi-.
20 TO4 itat; K2, BL1 ata.
21 TO1 sakam; K2, BL1 akalam.
22 TO4 ca/ lācala; BL2 ca/ lāca-; K2 and BL1 add. a central dot.
23 The rendering follows the Sandhi rule. B jagat śūnyam; TO1, TO3, K1, N1, BL2 jagac chūṇyam; TO2 jagajac chunyam; TO4 jaga chunyam; K2 jaga chunem; BL1 jagac chunyam.
24 B om. //. TO2, N1 /; BL1 add. a central dot.
25 TO1, TO3, K1, BL2 śūnyatāṃ jñāna-; TO2 sunyatā-; BL1 -jñānavajra•svabhāvātmako.
26 The rendering follows the Sandhi rule. B 'haṃ.
27 K2 add. //.
28 TO1, TO3, K1, BL2 om.
29 TO1 śūnyatādhitiṣṭhet/ adhitiṣṭhet; TO3 śūnyatādhiṣṭhet/ adhitiṣṭhet/; TO2 adheṣṭhet/; TO4 adheṣṭhet/ adhitiṣṭet/ adhitiṣṭet/; K1, BL2 śūnyatādhiṣṭhet// adhitiṣṭhet//; K2 adhitiṣṭhet//; BL1 adhiṣṭhet•.

adhiṣṭhāya[1] prakṛtiviśuddhāḥ[2] [(3-]sarve[4] ime[5] dharmās tathāham ity[6] avalokya[7] oṃ
svabhāvaśuddhāḥ[8] sarvadharmāḥ[9] svabhāvaśuddho[10] 'ham[11] iti[12] paṭhet/[13]
(4.1) tato[14] vijñānamātrātmako[15] bhāvakaḥ[16-3)] pūrvapraṇidhisañcoditaḥ[17]
paṃkārapariṇataviśvavarṇakamale[18] akārajaṃ[19] pūrṇaśaśimaṇḍalam[20] amalaṃ[21] tatropari[22]
hrīḥkāram[23] atiprabhāsvaraṃ[24] sphuratkiraṇasamūhavyāptanabhaḥsthalaṃ[25] vibhāvya[26]
tatpariṇataṃ[27] svabījagarbhaṃ[28] nālālaṅkṛtaṃ[29] vikacakamalam[30] avalokayet/[31] [(32-]tata
etat[-32)] sakalapariṇatam[33] ātmānaṃ[34] bhagavantaṃ[35] dhyāyāt/[36] himakarakoṭikiraṇāvadātaṃ[37]

---

1 K1 adhisthāya.
2 K1 add. //. K2 -viśuddhaḥ//; BL1 -viśuddhaḥ.
3 K1 om.
4 TO1, TO2, TO3, N1 sarvva; TO4, BL2 sarva; K2 sarvvam; BL1 sarvam eva.
5 TO1, TO3, TO4, BL1, BL2 om.; K2 eva.
6 BL1 ite; BL2 add. eva.
7 TO1, TO3, TO4 evalokya/; TO2 and K2 add. //. TO4 and N1 add. /. BL1 valaukya•; BL2 lokya//.
8 K2 -suddhāḥ.
9 K2, BL1 -dharmmā•.
10 K2 suddho; BL2 śuddham.
11 BL2 om.
12 K2 add. a central dot.
13 TO1, TO2, TO3, K2, BL2 //; TO4 baṭhet//; BL1 a central dot.
14 BL2 tataḥ.
15 BL2 -kaḥ/.
16 TO1 and TO3 add. /. BL2 om.; K2 -ka•.
17 TO1, TO3, K1, N1 and BL2 add. /. K2 -ta•; TO2 codhitaḥ.
18 TO1 -parīṇataviśvavarṇa-; TO2 -pariṇataṃ vivarṇa-; K1 -pariṇata•viśvavarṇakamale•;
K2 -pariṇata•viśvavarṇakamale; BL2 add. a central dot.
19 TO3, TO4, K1, N1 aṃkāra-; K2, BL1 hūṃkāraja.
20 TO1, TO2, K1, N1 and BL2 add. /. TO4 add. //.
21 TO1, TO3, K1, K2, BL2 om.; N1 add. /.
22 TO2, TO3, TO4 tatopari.
23 K2 hrīkāram.
24 TO1, TO2, TO3, K1, N1 and BL2 add. /. TO4 add. //.
25 TO1 -bhastala; TO2 sphulatkiraṇasamūhavyāptanabhastalaṃ; TO3, TO4, K1, BL1, BL2 -bhastalaṃ;
K2 -nabhastalaṃ•; N1 sphāratkiraṇasamūhavyāptanabhasthalaṃ
26 TO1 and TO3 add. /.
27 K1 and BL2 add. a central dot. N1 tapa-.
28 TO2, TO4, K2, BL1 svabījagarbha; K1 add. a central dot.
29 TO2 nānālaṃkṛta; TO4 add. /. K1 and BL2 add. a central dot.
30 TO2, TO3, K1, BL2 vikacakanālam; TO4 vikacakanālay; BL1 vikarakamalam
31 TO4 //; K1, BL2 eva lokayet//; BL1 has a central dot.
32 K1 tatra etat; K2 tata cet; BL1 tata cetat/.
33 TO1 sakalapalaṇatam; TO3, TO4 -paraṇa-; K1 sakala•pariṇatam; K2, BL1 sakara-; BL2 sakala•paraṇata.
34 BL2 tmānaṃ.
35 TO1, TO2 -anta.
36 B om. /. K1, K2, N1 and BL2 add. //. BL1 add. a central dot.
37 TO1 himakarakoṭiraṇāvadātaṃ; TO2, TO4, N1 -dāta; K1, BL2 himakalakoṭi-; K2 -dāṭa; BL1
himakarakoṭikiraṇāvaḍāta.

deham[1] ūrdhvajaṭāmakuṭaṃ[2] amitābhakṛtaśekharaṃ/[3] viśvanalinaniṣaṇṇaṃ[4] śaśimaṇḍale[5] ardhaparyaṅkaniṣaṇṇaṃ[6] sakalālaṅkāradharavigrahaṃ[7] smeramukhaṃ[8] dviraṣṭavarṣadeśīyaṃ/[9] dakṣiṇe[10] varadakaraṃ[11] vāmakareṇa[12] sanālakamaladharaṃ[13] karavigalatpīyūṣadhārābhyavahārarasikaṃ[14] tadadhaḥ[15] samāropitordhvamukhaṃ[16] mahākukṣim[17] atikṛśam atiśitavarṇaṃ[18] sūcīmukhaṃ[19] tarpayantaṃ[20] śrīmatpotalakācalodaranivāsinaṃ[21] karuṇāsnigdhavilokanaṃ[22] śṛṅgārarasaparyupāsitaṃ[23] atiśāntaṃ[24] nānālakṣaṇālaṅkṛtaṃ/[25]

(4.2.0) tasya puratas tārā[26] dakṣiṇapārśve[27] sudhanakumāraḥ/[28]

---

1 TO2, TO3, K1 and N1 add. /. TO4 add. //. K2, BL1 and BL2 add. a central dot.
2 TO1, TO4, BL2 urujaṭā-; TO2 urūjaṭāmakuṭa; TO3 urddhvajaṭā-; K1 add. urujaṭāmakuṭaṃ•; N1 ūrujaṭāmukuṭaṃ/.
3 B amitābhaśekharaṃ; TO1 amitābhākṛtaśeṣaraṃ/; TO4 amitābhakṛtaśeṣaraṃ; K1 amitābhaṃ kṛtasekharaṃ•; K2 amitāṃ bhasekharaṃ; BL1 amitāṃbhaśeṣaraṃ; BL2 a central dot.
4 TO1 viśvanalinanirṇṇa; TO2 vilalitenisaṇṇa; TO3 -niṣaṇṇa; TO4 visvenāsananiṣaṇṇa; K1 viśvanalina •nikharṇaṃ•; K2 viśvanalinalivarṇa; N1 viśvanalinaniṣaṇṇa; BL1 viśvanalinanīvarṇa; BL2 viśvanalina •nikharṇṇaṃ•.
5 K2 om.; BL1 -lo.
6 TO1 -paryyaṅkaṃniṣaṇṇavīta; TO2 -paryyaṅkaṅkaniṣaṇṇa; TO4 -paryaṅkaniṣaṇaṃ; K1 -paryyaṅkaniṣaṇaṃ •; BL2 add. a central dot. K2 śaśimaṇḍalorddhaparyyaṃkaniṣarṇaṃ; N1 -niṣaṇṇa; BL1 rdha-.
7 TO1 -lāladharavigrahaṃ//; TO2 ṣatalāradharavigrahaṃ/; TO3 illegible before -lāladharavigrahaṃ//; TO4 satalālaṃkāradharavigrahaṃ//; K1, BL2 vatalāladharaṃ vigrahaṃ/; K2 śakara•laṅkāradharavigrahaṃ; N1 add. /. BL1 śakarālaṅkāladhara-.
8 TO4, K1, BL2 smaramukhaṃ; K2 smarasukhaṃ; BL1 smaramuṣaṃ.
9 B om. /. TO1 -śiyaṃ/; TO2 dviraṣṭavarṣaśāyaṃ/; K2, BL1 dviraṣṭavarṣadehaṃ•.
10 TO3, TO4 dakṣṇena; K1 dakṣiṇa; N1 dakṣinena.
11 TO1 valakaraṃ/; TO3 varakanaṃ/; TO4 vadakaraṃ/; K1, BL2 varatakaṃ/; K2 and BL1 add. a central dot. N1 add. /.
12 TO1, TO3, K2, BL1 vāmekareṇa; BL2 vāmakalena.
13 TO1 sanārakamaradharaṃ; TO2 and TO3 add. /. TO4 sanālakaledharaṃ//; K2 and BL1 add. a central dot. K1, N1 and BL2 add. /.
14 TO1 karavigatpīyūkhadhāvyavahārarasika; TO3 karavigatpāyūṣadhārāvyavahārarasika; TO4 karavigatpāyūṣadhārāvyavahārarasika; K1 karavigatpīyūṣadhārā•bhyavahārarasivā •; K2 karavigaritapiyūṣadhārābhya •vahārarakta; N1 -ka; BL1 karavigaritapīyūṣadhārābhyavahārarakṭadharmmam; BL2 karavigalpīyūṣadhārā•vyavahārarasivā•.
15 TO2 add. /. K1 tadanu; K2, BL1 om.
16 TO1 and TO3 add. /. TO2 sasāropi-; TO4 samāropitordhvamūkhaṃ; K1 samālepitordhvamukhaṃ//; K2 dharmmamarorddhvamukhaṃ; BL1 ārorddhamuṣaṃ; BL2 samālepitordhvamukhaṃ//.
17 TO2 mahākuṣṭim; K2 mahākṛtkim; BL1 mahākṛtsna.
18 B, TO1, TO3, TO4, N1 atiśitivarṇaṃ; TO2 atiśivarṇaṃ/; K1 ati/ śitavarṇaṃ; K2 ativarṇa; BL1 tivarṇa; BL2 ati•śitavarṇaṃ.
19 TO1, TO3 sūcīmukhan; TO2 sucīmukha; K1 sūcīmukha; K2 sucimukhaṃ; BL1 sucimuṣaṃ.
20 TO2 tarppayanta/; K1 paryyayantaṃ•; K2 taparyyeyantaṃ; N1 add. /. BL2 paryyantaṃ.
21 TO1, TO2, TO3 -lakāvalodaranivāsinaṃ/; TO4 and N1 add. /. K1 -kāvalodalanivāsitaṃ/; K2 -pātālakāclodalaṇivāsinaṃ; N1 -navāsinaṃ; BL1 śrīmatpātalakācalodala-; BL2 śrīmatpotalakāvalodalanivāsinaṃ/.
22 TO1, TO2, TO3, BL2 karuṇāsnigdhavalokanaṃ/; TO4 karuṇāsnigdhāvilokanaṃ/; K1, N1 karuṇāsnigdhāvalokanaṃ/; K2 -lokaraṃ//; BL1 karuṇāsnigdhāvalokanaṃ•.
23 TO1 śṛṅgāralasaparyupāsitaṃ; TO2, TO4 and N1 add. /. K1 śṛṃgārasaparyyupāśitaṃ/; K2 śṛṅgārarasaparyyūpāsitaṃ; BL2 śṛṅgārasaparyupāśitaṃ//.
24 K1 and BL2 add. /. K2 asitaṃ atiśāntaṃ •; N1 atiśāntan.
25 TO1, TO3 and TO4 om. /. K1, K2, BL1, BL2 a central dot.
26 TO1, TO2, TO3, TO4, K1 and BL2 add. /.
27 TO1 -pāśa; TO3 -pāśe; TO4 dakṣiṇapārśe; K1 dakṣiṇe pārśve•. BL2 dakṣiṇe pārśve.
28 K2 -ra//; BL1 -raṃ •.

(4.2.1) tatra tārā śyāmā[1] vāmakaravidhṛtaṃ[2] sanālam utpalaṃ[3] dakṣiṇakareṇa[4] vikāśayantī[5] nānālaṅkāravatī[6] abhinavayauvanodbhinnakucabhārā/[7]

(4.2.2) sudhanakumāraś[8] ca[9] kṛtāñjalipuṭaḥ[10] kanakāvabhāsidyutiḥ[11] kumārarūpadhārī[12] vāmakakṣavinyastapustakaḥ[13] sakalālaṅkāravān/[14]

(4.2.3) paścime[15] bhṛkuṭī[16] hayagrīva uttare/[17] tatra[18] bhṛkuṭī[19] caturbhujā[20] hemaprabhā[21] jaṭākalāpinī[22] vāme[23] tridaṇḍīkamaṇḍaludhārihastā[24] dakṣiṇe[25] vandanābhinayākṣasūtradharakarā[26] trinetrā/[27]

---

1 TO1, TO2, TO3, TO4, K1, N1 and BL2 add. /. K2 śyāmavarṇā; BL1 śyāmavarṇaṃ.
2 TO1, K1 and BL2 add. /. TO4 illegible between vā- and -karavidhṛtaṃ. K2, BL1 vāmekaravidhṛtaṃ.
3 TO1, TO2, TO3 and TO4 add. /. K1 utparam/; BL2 utparaṃ/.
4 K2 dakṣiṇe kare; BL1 dakṣiṇakare.
5 TO1, TO3, TO4, K1, N1 and BL2 add. /. TO2 add. //. K2 -vikāsayentī.
6 TO1, TO3, TO4 and N1 add. /. TO2 -laṃkāvatī/; K1 -laṃkāravatāṃ/; K2 -laṅkālavatī; BL1 nānālaṅkālavati•; BL2 -laṅkālavatāṃ/.
7 TO1, TO3 abhinavayauvanayauvanodbhinna-; TO4 abhinavayauvanayauvanodbhinnakucabhārā//; K1 atinavayauvanayauvanodbhavakucabhārā; K2 abhinayayauvanohinnakucatārā•; BL1 abhinavayauvanohinnakucatarā•; BL2 abhinavayauvanayauvanodbhivakucabhārā/.
8 TO2 śudha-; K2, BL1 -rañ; BL2 -mālaś.
9 K1, K2 and BL2 add. a central dot.
10 TO1,TO2 kṛtāñjalipūtakaḥ/; TO3, K1, N1 and BL2 add. /. TO4 kṛtāṃjaliputaḥ/; K2 kṛtāñjalipuṭa •; BL1 kṛtāñjalipuṭaḥ.
11 TO1, TO3 kanakāvabhāsadyutiḥ/; TO4 kanakāvabhāsidyutiḥ//; K1, BL2 kanakāvabhāsadyutiḥ//; K2, BL1 kanakāvabhāsidyuti; N1 add. /.
12 TO4 -dhāraṃ; TO1, TO2, K1, N1 and BL2 add. /. K2 kumārarūpadhāraṃ •; BL1 -rūpadhāra.
13 TO1 -vinyasthapūstakaḥ; TO3 and N1 add. /. TO4, K1 and BL2 add. //. K2 vāmakakṣe vi-; BL1 vāmakakṣavinesta •pustakaḥ.
14 K2 savatvālaṅkāravān•; BL1 savatvālaṅkālavān.
15 K2 -ma.
16 K1 add. a central dot. K2 -ti•.
17 K2, N1 and BL1 om. /.
18 TO2 tataḥ.
19 TO1 bhṛtī; K2 bhṛkuṭi.
20 TO4 add. //. K1, N1 and BL2 add. /.
21 TO2 and N1 add. /. TO4 hamaprabhā/; BL2 add. a central dot.
22 TO1, TO3, K1, N1 and BL2 add. /. K2 jatākalāpinī//; BL1 add. a central dot.
23 K1, K2, BL1, BL2 vāma.
24 TO1 -maṇḍī/ kamaṃḍaludhārihastā/; TO2 and TO4 add. /. TO3 tridaṇḍī/ kamaṇḍaludhārihastā/; K1 triḍaṇḍī/ kamaṃḍarudhārihastā/, K2 tridaṃdikamaṃḍaludhārihastā//; N1 add. /. BL1 -kamaṇḍalusudhārihastā; BL2 triḍaṇḍī/ kamaṇḍarudhārihastā/.
25 TO2 dakṣiṇa.
26 TO1 -kṣatrasūdha-; TO2 -dharakarāṃ; TO3 -dharakanā/; TO4 add. //. K1, BL2 vandanābhinayā•akṣasūtradharakarā/; K2 vandanābhinayokṣasūtradharakaro; N1 add. /. BL1 -sutradharakaro.
27 TO3, TO4 //; K2 and BL1 om. /.

(4.2.4) hayagrīvo[1] raktavarṇaḥ[2] kharvalambodaraḥ[3] ūrdhvajvalatpiṅgalakeśaḥ[4] bhujagayajñopavītī[5] kapilataraśmaśruśreṇīparicitamukhamaṇḍalaḥ[6] raktavartulatrinetraḥ[7] bhrūkuṭīkuṭilabhrūkaḥ[8] vyāghracarmāmbaraḥ[9] daṇḍāyudhaḥ[10] dakṣiṇakareṇa[11] vandanābhinayī/[12]

(4.2.5) ete sarva eva[13] svanāyakānanapreritadṛṣṭayo[14] yathā śobham[15] avasthitāś[16] cintanīyāḥ/[17]

(4.3) tataḥ svahṛdi[18] śaśimaṇḍalopari[19] hrīḥkāraṃ[20] vibhāvya[21] tasmāc[22] ca nānākārān[23] raśmīn[24] (25-saṃsphārya[26] traidhātukam[27] āpūrya[28] sarvasattvān[29] lokeśvarapade[30] pratiṣṭhāpya[31] tān[32]

---

1 K2 hayegrivo.
2 TO2 and N1 add. /. TO4 add. //. K1, BL2 -varṇaṃ/.
3 TO2 and N1 add. /. TO4 add. //.
4 TO1 -piṃgarakeśaḥ/; TO2, TO3 and TO4 add. /. K1 -jvaratpiṃgalakeśaḥ/; K2 -śa •; N1 add. /. BL1 -jvalotpiṅgala-; BL2 -jvaratpiṃgalakeśaḥ/.
5 TO1 bhujagaryajñopavitī/; TO2 bhujaṃgaya-; TO3 -vīti; TO4 add. /. K1 bhujaṃgayajñopavīti; N1 add. /. BL2 bhujaṃgayajñopavīti/.
6 TO2 kilataraśmaśruṇī-; TO3 and N1 add. /. TO4 kapilataraśmaśkaśreṇīparicitamukhamaṇḍalaḥ//; K1 kapilatalaśmaśruṇoṇīparicitamukhamaṇḍaladhāraḥ/; K2 kapilatalaśmasktastreṇipariritamukhamaṇḍalaṃ•; BL1 kapilatalaśmaśruśrenipariritamukhamaṇḍalaṃ •; BL2 kapilatalaśmaśruśaśīparicitamukhamaṇḍalakāraḥ/.
7 TO3 and N1 add. /. TO4 raktavattulanitrinetraḥ/; K1, BL2 raktavarturatriṇetraḥ/.
8 TO1 bhṛkuṭīkuṭilabhrūkaḥ; TO2 and N1 add. /. TO4 bhrūkuṭīkuṭīlabhrūkaḥ//; K1 bhrikuṭīkuṭilabhrukaḥ; K2 bhṛkuṭikutalī•bhrūka •; BL1 bhrūkuṭīkuṭalībhrūkaḥ; BL2 bhrikuṭīkuṭilabhrūkaḥ.
9 TO1 -carmmāmbarā; TO2 -carmmāṃbara; TO3, TO4 and N1 add. /. K2, BL1 -carmmāmbara •.
10 TO2, TO4 and N1 add. /. K2, BL1 om.
11 K2 -karena; BL1 dakṣinakarena.
12 K1, BL2 //; K2 vandanābhīnayī •; BL1 has a central dot.
13 K1, BL2 om.
14 TO4 svarānāya-; K1 svanāyakānanenapreritadṛṣṭayo•; BL1 svanāyakānnapreritadṛṣṭayā; BL2 svanāyakānnena •preritadṛṣṭayo •.
15 TO1 śobha; TO2 śobati.
16 TO1, K1 sthitāś; TO2 sthitā; TO4 avasthitāṃś; BL2 asthitāś.
17 TO1 om. /. TO3, TO4, K1, BL2 //; K2 ciṁtaniyā•; BL1 cintaniyā.
18 BL1 svahṛdī.
19 TO1 -parī; K1 add. a central dot . K2 -pa; BL1 śaśīmaṇḍalopari; BL2 śaśīmaṇḍalopari•.
20 TO1 -kāra; K1 hrīkāraṃ.
21 TO1, TO2, TO4 and N1 add. /. TO3 add. //. K1, K2, BL2 -yaḥ//; BL1 add. a central dot.
22 BL1 tasmā.
23 TO1 nānyakān; TO3, K1 nānākān; TO4 nākārān; K1 add. a central dot. BL2 nānākān •.
24 K2, BL1 rasmin.
25 K1, BL2 om.
26 TO2 sasphāryya; TO3 saphāryya; K2 -yye; BL1 sasphārya.
27 TO2 traidhākam.
28 TO1 māpūrya; K2, BL1 āvṛtya.
29 K2 sarvvasatvāna; BL1 sarvvasarvasatvān.
30 BL1 alokepade.
31 K2 pratiṣṭhāpe; N1 add. /.
32 K2 add. a colon .

raśmīn punas[1-25)] tatraiva[2] bījākṣare[3] praveśayet/[4] punas[5] tatkiraṇair[6] eva[7] jñānasattvam[8]
ākṛṣya[9] samayasattvena[10] saha[11] kṣīranīrayor[12] iva ekarūpatāṃ dhyāyāt/[13]

(4.4) tataḥ kāyavākcittaviśuddhyā yathā kramaṃ[14] śirasi sitam[15] oṃkāraṃ/[16] kaṇṭhe raktam
āḥkāraṃ/[17] hṛdi kṛṣṇahūṃkāraṃ[18] vicintayet/[19]
amī[20] cānavarataniḥsaradanantakiraṇājālavidhvastanikhilasattvarāśikaluṣasaṅghātā[21] iti
bhāvanāṃ[22] yathāśakti sphuṭīkuryāt/[23]

(5) pāṭavaṃ[24] dhāraṇāṃ[25] prajñāṃ[26] saubhāgyārogyasampadam/[27] labhate bhāvanāyogāt[28]
sākṣāt[29] kāraṃ[30] ca vīryavān//[31]

---

1 TO1 puna; K1 punaḥ; K2 puras; BL2 punan.
2 TO1 tattaiva; K2 add. a central dot. N1 tatreva; BL2 tatrīva.
3 K1 -ram; BL1 -ra; BL2 -reṇa.
4 TO1, TO3, K1, BL2 //; K2 om. /. BL1 -yat•.
5 BL1 puṇas.
6 K1 tatkiranaiva; K2 tatkīraṇai•reva; BL2 tatkiraṇai •va.
7 K1, K2, BL2 om.
8 K2, BL1 jñānasam.
9 K2 and BL2 add. a central dot.
10 K1 -satvena •; BL2 add. a central dot.
11 K1, BL2 sahī.
12 TO2 kṣīraṇīrayor; K1 kṣiraṇilayor; K2 kṣīṇilayor; BL1 kṣīranīlayor; BL2 kṣiraṇīlayor.
13 K1, BL1, BL2 //; K2 has a central dot.
14 K1 and BL2 add. //. K2, BL1 -ma.
15 B sitaṃ; K2 tam.
16 B om. /. K2, BL1 aukāraṃ.
17 B and TO1 om. /. K2, BL1 ākāraṃ •.
18 TO2 -hūṃkāra; BL2 kṛṣṇa •hūṃ-.
19 TO1, TO3, TO4 //; K2 and BL1 have a central dot.
20 K2 ami.
21 TO1 rānavarataniḥsaradanatukiraṇajālavidhastanikhilasatvarāśikaruṣasaṃghātāḥ; TO2 -kiraṇajālavidhvastanikhilasatvarāsikaluṣasaṃghātāḥ/; TO3 rānavarataniḥsaracamatu-kiraṇajālavidhastanikhilasatvarāśikalūṣasaṃghātāḥ; TO4 rānavarataniḥsaravanantra-kiraṇājālavidhvastanikhilasatvarāśikaluṣasaṃghātāḥ//; K1 rānavarataniḥsaravanatu •kiraṇa-jālavidhastanikhilasatvarāśi•kaluṣasaṃghātāḥ//; K2 cānvarataniḥsaradaṃtakiraṇa-jālavidhostatikhilasatvarāsikarukasahastā•; N1 -saṃghātāḥ/; BL1 cānavarataniḥsaradanta-kiraṇājālavidhvastaniṣilasatvarāsikaluṣasahatāḥ; BL2 rānavarataniḥsaravananta •kiraṇajāla-vidhastanikhilasatvarāśi•kaluṣasaṅghātāḥ//.
22 TO1, K2, BL1 -nā; TO3 bhāvānāṃ; BL2 add. //.
23 TO1, TO3, TO4, K1, N1 //; TO2 sphaṭīkuryāt//; K2 sphuṭikuryyāṭ; BL1 om. /. BL2 sphuṭikuryyāt//.
24 TO1, TO3 -van; TO2 -va; K1 pātavaṃ; K2 pādavaṃ; BL2 pātavan.
25 TO1, K1 dhānanāṃ; TO4 dhānaṇāṃ; K1 dhāraṇāṃ•; K2, BL1 dhāraṇā; BL2 dhānanāṃ •.
26 TO1, TO4, K2, BL1 prajñā.
27 TO1 -rogye saṃpadaṃ//; TO2 -roga-; K1 a central dot. K2 saubhāgyarogesampadaṃ; BL1 saubhāgerogasaṃpadaṃ•.
28 K2 bhāvanoyogā; BL1 -yogā.
29 TO1, TO3, K1, BL2 sākṣat.
30 TO1, TO3, K1, BL2 karaṇañ; TO4, K2, N1, BL1 -kārañ.
31 TO4 /; K2 vīryyevān; BL1 add. a central dot.

(6) bhāvanākhinnas[1] tu[2] mantram[3] ekāgracetasā[4] japet/[5] tatrāyaṃ[6] mantraḥ//[7] oṃ hrīḥ svāhā/[8] amī[9] ca varṇāḥ śaradamalatārakāmālikeva[10] prabhāsvarāḥ[11] sphuradanekaraśmayaḥ/[12] japakhedāt[13] tu[14] puṇyaṃ[15] pariṇamayotthāya[16] yathāsukhaṃ[17] devatāhaṅkāram[18] udvahan[19] viharet/[20]

(7) vidhāya[21] sādhanaṃ[22] hṛdyaṃ[23] śrīmallokeśvarasya[24] yat/[25]
mayā puṇyaṃ[26] samāsādi[27] tenāstāṃ[28] tatpadaṃ jagat//[29]
//iti[30] khasarpaṇasādhanaṃ[31] samāptam/[32]
kṛtir[33] iyaṃ[34] padmākaramatipādānām//[35]

---

1 TO1, TO2, TO3, TO4, K1, K2, BL1, BL2 -khinno; N1 bhāvanakhinno.
2 TO1, TO2, TO3, TO4, K1, N1, BL2 om.; K2, BL1 tum.
3 K2, BL1 om.
4 TO2 -cettasā; K1, BL2 ekāgra •cetasā; K2, N1, BL1 ekāgrato cetasā.
5 TO1, TO2, TO3, TO4, K1, K2, BL1, BL2 //.
6 TO1 tatrayaṃ; TO3 tatrāyan; TO4, K2, BL1 tatrāya; N1 tatraya.
7 B and K2 om. //. TO2 mantra//; N1 add. /.
8 TO1, TO2, TO3, TO4, K1, K2, N1, BL1, BL2 //.
9 K2 ami.
10 K1, BL2 daśadamalatālakāmālikeva; K2 śaramalatālakālikeca; BL1 śaradamalatālakālikeca.
11 BL1 -varā•.
12 TO1 and BL1 om. /. TO4 spharadanakaraśmayaḥ//; K2 -ye.
13 TO1 japedārt; TO2 japakṣadāṃ; TO3 japedājapekhedā; K1 japeddātradā; K2, BL1 -dā; BL2 japedāt.
14 TO1, TO4 ta; K1 om.; BL1 add. a central dot.
15 TO2 puṇya; K2, BL1 puṇye; BL2 add. a central dot.
16 B pariṇamaya utthāya; K1 pariṇāmayotthāya •; K2 parimadhyotthāya; BL1 parimadhyotthāya; BL2 add. a central dot.
17 TO1, N1 -sukha; K1 -mūkhaṃ; K2 yāsukhaṃ; BL1 yāsuṣa.
18 TO4 -haṃkāra.
19 K2, BL1 udvaharet•; BL2 add. a central dot.
20 TO2, TO3, TO4, N1, BL2 //; K1 om. /. K2, BL1 om.
21 BL1 vidhā.
22 TO1 -ne; K2, BL1 sāṃ na.
23 K2, BL1 -ya; BL2 add. a central dot.
24 K2 śrīmalo-.
25 TO2 yet/; K2 yet//; N1 om. /. BL1 has a central dot.
26 TO1 pūṇya; TO2 pūṇyaṃ; K2 puṇye.
27 K1 and BL2 add. a central dot. K2 māsādi•; BL1 āsādi.
28 TO1, TO3, K1, N1, BL2 -staṃ; K2, BL1 -stā.
29 TO1, TO2, TO3, TO4, K1 and N1 om. //.
30 TO4 / iti; K1 om. //.
31 K2 sādhanasamucaye khasarpaṇalokeśvarasya sādhanasaptatriṃśaty adhikaśatatamapaṭalaḥ//137//; BL1 sādhanasamuccaye khasarpaṇalokeśvarasya sādhanasaptatriṃśaty adhikaśatatamapatala//137.
32 TO1, N1 //; TO2, TO3, TO4, K1, BL2 // //; K2, BL1 om.
33 B, TO4, N1 kṛtiḥ; TO1, TO3, K1, BL2 kṛti; K2, BL1 om.
34 B, TO1, TO3, K1, K2, N1, BL1, BL2 om.
35 TO2 paṇḍitaḥpadmākaramatipādānāṃ; K2, BL1 om.

## 2.3 Khasarpaṇalokeśvarasādhana (Bhatt. no. 15)

(0) namaḥ śrīkhasarpaṇāya//[1]

(1) iha śubhaṅkaranāmā[2] upāsakaḥ[3] śubhakarmakārī[4] karuṇāyamānaḥ[5] sa kila potalakagamanodyataḥ[6] gacchan[7] khāḍīmaṇḍale[8] khasarpaṇanāmā[9] grāmo 'sti[10] tatroṣitaḥ/[11] tasya tu bhagavadāryāvalokiteśvareṇa[12] pratyādeśo[13] dattaḥ/[14] mā gaccha[15] tvam ihāsmān[16] vairocanābhisaṃbodhitantrarājakrameṇa[17] sthāpaya[18] tena mahān[19] sattvārtho[20] bhaviṣyati/[21] tatrāsau[22] bhagavantaṃ[23] (24-śīghram[25] eva[26] kāritavān[27] ity eṣā[28] śrutiḥ/[29]

---

1 B /, TO1 śrīkhasarppaṇāyaḥ//; K1, BL2 khasarppāya//.
2 K1 śubhakaraṇāmā; BL2 śubhakaraṇāmā •.
3 TO1 -kāḥ.
4 K1 add. a central dot.
5 TO1 -yamaḥ/; TO2 -yamāṇaḥ; TO3, K1, N1 and BL2 add. /.
6 TO2 and N1 add. /. TO4 add. //.
7 K1 gachan.
8 TO1 khātimaṇḍale; TO2, TO3 khātīmaṇḍale; K1, BL2 sukhāvatī•maṇḍale.
9 TO1 khasarppanaṇāmā; TO2 -māṃ/.
10 TO3, K1 and BL2 add. /.
11 TO1 tatropītaḥ; TO3, TO4 tatropitaḥ; K1 tatrāpitas; BL2 tatrāpitaḥ.
12 The rendering follows the Sandhi rule. B, TO1, TO2, TO3, TO4, K1, N1, BL2 bhagavatāryāva-.
13 TO1 -śva.
14 TO1 om. /. TO4 //.
15 K1 gachan.
16 K1 add. a central dot.
17 TO1 vairocaṇābhi-; TO4 vairocanābhisambodhitatrarāja-; K1 vairocanābhiḥsambodhimaṃtra-; N1 vairocanābhisambodhi-; BL2 vairocanādibhi-.
18 TO2 sthāpaye; K1 and BL2 add. a central dot.
19 K1, BL2 mahāsatvān.
20 K1 satvān.
21 TO1, TO2, TO3 //.
22 TO1, TO2, TO3, BL2 tato sau; TO4, K1 satosau.
23 TO2 bhagavan; N1 bhāgavantaṃ; K1 and BL2 add. a central dot.
24 TO2 om.
25 TO4 śrīghram.
26 TO1 meva.
27 TO4, K1, N1 and BL2 add. /.
28 TO1 ekhāṃ; TO3 eṣāṃ; K1, BL2 evaṃ.
29 TO1, TO3 and BL2 om. /. TO4 //; K1 has a central dot.

(2) tatra bhagavataḥ sādhanāya[1] dṛṣṭisampattiḥ[2] kriyate/[3] tathāhi varaṃ bhikṣoḥ śīlavipattir[4] na[5] punar[6] dṛṣṭivipattir[7] iti[8] atas[9] tatra[10] tāvat kṣaṇikān[11] nirātmakān[12] sarvadharmān[13-24)] vyavalokya[14] vyapagatasakalavikalpaḥ[15] kṛpāśayo[16] 'ho batāmī[17] sattvāḥ kleśakarmādibhir[18] upadrutāḥ[19] tato jātijarāmaraṇaduḥkhair[20] atīva pīḍyamānāḥ[21] santo 'nekaprakāraduḥkham[22] anubhavanti/[23] tato 'haṃ[24] lokeśvaro[25] bhūtvā teṣāṃ[26] duḥkhādy apanayāmi[27] sarvajñajñāne pratiṣṭhāpayāmi/[28] ity evaṃ pratijñāśayaṃ[29] kṛtvā

(3.1) svahṛdi[30] paṃkārajasahasradalapadmavaraṭakamadhye[31] akārajaṃ[32] candramaṇḍalopari[33] āḥ[34]-tāṃ[35]-sūṃ[36]-bhṛīṃ-hāṃ iti pañcabījāni vinyasya[37]

---

1 TO1 sādanyaya; K1 and BL2 add. a central dot.
2 K1 -patti.
3 TO4 kiyate/; K1, BL2 //.
4 TO4 śīlavipatti.
5 TO4 om.
6 K1 punaḥ•; BL2 puna•.
7 K1, BL2 dṛṣṭirvvipattir.
8 TO1, TO3, K1 and BL2 add. //. TO4 and N1 add. /.
9 K1, BL2 atras.
10 K1 tatras.
11 TO1, TO3 kaścikān; TO4 kṣaścikān; K1, BL2 kaścikān•.
12 BL2 add. a central dot.
13 K1 and BL2 add. a central dot.
14 K1, BL2 -kyā•.
15 TO4 -gatasarvavikalavikalpaḥ; K1, BL2 vyapagata•sakala-; N1 -gatāmsakalavikalpaḥ.
16 TO1 kṛpāsayo.
17 B bata amī; K1, N1 matāmī.
18 TO2 -karmmādibhi; K1, BL2 kleśakalpādibhir.
19 B add. a comma. TO1 and TO4 add.//. K1, BL2 upadruvāḥ/; TO2, TO3 and N1 add. /.
20 TO2 jātirāmaraṇa-.
21 TO2 pītsumanāḥ.
22 TO4 -praraduḥkham; TO2 -duḥkhan; BL2 -dūkam.
23 TO1, TO3, TO4, K1, BL2 //; TO2 bhavaṃti/.
24 TO4 ha; N1 add. /.
25 TO2 lokeśvarā; TO4 lokeśvarau.
26 K1 and BL2 add. a central dot.
27 TO2, TO3 and N1 add. /. TO4 epanayāmi/; K1 apraṇāyāmi/; BL2 apaṇayāmi/.
28 K1, BL2 //.
29 TO2 pratijñāmamayaṃ.
30 K1 and BL2 add. a central dot.
31 TO1 -madhya; TO2 -ya; K1 paṃkāraja•sahasradalapadmavaratakamadhye•; BL2 paṃkāraja•sahasradalapadmavaratakamadhye•.
32 TO1, TO2, TO3, K1, BL2 akāraja; N1 akāra.
33 K1 add. a central dot. BL2 -maṇḍaropari•.
34 TO1, TO3, TO4, K1, BL2 āṃ; TO2 ā; N1 oṃ.
35 TO2 trā.
36 TO2 su.
37 TO1, TO2, TO3, TO4, K1, N1 and BL2 add. /.

(3.2) etadraśmimālābhiḥ sañcodyānīya[1] tān gurubuddhabodhisattvān[2] gaganatale[3] purovartinaḥ[4] kṛtvā vandanāpūjāpāpadeśanātriśaraṇagamanādisaptavidhāṃ[5] pūjām[6] ekādaśavidhāṃ[7] vā[8] kṛtvā[9] maitrīkaruṇādicaturbrahmavihārabhāvanāṃ[10] kuryāt/[11]

(3.3) tataḥ oṃ[12] śūnyatājñānavajrasvabhāvātmako[13] 'ham[14] ity uccārya śūnyatābodhiṃ[15] kṛtvā[16] bhagavān[17] avalokiteśvaro[18] yogātmanā[19] bhūyate/[20]

(4) sa ca śaratkāṇḍagauraḥ[21] jaṭāmakuṭī[22] śirasi[23] amitābhadhārī sarvālaṅkārabhūṣitaḥ[24] ratnasiṃhāsanopari[25] sahasradalapadmasthaḥ[26] lalitākṣepaḥ dvibhujaikamukhaḥ[27] vāmena padmadhārī[28] dakṣiṇenāmṛtadhārāsravadvaradaḥ[29] sattvaparyaṅkāsīnaḥ/[30]

(5.1) agratas tārā[31] kanakaśyāmavarṇā/[32] unnatapīnapayodharā[33] sarvālaṅkārabhūṣitā/[34] utpalakalikāsannakaradvayārpitanetrā/[35]

---

1 K1 and BL2 add. a central dot.
2 TO2 illegible between gurubu- and -bodhisatvān.
3 TO1, TO3, TO4 gagaṇatale; K1, BL2 gagaṇatale•.
4 TO1 pūrovarttanaḥ; TO3, BL2 purovarttanaḥ; K1 punovarttanaḥ.
5 TO1 -gamaṇādisaptavidhāṃ; TO2 -gamanādisaptavidhā; K1 vandanāpūjā/ pāpadeśanā-triśaraṇagamanādi•saptavidhāṃ; BL2 -pāpadeśanā•triśaraṇagamanādi•saptavidhāṃ.
6 BL2 pūjā•.
7 TO1 ekādaśavidhām; TO2, K1 ekādaśadhāṃ; TO3, TO4 ekādaśadhām; N1 ekādasavidhām; BL2 mekādaśadhāṃ.
8 K1 and BL2 om. vā and add. a central dot.
9 BL2 add. a central dot.
10 TO1 maitrīkaruṇādi/ catubahmavihārībhāvanā; TO2, TO3, TO4, N1, BL2 -vihārībhāvanāṃ; K1 -catubrahmavihārībhāvanāṃ.
11 TO1 kūryyāt//; K1, BL2 //.
12 TO1, TO2, TO3, TO4, K1, N1, BL2 om.
13 TO3 śūnyatāṃ jñāna-; K1 śūnyatāṃ jñānasatvavajra-; BL2 śūnyatāṃ jñānasatva•vaja-.
14 The rendering follows the Sandhi rule. B 'haṃ.
15 TO1, TO3 -bodhi; K1, BL2 śūnyatābodhisatvā•.
16 K1, BL2 om.
17 N1 add. /.
18 TO2 valokiteśvaro.
19 TO1, TO3, N1, BL2 yoginātmanā; TO4 yogitātmanā.
20 TO1, TO3, TO4, K1, BL2 //.
21 TO1 -gaura; N1 śarakhāṇḍagauraḥ; TO4, K1, BL2 sarat-.
22 TO1 jaṭāmutī; K1 add. a central dot.
23 TO1 si.
24 TO1, TO3 sarvvāraṃkārabhūṣitaḥ/; TO4, K1, N1 and BL2 add. /.
25 TO1 -parī; K1 add. a central dot.
26 TO1 -sahasradarapadmasthaḥ/; TO2, TO3, TO4, K1, N1 and BL2 add. /.
27 TO2 dvitubhujaikamukhaḥ/; TO4 add. //. K1 -bhujaivamukho; N1 add. /. BL2 -bhujaikamukho.
28 TO1, TO3 and N1 add. /. TO2 -dhārīnaṃ; K1, BL2 -dhārī•.
29 TO1 dakṣiṇenāmṛtaśravad-; TO2 dakṣiṇenāmṛtadhārāśravadvaradaḥ/; TO3 dakṣiṇenāmṛtaśravadvaradaḥ/; TO4 dakṣiṇenāmṛtadhārāśruvadvaradaḥ/; N1 add. /. K1, BL2 dakṣiṇenāmṛtaśravadvaradaḥ//.
30 TO1 -paryyaṅkāsīna/; K1, BL2 //; N1 -paryaṅkāsīna//.
31 K1 and BL2 add. /.
32 B om. /. TO1, TO3 -varṇāḥ; K1, BL2 -varṇāḥ/.
33 TO1, TO3 -rāḥ; K1, BL2 -rāḥ/; TO2 and N1 add. /.
34 B om. /. TO1, TO4 sarvālakārabhūṣitā/; K1, BL2 //.
35 TO1 -dvayāpitanetrā/; TO3, TO4, K1, BL2 -karadvayāpitanetrā/.

(5.2) tadanu[1] sudhanakumāraḥ[2] kanakojjvalaḥ[3] ratnābharaṇo ratnamakuṭī[4] vāmakakṣāvasaktakamalikaḥ[5] kṛtāñjalipuṭaḥ/[6]

(5.3) tadanu bhṛkuṭī[7] jaṭāmakuṭinī[8] mūrdhni[9] caityālaṅkṛtā[10] kanakojjvalā[11] raktavastraparidhānā[12] dakṣiṇahastena[13] namaskāraṃ[14] kurvāṇā/[15] apareṇākṣamālādharā[16] vāmakarābhyāṃ[17] tridaṇḍīkamaṇḍaluvyagrā/[18]

(5.4) tadanu hayagrīvo jvaladbhāsuraḥ[19] piṅgalordhvakeśaḥ[20] nāgābharaṇo[21] raktavarṇaḥ[22] lambodaro[23] vyāghracarmāmbaraḥ[24] daṇḍahastaḥ/[25]

(5.5) evaṃ pañcātmako[26] bhagavān bhāvanīyaḥ[27] saparivāraḥ[28] pūjayitavyo[29] 'py evaṃ[30] vidhaḥ/[31]

---

1 TO4 tadanū.
2 TO1, TO2, TO3, TO4, K1, N1 and BL2 add. /.
3 TO1-kodjāraḥ; TO2 -kojvalaḥ; K1 add. //. TO3, TO4 and N1 add. /. BL2 -kojvalaḥ//.
4 TO1, N1 ratnamukṭī/; TO2 add. /.
5 TO2, TO3, TO4 and N1 add. /. K1 add. //. BL2 -saktamalikaḥ//.
6 TO1 om. /. TO2 -pūṭaḥ; K1, BL2 //.
7 K1 and BL2 add. a central dot.
8 TO1 jaṭāmuku-; TO2, N1 jaṭāmukuṭinī/; TO4 add. /.
9 TO1 murdhni; TO2 mūrdhna; K1 //.
10 TO1 caityālakṛtā/; TO2, TO3 and N1 add. /. K1 bhyālaṃkṛtaṃ/; BL2 tyālaṅkṛtā/.
11 TO1, TO2, TO4 -kojvalā; TO4 kenakojvalā/; K1 and BL2 add. a central dot.
12 TO1, TO2, TO3, N1 and BL2 add. /. TO4 raktavastraparidhārā/; K1 raktavastravaridhānā/.
13 TO2, K1 -haste.
14 TO2 illegible after namaskā-.
15 B om. /. TO2 kurvvāṇā/; K1, BL2 //.
16 TO1 -mālādhalā; TO2, TO3, K1, N1 and BL2 add. /. TO4 apareṇākṣemālādharā/.
17 K1 and BL2 add. a central dot.
18 K1 -kamaṇḍaruvyagrā//; BL2 -maṇḍaruvyagrā//.
19 K1 add. /. N1 -ra; BL2 -bhāsuraṣe.
20 TO2, TO4 and N1 add. /. BL2 piṃgalordvakeśaḥ.
21 TO4 rāgābharaṇo; BL2 nāgābharano.
22 TO2, TO3, TO4 and N1 add. /. K1 -ṇo; BL2 -ṇa.
23 TO1 -dalo; TO2, BL2 -rā; K1 add. a central dot.
24 TO4 -carmmambaraḥ/; N1 add. /.
25 TO1 daṇḍadastaḥ; TO4, K1, BL2 //.
26 K1 add. a central dot.
27 TO2 and N1 add. /. TO4 add. //.
28 TO4 add. //.
29 K1 and BL2 add. a central dot.
30 K1, BL2 edaṃ; N1 evam.
31 TO1 and TO2 om. /. TO4 //.

(6.1) tataḥ[1] kṛtamaṇḍale[2] tatrādau maṇḍalaṃ[3] kṛtvā[4] rakṣāṃ[5] kuryāt/[6] oṃ maṇidhari[7] vajriṇi[8] rakṣa rakṣa[9] māṃ hūṃ[10] phaṭ svāhā/[11] oṃ vajrarekhe[12] hūṃ[13] maṇḍalamantraḥ/[14]
(6.2) oṃ āgaccha[15] bhagavan[16] maṇḍalakasiṃhāsane[17] oṃ āḥ iti mantrakṛto[18] 'dhyeṣaṇāyāṃ[19]
(6.3) kṛtamaṇḍalamadhyasiṃhāsanopari[20] sahasradalapadmasthaṃ[21] pañcātmakaṃ pūjayed iti/[22] tatra pūjāmantraḥ//[23] oṃ vajrapuṣpe hūṃ/ oṃ vajradhūpe[24] hūṃ/[25] oṃ vajragandhe hūṃ/[26] oṃ vajrāloke[27] hūṃ/ oṃ vajrāhāre[28] hūṃ/[29] iti saṃpūjya[30] saṃstutya[31] mantrajāpaṃ[32] kuryāt/[33] oṃ sarvatathāgatapūjāmeghaprasarasamūhe[34] hūṃ/[35] pūjādhiṣṭhānamantraḥ[36] oṃ

---

1 K1, BL2 tatra.
2 TO1, TO2, TO3, TO4 and N1 add. /. K1 and BL2 add. //.
3 K1 maṇḍala.
4 BL2 add. a central dot.
5 TO1 rakṣā.
6 TO1, TO3, K1, BL2 //.
7 TO2 maṇidhara.
8 TO3 vajaṇi; K1 vajriṇī.
9 TO2, TO3, TO4 om.
10 K1 and BL2 add. hūṃ.
11 TO2, TO4, K1, N1, BL2 //.
12 TO4 -lekhe.
13 TO1, TO2 and TO3 add. /. K1 and BL2 add. //.
14 TO1, TO3, K1, BL2 //; TO4 -mantra//; N1 om. /.
15 K1 āgacha.
16 TO4 bhagavana; K1 om.; BL2 add. //.
17 K1 and BL2 add. a central dot.
18 TO2 mantraṃ kṛtā; TO3, BL2 mantrakṛtā; TO4, K1 maṃtrakṛtā.
19 TO3, TO4, K1 dhyeṣaṇayāṃ; BL2 dhyeṣaṇayāṃ•.
20 K1, BL2 -madhye•siṃ-.
21 TO1 sahasradarapadmastha; TO3, TO4, BL2 -stha; TO2 add. //. K1 -stha•.
22 TO1, TO2, TO3, TO4 //.
23 B pūjāmantrāḥ; TO3 -mantra; N1 /.
24 TO4 vajradhupe.
25 TO4 //.
26 TO4 //.
27 TO1 vajāroke; K1 vajralokite; BL2 vajalokite.
28 K1 vajrahare.
29 TO1, TO2 //.
30 TO1 sapūjya.
31 BL2 add. a central dot.
32 TO4 maṃtrajāpa.
33 TO1, TO3, TO4, K1, BL2 //.
34 TO1 -prasalasamūhe.
35 K1, BL2 //.
36 TO1, TO2 and N1 add. /. TO3 add. //. TO4 -mantra//; K1 puṣpādhisthānamaṃtraḥ//; BL2 puṣpādhiṣṭhānamantraḥ//.

āḥ[1] tāṃ[2] sūṃ bhṛīṃ hāṃ[3] phaṭ[4] svāhā/[5] oṃ sarvatathāgatasulalitanamitair[6] namāmi[7] bhagavantaṃ[8] jaḥ hūṃ vāṃ hoḥ[9] pratīccha[10] kusumāñjaliṃ[11] nātha hoḥ[12] iti vandanāmantraḥ/[13]

(6.4) oṃ muḥ svāhā[14] iti[15] visarjanamantraḥ/[16]

(6.5) oṃ kha[17] kha khāhi[18] khāhi gṛhṇa gṛhṇa[19] gṛhṇantu[20] sārvabhautikā[21] imaṃ[22] baliṃ[23] svāhā[24] iti balimantraḥ/[25]

(6.6) atha pūjārambhakāle[26] evam uccārya cittaṃ[27] śodhanīyaṃ[28] yat sarvaduścāritebhyo[29] viratiṃ[30] karomi[31] sarvabuddhabodhisattvaśikṣāṃ[32] śikṣiṣye[33] yāvat pūjāvidhiṃ[34] na samarthayāmi/[35] yady evaṃ[36] na kriyate[37] tadā[38]·rāgajaṃ[39] dveṣajaṃ[40] mohajaṃ[41] kuśalamūlaṃ syāt/[1] iha sarva eva[2] sattvā[3] rāgadveṣamohāśayāḥ/[4] tathāhi

---

1 TO1, TO2, TO3, TO4, K1, N1 āṃ.
2 TO1, TO3, K1, BL2 trāṃ.
3 TO1, TO2, TO3, TO4, K1, N1, BL2 hūṃ.
4 B and N1 add. phaṭ.
5 TO1, TO3, TO4, K1, N1, BL2 //.
6 TO1 -tathāgatasurarītamitai; TO3 -tathāgatasulalitamitair; K1 -tathāgatasulalitair; BL2 -tathāgatasuralitair.
7 TO2 nami.
8 TO4 bhaktagavantaṃ.
9 TO1 hūḥ; K1 and BL2 add. /.
10 TO1 praticcha.
11 TO1 kusumāṃjarī; TO2, TO3, TO4, N1 -lin; K1 kuśmāṃjali; BL2 kuśumāñjali.
12 TO2, TO4, K1 and BL2 add. //. N1 add. /.
13 TO1 vandaṇāmantra//; TO4 -mantra//; K1, BL2 //.
14 TO1,TO3, K1 and BL2 add. //. TO2 add. /.
15 K1, BL2 om.
16 TO2, K1, BL2 //.
17 TO2 om.
18 TO1, TO2, TO3, TO4, BL2 om.
19 TO1, TO2, TO3, TO4 om.
20 BL2 add. a central dot.
21 TO1, TO2 sarvvabhautikā; TO4 sarvabhautikā; N1 sārvabhauti.
22 TO1, N1 imam.
23 TO4 bali.
24 TO1, TO2, TO3, K1, N1 and BL2 add. //. TO4 add. /.
25 TO1, TO4, K1, N1, BL2 //.
26 TO4 pūjāraṃmbhakāla (anusvāra insertion); K1 pūjālaṃbhakale; BL2 pūjālaṃbhakāle.
27 TO2 citta.
28 TO1, TO2, TO3, TO4, K1, N1 and BL2 add. /.
29 TO1, TO2, TO4, N1, BL2 -duścaritebhyo.
30 TO1 viratiñ; TO2 virati; TO3 viratiṅ.
31 B add. a comma. TO1, TO3 karosi//; TO2 and TO4 add. /. K1, BL2 karosi.
32 TO2 -bodhisatvāsikṣā; K1 -bodhisattvaśiṣyām; BL2 -bodhisattvaśiṣyām•.
33 B add. a comma. TO1 and TO3 add. //. TO2 sikṣiṣye/; TO4 and N1 add. /. K1, BL2 śiṣye.
34 TO1, TO4, BL2 -vidhi.
35 TO1 samadhayāmi//; TO3 samanthayāmi//; K1 samaṃvayāmi//; N1 samanvayāmi/; BL2 samaṃdhayāmi//.
36 N1 evan.
37 TO1, TO2, TO3, TO4, K1, N1 and BL2 add. /.
38 TO2 tad.
39 TO2 gajaṃ; K1 and BL2 add. a central dot.
40 K1 and BL2 add. a central dot.
41 K1 and BL2 add. a central dot.

syāt/[1] iha sarva eva[2] sattvā[3] rāgadveṣamohāśayāḥ/[4] tathāhi rāgajakuśalamūlena[5] nandopanandau nāgarājānau[6] dveṣajena[7] rāgajena[8] mohajena[9] vaiśravaṇo[10] yakṣo[11] bhūtaḥ/[12] ity ato[13] rāgadveṣamohādīn[14] parihṛtya cittaviśuddhyā[15] karuṇāmayacittena[16] sarvāṇy eva[17] dānādikuśalamūlāni[18] kartavyāni/[19]
//iti khasarpaṇasādhanaṃ[20] samāptam//[21]

---

1 K1, BL2 //.
2 TO2 om.
3 BL2 add. a central dot.
4 TO1, TO4 -mohaśayāḥ//; TO2 om. /. TO3 //; K1 -moha•śayā; BL2 rāgadveṣa•moha •śayā.
5 TO1 rāgajakuśaramūlena//; TO2 rāgajaṃkuśa-; K1 rāgaja•kuśalamūlena; BL2 rāgaja•kuśalamūlena•.
6 B add. a comma. TO2, TO3 and N1 add. /. TO4 add. //.
7 TO2 dveṣajeṇa; K1 add. a central dot.
8 B rāvaṇaḥ and a comma. TO1, TO3 rāgena; TO2, N1 rāmaṇa/; TO4 rāgeṇa; K1 and BL2 add. a central dot.
9 TO2 mahajeṇa; K1 add. a central dot.
10 TO2 -ṇā.
11 BL2 add. /.
12 TO1 om. /. TO2 //.
13 K1, BL2 anto.
14 K1 add. a central dot. BL2 rāgadveṣa•mohādīn•.
15 TO2 cittaśuddhyā; K1 and BL2 add. a central dot.
16 TO2 -citteṇa; BL2 add. a central dot.
17 TO4 ava.
18 TO1 dānādikusalamūlāni; BL2 dānādi•kuśala-.
19 TO1 kattavyāni; TO2, TO3 and TO4 om. /. K1, BL2 //.
20 TO1 khasarppasādhana; TO2 khasarppaṇasādhana; TO3, BL2 khasarpasādhanaṃ; K1 khasappasādhanaṃ.
21 K1 and BL2 add. māghasya//.

## 2.4 Khasarpaṇalokeśvarasādhana (Bhatt. no. 16)

(0) namaḥ khasarpaṇāya/[1]

(1) prathamaṃ tāvan mantrī sukhāsanopaviṣṭaḥ

(2.1.1) svahṛdy[2] akāreṇa candramaṇḍalaṃ[3]

(2.1.2) tataḥ hrīḥkāraṃ sitavarṇaṃ[4] tadudbhūtasitaraśmibhir[5] agrato[6] 'mbare[7] gurubuddhabodhisattvān paśyet/[8] tān[9] svahṛdbījaraśmibhiḥ saṃpūjya[10] pāpadeśanādikaṃ[11] kuryāt/[12]

(2.1.3) oṃ śunyatājñānavajrasvabhāvātmako 'ham iti adhiṣṭhayet/[13] ātmānaṃ śunyatāyāṃ[14] vyavalokya[15]

(2.2.1) pūrvoktahrīḥkāreṇa[16] sphuraṇasaṃharaṇakrameṇa[17] lokeśvararūpam ātmānaṃ bhāvayet//[18] sarvāṅgasitavarṇaṃ[19] jaṭāmukuṭamaṇḍitam[20] amitābhakṛtaśekharaṃ[21] sarvābharaṇabhūṣitaṃ[22] ardhaparyaṅkinaṃ dakṣiṇe[23] varadahastaṃ vāme padmadharaṃ padmacandrāsanastham/[24]

(2.2.2) dakṣiṇapārśve āryavasudhārāsudhanau[25] vāmapārśve bhṛkuṭīhayagrīvau/[26]

(2.2.3) bhagavataḥ[27] śirasi candre oṃ kaṇṭhe āḥ[28] hṛdi hūṃ[29] evaṃ vibhāvayet/[30]

---

1 K1 khasapanāya; BL1 om. /.
2 The rendering follows the Sandhi rule. B, K2, BL2 svahṛdi.
3 K2 add. //.
4 K2 sītavarṇaṃ•; BL1 sitavarṇa.
5 K2 tadubhūtāśitarasmibhīr; BL1 adudbhūtāsitarasmibhir.
6 BL1 agratvato.
7 K2, BL1 mbara.
8 K2 has a central dot. BL1 paśyat•.
9 K2, BL1 tā.
10 B mampūjya.
11 K2 -kaṅ.
12 K2, BL1 //.
13 K2 adhiṣṭayat//; BL1 a central dot.
14 K2 -tāyā; BL1 has a central dot.
15 K2, BL1 -loka.
16 K2 add. a central dot.
17 K2 -saṃharanakrameṇa.
18 B om. //. BL1 add. a central dot.
19 K2, BL1 sarvāṅgasītavarṇa.
20 K2 jaṭāmakuṭamaṇḍitam; BL1 jaṭāmukutamaṇḍitaṃ.
21 K2 add. a central dot. BL1 amṛtābhakṛtaśeṣaraṃ.
22 K2 sarvāvaraṇa-; BL1 add. a central dot.
23 K2, BL1 -ṇa.
24 K2 and BL1 om. /.
25 B add. a comma. K2 āryyevasuṃdhārāsudhanau.
26 K2 om. /. BL1 bhṛkuṭihayagrīvau.
27 K2 add. //. BL1 -vata•.
28 K2 ā.
29 K2 add. a central dot.
30 K2, BL2 -yat; BL1 om. /.

(3) dhyānāt[1] khinno yogī mantraṃ japet/[2] tatrāyam[3] mantraḥ//[4] oṃ hrīḥ[5] svāhā/[6] [(7-]//āryāvalokiteśvarakhasarpaṇasādhanaṃ samāptam iti//[7)]

---

1 K2, BL1 dhyānā.
2 K2 and BL1 om. /.
3 K2 trāyaṃ; BL1 tatrāya.
4 B and BL1 om. //.
5 K2 hrī.
6 K2 om. /.
7 K2 //āryyāvalokiteśvarakhasarpaṇasādhanam iti// // iti sādhanasamucaye khasarpanasādhana pañcatriṃśaty adhikaśatatamapaṭala//135//; BL1 //āryyāvalokiteśvarakhasarpaṇasādhanam iti// // iti sādhanasamucaye khasarpaṇasādhana paṃcatriṃsatedhīkaśatatamapaṭalaḥ//135//.

## 2.5 Khasarpaṇalokeśvarasādhana (Bhatt. no. 24)

(0) namaḥ khasarpaṇāya//[1]

(1) natvā khasarpaṇaṃ[2] nāthaṃ[3] nāthabhūtaṃ[4] ca duḥkhinām/[5] saṃkṣiptād[6] vistaraṃ[7] kiñcit sādhanaṃ tasya likhyate//[8]

(2) prathamaṃ[9] tāvan[10] mantrī[11] pāṇipādādikaṃ vāriṇā[12] prakṣālya[13] paramaśucir[14] bhūtvā[15] vijanagiriguhāyāṃ[16] sthāne[17] śucau vā[18] kvacic[19] cittānukūle[20] mṛduviṣṭarāsanopaviṣṭaḥ[21]

(3.1) svahṛdi prathamasvarapariṇataṃ nirdoṣadoṣākaramaṇḍalam[22] ālokya[23] cetasā tanmadhye[24] śaradindugatakiraṇāvalīprojjvalaṃ[25] hrīḥkārabījaṃ[26] paśyet//[27]

(3.2) tato 'pi hrīḥkārabījān[28] niḥsṛtya jaganmohatamastomadhvaṃsakāribhir[29] aṅkuśākārair[30] marīcivisarair[31] daśasu[32] dikṣu[33] ye cānantalokadhātavo[34] 'vatiṣṭhante/[35] tān sarvān

---

1 B, K1 /; TO1 khasappaṇāya//.
2 TO2 khasarppaṇa; TO4 khasarppaṇan.
3 TO4 nāthan; BL2 add. a central dot.
4 TO4 -bhūtañ.
5 TO1 dukhinām/; TO3, TO4 -ṇāṃ.
6 B saṃkṣiptāt; TO1 sakṣiptā; TO3, TO4, K1, BL2 saṃkṣiptā.
7 TO1 vistara.
8 TO2, TO4 /.
9 TO1 -ma; TO2 -man.
10 TO1, TO2, BL2 tāvat.
11 BL2 add. a central dot.
12 K1 cāriṇā.
13 BL2 add. a central dot.
14 TO1 paramasucir.
15 BL2 add. //.
16 TO1 vijinagiriguhāyā; BL2 add. a central dot.
17 K1 sthāme.
18 K1 and BL2 add. a central dot.
19 B, TO1, K1, BL2 kvacit; TO4 kvaci.
20 TO2 -kure; BL2 add. a central dot.
21 B mṛduviṣṭarāmalopaviṣṭaḥ; K1 mṛduviṃbharāvāsanopaviṣṭaḥ; BL2 mṛduviṃbharāvāsano •paviṣṭaḥ.
22 TO1 niddokhadokhākaramaṇḍalam; TO2 nidoṣa-; K1 nirdoṣadoṣākalamaṇḍalam; BL2 nirdoṣadoṣakalamaṇḍalam.
23 TO1 ārokya; BL2 add. a central dot.
24 TO1tatmadhya; TO2 tatmadhye; BL2 add. a central dot.
25 B śaradindugataṃ kiraṇāvalīprojjvalaṃ; TO1 śaradinduśataprojalaṃ; TO2 śarandiśanakiraṇāvalīprojjvalaṃ; TO4 śaradinduśatakiraṇāvalīprojjvalaṃ; K1 śaradinduśataprajvālaṃ •; BL2 śaradigśatakiraṇāvalīprajvālaṃ.
26 TO1 hrīkāra-; K1, BL2 hrīḥkārajaṃ.
27 B /; TO1 paśyat//; TO2 paśyat/.
28 B hrīḥkārabījāt; TO1 hrīkākārabījān; K1, BL2 hrīkārabījān.
29 TO1 jaganmohatasastomathvansakāribhir; TO2 jagatmohatamastomadhvansakārībhir; TO3 jaganmohatamastomathansa-; K1 jaganmohatamastomathanmakāribhir; BL2 jaganmohatamastomathamsakāribhir.
30 TO1 aṅkuśākāram; TO2 aṃkusākāra; K1 and BL2 add. a central dot.
31 TO1 maricivisarai; TO2 marīcivimarair; K1 mmāricivisarair; BL2 mmāricīsarair•.
32 TO1, TO3, K1 daśa; TO2 ddaśasu; BL2 ddaśa.
33 K1 add. a central dot.
34 B, TO2 -dhātavaḥ; TO4 vānaṃtalokadhātavo.
35 B avatiṣṭhante; TO1 'vatiṣṭhate//; TO2 avatiṣṭhante/; TO4 'vatiṣṭhaṃta//; K1, BL2 //.

prakāśya[1] tatra sthitā[2] apy asaṃkhyeyā[3] aprameyāś ca gurubuddhabodhisattvā[4] nabhodeśe cākṛṣya[5] saṃsthāpyante//[6]

(3.3.0) paścāt teṣāṃ[7] nabhodeśavartināṃ[8] paramakāruṇikānāṃ[9] gurubuddhabodhisattvānāṃ[10] puṣpadhūpadīpagandhamālyavilepanacūrṇacīvaracchatradhvajaghaṇṭāpatākādibhir[11] atiśayavatīṃ[12] pūjāṃ[13] vidhāya pāpadeśanāṃ[14] kuryāt//[15]

(3.3.1) [(16-]yat kiṃcid[17] asyāṃ jātāv anyāsu[18] vā jātiṣṭhanādinidhane[19] jātisaṃsāre[20] saṃsaratā mayā pāpakaṃ karma kāyena[21] vācā manasāpi[22] kṛtaṃ[23] kāritaṃ kriyamāṇam[24] anumoditaṃ[25] tatsarvaṃ[26] bhagavatāṃ[27] trailokyamahotsavānāṃ[28] gurubuddhabodhisattvānāṃ[29] purataḥ pratideśayāmīty[30] anena vidhinā[31] pradeśya[32] punar akaraṇasaṃvaraṃ[33] pratigṛhya puṇyānumodanāṃ[34] kuryāt//[35-16)]

---

1 TO2 prakāvya; K1 and BL2 add. a central dot.
2 K1, BL2 sthito.
3 TO4 -khyayā; K1 -khyayā•; BL2 add. a central dot.
4 TO2 -bodhima.
5 TO4 vākṛṣya; K1 add. a central dot.
6 B, TO1, TO2, TO3, TO4 /; K1 sasthāpyante//.
7 TO2 teṣān; TO4 taiṣān.
8 TO4 -varttinā; K1 and BL2 add. a central dot.
9 TO2 -kāruṇikāṇāṃ; K1 -kāruṇi.
10 BL2 add. a central dot.
11 TO1 puṣpadhūpadīpadīpagandhamālyavilepanacūrṇacīvaracchatradhvajaghaṇṭāpatākābhider; TO4 -cīvarachatra-; K1 -cīvarachatradhvajapatākāghaṇṭhādibhir; BL2 -cīvaracchatradhvajapatākāghaṇṭādibhir.
12 TO1 atiśayavatiṃ; TO4 atiśayavatī; BL2 add. a central dot.
13 TO4 pūjām; K1 pūjā.
14 TO1 -nā; K1 -naṃ.
15 B /.
16 TO2 om.
17 B, TO2, TO4 kiñcit; TO1 kīcid; BL2 kicid.
18 BL2 jātā•vanyāsu.
19 K1, BL2 jātiṣṭhanādinidhane•.
20 BL2 add. a central dot.
21 TO4 kāyana; K1 and BL2 add. a central dot.
22 BL2 add. a central dot.
23 BL2 add. a central dot.
24 TO1, TO3, K1, BL2 kriyamānam.
25 K1 and BL2 add. a central dot.
26 TO4 tatsarva.
27 K1 and BL2 add. a central dot.
28 TO1 tailokya-; K1 and BL2 add. a central dot.
29 K1 and BL2 add. a central dot.
30 TO1 pratideśayām ity; TO3 pratideśeyāmīty.
31 K1 and BL2 add. a central dot.
32 TO1 pratideśe; TO3, TO4 pratideśya; K1 and BL2 add. a central dot.
33 TO1, K1, BL2 akaraṇaṃ saṃvaraṃ; TO3 akaraṇaṃ samvaraṃ.
34 TO1 puṇyānumodanā.
35 B, TO1, TO3 /.

(3.3.2) saṃbuddhapratyekaśrāvakānāṃ[1] tatsutānām api[2] bodhisattvānāṃ[3] sattvānām api trailokyodaravartināṃ[4] yad eva kuśalaṃ tatsarvam[5] anumodayāmīti//[6]

(3.3.3) tadanu ratnatrayaśaraṇagamanam/[7] buddhaṃ[8] śaraṇaṃ gacchāmi[9] dvipadānām agryam/[10] dharmaśaraṇaṃ gacchāmi[11] virāgāṇām[12] agryam/[13] saṅghaśaraṇaṃ[14] gacchāmi[15] gaṇānām agryam[16] iti//[17]

(3.3.4) paścān[18] mārgāśrayaṇam/[19] mārgaḥ[20] sambuddhoktaḥ[21] sa[22] cāśrayaṇīyo[23] mayā nānya[24] iti//[25]

(3.3.5) tadantaram[26] adhyeṣaṇāṃ[27] kuryāt/[28] sattvārtham[29] āsaṃsāraṃ[30] kurvantu[31] bhagavantaḥ saṃbuddhās[32] tatsutā[33] api[34] mahābodhisattvās[35] tiṣṭhantu mā[36] parinirvāntv[37] iti//[38]

---

1 B, TO4 -śrāvakabuddhānāṃ; TO1 sabuddhapratyekaśrāvakānāṃ; TO2 sabuddha-; K1, BL2 add. a central dot.
2 BL2 add. a central dot.
3 BL2 add. a central dot.
4 TO1 tailokodaravarttināṃ; TO3, TO4, K1 trailokodaravarttināṃ; BL2 trailokodaravarttināṃ•.
5 B tatsarvvaṃ; BL2 tatsarvva.
6 B, TO1, TO2, TO3, TO4 /; K1 anumodayāmi iti//.
7 K1 -śaraṇaṃ gamanaṃ/.
8 TO1, TO2, K1, BL2 buddha.
9 TO2, TO4 gachāmi; K1 and BL2 add. a central dot.
10 B om. / and add. a comma. TO2 agyaṃ/; BL2 add. a central dot.
11 TO4 gachāmi.
12 TO1 vīrāṇām; TO2 vīrāgāṇāmm (anusvāra insertion); K1 virāganām; BL2 virāgānām.
13 B om. / and add. a comma. TO1 om. /. TO2 agyaṃ/; K1 pravaraṇaṃ •; BL2 pravaraṇaṃ/.
14 TO2 saṅghaṃ śaraṇa.
15 TO4 gachāmi.
16 TO2 agyaṃ; K1 and BL2 add. //.
17 B /; K1 and BL2 om.
18 TO1, TO2, TO3, BL2 paścāt.
19 TO1 //; TO2 mārggāśrayanaṃ/; TO3 illegible after mārgāśraya-. K1 om. /.
20 TO3 illegible; K1, BL2 mārgga.
21 TO2, K1 and BL2 add. /. TO4 add. //.
22 BL2 om.
23 TO1, TO2 cāśrayanīyo; K1 cāgrayaṇīyo.
24 TO2 nānyam.
25 B, TO2, TO4 /.
26 K1 tadantaramadhye.
27 TO2 adhyaṣaṇāṃ; K1 adhye ganṭhāṃ; BL2 addhe ghaṇṭāṃ.
28 K1, BL2 //.
29 TO1, TO2 satvātham.
30 TO1 āsaṇāraṃ; TO3, K1, BL2 āsaṃsāra.
31 TO1 kuvvanto; TO2, TO3 kurvvanto; TO4 kurvanto; K1 kurvvanto •; BL2 kurvanto•.
32 TO1 sabuddhās; TO2 sarvvabuddhās; K1 saṃbuddhāḥ; BL2 saṃbuddhyāḥ.
33 K1, BL2 statsutā.
34 TO3, K1 and BL2 add. /.
35 TO1 -satvān.
36 B add. mā.
37 B parinirvāṇād; TO1 parīnirvvāstv; TO2 parinirvvādd; K1, BL2 parinirvvāsv.
38 B, TO1, K1, BL2 /.

(3.3.6) tadanu yācanāṃ[1] tathāvidhāṃ[2] niruttaradharmadeśanāṃ bhagavantas[3] tathāgatā deśayantu[4] yayā[5] tvaritam eva sattvāḥ saṃsārāgādhasāgaraṃ[6] tarantīti//[7]

(3.3.7) tadanu yācanānantaraṃ[8] puṇyapariṇāmanāṃ[9] kuryāt/[10] saptavidhānuttarapūjayā yad[11] eva kuśalam[12] utpannaṃ[13] tad eva saṃbodhaye[14] pariṇāmayāmīti/[15] athavā samāsataḥ saptavidhānuttarapūjāsūcakān[16] ślokān[17] amūn[18] paṭhet//[19]

(3.3.8) kāyena[20] vācā manasā kṛtaṃ yat
pāpaṃ jinānāṃ[21] purato diśāmi/[22]
lokatrayāṇāṃ[23] kuśalaṃ[24] tu sarvaṃ[25]
nityaṃ pramodād anumodayāmi//[26]
ratnatrayaṃ yāmi[27] sadāham atra
mārgaṃ[28] jinoktaṃ śaraṇaṃ[29] śraye ca/
sattvārtham[30] atrāpi kurvantu buddhāḥ
sutāś[31] ca teṣāṃ satataṃ bhavasya//[32]
tiṣṭhantu yāvat[33] sthitir eva tāvan[34]

---

1 TO1, TO3, K1 and BL2 add. //. TO2 and TO4 add. /.
2 TO1 tathāvidhi; TO4 tathāvidhānaṃ; K1, BL2 tathāvidhā.
3 TO2 bhavantas.
4 TO1 deśayatu.
5 TO1 mayā.
6 TO1 sasārāgrādhasāran; TO3 -gādhasāgaran; K1, BL2 -gāḍhasāgaraṃ.
7 B, TO3, TO4 /, TO1, TO2 tarantiti/.
8 TO1 and TO3 add. /. K1 and BL2 add. //.
9 TO1, BL2 puṇyapariṇāmaṇāṃ.
10 TO1, TO3, K1, BL2 //.
11 K1, BL2 yad•.
12 TO1 kuśaram.
13 K1 and BL2 add. a central dot.
14 TO1, TO2 saṃbodhaya; TO4 saṃbodhiye.
15 TO1, TO4 pariṇāmayām iti//; TO3, K1 //.
16 TO4 -pūjāsu ca kān; K1, BL2 -pūjāśūcakān.
17 K1 and BL2 add. a central dot.
18 TO1 amūna; TO4 amṛn; K1, BL2 mūla.
19 B om. //. TO4 pathet//.
20 TO1, TO4 kāyana.
21 BL2 add. a central dot.
22 TO2 diśāsi/.
23 TO1 lokatrayātraṇāṃ.
24 TO1 kuśaraṃ; TO2 -lan.
25 TO1, TO2 sarvva; TO4 sarvvan; BL2 add. a central dot.
26 TO4 /.
27 TO1 yāyāmi.
28 TO1 mārgga; TO3 māgraṃ; K1, BL2 magnaṃ.
29 TO1 śaraṇa.
30 TO1 satvātham.
31 K1 sutaś.
32 TO2 bhavisya/; K1, BL2 /.
33 TO2, BL2 yāva.
34 B, K1 tāvat.

nirvāntu[1] mā[2] te[3] pitaraḥ prajānām/[4]
saṃdeśanāṃ[5] te nanu[6] tādṛśīṃ[7] vā[8]
dharmasya kurvantu mahāprabhāvāḥ//[9]
saṃsārasindhoḥ[10] sahasāpi[11] sattvāḥ[12]
pāraṃ[13] yathā[14] yānti sukhaṃ prabhūtam/[15]
puṇyaṃ prabhūtaṃ[16] yad ihāpi[17] sarvaṃ[18]
saṃbodhaye[19] tat pariṇāmayāmi//[20]
jinebhyas tatsutebhyaś ca[21] gurubhyo jagatām[22] aham/[23]
ātmānaṃ[24] sarvabhāvena[25] niryātayāmi šarvadā//
ity amībhiḥ[26] saptavidhāṃ[27] pūjāṃ[28] vidhāya//[29] oṃ āḥ hūṃ mur iti visarjayet//[30]

---

1 TO4 nitvātu.
2 B māṃ; TO1, TO3, TO4, K1, BL2 om.
3 TO4 om.
4 TO2 prajānaṃ.
5 TO1 sadeśanā; TO4 sandeśanāṃ; K1, BL2 deśanāṃ.
6 TO2 nunu.
7 TO1 tādṛśim; TO3, TO4 tādṛśīm; K1 tatṛśīm.
8 K1 and BL2 add. a central dot.
9 TO1, TO2, K1, BL2 /.
10 TO2, TO4 sansāra-.
11 K1, BL2 sahasopi.
12 K1 śrutvā; BL2 śratvāḥ.
13 TO1 pāra.
14 TO1, TO3, TO4, BL2 yayā; TO2 prayā; K1 yā.
15 TO4, K1 prasūtaṃ/.
16 TO4, K1 prasūtaṃ.
17 TO1 hāpi.
18 TO2 sarvva.
19 TO1 saṃbodhaya; TO4 saṃbodhayaṃ.
20 TO1, TO2, TO3, K1 /; BL2 has a central dot.
21 K1 and BL2 add. a central dot.
22 TO1 jagam.
23 TO1, TO3 //.
24 K1 ātmāna.
25 BL2 add. a central dot.
26 BL2 bhiḥ.
27 TO2 -vidhā.
28 TO1, TO3, K1, BL2 pūjā.
29 B, TO2 and TO3 om. //. TO4 viya.
30 B, TO1, TO3 /; TO2 visajayet/.

(3.4) tadanantaram[1] apramāṇāni[2] catvāri maitrīkaruṇāmuditopekṣāṇi[3] vakṣyamāṇakrameṇa[4] dhyāyāt/[5] tatreyaṃ[6] maitrī[7] sarvasattveṣv[8] atiśayitahitaikaputrakasnehalakṣaṇā/[9] karuṇā tu[10] kīdṛśī[11] agādhāpārasaṃsārasāgaramadhye[12] patitānantasattvadhātūn[13] samuddharāmīty[14] adhyāśayaḥ/[15] muditā[16] punaḥ[17] kīdṛśī[18] dhātutrayāvasthitānāṃ[19] sattvānāṃ[20] yāni sucaritāni[21] teṣu tadbhogaiśvaryādiṣv[22] hṛṣṭacittatā/[23] keyam upekṣā[24] pratidhānunayanibandhanam[25] apahāya[26] hitāhiteṣu[27] sattveṣu paramahitācaraṇaṃ[28]

(3.5) catuḥpramāṇabhāvanānantaraṃ[29] sarvadharmaprakṛtipariśuddhatāṃ[30] cintayet/[31] sarva[32] evāmī[33] dharmāḥ prakṛtyā svarūpeṇa[34] pariśuddhāḥ/[35] aham api prakṛtipariśuddha

---

1 TO4 tadasantaram.
2 BL2 add. a central dot.
3 TO1, TO3, TO4, K1, BL2 -muditopekṣāmi; TO2 -muditopekṣāni.
4 TO1, K1 vakṣyamānakrameṇa; TO2 lakṣaṇavakṣamānakrameṇa; K1 om.
5 TO1, TO3, TO4, K1, BL2 //.
6 K1, BL2 tatrāyaṃ.
7 TO1 and TO3 add. /. TO4 maitraṃ/; K1 and BL2 add. //.
8 B sarvasattveṣu; TO2 -satvethat; K1 sarvvabuddhair; BL2 sarvvabuddheti.
9 TO1 -putrasnehalakṣaṇā//; TO2 aniṇayitahitaikaputraśneha-; TO3 -putram nehalakṣaṇā//; TO4 atiṇayitahitaikaputrasnehalakṣaṇā//; K1 iti sahitaikaputrasnehalakṣaṇā//; BL2 sahitahitekaputrasnehalakṣaṇā//.
10 TO4 tta.
11 TO2 kīdṛsī/; TO3 add. //. TO4 and K1 add. /. BL2 add. a central dot.
12 TO1, TO2 -madhya; TO3 agādhāpārasaṃsārasārasāgaramadhye; TO4 agādhāpārasaṃsārasārasāgaramadhya; K1, BL2 agāḍhāpārasaṃsārasāgaramadhye.
13 K1 patitānanta/ satvadhātūn•: BL2 patitānanta•satvadhātūn•.
14 TO1 asamurddharām ity.
15 TO1 adhyāśayataḥ//; TO2 add. //. TO4 adhyāśayataḥ/; BL2 om. /.
16 TO1, TO3, K1, BL2 muditāḥ.
17 TO1, TO4 puna.
18 TO1 kīdṛśi//; TO3 kīdṛśā//; TO4 and K1 add. /. BL2 add. //.
19 TO1 -nā; TO2 dhātutrayavyavasthitānāṃ; BL2 add. a central dot.
20 K1 and BL2 add. a central dot.
21 TO1, TO4 sucitāni; K1, BL2 sucitāni•.
22 The rendering follows the Sandhi rule. B, TO1, TO3 -ādiṣu; TO2 -ādisu; TO4 tabhogaiś-; K1 tadbhogesyayyādiṣu; BL2 gadbhogesyāryyādiṣu.
23 TO1, TO3, TO4, K1, BL2 //.
24 TO1, TO2, TO3 and TO4 add. /. K1 add. a central dot.
25 TO3 pratidhātūnanayananibaṃdhanam; K1 pratighātūn• nayanam iva dhanam; BL2 pratighāttana•nayanam ivaṃ dhanam.
26 K1 add. a central dot.
27 K1 add. a central dot.
28 TO1 -hitāvaraṇāṃ; TO2 add. /. TO3, TO4 -hitācaraṇāṃ; K1 -hitāvaraṇāṃ•; BL2 -hitāvaraṇāṃ•.
29 TO1 caturapramāṇabhāvaṇān antara; TO2 caturapramāṇabhāvanāntaraṃ; TO3 caturapra-; TO4 caturapramāṇabhāvanān aṃtaraṃ; K1 caturapramāṇaṃ•bhāvanān antaraṃ; BL2 caturapramāṇa-.
30 TO2 sarvvadharmmapratipariśuddhatāñ; TO4 sarvadharmaprakṛtipariśuddhatāñś; K1 sarvvadharmmaprakṛti•viśuddhatāṃ; BL2 sarvvadharmmaprakṛtiviśuddhatāṃ.
31 TO1, TO3, TO4, K1, BL2 //.
32 TO4 sarvevāmī.
33 TO4 om.; K1 evāsī.
34 BL2 add. a central dot.
35 B and TO3 om. /. TO1 parīśuddhāḥ; TO4 //; BL2 pariśuddhyāḥ.

ityādikam āmukhayet/[1] imām eva[2] sarvadharmaprakṛtipariśuddhatāṃ/[3] oṃ[4] svabhāvaśuddhāḥ sarvadharmāḥ[5] svabhāvaśuddho 'ham ity anena[6] dṛḍhīkuryāt//[7] na ca prakṛtipariśuddhe[8] sarvadharme[9] sadyo[10] muktiprasaṅgo[11] durvāraḥ[12] syāt/[13] satyaṃ[14] param ayaṃ prasaṅgo 'saṅgata[15] eva/[16] kuto[17] 'saṅgataḥ[18] saṃsārahetukarāgādimalaśavalatvāt[19] sarvadharmāṇām/[20] kathaṃ[21] punaḥ[22] tadapagamaḥ[23] syād[24] viśiṣṭamārgabhāvanayā/[25] tayā sa[26] niruddhyate/[27] ata evāha bhagavān[28] nirodhaḥ sākṣāt kartavya[29] iti/[30] tasmāt[31] prakṛtipariśuddhāḥ[32] sarvadharmā ityādi[33] vacanam[34] upapannam[35] eva[36] ity alaṃ[37] bahubhāṣitayā/

---

1 TO1, TO3, TO4, K1, BL2 //.
2 BL2 meva.
3 B om. /. TO1 -kṛtipariśuddhatā//; TO2 -kṛtiparisuddhatāṃ/; TO3, K1 //; BL2 -kṛti•pariśuddhatāṃ//.
4 TO2 om.
5 TO2 om.
6 TO4 arera; BL2 add. a central dot.
7 B, TO1, TO2, TO3 /.
8 TO1 -śudhina; TO3, K1, BL2 -śuddhina; TO4 -śuddhena.
9 TO4 -dharma.
10 K1, BL2 nadyo.
11 TO2 muktipasaṃgo.
12 TO1 durvvāra.
13 TO1, TO3, K1, BL2 //.
14 TO1 satya.
15 TO1, TO3, K1, BL2 asaṃgata; TO2, TO4 asaṅgata.
16 K1, BL2 //.
17 TO1 add. kuto. TO4 kutā.
18 TO1, TO3, TO4 asaṃgataḥ//; TO2 asaṃgataḥ/; K1 and BL2 add. //.
19 TO1 sasārahetukarāgādimarasavalatvāt; K1 saṃsārahetukerāgādimalaśavalatvāt/; TO4 saṃsārahettaka-; BL2 saṃsārahetuke rāgādimalaśavalatvāt•.
20 TO1 sarvvadharmmāṇā//; TO3, K1, BL2 //.
21 TO1, TO2 katha; TO4 katham.
22 TO2, TO4 punas.
23 K1 samudayagama; BL2 sadayugama.
24 The rendering follows the Sandhi rule. B, TO1 syāt; TO2, TO3, TO4 syāt/. K1 and BL2 syāt //.
25 TO1, TO3 -mānnabhāvanayā/; K1 viśiṣṭamātravanayā/; BL2 viśiṣṭamānnavanayā/.
26 TO4 om.
27 TO1, TO3, K1, BL2 //; TO4 niruddhyata/.
28 K1 and BL2 add. a central dot.
29 TO1 kattavya.
30 K1, BL2 //.
31 TO3 illegible after tasmā-.
32 TO3 illegible before -tipariśuddhāḥ.
33 BL2 add. a central dot.
34 TO4 vacana.
35 TO2 upannam.
36 TO1, TO3, K1 and BL2 add. //. TO2 and TO4 add. /.
37 TO4 ulaṃ.

(3.6) sarvadharmaprakṛtipariśuddhatām[1] āmukhīkṛtya[2] sarvadharmaśūnyatāṃ dhyāyāt/[3] tatreyaṃ śūnyatā[4] manomātram evedaṃ[5] tena tenākāreṇa[6] prakāśātmakaṃ[7] pratibhāsate//[8] yathā svapne[9] nāsti[10] manaso bāhyaṃ[11] manogrāhyaṃ/[12] grāhyābhāvād[13] grāhakam api mano nāsti/[14] tataś[15] ca manaḥsvarūpāḥ sarvadharmāḥ/[16] teṣāṃ[17] grāhyagrāhakādisakalakalpanāprapañcaśūnyatātattvaṃ[18] paramārtha[19] iti yāvat//[20] ayam arthaḥ/[21] advaitaprakāśamātrātmakaṃ[22] sacarācaraṃ[23] jagad iti[24] cintanīyam/[25] imām eva[26] śūnyatāṃ[27] oṃ śūnyatājñānavajrasvabhāvātmako[28] 'ham[29] ity amunā[30] mantreṇādhitiṣṭhet/[31]

---

1 TO2 sarvvadharmmaprakṛtipariśuddhitām; K1, BL2 sarvvadharmmaprakṛtipariśuddhatā•.
2 K1 and BL2 add. a central dot.
3 TO1, TO3, K1, BL2 //.
4 TO1, TO3, TO4, K1 and BL2 add. //.
5 K1 and BL2 add. a central dot.
6 TO4 tenākāraṇa; K1 tenokāreṇa; BL2 add. a central dot.
7 K1 add. a central dot.
8 B om. //. TO4 /.
9 TO1, TO3 and TO4 add. /. K1 and BL2 add. //.
10 TO4 rāsti.
11 K1 and BL2 add. a central dot.
12 B and K1 om. /.
13 B, BL2 grāhyābhāvāt/; TO1, TO3 grāhyābhāvāt; TO2 -vā; TO4, K1 -vāñ.
14 TO1, TO3 //.
15 BL2 tataḥ.
16 TO4 //.
17 TO1 teṣā.
18 K1 grāhya•grāhakādisakalakalpamātraprapañca•śūnyatātatvaṃ; BL2 grāhya•grāhakādisakalakalpanāprapañca•śūnyatātatvaṃ.
19 K1 and BL2 add. a central dot.
20 B, TO2, TO4 /.
21 B artha; TO2 om. /. K1, BL2 //.
22 K1, BL2 advaitaprakāśamātrākaṃ.
23 K1 add. a central dot. BL2 saṃcarāçaraṃ•.
24 K1 add. a central dot.
25 TO1 cintaniyam; TO2 cintaniyaṃ; K1, BL2 //.
26 TO2 evaṃ.
27 K1 and BL2 add. //.
28 TO1, TO3, K1 śūnyatāṃ jñāna-.
29 B 'haṃ.
30 TO2 anunā.
31 TO4 mantreṇā/ dhitiṣṭhet/; K1 maṃtreṇādhiṣṭhitan//; BL2 //.

(4.1) tadanu[1] kalaṅkāṅkanirmuktakṣapākaramaṇḍalārudhāc[2] chubhrātiśubhrād[3] hrīḥkārabījād[4] bhagavantaṃ[5] śrīmatkhasarpaṇalokeśvaraṃ[6] śaradamalahariṇāṅkamaṇḍalaśatodayātiśubhradehaṃ[7] parama-śṛṅgārojjvalaramaṇīyamūrtiṃ[8] nānāratnādyābharaṇavirājitavigrahaṃ[9] jaṭāmakuṭadhāriṇaṃ[10] vikasitapuṇḍarīkalocanaṃ[11] bhagavadamitābha-jinaratnaviśobhitaśirodeśaṃ[12] himavālukāsalilakṣālitāvadātāmbarāvṛtaśarīraṃ[13] śakaṭacakrapramāṇātikamanīyasitāmbhoruhoparisthita-niṣkalaṅkavidhumaṇḍalāsanasthaṃ[14] ardhaparyaṅkiṇaṃ[15] savyakareṇa varadaṃ[16]

---

1 TO2 tadana.

2 The rendering follows the ablative case in TO1, TO2, TO4 and BL2. The rendering follows the Sandhi rule. B kalaṅkāṅkanirmuktakṣapākaramaṇḍalārudhaṃ; TO1 kalaṃkāṅkanimmuktakṣepākaramaṇḍalārūḍhāt; TO2 kalaṅkākanirmmuktakṣāpākaramaṇḍalārudhāt; TO3 kalaṃkāṅkanimmuktapākaramaṇḍalārudhān; TO4 -kṣapākaramaṇḍalārūḍhāt; K1 kalakāṅkanimuktakṣapākalamaṇḍalarūḍān •; BL2 kalakāṅkanimuktakṣapākalamaṇḍalārudhāt.

3 The rendering follows the ablative case in TO2. The rendering follows the Sandhi rule. B śubhrātiśubhraṃ; TO1 śubhātiśubhāt/; TO2 śubhrātiśubhrāt; TO3 śubhātiśubhāt/; K1 add. /. TO4 śubhātiśubhāt; BL2 śubhāniśubhān/.

4 B -bījaṃ; TO1 hrīkārabījāt; TO2 -bījā.

5 BL2 add. a central dot.

6 TO1, TO2, TO3 and TO4 add. /.

7 TO1 śaradamahariṇāṅkamaṇḍalaśatodayātiśubhradehaṃ/; TO2 add. //. TO3 śaradamahariṇāṅkamaṇḍalaśatodayātiśubhradehaṃ/; TO4 add. /. K1 śaradamahakāriṇāṃ•kamaṇḍala •satodayātiśubhradehaṃ//; BL2 śaradamakāriṇāṃ•kamaṇḍala•satodayāti-śubhradehaṃ//.

8 TO1 -mūtti/; TO2 -mūrti/; TO3 -mūrtti/; TO4 paramaśṛṅgārojvalaramaṇīyamurtti/; K1 paramaśṛṅgārojvala •ramaṇīyamūrttiḥ//; BL2 add. //.

9 TO1 -virajitavigrahaṃ/; TO2 and TO3 add. /. TO4 -vigraha/; K1, BL2 -virājitagrahaṃ/.

10 TO1, TO2 and TO3 add. /. TO4 jaṭāmukuṭadhāriṇaṃ/; K1 and BL2 add. //.

11 TO1, TO2, BL2 -puṇḍarīkarocanaṃ/; TO3 vikapuṇḍarīkalocanaṃ/; TO4 add. /. K1 vakasitapuṇḍarīkarocanaṃ/.

12 TO1 -deśa/; TO2 amitābhajīnaratnaviśobhitāśirodesaṃ//; TO3 add. /. K1, BL2 amitābharatnaviśobhitaśirodeśaṃ/.

13 The rendering follows TO1, TO3, TO4, K1 and BL2: hima-. B hemavālukāsalilakṣālitāvadātāmbarāvṛtaśarīraṃ; TO1 himavālukāśalilakṣāritāvadātāmbaravṛtaśarīraṃ/; TO2 hemavālukāśalilakṣālitāvadātāṃbūrāvṛtaśarīraṃ; TO3 himavālukāśalilakṣāritāvadātāmbarāvṛtaśarīraṃ/; TO4 himavālukāśalilakṣālitāvadātāmbarāvṛtaśarīraṃ/; K1 himavālukāśarirakṣālitāvadātambaravṛtaśarīraṃ/; BL2 himavālukāśarirakṣāritāvatāmbaravṛtaśanīlaṃ/.

14 The rendering follows TO1, TO3, TO4, K1 and BL2: śakaṭacakrapramāṇāti- and TO1, K1 and BL2: -sthitaniṣkalaṅkavidhumaṇḍalāsanasthaṃ. B śakaṭacakrapramāṇam atikamanīyasitāmbhoruhoparisthitaṃ niṣkalaṅkavidhumaṇḍalāsanasthaṃ; TO1 śakaṭacakrapramāṇātikamaṇiyasitāṃbhoruhoparisthitaniṣkalaṃkavidhumaṇḍalāsanasthaṃ/; TO2 satacakrapramāṇimātikamanīyaśitāṃbhoruhoparisthitaniṣkalaṅvidhumaṇḍalāsanasthaṃ/; TO3 illegible between śakaṭacakrapramāṇātikamanīyasitāṃbhoruhoparisthitani- and -laṅkavidhumaṇḍalāsanasthaṃ/. TO4 śakaṭacakrapramāṇātikamanīyasitāmbhoruhoparisthitaniṣkalaṃvidhumaṇḍalāsanasthaṃ/; K1 śakaṭacakrapramāṇātikamanīya•sitāṃbhoruhoparisthitaniṣkalaṅkavidhumaṇḍalāsanasthaṃ/; BL2 śakaṭacakrapramāṇātikamanīya •sitāmbhoruhoparisthitaniṣkalaṃkavidhumaṇḍalāsanasthaṃ/.

15 B arddhaparyyaṅkinaṃ; TO1, TO3, K1 arddhaparyaṅkinaṃ/; BL2 ardhaparyyaṅkinaṃ/.

16 TO1, TO3, TO4, K1 and BL2 add. /. TO2 valadaṃ/.

avasavyena[1] vikasitamanohārisitāravindadharaṃ[2] evaṃ[3] bhūtaṃ bhagavantaṃ[4] niṣpādya tadrūpam ātmānaṃ[5] vibhāvayet//[6]

(4.2) bhagavato[7] dakṣiṇapārśve[8] cāryatārāsudhanau[9] vāmapārśve ca bhṛkuṭīhayagrīvau cintanīyāv[10] iti/[11]

(4.3) śirasi niṣkalaṅkendumaṇḍalopary[12] oṃkāraṃ[13] tadanu kaṇṭhe vimalasomamaṇḍalopary[14] āḥkāram/[15] hṛdaye[16] tv[17] amalakumudabandhumaṇḍalopary[18] hūṃkāraṃ[19] paśyet/[20] tadanena krameṇa[21] yāvad[22] icchati[23] tāvad[24] bhāvayet/[25]

(4.4.1) tadanantaram[26] asyaiva[27] samayasattvarūpasya bhagavato lokanātharūpasya[28] hṛdisthakalaṅkāṅkaviviktaśaśimaṇḍaloparisthitakārtikendu-kundasannibhahrīḥkārabījavinirgatāparyantaraśmivisarais[29] trailokyājñā-

---

1 TO1 avasavyeṇa; TO3 avasavyaṇa.
2 TO1, TO3 -manohārisitārivindadharaṃ//; TO2 add. /. TO4 -manohārisitārivindadharaṃ/; K1, BL2 -manohāri•sitādivindadharaṃ/.
3 TO1 evam.
4 K1 bhagavavantaṃ.
5 TO2 alānaṃ.
6 B, TO2 /; TO1 vibhāvayat//; TO4 om. //.
7 TO1 bhagavanta; TO4 bhagavaṃtā.
8 TO1 -pāśve; TO4 dakṣaiṇapārśve.
9 TO3, K1 and BL2 add. /. TO4 cāryatāvāsudhanau/.
10 TO2 cintaṇīyāv; TO3, TO4, BL2 cintayāv; K1 cintayāmīti//.
11 TO1, TO3, BL2 //; K1 om.
12 The rendering follows the Sandhi rule. B, TO1, TO2, TO3, TO4, K1, BL2 -maṇḍalopari.
13 B add. a comma. TO1, TO3 and TO4 add. /. TO2 -ra/.
14 The rendering follows the Sandhi rule. B, TO1, TO3, TO4, BL2 vimalasomamaṇḍalopari; TO2 vimarasamamaṇḍalopari; K1, BL2 vimalasomaṇḍalalopari.
15 B om. / and add. a comma.
16 TO2 -ya.
17 TO1 tvaṃ; TO4 tvam; K1, BL2 tu.
18 The rendering follows the Sandhi rule. B -pari; TO1 marakumudabaṃdhumalopari; TO2 analakumundhamaṇḍalopari; TO3 amalakumudabaṃdhumalopari; TO4 amakumudabaṃdhumalopari; K1 amalakumudabandhumeropari; BL2 kumudabandhumaropari.
19 TO1 hūṃkāra.
20 TO1, TO2 paśyat/; K1 om. /. BL2 //.
21 TO2 kameṇa; TO4 kramena.
22 K1, BL2 yāva.
23 TO2, TO4 ichati; K1 chati; BL2 cchati.
24 TO1, TO4 tāva.
25 K1, BL2 //.
26 TO4, BL2 tadanantam.
27 TO2 asy eva.
28 TO1, TO3, TO4, K1, BL2 lokanāthasya.
29 TO1 hṛdisthakarakāviviktaśaśimaṇḍaloparisthitakāttikendukundasanibhaṃhrīkārabīja-vinniggatāpayantaraśmiviśarai; TO2 hṛdisthakamalaṃkalaṃkāṃkaviviktaśaśimaṇḍalopari-sthitakārttikendukundasannirahrīḥkārabījanirggatāparyantarasmivisarais; TO3 hṛdistha-kalaṃkāviviktaśaśimaṇḍaloparisthitakārttikendukundasannibhahrīḥkārabījavinirggatāparyantaraśmivisarais; TO4 -kendukuṇḍasannibhahrīḥkārabījavinirgatāparyaṃtaraśmivisanais; K1 hṛdisthakalaṃkāviviktaśaśīmaṇḍaloparisthitakārttikendu•kundasaṃnibhaṃ•hrīḥkārabījavinirggato•paryyantaraśmivisarais; BL2 hṛdisthakalaṃkāviviktaśaśīmaṇḍaloparisthita-kārttikendu•kundasannibhaṃ•hrīḥkārabījavinirggato•paryyāntaraśmivisarais.

nāndhakārāpahāribhir[1] gatvā[2] anādisaṃsiddho[3] bhagavān[4] jñānasattvarūpaḥ sudūrād[5] dvīpadeśād[6] ānīyate/ samānīya[7] tam[8] eva[9] bhagavantaṃ[10] purato nabhaḥpradeśe[11] ca[12] saṃsthāpya[13] nānāratnakhacitacāmīkarādibhājanāvasthitasugandhodakena[14] surabhikusumena[15] ca[16] tasyaivānītajñānasattvarūpasya[17] bhagavato lokanāthasya[18] caraṇārghaṃ[19] dattvā[20] tadanu divyapuṣpadhūpadīpanaivedyagandha-mālyavilepanacūrṇacīvaracchatradhvajaghaṇṭāpatākādibhir[21] bāhyaguhyapūjānivahair[22] nānāprakārais tam eva bhagavantaṃ[23] jñānasattvātmakam arcayet/[24] punaḥ punar abhyarcya[25] stutvā ca[26] jaḥ hūṃ vaṃ hor[27] ity anenākṣaracatuṣṭayena[28] mudrāṃ darśayet/[29]

---

1 TO1 -bhis; TO4 trailokyājñānaṃdhakārāpahāribhir.
2 TO3 ggavā; TO4 gavā; K1 and BL2 add. a central dot.
3 BL2 add. a central dot.
4 BL2 add. a central dot.
5 TO2 sudurād; TO4 surādūrā; K1, BL2 siṃdūrā.
6 TO1 dvivaṃdaśād; TO2, TO4 dvipadeśād; TO3, K1, BL2 dvipaṃ deśād.
7 TO2 add. /.
8 TO1, TO3, TO4 te; K1 ta/.
9 TO1 mucchunaṃ; TO3, TO4, K1 meva.
10 TO2 -vanta; BL2 add. a central dot.
11 K1, BL2 nabhaḥsthaladeśe.
12 TO1 add. /. TO4 va.
13 TO2 saṃsthāppya; K1 and BL2 add. a central dot.
14 TO2 -sugandhodakeṇa/; TO4 add. sugaṃdhodakena; K1 -sthita•sugaṃdhodakena•; BL2 nānāratnakhacitacāmī•karādibhājanāvasthita•sugandhodakena•.
15 TO2 su/ rabhikusumena; TO4 -kusumeva; K1 add. /.
16 TO1, TO3, TO4, K1 and BL2 add. /.
17 TO1, TO3, TO4 -jñānasatvasya; K1, BL2 -jñānasatvasya•; TO2 tasmaivyanītajñānasatvarupasya.
18 K1 and BL2 add. a central dot.
19 TO4 -ghan.
20 TO2 add. /. K1 and BL2 add. a central dot.
21 TO1 -gandhamālyavirepanacūrṇacīvaracchatraghaṇṭāpatakādibhir; TO2 divyapuṣpa-dhupadīpanaivedyagandhamālyavilepanacūrṇacivaracchatradhvajaghaṇṭāpratākādibhir; TO3 divyapuṣpadhūpadīpanaivedyagandhamālyavilepanacūrṇacīvaracchatraghaṇṭāpatākādibhir; TO4 divyapuṣpadhūpadīpanaivedyagaṃdhamālyavilepanacūrṇacīvarachatradhvajaghaṇṭāpatākādibhi; K1 divyapuṣpadhūpadīpanaivyadyagaṃdhamālyavilepanacūrṇacīvarachatraghaṇṭāpatākābhir; BL2 divyapuṣpadhūpadīpanaivyadya•gandhamālyavilepana•cūrṇacīvaracchatraghaṇṭāpatābhir.
22 TO1 bāhyaguhyam pūjānivaher; TO2 -pujānivahain; K1 add. a central dot. BL2 bbāhyaguhyapūjānivahair•.
23 K1 and BL2 add. a central dot.
24 TO1 //; TO2 abhyarcyā; TO3, TO4, K1 //; BL2 accaryet//.
25 TO1 abhyacya; TO2 abhyacya/; BL2 add. a central dot.
26 TO2 nāva; K1 and BL2 add. a central dot.
27 B hoḥ; TO2 hoḥr; K1, BL2 hoḥ/.
28 TO4 anenākṣarastayena.
29 TO4, K1, BL2 //.

(4.4.2) kiñcid ucchritaṃ[1] saṃpuṭāñjaliṃ[2] kṛtvā[3] madhyame[4] sūcīkuryāt//[5] śeṣāś cāṅgulīḥ[6] kiñcit saṅkocya[7] sammukham asaṃśliṣṭā[8] dhārayet/[9] aṅguṣṭhau tarjanīdvayasamīpe sthāpayed iti vikasitakamalamudreyam/[10]

(4.4.3) anayā[11] mudrayā tam evānītaṃ bhagavantaṃ[12] jñānasattvalakṣaṇaṃ[13] paritoṣyāpi samayasattvarūpe bhagavaty[14] antarbhāvya[15] oṃ āḥ[16] hūṃ ity anenānayor[17] advaitam adhimuñcet//[18]

(4.5) tadanantaraṃ kalaṅkapaṭalanirmuktaśubhrāṃśumaṇḍalamadhyāva-līnāmanauṣadhīśamaṇḍalaśatakaranikarojjvalahrīḥkārabījavinirgatā[19] asaṃkhyeyā[20] aprameyāś[21] ca bhagavantaḥ[22] śrīkhasarpaṇalokeśvarabhaṭṭārakadaśadigvartino[23] 'nekalokadhātūn[24] avabhāsya[25] tatra sthitānām[26] api[27] sattvānāṃ[28]

---

1 TO1, TO3 ucchunaṃ; TO4 uchunaṃ; K1 ucchuna; BL2 ucchana.
2 TO1 saputañjaliṃ.
3 BL2 add. a central dot.
4 K1 madhyeme.
5 B om. // and add. a comma. TO2, K1, BL2 /.
6 B cāṅgulyaḥ; TO2 cāṃgulī.
7 K1 and BL2 add. a central dot.
8 TO1, TO4 asaṃśliṣṭāḥ//; TO2 asaṃśliṣṭāḥ; TO3 asaṃśliṣṭāḥ/; K1 samāśliṣṭhāḥ//; BL2 samaṃśliṣṭāḥ//.
9 B om. / and add. a comma. TO1 om. /. K1 and BL2 add. //.
10 TO1 vikasitakarmaramudreyaṃ/; TO2 vikāsitakamalamudreyaṃ/; TO4, K1, BL2 //.
11 TO1 antayā.
12 TO2 -tañ; K1 and BL2 add. a central dot.
13 TO1 -salakṣaṇaṃ; BL2 add. a central dot.
14 K1 bhavagatya.
15 TO1 antabhāvya; K1 bhāvya/; BL2 arbhāvya/.
16 TO4 ā.
17 K1 -yār; BL2 anenayār.
18 TO2 /; TO3, BL2 adhimucet//; K1 adhimucyet//.
19 The rendering follows TO1, TO3, TO4, K1 and BL2: -madhyāvalināmanauṣadhīśamaṇḍala-. B kalaṅkapaṭalanirmuktaśubhrāṃśumaṇḍalamadhyāvalīnāṃ anauṣadhīśamaṇḍala-śatakaranikarojjvalahrīḥkārabījavinirgatā; TO1 karakaṅkapaṭarananirmmuktaśubhāśu-maṇḍalamadhyāvalināmanauṣadhīśamaṇḍalaśataranikarorjjvalahrīḥkārabījavinirggatā; TO2 kalaṅkapaṭalaniṃmuktaśubhrāṃśumaṇḍalamadhyāvalīnāmalauṣadhiśamaṇḍalaśatakaraśikarojvalahrīḥkārabīja-vinirgatā; TO3 illegible between kalaṅkapaṭalanimmuktaśubhrāṃśu-maṇḍalamadhyāvalīnāmanauṣadhīśamaṇḍalaśatakaranikarojjvalahrīḥkārabījavi- and -tā. TO4 kalaṅkapaṭalananirmuktaśubhrāṃśumaṇḍalamadhyāvalīnāmanauṣadhīśamaṇḍalaśatakara-nikarojjvalahrīḥkārabījavinirgatā; K1 karaṃkapaṭalananirmmuktaśubhāṃśumaṇḍala-madhyāvalīnāmanauṣadhīśamaṇḍala •śatakaranikalojvalahrīḥkārabījavinirggato; BL2 karaṃkapaṭalananirmuktaśubhāṃśumaṇḍalamadhyāvalīnāmanauṣadhīśamaṇḍala •śatakaran •kalojjvalahrīḥkārabījavinirggato.
20 TO1 asakheyāś; K1 and BL2 add. a central dot.
21 TO1 om.
22 B, TO1 bhagavataḥ.
23 TO1 -digvattino; TO2, TO4, K1, BL2 -bhaṭṭārakādaśa-.
24 TO1 -tun.
25 BL2 add. a central dot.
26 TO1, TO2 sthitānā.
27 TO1, TO2 nāpi.
28 TO2 satvānā; BL2 add. a central dot.

svarṇamāṇikyamuktārājapaṭapravālavaiḍūryendranīlādiratnavarṣaṇena[1] dāridryādiduḥkham[2] apaharanti/[3] niruttarakṣaṇikanairātmyādidharmadeśanāyāḥ[4] pīyūṣadhārāprabandhena[5] tān[6] santarpayanti/[7] punaḥ punar[8] anavaratanānāprakāraṃ[9] parārthaṃ[10] kṛtvā[11] jagad api bhagavallokeśvararūpeṇa[12] (13-niṣpādya[14] tatrāpi[15] himārcimaṇḍalamadhyavartini sphaṭikamaṇikiraṇasaṅkāśahrīḥkārabīje[16] 'ta[17] eva bhagavantaḥ samāgatyāntarbhavantīty[18] evam-13) ādisphuraṇasaṃharaṇakrameṇa[19] yāvat[20] (21-khedo na jāyate tāvad[22] bhāvayet/

(5) tatrāpi[23] bhāvanākhinno[24-21)] mantraṃ japet/[25] tatrāyaṃ mantraḥ[26] oṃ hrīḥ svāhā/[27] mantro[28] 'yaṃ[29] bhagavato lokanāthasya[30] hṛdayam/[31] asādhāraṇaprabhāva[32] evāsau mantrarājaḥ[33]

---

1 TO1 svarṇamāṇikyamurktārājapaṭūpravāravaiḍūryandranīrādiratnavarṣaṇena; TO2 svarṇamāṇikyamuktārājapaṭṭapravālavaiḍūryya indranīrādiratnavarṣaṇena; TO4 -paṭv apravālavaiḍūryandra-; K1 svarṇamānikyamuktārājapaṭṭapravādavaiḍūryya indranīlādiratnavarṣeṇa; BL2 svarṇamānikyamuktārājapaṭṭa•pravādavaidūryya indranīlādiratnavarṣaṇa
2 TO2, TO4 dāridyādiduḥkham; BL2 dāridrādiduḥkham.
3 TO2 //; K1 and BL2 have a central dot .
4 TO1 -dharmmadeśanāyā; TO3 -dharmadeśanāyā; K1 -dharmmadeśanāyā•; TO2 -dharmadeśanā; TO4 -dharmadeśanāyau; BL2 -nairātmyādi •dharmadeśanāyā•.
5 TO4 pṛyūṣadhārā-; K1, BL2 pīyūṣadhārā•pra-.
6 K1 and BL2 add. a central dot.
7 TO2 saṃtarparyati; K1, BL2 //.
8 TO1, TO3 puna; TO2 ru; K1 punaś; BL2 punaḥ.
9 TO1, TO3 caraṇatanānāprakāraṃ; TO2 -kāram; TO4 ananananāprakāram; K1, BL2 caraṇatanānāprakāraṃ•.
10 TO1 parārtha.
11 TO1 om.; BL2 add. a central dot.
12 BL2 -lokeśvararūpe.
13 K1, BL2 om.
14 TO1 and TO3 add. /.
15 TO4 tatropi.
16 TO1 -maṇikiraṇasaṃkāsahrīkārabīje; TO2 -maṇikamaṇikiraṇasakāśahrīḥkārabīje; TO3 -maṇikiraṇasaṃkāśahrīḥkārabīje; TO4 -maṇinikarasaṃkośahrīḥkārabījet.
17 B, TO1, TO2, TO3, K1, BL2 ta; TO4 om.
18 TO2 samāgatyāntabhavantīty.
19 TO4 ādistharaṇasaṃ-; K1, BL2 krameṇa.
20 TO1 and TO3 add. //. TO4 illegible before -vat. K1 and BL2 add. /.
21 K1, BL2 tatravibhāṣaṇāt//; khinno.
22 TO2 add. bhāva.
23 TO1, TO2, TO4 tatopi.
24 TO1, TO3 bhāvanāt/ khinno; TO4 bhāvaṇāt khinno.
25 K1, BL2 //.
26 TO1, TO2, TO3 mantra//; TO4, K1 and BL2 add. //.
27 TO1, TO2, TO3, TO4, K1, BL2 //.
28 TO2 tatrāyam; TO4 maṃtrāyaṃ.
29 TO1 yaṃ; TO2, TO4 om.
30 BL2 add. a central dot.
31 TO2 om. /. K1, BL2 //.
32 TO2 asādharaṇa-; K1 and BL2 add. a central dot.
33 TO2, TO3 and K1 add. /. TO4 and BL2 add. //.

sarvair[1] eva jinavarair abhyarcitaḥ[2] satkṛto namaskṛtaś[3] ceti/[4] samādher[5] utthito[6] jagal
lokeśvararūpaṃ[7] vīkṣya[8] tadahaṅkāreṇa[9] yatheṣṭaṃ[10] vihared[11] iti/[12]
(6) prāyo 'nena[13] vidhinā[14] bhagavantaṃ[15] cintayet[16] khaḍgāñjanādipramukhasakalā[17]
mahāsiddhayaḥ[18] samāgatya[19] pādayoḥ[20] patanti[21] kiṃ[22] punaḥ kṣudrasiddhayaḥ/[23] api[24] tu
tāś[25] ca nitarām[26] eva//[27] ye vijanavanaśmaśānagiriguhāsīnā[28] bhagavantaṃ bhāvayanti[29] te
cācirād[30] eva niyatam[31] atra[32] bhagavantaṃ[33] paśyanti/[34] svayam eva[35] bhagavāṃs[36] teṣām[37]

---

1 TO1 savver; TO4 savair.
2 TO1 abhyaccitaḥ; TO2 -taṃ; K1 and BL2 add. //.
3 BL2 namaskṛteś.
4 TO1, TO3 and TO4 om. /. TO2, K1, BL2 //.
5 TO1 samādheyy?; TO2 samādheyy; TO3, TO4, K1, BL2 samādhevy.
6 TO2 attheto?; K1 and BL2 add. a central dot.
7 TO2 -rupa.
8 TO2 vākṣya.
9 K1 tahaṅkāreṇa; BL2 gahaṃkāreṇa.
10 TO2 ṣṭaviṣṭa; K1 and BL2 add. a central dot.
11 B, TO1, TO3, K1, BL2 viharet; TO2 viharāt.
12 TO1, TO3, TO4, K1, BL2 //; TO2 māra.
13 TO1 neṇa.
14 K1, BL2 vidhānā.
15 TO1 bhavatañ; TO2 bhagavanta; TO3 bhavantañ; TO4 bhagavaṃtañ; K1, BL2 bhavanti •.
16 TO1, TO2, TO3 cintayataḥ; TO4 ciṃtayataḥ; K1 tatkiṃcataḥ/; BL2 tatkiñcitaḥ/.
17 TO2 khaḍgāñjanādipramakhasakalā; K1 khaḍgoñjanādipramukhasakalā; BL2 khaḍgāñjanādi•pramukhasakalā
18 TO1 and TO3 add. /. K1 and BL2 add. //.
19 BL2 samāgatyaḥ.
20 TO1 pādayāḥ.
21 B add. a comma. TO1, TO2, TO3 and TO4 add. /. K1 paṭhanti//; BL2 paṭanti//.
22 TO4 kim.
23 B om. /. TO2, TO4, K1, BL2 //.
24 K1 add. //.
25 K1 taś.
26 TO1, TO3, BL2 niratarām.
27 B, TO2 /.
28 TO2 vyajanavaraśmasānagīriguhāsīno.
29 K1 and BL2 add. /.
30 B, BL2 ca acirād; TO4 vācirād.
31 TO2, TO4 niyata; BL2 niyata•.
32 TO2, TO4 maṃtra; BL2 matra.
33 TO1 bhagavanta; TO2 bhagavataṃ.
34 TO1, TO3 //.
35 TO2 meva.
36 TO1, TO2 -vās.
37 B, TO1, TO2 teṣāṃ; BL2 add. a central dot.

āśvāsapraśvāsādikaṃ[1] dadyāt/[2] yātu[3] kiṃ[4] bahuvacanīyaṃ[5] paramātidurllabhaṃ[6]
buddhatvam[7] api teṣāṃ[8] pāṇitalāvalīnabadarakaphalam[9] ivāvatiṣṭhati[10] iti/[11]
(7) kiñcid vistaraṃ[12] śrīkhasarpaṇalokeśvarasādhanaṃ[13] samāptam/[14]
śrīkhasarpaṇanāthasya[15] kṛtvā[16] sādhanam[17] uttamam/[18]
yat puṇyam arjitaṃ[19] tena[20] yātu lokaḥ[21] puraṃ[22] muneḥ//[23]
/kṛtiḥ[24] sthavirānupamarakṣitānām//[25]

---

1 TO2 āśvāsapaśvāsādikaṃ; TO4 āśvāsādikaṃ.
2 TO1, TO3, K1, BL2 //.
3 TO1, TO3, K1, BL2 yāvat; TO4 yātta.
4 TO4 kim; K1, BL2 kiñcid.
5 TO1, TO3 and TO4 add. /. TO2 -niyaṃ/; K1 and BL2 add. //.
6 TO1, TO4 paramātidullabha; TO2 paramādidurllabha; K1 and BL2 add. //.
7 B, TO1, TO2, TO3, TO4, BL2 buddhatvaṃ.
8 TO1 teṣā; TO2 tekhāṃ.
9 TO1 -pharam; TO2 pāṇitalāvalīnapunīnabadarakaphalam; K1, BL2 pāṇitalāvalīnabadalakaphalam.
10 TO1, TO2 ivāvatiṣṭhata; TO3, TO4 -ṣṭhata; K1 ivābhavatiṣṭhate; BL2 ivāvatiṣṭhate.
11 TO1, TO3 and TO4 om. /. K1 om.; BL2 ti.
12 TO2 add. //.
13 TO1 śrīkhasappaṇalokeśvarasādhana.
14 TO1, TO3, TO4 // //; K1, BL2 samāptaṃ// // māghasya// //.
15 TO1 śrīkhasappaṇanāthasya; BL2 add. a central dot.
16 TO1 kṛtvānan.
17 TO1 om.
18 K1, BL2 //.
19 TO2, TO4 -tan.
20 TO1 te; BL2 add. a central dot.
21 TO1 rokaḥ.
22 TO1 pura.
23 TO1, TO2, BL2, K1 mune// //; TO3 // //; TO4 punaḥ// //.
24 TO1 om. /. TO2 kṛtti; TO3 and TO4 om. /. K1 kṛṣtiṣṭa; BL2 kṛti.
25 TO1, TO3, TO4 stha arupamarakṣitānāṃ//; TO2 sthe anupamarakṣitānām//; K1 anupramarakṣitānāṃ// //; BL2 ṣṭha anuprasarakṣitānāṃ//.

## 2.6 Khasarpaṇalokeśvarasādhana (Bhatt. no. 26)

(1) prathamaṃ[1] tāvan[2] mantrī sukhāsanopaviṣṭaḥ[3]

(2.1.1) svahṛdi paṃkārapariṇatāṣṭadalakamalasyopary[4] akārapariṇāmena[5] candramaṇḍalaṃ[6] tasyopary[7] hrīḥkāraṃ[8] saraśmikaṃ dṛṣṭvā[9] (10-tena raśminākṛṣyākaniṣṭhabhuvanavartilokeśvaraṃ[11] purato nabhaḥsthale[12] dṛṣṭvā[13-10])

(2.1.2) pāpadeśanādikaṃ kuryāt/[14] tadyathā[15] pāpadeśanā[16] puṇyānumodanā[17] puṇyapariṇāmanā[18] triśaraṇagamanaṃ[19] ātmabhāvaniryātanā[20] adhyeṣaṇā[21] bodhicittotpādanaṃ kṛtvā[22] caturbrahmavihāravān[23] bhāvayet/[24] maitrīkaruṇāmuditopekṣāḥ/[25]

(2.1.3) tataḥ śūnyatāṃ bhāvayet/[26] oṃ śūnyatājñānavajrasvabhāvātmako[27] 'ham/[28]

---

1 TO1 prathama; TO2 prathaman.
2 B, TO2, K1, BL2 -vat.
3 TO4 -nopraviṣṭaḥ.
4 The rendering follows the Sandhi rule. B, TO1, TO3, TO4, K1, N1 -yopari; TO2 -kamarasyopari; BL2 add. a central dot.
5 TO1 akārapariṇāmeṇa.
6 TO2, TO4 and N1 add. /. BL2 add. a central dot.
7 The rendering follows the Sandhi rule. B, TO1, TO2, TO3, TO4, K1, N1, BL2 tasyopari.
8 K1 and BL2 add. a central dot.
9 TO1 dṛṣṭā; K1 and BL2 add. a central dot.
10 TO4 om.
11 TO1 raśminākṛṣṭākanibhuvanavattilokeśvaraṃ; TO3, TO4, N1 raśminākṛṣṭākaniṣṭhabhuvanavarttilokeśvaraṃ; K1 raśminākṛṣṭākaniṣṭhabhuvanavartti•lokeśvaraṃ; BL2 raśminākṛṣṭhā •kaniṣṭhabhuvanevartti•lokeśvaraṃ.
12 The rendering follows Tib. T3: nam mkha'i mthil du. B nabhaḥsthalaṃ; TO1 nabhaṣṭhara; TO2 nabhastalā; TO3 nabhaṣṭharaṃ; K1 nabhaṣṭaraṃ; N1 nabhastalaṃ; BL2 nabhaṣṭharaṃ.
13 K1 and BL2 add. a central dot.
14 K1, BL2 //.
15 K1 and BL2 add. //.
16 B add. a comma. TO1, TO3 pāpadeśanā//; TO2, TO4, N1 pāpadeśanā/.
17 B add. a comma. TO1, TO2, TO3, TO4, N1 and BL2 add. /. K1 -modanāṃ/.
18 B add. a comma. TO1, TO3, TO4 and N1 add. /. TO2 puṇyapariṇāmaṇāṃ/; K1, BL2 punaḥ pariṇāmanā/.
19 B add. a comma. TO1, TO3, TO4, N1, K1 -mana/; TO2 -manaṃ/; BL2 -man.
20 B add. a comma. TO1, TO2, TO3 and N1 add. /. TO4 -niyātanā/; K1 ātmābhāvaniryātanā/; BL2 ātmābhāvaniryyātanā/.
21 B add. a comma. TO2, TO3, K1, N1 and BL2 add. /. TO4 adhyiṣyaṇā/.
22 BL2 add. a central dot.
23 TO1 catubrahma-; TO3, TO4 -vihārān; K1, BL2 brahmacaryyavihārān; N1 caturbrahmavihārān.
24 B om. /.
25 TO1-muditā/ upekṣā/; TO2, TO3, TO4 maitrī/ karuṇā/ muditā/ upekṣā/; K1 -muditā upekṣāḥ//; N1 -mudita/ upekṣā/; BL2 -muditopekṣā//.
26 B om. /. TO1, TO4, K1, BL2 //.
27 TO3, K1 śūnyatāṃ jñāna-.
28 TO4, K1 //.

(2.2) pratibhāsamātraṃ[1] tena[2] raśminā[3] svakāyaṃ[4] vyavalokya[5] hṛdi madhye[6] paṃkārajāṣṭadalapadmasyopary[7] akāreṇa[8] candramaṇḍalaṃ[9] tasyopari[10] raktahrīḥkāraraśminākṛṣṭasarvatathāgatapraveśenātmānaṃ[11] lokeśvararūpaṃ[12] vibhāvayet/[13] śuklavarṇaṃ[14] jaṭāmukuṭinaṃ[15] dakṣiṇahastavaradaṃ[16] taditaraśubhrapadmahastaṃ[17] ardhaparyaṅkiṇaṃ[18] sarvālaṅkārabhūṣitaṃ[19] amitābhamakuṭinaṃ[20] dvātriṃśallakṣaṇadharaṃ[21] aśītyanuvyañjanaṃ[22] candrāsanaṃ[23] candraprabham[24] ātmānaṃ vibhāvayet/[25]

(2.3) tato dakṣiṇe[26] āryatārāsudhanau/[27] vāme[28] bhṛkuṭīhayagrīvau/[29]

(2.4) pūrve[30] vairocanaḥ/[31] dakṣiṇe ratnasambhavaḥ/[32] paścime[33] amitābhaḥ/[34] uttare[35] amoghasiddhiḥ/[36]

---

1 BL2 add. a central dot.
2 B, TO2, N1 om.
3 B, TO2, N1 om.; TO4 raśmi.
4 TO2 -ya.
5 K1 and BL2 add. a central dot.
6 TO1 om.; TO2, TO3, K1, BL2 madhya.
7 The rendering follows the Sandhi rule. B, TO2, TO3, TO4, K1, N1, BL2 paṃkārajāṣṭadalapadmasyopari; TO1 pakārajāṣṭadarapadmasyopari.
8 TO1, TO3, K1, BL2 akāre.
9 TO2, TO3 and N1 add. /. TO4 add. //. K1 and BL2 add. a central dot.
10 BL2 add. a central dot.
11 TO1 raktahrīkāra-; TO3 raktaḥ hrīḥkāra-; TO4 -praveśanātmānaṃ; K1 -praveśam ātmānaṃ; BL2 -kṛṣṭa•sarvatathāgatapraveśemātmānaṃ.
12 N1 -rūpam; BL2 lokeśvaraṃ rūpaṃ.
13 TO1, TO3, K1, BL2 //.
14 TO1 śuklavarṇa; BL2 add. a central dot.
15 TO2, TO4 jaṭāmakuṭinaṃ; K1 and BL2 add. a central dot.
16 K1 and BL2 add. /.
17 TO1, TO3, N1 and BL2 add. /. TO2 -śubhapadmahastaṃ/; TO4 -śutrapadmahastaṃ/; K1 -śuvibhrapadmahastaṃ/.
18 B -paryyaṅkinaṃ; TO2 add. /. TO3 -paryaṅkinaṃ; TO4 -paryaṃkinaṃ/; K1 -paryaṅkitaṃ/; BL2 -paryyaṅkinaṃ/.
19 TO1 sarvvālakārabhūṣita/; BL2 sarvvāraṅkārabhūṣitaṃ/; TO3, TO4 and N1 add. /. K1 sarvāraṅkārabhūṣitaṃ/.
20 TO2 -na; TO4, K1 and BL2 add. /. N1 -mukuṭinaṃ/.
21 TO1, TO2, TO3 and N1 add. /. TO4 dvātriṃśalakṣaṇadharaṃ/; K1 add. a central dot. BL2 dvātriśallakṣaṇadharaṃ•.
22 TO1, TO3, TO4 and N1 add. /. TO2 aśityanuvyaṃjanaṃ/; K1 aśītyānuvyaṃjanaṃ/; BL2 aśītyānuvyañjanaṃ.
23 TO1, TO2, TO3 and TO4 add. /. N1 candrāsana/.
24 TO2 -prabhām.
25 TO1, TO3, K1, BL2 //.
26 TO4 -ṇai/.
27 B om. / and add. a comma. K1 om. /.
28 N1 add. /.
29 B om. / and add. a comma. TO3 om. /. K1 bhṛkuṭihayagrīvau/; BL2 bhṛkuṭihayagrīvau//.
30 TO2 pūrvva; BL2 add. a central dot.
31 B om. / and add. a comma. TO1, TO3, TO4 vairocana; K1 -no; BL2 vairocana•.
32 B om. / and add. a comma.
33 TO2 paścima.
34 B om. / and add. a comma. TO4 //; K1 amitābha; BL2 amitābha•.
35 TO1 urttare.
36 B om. / and add. a comma. TO4, K1, BL2 //.

(2.5) āgneyāṃ[1] locanā/[2] nairtyāṃ[3] māmakī/[4] vāyavyāṃ[5] pāṇḍarā/[6] aiśānyāṃ[7] vajradhātvīśvarī//[8]

(3) tato hṛdbījaraśmināḳṛsya[9] jñānasattvaṃ[10] praveśayet/[11]

(4) cakṣurādyadhiṣṭhānaṃ[12] kāyavākcittādhiṣṭhānaṃ[13] kṛtvā[14] abhiṣekaṃ prārthayet/[15] yathāhi jātamātreṇa[16] snāpitāḥ sarvatathāgatāḥ/[17] tathāhaṃ snāpayiṣyāmi[18] śuddhaṃ[19] divyena vāriṇā//[20] oṃ[21] sarvatathāgatābhiṣekasamayaśriye[22] hūṃ phaṭ svāhā/[23]

(5) locanādidaśadevatāṃ[24] saṃsphārya[25] pūjāstutiṃ kṛtvā[26] mantram ājapet/[27] tatrāyaṃ mantraḥ/[28] oṃ hrīḥ[29] svāhā/[30]

//khasarpaṇasādhanaṃ[31]

---

1 TO2 āgneryyā; N1 add. /.
2 B om. / and add. a comma. TO1 and TO3 om. /.
3 TO2 nairtyā; N1 add. /.
4 B om. / and add. a comma. TO1 māmaki/; TO2 māmaki.
5 TO2 vāyavyā; N1 add. /.
6 B om. / and add. a comma. TO1, TO3 and TO4 om. /. TO2 pāṇḍalā/.
7 TO1, TO2 aiśānyā.
8 B, K1, N1 /; TO1, TO2 vajadhāteśvarī/; TO3 vajedhāteśvarī/; TO4 vajradhātveśvarī/; BL2 vajadhātveśvarī//.
9 TO2 -mir ākṛṣya; K1, BL2 -ākṛ.
10 TO4 jāna-; BL2 jñā•nasatvaṃ.
11 TO1, TO3, K1 //; TO2 praveyet/; BL2 praveśeyet//.
12 TO1, TO2, TO3, TO4, K1, N1 and BL2 add. /.
13 K1 vāyavākcittadhiṣṭhānaṃ; BL2 rkayavākcittadhiṣṭhānāṃ.
14 TO2 add. /. BL2 add. a central dot.
15 N1 prāvvayet/.
16 TO2 -mateṇa.
17 TO1, TO3, TO4 and BL2 om. /. K1 -tathāgatās.
18 TO2 snāpiṣyāmi.
19 TO4 śuddhan.
20 TO1, TO2, TO3, K1, N1, BL2 /.
21 TO1 add. ā. K1 and BL2 add. āḥ.
22 TO1 sarvvatathāgabhiṣekasamaśriya; TO2 -samayaśriya; TO3 -samaśriye; BL2 -samaye śriye.
23 TO1, TO2, TO3, TO4, K1, N1, BL2 //.
24 TO1 locanādaśadevatāṃ; TO2 locanādidiśadikṣadevatīḥ; TO3, N1 locanādidaśadevatīṃ; TO4 -devatī; K1, BL2 rocanādidaśadevatīṃ.
25 TO2 add. /. K1, BL2 satvāryya.
26 K1 and BL2 add. a central dot.
27 TO1, TO3, K1, BL2 //.
28 B om. /. TO1, TO3, K1, N1 //; BL2 mantraṃ//.
29 TO1 hrī.
30 TO1, TO3, K1, BL2 //; TO2 and N1 om. /.
31 TO1, TO3 -sādhana; TO2 //iti khasarppaṇasādhanaṃ.

## 3 Vajradharmasya sādhanopāyikā (Bhatt. no. 10)

(1) hṛccandre[1] nyasya[2] hrīḥkāraṃ[3] dharmanairātmyabhāvanam/[4]
kṛtvā saṃsphārya[5] tasmāc[6] ca[7] raktaraśmīn[8] nabhaḥsamān//[9]
taiś ca lokeśvarākāraṃ[10] jagat sthāvarajaṅgamam/[11]
kṛtvā[12] sambodhisattvārthajātaṃ[13] hṛdi praveśya[14] ca//[15]
taṃ[16] hrīḥkāraṃ[17] parāvṛtya jhaṭiti[18] jñānayogataḥ/
(2) taṃ sitaraktavarṇaṃ[19] tu[20] padmarāgasamadyutim//[21]
pañcabuddhamakuṭadharaṃ[22] harṣeṇotphullalocanam/[23]
vāmato garvayā[24] nālaṃ[25] dhṛtvā ṣoḍaśapatrakam//[26]
padmaṃ vikāśayantaṃ[27] ca hṛdi dakṣiṇapāṇinā/[28]
mayūropari[29] madhyasthe[30] niṣaṇṇaṃ[31] candramaṇḍale//[32]
sattvaparyaṅkam ābhujya[33] saśṛṅgārarasotsavam/[34]

---

1 TO3 illegible between hṛ- and -re.
2 TO3 nyasye.
3 TO1, TO2, TO3, TO4 -kāran; K1, BL2 -kāra.
4 TO2 -nairātmābhāvanam/; TO4, BL2 //; K1 om. /.
5 TO1 sasphārya; TO2 saṃhāryya; K1, BL2 saṃsthāpya; N1 illegible after saṃ- .
6 N1 illegible before -māc.
7 K1 and BL2 add. a central dot.
8 TO4 -raśmīna; N1 raktaraśmi.
9 N1 /.
10 K1 and BL2 add. a central dot.
11 TO1, TO3 sthāvarajaṃ maṃ//; K1, BL2 thāvarajaṃgamaṃ.
12 BL2 add. a central dot.
13 B sambodhisattvārthaṃ jātaṃ; TO1, TO3, TO4 saṃbodhisatvārthajātaṃ; K1 saṃbodhisatvārtha•jātaṃ; N1 saṃbodhisattvāthajātaṃ; BL2 sambodhisatvārtha •jātaṃ; TO2 -jāta.
14 K1, BL2 paśye.
15 TO1, TO3 /; TO2 om. ca/; K1 and BL2 om. //.
16 TO2 ta.
17 TO1 hrīḥkāra.
18 TO1 jhatiti; K1, BL2 jhatiṭi.
19 B, TO3, TO4, K1, BL2 sitaṃ raktavarṇaṃ; TO1 sitaṃ raktavarṇa; N1 sitaṃ raktavarṇan.
20 K1 and BL2 add. a central dot.
21 TO1 -samadyuti/; TO2 padmarāgamayadyutiṃ//; TO3 /; TO4 -samadyutiḥ//; N1 padmarāgamayaṃ dyutiṃ//; BL2 -samadvtiṃ/.
22 TO1, TO2, TO3, TO4 -mukuṭaṃ; N1 -makuṭaṃ; K1, BL2 -makuṭaṃ•.
23 TO1 hatṣotphurrallocana/; TO2, TO4 harṣotphullalocanam//; TO3 harṣotphullalocanam/; K1 harṣotphullarocanaṃ•; N1 harṣodphellalocanam/; BL2 harṣophullarocanaṃ•.
24 B sparddhayā.
25 TO2 nāraṃ; K1 and BL2 add. a central dot.
26 TO1, TO2, TO3, K1, N1, BL2 /.
27 TO3, TO4, K1, N1, BL2 -tañ.
28 TO1, TO3 dakṣiṇapāninā/; TO4 //; K1 and BL2 om. /.
29 TO4 mayuropari.
30 K1, BL2 sthe•.
31 TO1, TO2, K1, BL2 niṣaṇṇa.
32 TO1 om. //. TO2, TO3, TO4, K1, N1, BL2 /.
33 BL2 add. a central dot.
34 TO1, TO3, TO4 //; TO2 śṛṅgārarasotsavam/; K1 saśṛṃgārasasotsavaṃ/; BL2 saśṛṅgārasamotsavaṃ/.

caityāntaḥsthamahākarmakūṭāgāravihāriṇam/[1]
bhāvayed vajradharmāgryaṃ[2] nityaṃ bodhim[3] avāpnuyāt//[4]

(3) bhāvanākhinno[5] hṛccandre[6] nyasya mālām ivāvikṣiptacitto[7] japet/[8] tatrāyaṃ japyo mantraḥ//[9] oṃ vajradharma hrīḥ/[10]
//sādhanopāyikā[11] saṃkṣiptā[12] vajradharmasya//

---

1 TO1 caityāntasthamahākarmmakūṭāgāravihāriṇam; TO2, K1, N1 caityāntasthamahākarmmakūṭāgāravihāriṇam/; BL2 caityāntasthamahākarmmakūṭāgāravihāraṇam/; TO3 caityāṃtasthamahākarmmakūṭāgāravihāriṇam.
2 TO1, TO2, TO3 vajadharmmāgran; TO4 vajadharmāgran; K1 vajradharmāgran •; N1 vajradharmmāgran; BL2 vajadharmmāgran•.
3 N1 illegible before -dhim.
4 TO1, TO3, N1 /.
5 K1, BL2 bhāvanāṣinna.
6 K1 and BL2 add. a central dot.
7 TO2 ivāvilikṣiptacitto.
8 TO1, TO2 //.
9 B om. //. TO2 mantra//; TO3 /; BL2 mmantraḥ// //.
10 TO1, TO2, TO3, TO4 and N1 om. /. K1, BL2 //.
11 N1 -payikā.
12 K1 and BL2 add. ca•.

# 4.1 Ṣaḍakṣarīlokeśvarasādhana (Bhatt. no. 6 Ṣaḍakṣarīmahāvidyāsādhana)

(0) [(1-]āryaṣaḍakṣarīmahāvidyāyai namaḥ/[-1)]

(1.1) ādau tāvan[2] mantrī[3] sukhāsanopaviṣṭaḥ[4] mukhaśaucādikaṃ[5] kṛtvā[6]

(2.1.1) [(7-]svahṛdi[8] candrasthasitahrīḥkāravinirgataraśmibhir[9] gurubuddhabodhisattvān[10] purato[11-7)] dṛṣṭvā[12] sampūjya triśaraṇagamanādikaṃ[13] kuryād[14] ratnatrayaṃ[15] me śaraṇam ityādinā//[16]

(2.1.2) yāvantaḥ[17] sattvāḥ[18] sattvasaṃgraheṇa[19] saṃgṛhītāḥ[20] aṇḍajā[21] vā[22] jarāyujā[23] vā[24] saṃsvedajā[25] vā[26] aupapādukā[27] vā[28] rūpiṇo vā[29] [(30-]arūpiṇo vā[-30)] saṃjñino[31] vā[32] asaṃjñino[33]

---

1 TO1, TO2, TO3, TO4, K1, N1, BL2 om.; K2 āryaṣaḍakṣarīvidyāyai namaḥ//; BL1 āryyaṣaḍakṣarīmahāvidyāyai namaḥ//.
2 TO2, TO3, BL2 -vat.
3 BL1 add. a central dot.
4 TO1 -praviṣṭaḥ; TO2 and N1 add. /. TO4 add. //. BL1 -viṣya•.
5 TO2, K2, BL1 mukhasau-.
6 K1 and BL2 add. a central dot.
7 K2, BL1 om.
8 TO4 hṛdi.
9 TO1 -kāvinir-; TO4 -mibhi; K1 -vinirgata•raśmi; BL2 -nirggataḥ raśmi-.
10 N1 add. /. BL2 -sattvā •.
11 BL2 tpirato.
12 B, K2, BL1 buddhādīn dṛṣṭvā; TO1 dṛvā.
13 TO1, TO3 -ṇagamaṇādikaṃ; TO4 -ṇamanādikaṃ; K2 -ṇāgamaṇādikaṃ.
14 TO1, TO3, K1, K2 kruyāt//; TO2 add. /; TO4 kruyāt/; N1 krayāt/; BL1 kruyāt; BL2 add. //.
15 TO2, K1 -ya; K2 ratnaṃ traya.
16 B, TO2, TO4, N1, BL2 /; K1 om. //. K2 ādi; BL1 ityādi.
17 TO1, TO2 -ta.
18 TO2 -vā.
19 B sattvasaṃgrahena; TO1 sagraheṇa; K1 satvasaṃgṛhītena; K2 satvaṃ saṅgrahena; BL1 sattvaṃ saṃgraheṇa; BL2 satvvasaṃgṛhītāḥ.
20 TO1 sagṛhītāḥ; TO2, TO4 and N1 add. /. K2 saṅgrihītā; BL1 sadgrihitāḥ; BL2 -tena.
21 BL1 andajā•.
22 TO4, K1 and BL2 add. a central dot. N1 add. /.
23 K2 jalāyujā.
24 TO1 va; TO4 and N1 add. /. K1 and BL2 add. a central dot.
25 TO1 sasvedajā; K2, BL1 svedajā.
26 TO2, TO4 and N1 add. /. K1 and BL2 add. a central dot.
27 TO2 -dujā.
28 TO4 add. /. K1 and BL2 add. a central dot.
29 TO2, TO4 and N1 add. /.
30 TO2 arūpino vā/; TO4 om.; K2 arūpiṇau vā•; BL2 arūpiṇo vā•.
31 TO1, TO3, K1, BL2 saṃgino; BL1 saṃjñīno.
32 TO1 va; TO4 and N1 add. /. K1 add. a central dot.
33 TO1 asaṃpino; TO3, K1, K2, BL2 asaṃgino; BL1 asaṃjñīno.

vā[1] naivasaṃjñānāsaṃjñino[2] vā[3] yāvat[4] kaścit[5] sattvadhātuḥ prajñapyamānaḥ[6] prajñapyate[7] sarve[8] mayā anupadhiśeṣanirvāṇadhātau[9] pratiṣṭhāpayitavyā[10] iti//[11]

(2.1.3) tataḥ oṃ[12] svabhāvaśuddhāḥ sarvadharmāḥ svabhāvaśuddho[13] 'haṃ[14] iti vāratrayam[15] uccārayet/[16] tadanu śūnyatāṃ[17] muhūrtam[18] ālambayet/[19]

(2.1.4) tadanantaraṃ[20] svahṛdaye[21] sitapadmopari candramaṇḍalaṃ[22] tasyopari[23] sitahrīḥkāraṃ[24] tato niścaradanekaraśmiśatasahasraṃ[25] dhyātvā[26] (27-tena sarvasattvānām aśeṣānādikālasañcitaṃ-27) rāgādikleśasamūhaṃ[28] viśodhyante/[29] tat[30] punas tatraiva praveśayet/[31]

---

1 TO1, TO2, TO3, TO4 and N1 add. /. K2 and BL2 add. a central dot.

2 TO2 na iva saṃjñānāvasaṃjñino; K1 naivasaṃginovānāsaṃgino; K2 naivasaṅgino; BL1 naivasaṅgīno; BL2 naivasaṃgino.

3 TO1, TO2, TO3, TO4 and N1 add. /. K1 add. //. K2 and BL2 add. a central dot. nā saṃgito vā//.

4 TO4 yāvān.

5 TO1 kaśçi; K1, BL2 kacit; K2, BL1 om.

6 K2, BL1 prajñamānaḥ; BL2 prajñāpya-.

7 TO1, TO2 and TO3 add. /. TO4, K1 and BL2 add. //. K2 prajñapete te; N1 prajñapya/; BL1 prajñepyete te.

8 TO1, TO2, TO3, N1, BL2 sarvvo; TO4, K1 sarvo; K2 sarvve•.

9 TO2 anupadhiśeṣonirvvāṇadhātau; TO3, K1 anupadhiśeṣeṇa nirvvāṇadhātau; TO4, N1 anupadhiśeṣenirvāṇadhātau; K2 apadhiseṣeṇirvānadhātau; BL1 anupadhiṣeṣanir-; BL2 anupadhiśeṣeṇa nirvāṇadhātau.

10 TO1, TO3, TO4, K1 -payitavyāḥ//; TO2 -payitavyaiḥ//; K2 -payatavyā; N1 -payitavyaḥ/; BL1 pratisthāpayītavyā; BL2 pratisthāpayitavyāḥ.

11 B /; TO1, TO2, TO3, TO4, K1, N1, BL2 om.

12 K1 om.

13 K1, BL2 śubhāva-.

14 K1 add. a central dot.

15 K2 -traye•.

16 TO1, TO3, K1, BL2 //; TO2 mūccarayet/; K2 mucāryye; BL1 uccāryya.

17 K1, BL2 -tā; K2 sūnyatā; BL1 sunyatā.

18 K2, BL1 muhūrtamātraṃ; BL2 mūhūrtam.

19 TO1 alambayet//; TO2, TO3, K1, BL2 //; K2, BL1 dhyātvā and a colon.

20 TO1 tadanantara; TO3 tadantara; K1 tadāśvinemṛtamartyasya ṣaḍakṣarīsu mūrtikātasya dhyānaṃ pravakṣyāmi jinendreṇa yathoditaṃ sarvālaṃkārabhūṣādyaṃ śuklavarṇaṃ caturbhujāṃ vāmapāṇau padmadharaṃ dakṣiṇenākṣasūtrakaṃ bhujābhyāṃ dakṣavāmābhyāṃ hṛdipuṭāṃjaliṃ smaret antaraṃ; K2, BL1 tadanu.

21 TO1, TO2, TO3, TO4, K1, N1, BL2 hṛdaye; BL1 -ya.

22 TO2 and N1 add. /. TO4 add. //. K2 catumaṇḍalaṃ; BL1 catumandalaṃ; K1 and BL2 add. a central dot.

23 K2 tasyoparī.

24 TO1 site/ hrīḥ; TO3 add. /. K2 sītahrīḥ- ; BL1 sitaḥ hrīkāraṃ.

25 K1, BL2 -raśmisata-; K2 nekarasmiśatasahaśraraśmibhiś ca; BL1 'nekarasmiśatasahaśraraśmibhiś ca.

26 K2 add. a colon. BL2 add. a central dot.

27 TO1 tenāśeṣānādikālaṃsancita; TO2 tenāśeṣānādikālasañcita; TO3 tenāśeṣānādikālaṃsancita; TO4 tenāśeṣānādikālaṃsamcita; K1 tenāśeṣādinkālaṃ saṃvīta; K2 nāmaśeṣāṇādikālasaṃcitaṃ•; N1 tenāśeṣānādikān asañcita; BL2 tenāśeṣāditkālaṃ •saṃvīta.

28 B, TO2, TO3, TO4, N1 and BL2 add. sattvānāṃ. TO1 -śamūhaṃ sattvānāṃ; K1 rāgādi•kleśasamūhaṃ sattvānāṃ; K2 -śasamūha; BL1 -mūha.

29 TO1, TO2, TO3, TO4, K1, N1 -yataṃ; K1 -yantaṃ•; K2 viśodhā; BL1 viśodhya; BL2 -taṃ•.

30 TO1, TO2, TO3, TO4, K1, N1, BL2 om.; K2, BL1 tan.

31 TO1 praveśat, TO2 om. /. TO3, BL2 praveśet; TO4 praviśayet; K1 praveśa; K2, N1 praveśaye; BL1 -ye.

(2.2.1) tatpariṇatam[1] ātmānaṃ[2]lokeśvararūpaṃ[3] sarvālaṅkārabhūṣitaṃ[4] śuklavarṇaṃ[5] caturbhujaṃ[6] vāmataḥ[7] padmadharaṃ[8] dakṣiṇato akṣasūtradharaṃ[9] aparābhyāṃ[10] hastābhyāṃ[11] hṛdi saṃpuṭāñjalisthitaṃ[12] dhyāyāt//[13]

(2.2.2) dakṣiṇe[14] maṇidharaṃ[15] tadvadvarṇabhujānvitaṃ[16] padmāntaroparisthaṃ[17] vāme[18] tathaivāparapadmasthāṃ[19] ṣaḍakṣarīmahāvidyām//[20]

(2.3.1) tataḥ[21] oṃ mahāsukha[22] vajrasattva[23] jaḥ[24] hūṃ vaṃ hoḥ[25] suratas tvaṃ[26] (27-alalalalala hoḥ-27) aḥ[28] aḥ[29] aḥ aḥ[30] ity adhiṣṭhānamantrarājam[31] uccārayet//[32]

---

1 B tatpapariṇatam; K2, BL1 tatpariṇamyam.
2 K2 ātmāṇaṃ.
3 K1 and BL2 add. a central dot.
4 TO1 sarvālakāra-; TO2 and TO4 add. /. K2, BL1 and BL2 add. a central dot.
5 TO1, K2, BL1 -varṇa; K1 and BL2 add. a central dot.
6 TO1, TO2 carbhujaṃ; TO3, TO4, K1 and N1 add. /. K2, BL1 and BL2 add. a central dot.
7 K2 -ta•.
8 B add. a comma. TO1, TO3, TO4, K1 and N1 add. /. BL2 -dharāṃ.
9 B add. a comma. TO2 kṣa-; TO2, TO3, TO4, K1 and N1 add. /. K2 add. a central dot. BL1 akṣasutradharaṃ•; BL2 akṣasutradharaṃ/.
10 TO1 -yā; K1 and BL2 add. a central dot.
11 TO2 -yā.
12 TO1, TO2 -pūṭā-; K2 saṃpūṭāñjalisthitaṃ•; BL1 add. a central dot. BL2 -liṃ sthitaṃ•.
13 B, TO2, TO4, N1 /, K2, BL1 om.
14 TO2 -ṇa.
15 TO2 mahāmaṇi-; K1, K2 and BL2 add. a central dot.
16 TO1 and BL2 add. /. TO2, TO4 tadvarṇa-; TO3, K1 tadvarṇabhujānvitaṃ/; K2 -bhūjā-.
17 TO1, TO2, TO3 and TO4 add. /. K1, BL2 padmontaroparisthaṃ/; K2 padmopariṣṭhaṃ; N1 illegible after padmānta-. BL1 padmoparisthaṃ.
18 BL1 vāma.
19 B tathaiva aparapadmasthāṃ; K1 tathaivāparapadmasthaṃ/; K2 tathaivaparapadmastha; N1 tathaivāparapadmasthā; BL1 tathevaparapadmastham•; BL2 add. /.
20 B ṣaḍakṣarīṃ mahāvidyām/; TO1, TO3, N1 ṣaḍakṣarīm mahāvidyām/; TO2 /; TO4 ṣaḍakṣarīm mahāvidyām.
21 N1 add. /.
22 K2 mahāśuṣa; BL1 mahāsuṣa.
23 K1 vajrasatvaḥ; BL2 vajasatvaḥ; K2 mayesatva; BL1 mayasatva.
24 K2 -ja.
25 K2 ho.
26 K2 tha; BL1 yaṃ.
27 TO2 alalala hoḥ; TO3, TO4, K1, K2, N1, BL1, BL2 alalalala hoḥ.
28 TO1 a.
29 TO1 a.
30 TO3, K1 and BL2 add. /.
31 TO2 adhisthāna-; K2 adhisthānamaṃtram; BL1 adhisthānamantram; BL2 adhiṣṭhānamantraṃ rājam.
32 B, TO2, TO4 /; K2 and BL1 have a central dot.

(2.3.2) evaṃ dhyātvā[1] tato[2] lokeśvarātmahṛdayacandramaṇḍalād[3] akṣasūtrākāraṃ[4] śuklavarṇaṃ[5] mukhena[6] nirgatya[7] nābhau praviśantaṃ[8] cakrabhramaṇayogena[9] imaṃ[10] mantrarājaṃ[11] sarvabuddhahṛdayacintāmaṇikalpaṃ[12] paśyed[13] animittayogena/[14] tato japaṃ[15] kṛtvā[16] bhramaṇapraveśanādikaṃ[17] prāpyācireṇaiva[18] kālena[19] śrāddhaḥ[20] kṛpāvān gurubhakto[21] yogī[22] sidhyati/[23] oṃ maṇipadme[24] hūṃ[25] iti[26] jāpamantraḥ//[27]

(3) tata[28] utthānakāle[29] imaṃ[30] mantrarājam[31] uccāryottiṣṭhet/[32]

---

1 K2, BL1 dhyānaṃ kṛtvā.
2 K2, BL1 om.
3 TO1, TO3, N1 lokeśvarātmahṛdaye candramaṇḍalād; TO4 lokeśvarātmatmahṛdaya-; K2 lokeśvarātmahṛdaye candramaṇḍalād; K1 lokeśvarohṛdayacandra-oṃ-maṇḍalā; BL1 -hṛdaye candra-; BL2 lokeśvaro hṛdayacandraṃ oṃ-maṇḍalā•.
4 TO1 akṣasūtrakāraṃ; TO3 akṣasūtrokāraṃ; K1 and K2 add. a central dot.
5 TO1, TO3, K2 -ṇa.
6 TO1-eṇa; K1 and K2 add. a central dot.
7 K1 nirga; BL2 nirgata.
8 TO2 paviśantaṃ; K1 and BL2 add. a central dot. K2 pravisantaṃ; BL1 pravīsan na.
9 TO2 -manayogena; K2, BL1 -meṇa yogeṇa; BL2 add. a central dot.
10 TO1, TO3, TO4, K1, BL2 iyaṃ; K2, BL1 idaṃ.
11 TO2 -jā.
12 TO1 -yacintāmanikalpa; K2 -yaṃ cintāmaṇi•kalpa; N1 sarvvaṃ buddha-; BL1 -hṛdayaṃ cintāmaṇīkalpa.
13 TO1, K2 paśyad.
14 TO4 animittayogenā; K1, BL2 //; K2 animita•yogena; BL1 om. /.
15 TO1 japa; K1, K2, BL2 jāpaṃ.
16 TO1, TO2, TO3, TO4, K1 and N1 add. /.
17 TO1 bhramaṇaveśanādikaṃ; TO2 bhramaṇakeśanādikaṃ; TO3, TO4, N1 bhramaṇāveśanādikaṃ; K1, BL2 bhramanāveganādikaṃ; K2 bhrameṇa pravaśādikaṃ; BL1 bhrameṇa praveśanādikaṃ.
18 TO3, TO4 prāpyādireṇaiva; K1 prāpyādiraiṇaiva; K2 -renaiva; BL1 prāpyācirenaiva; BL2 prāpyādicaiṇaiva.
19 TO1 kārena; TO2, BL2 kāreṇa; K1, K2 kāreṇa•.
20 K1 śrāddha•; K2 srāddha; BL2 śrārddha.
21 K2 add. a central dot.
22 TO1 yogi .
23 TO1, K1 // //; TO2, TO3, TO4, N1, BL1 //; K2 has a central dot and //. BL2 // //.
24 BL1 maṇīpadme.
25 TO1, TO2, TO3, TO4, N1 and BL1 add. //. K1 and BL2 add. // //. K2 add. a central dot.
26 TO1, TO2, TO3, TO4, K1, N1 om.
27 B /; TO1 -tra; TO2 -tra//; BL1 om. //.
28 TO2, K1, K2, BL1, BL2 tataḥ.
29 TO4 -lai; K1, BL2 -la.
30 TO1 i; K2, BL1 idaṃ; N1 kāmaṃ.
31 K1, BL2 mantraṃ rājaṃ; K2 maṃtraṃ; BL1 mantraṃ.
32 TO1 muccārayat tiṣṭhet//; TO2 uccārya tiṣṭhet//; TO3, K1, BL2 uccārayet tiṣṭhet//; TO4 uccārayāt tiṣṭhet//; K2 uccāryyet tiṣṭhet://; N1 uccāryo tiṣṭhet/; BL1 mucāryya utiṣṭhet//.

oṃ [(1-]vajrasattva samayam[-1)] anupālaya[2] vajrasattvenopatiṣṭha[3] dṛḍho me bhava[4] sutoṣyo me bhava[5] [(6-]supoṣyo[7] me bhava[8-6)] anurakto[9] me bhava[10] sarvasiddhiṃ[11] me prayaccha[12] sarvakarmasu ca[13] me cittaṃ[14] śreyaḥ[15] kuru[16] hūṃ ha ha ha ha[17] hoḥ[18] bhagavan[19] sarvatathāgatavajra mā me muñca[20] vajrībhava mahāsamayasattva āḥ/[21] evam uktvā yathāsukhaṃ[22] vihared[23] iti/[24]
//āryaṣaḍakṣarīmahāvidyāsādhanaṃ[25]

---

1 TO1 vajasattvasam; BL1 -yem.
2 TO4 -ye; K2 -yeḥ; BL2 add. a central dot.
3 B add. a comma. TO1 vajasatvonopatiṣṭha; TO2 -pratiṣṭha; TO3 vajasattvānopatiṣṭha; TO4 vajrasatvavenopatiṣṭhavajrasatvattvettvenopaviṣṭha; K1 vajrasatvatenopatiṣṭhaṃ •; K2 vajrasatvatvena pratiṣṭha; N1 satvavenopatiṣṭha; BL2 vajasattvo tenopatiṣṭhaṃ•.
4 B add. a comma. BL1 sā.
5 B add. a semicolon. K1 and BL2 add. a central dot.
6 TO2, BL1 om.
7 K1 -ṣo.
8 B add. a comma. K1 and BL2 add. a central dot.
9 K2, BL1 anurakṣo.
10 B add. a comma. K1 and BL2 add. a central dot.
11 TO1, TO2, TO3, K2, BL1, BL2 -siddhi.
12 B add. a comma. TO4 preccha; K1 and BL2 add. a central dot. K2 prayeccha; BL1 prayaṃccha.
13 K1, BL2 om.
14 TO2, K2, BL1 citta; K1 and BL2 add. a central dot.
15 TO2 śreyaṃ; BL2 śriyaḥ.
16 B add. a comma.
17 K1 and BL2 add. a central dot.
18 TO1, TO3, TO4 ho; BL1 om.; K1, BL2 •ho.
19 K2 -vān.
20 K1 and BL2 add. a central dot.
21 TO1, TO2, TO3, K1, K2, N1 //.
22 BL1 yathākhaṃ.
23 K1 virahed.
24 TO1, TO3, K1, BL2 //; TO4, N1 and BL1 om. /. K2 has a colon and //.
25 TO1, TO3 -na; K2 //iti sādhanasamuccaya āryyeṣaḍakṣarīmahāvidyāsādhana trāyatriṃśatyadhikaśatatamapaṭala //133//; BL1 iti sādhanasamucaye āryyaṣaḍakṣarīmahāvidyāsādhana trāyatriṃsaty adhikaśatatamapaṭalaḥ//133//.
26 K1 add. //āśvinasya//. K2, BL1 om.

## 4.2 Ṣaḍakṣarīlokeśvarasādhana (Bhatt. no. 7 Kāraṇḍavyūhāmnāyena racitaṃ sādhanaṃ)

(1.1) padmakulodbhavaṃ[1] nāthaṃ[2] sarvajñakṛtamaulinam/[3]
praṇamya[4] sādhanaṃ[5] vakṣye[6] sarvarogavināśanam/[7]
prathamaṃ[8] tāvad ācāryānugatā siddhiḥ/[9]
tasmāc[10] ca[11] sarvabhāvena gurum[12] pūjayed[13] yatnataḥ/[14]
guruṇā parituṣṭena karmasiddhiḥ[15] prajāyate//[16]
maṇḍalapraviṣṭasya[17] siddhir[18] anujñātā[19] ca sarvathā/[20]
svasamayasamvaraṃ[21] rakṣayan[22] sidhyate[23] dhruvam//[24]

(1.2) mukhaśaucādipūrvakaṃ[25] devagṛhe[26] paṭādigatabhaṭṭārakam[27] avatārya[28]

---

1 TO1, TO3, TO4, K1, N1, BL2 padmakulodbhavan; TO2 padmakulodbhava.
2 K1 add. a central dot.
3 TO4 //; K1, BL2 a central dot.
4 N1 illegible.
5 TO1 -na.
6 TO2 vakṣe; BL2 vakṣe•.
7 TO1,TO3, TO4, K1, N1 //; BL2 om. /; TO2 -vināsanam//.
8 TO1, TO2, TO3, K1, N1, BL2 -man.
9 TO1, K1 siddhi//; TO2 //; TO3, TO4 siddhi/.
10 TO1, TO2, TO3, TO4, K1, N1, BL2 tasmāt.
11 TO1, TO2, TO3, TO4, K1, N1, BL2 om.
12 TO2 gurū; K1 guru; BL2 om.
13 BL2 om.
14 TO1, TO3 and K1 om. /. TO4, N1 //; BL2 om.
15 TO1, TO3, K1 -siddhi; BL2 karma guru pūjayed yatnataḥ siddhi.
16 TO1, TO2, TO4, K1, N1, BL2 /.
17 K1 and BL2 add. a central dot.
18 TO2 siddhiḥ.
19 TO2 ranujñātā.
20 TO2, TO4, N1 //.
21 K1 svaramayasaṃvaraṃ; N1 svasamayam svaraṃ.
22 K1 and BL2 add. a central dot.
23 TO4 sidhyete.
24 TO1, TO2, N1 /.
25 TO2 mukhaśaucādipūrvvantaṃ; TO4 mukhaṇaucādi-; K1, BL2 mukhaśaucādikaṃ•pūrvvakaṃ•.
26 K1, BL2 -ha.
27 TO2 paṭādisata-; BL2 -bhaṭṭārakam•.
28 TO2 avatārā; K1, BL2 -ya•.

(2.1.1) svahṛdaye[1] ādyakṣareṇa[2] candramaṇḍalaṃ[3] tasyopary[4] aṣṭamasya caturthakaṃ bījaṃ[5] saptamadvitīyenāsanaṃ[6] prathamacaturthena maṇḍitaṃ[7] ṣoḍaśena saṃyuktaṃ[8] śuklavarṇaṃ[9] [(10-]manoramaṃ//[11]

(2.1.2) tato[-10)] viśvaraśmīn[12] niścārya[13] tai[14] raśmibhir[15] niṣpannān[16] gurubuddhamūrtīn[17] dṛṣṭvā[18] pūjayitvā[19] abhivandya[20] cānena[21] mantreṇa//[22]

oṃ vajrapuṣpe hūṃ/[23] oṃ vajradhūpe hūṃ/[24] oṃ vajradīpe hūṃ/[25]

[(26-]oṃ vajragandhe hūṃ/[-26)] oṃ vajranaivedye[27] hūṃ/[28]

(2.1.3) tato[29]

ratnatrayaṃ[30] me[31] śaraṇaṃ[32] sarvaṃ[33] [(34-]pratidiśāmy aghaṃ/[-34)] anumode[35] jagatpuṇyaṃ[36] buddhabodhau[37] dadhe manaḥ//[38]

---

1 K1, BL2 -ya•; N1 illegible.
2 TO4 ādyādyakṣareṇa; K1 ādyāntākṣareṇa; N1 illegible before -dyakṣareṇa. BL2 ādyānta •akṣareṇa.
3 TO1 -la; TO1, TO2, TO4 and N1 add. /.
4 The rendering follows the Sandhi rule. B, TO1, TO2, TO3, TO4, K1, N1, BL2 tasyopari.
5 TO1 bīja/; TO1, TO2, TO3, TO4 and N1 add. /. K1 and BL2 add. //.
6 TO2 -yanāsanaṃ, N1 -yenāśanaṃ/; TO3 and TO4 add. /. K1 and BL2 add. //.
7 TO1, TO2, TO3, TO4, K1, N1 and BL2 add. /.
8 TO3, K1 -ta; BL2 saṃyukta.
9 TO2, TO4 śuklavarṇa; K1 śuklavarṇam; BL2 add. a central dot.
10 N1 illegible.
11 B om. //. TO1, TO2, TO3 /.
12 TO1, TO2, TO3, TO4, N1, BL2 -ṃin; K1 -mi.
13 BL2 add. a central dot.
14 TO4 trairaśmibhir.
15 TO4 om.
16 TO1, TO4 nniṣpannān; K1 nniṣpannā; N1 niṣpānnān; BL2 nnipannā.
17 B gurūn sabuddhamūrttīn; TO1, TO2, TO3 saṃbuddha-; TO4 sambuddhamṛttīn; K1 gurubuddha•mūrttīn•; N1 sambuddha-; BL2 gurabuddha•mūttīna•.
18 K1 and BL2 add. a central dot.
19 K1 and BL2 add. a central dot.
20 TO1, TO2, TO3, TO4, K1 -dyā; BL2 add. /.
21 TO4 cārena.
22 B om. //. TO4 matra//; K1, BL2 mantraḥ//.
23 B om. / and add. a comma. TO4 //; TO2 add. oṃ vajagandhe hūṃ/.
24 B om. / and add. a comma.
25 B om. / and add. a comma.
26 B om. / and add. a comma. TO2 om.; BL2 oṃ vajagandhe hūṃ•.
27 TO1 -naivadya; TO3, BL2 -naivedya.
28 B om. /. TO1, TO2, TO3 //.
29 TO1 om.
30 TO2 -ye.
31 TO1 om.
32 K1 and BL2 add. a central dot.
33 TO1 sarvva; TO4 sarva.
34 TO1 pratīdiśāmeghaṃ/; K1 pratidiśāmy eghaṃ.
35 TO1, TO3 anumodya; TO2 anumedya; TO4 anumodye.
36 TO1 jagatapūnya; K1 add. a central dot. BL2 -pūṇyaṃ •.
37 BL2 boddha-.
38 TO1 and TO3 om. //. TO2, K1, BL2 /.

ābodheḥ[1] śaraṇaṃ yāmi[2] buddhaṃ[3] dharmaṃ[4] gaṇottamam/[5]
bodhau cittaṃ[6] karomy[7] eṣa[8] svaparārthaprasiddhaye//
utpādayāmi[9] (10-paramaṃ[11] varabodhicittaṃ nimantrayāmi[12-10)] bahusarvasattvān/[13]
iṣṭāṃ[14] cariṣye[15] varabodhicārikāṃ[16] buddho[17] bhaveyaṃ jagato hitāya//[18]

(2.1.4) iti/[19] praṇidhipūrvakaṃ[20] sarvadharmanairātmyaṃ[21] bhāvayet/[22] anena mantreṇa/[23]
oṃ[24] (25-śūnyatājñānavajrasvabhāvātmako 'ham/[-25)]
bījaṃ[26] māyopamākāraṃ[27] traidhātukam aśeṣataḥ/[28]
dṛśyate spṛśyate[29] caiva[30] yathā[31] (32-māyā hi[-32)] sarvataḥ/[33]
na copalabhyate[34] caiva[35] sarvasya jagataḥ sthitiḥ//[36]

---

1 TO1, TO3, TO4, K1, BL2 ābodhe.
2 K1 and BL2 add. a central dot.
3 TO4 buddha.
4 TO1 dharmmaṅ; TO3, K1, BL2 dharmma.
5 K1 om. /.
6 K1 citta.
7 N1 karom?.
8 TO2 aṣa.
9 TO1, TO3, TO4, N1 -mī.
10 TO1, TO3, TO4, K1, BL2 om.
11 TO2, N1 om.
12 TO2, N1 -mī.
13 TO1, TO3, K1 aṃgasarvva-; TO2 ahusarvvasatvān/; TO4 aṅgasarva-; BL2 aṃgasarvasattvān/.
14 TO1 iṣṭaṃ; TO2, TO4, N1 iṣṭāñ; K1, BL2 -ān.
15 TO2 cariṣya; K1, BL2 tariṣye.
16 K1 and BL2 add. a central dot.
17 K1 bodho; BL2 bodhau.
18 TO1, TO3, BL2, N1 hitāyeti//; K1 hitāyeti; TO2 hitāyati//; TO4 hiyeti//.
19 TO1, TO2, TO3, TO4, BL2, K1, N1 om.
20 TO2 pranidhi-.
21 TO4 -nairātmām.
22 B om. /. TO3 and BL2 add. //. K1 //.
23 TO1, TO3, K1, BL2 //; TO2 om. /.
24 TO2 om.
25 TO1 śūnyatāṃ jñānavajasvabhātmako 'haṃ; TO2 śūnyatājñānasvabhāvātmako ham/; TO3 śūnyatāṃ jñānavajasvabhāvātmako 'haṃ/; TO4 śūnyatāṃ jñānasvabhāvātmako haṃ/; K1 śūnyatāṃ jñānasatvasvabhāvātmako 'ham//; BL2 śūnyatāṃ jñānasatvam bhāvātmako 'ham//.
26 K1, BL2 bīja.
27 TO2 māyopamākāra; TO4 māyaupamākāraṃ; K1 and BL2 add. a central dot. N1 māyopamākāra vicintya.
28 TO4 aśeṣata//.
29 TO2, K1, BL2 -teś.
30 K1 and BL2 add. a central dot.
31 K1, BL2 tathā.
32 TO1 mādi; TO3, TO4, K1, BL2 māyādi.
33 TO1, TO2, TO3, TO4, N1 //.
34 TO2 coparabhyante.
35 K1 and BL2 add. a central dot.
36 TO1, TO2, TO3, TO4, K1, N1, BL2 sthitir.

ity adhimucya/[1] tato 'nādikālīnam[2] asatkalpanābījam[3] apanīya[4] svabhāvam[5] adhimuñcet/[6]
oṃ svabhāvaśuddhāḥ[7] sarvadharmāḥ svabhāvaśuddho 'ham//[8]

(2.2) tataḥ[9] pūrvoktabījaniṣpannaṃ[10] padmaṃ[11] tasyopary[12] hrīḥkāraṃ[13] tatsarvaniṣpanne[14]sati śrīmallokanāthaṃ vajrapadmagarbhacandrasthaṃ[15] vajraparyaṅkaṃ[16] śaśiprabhaṃ[17] kundenduvarṇam ujjvalaṃ[18] jaṭāmakuṭadharaṃ[19] śāntaṃ amitābhakṛtaśekharaṃ[20] vyāghracarmanivasanaṃ[21] caturbhujaṃ[22] nānālaṅkārabhūṣitaṃ[23] dakṣiṇakare[24] akṣamālādharaṃ[25] vāmakare[26] padmamaṇivibhūṣitaṃ[27] dvau hastau saṃyuktau[28] (29-sarvarājendramudrayā hṛdi saṃsthitaṃ/-29) tato 'haṅkāraṃ[30] kuryāt//[31] aham eva lokeśvara[32] iti//[33]

---

1 TO4 -yate/; K1 and BL2 om. /.
2 TO1 nādikārīnam; TO4 -linim; K1 -līna•; BL2 nādikālīn•.
3 K1 nasatkalpanābīja•; BL2 namas kalpanābīja•.
4 K1, BL2 pamanīya.
5 BL2 svabhāva•.
6 TO1-cete//; TO2 -muṃcat //; TO3, TO4, N1 //; K1 adhimucayat//; BL2 madhimucet//.
7 K1 add. kārtikemṛtamartyasya kāraṃḍavyūhamūrttikā tasya dhyānaṃ pravakṣyāmi yathā proktaṃ jinaiśvaraiḥ vajrapadmagarbhacaṃdravajraparyyaṃkasaṃsthitaṃ śaśikadeṃdudhavalaṃ jaṭāmakuṭamaṃḍitaṃ amitābhajatābhāraṃ vyāghracarmottarachadaṃ catubhuṃjam anekālaṃkārabhūṣaṇabhūṣitaṃ dakṣekṣamālinaṃ vāmopadmaṇivibhūṣitaṃ dvauhastau sarvarājendramudrayāhṛdisaṃpuṭau.
8 B /.
9 BL2 tata.
10 K1 and BL2 add. a central dot.
11 TO2 -ma.
12 The rendering follows the Sandhi rule. B, TO1, TO2, TO3, TO4, K1, N1, BL2 tasyopari.
13 TO1, TO3, K1, BL2 -ra.
14 B, TO2, K1 tatsarvvaṃ niṣpanne.
15 K1 -tha; BL2 -tha•.
16 TO2, TO3, TO4 -ka; K1 -ka•; N1 -kaḥ; BL2 -paryaṅga.
17 TO1 -bha; TO1, TO2, TO3, TO4 and N1 add. /.
18 TO1 ūrjjala; TO4 ujjalaṃ.
19 BL2 add. a central dot.
20 TO1, TO3, N1 and BL2 add. /. TO2 -kṛtasekharaṃ/; TO4 -kṛtaśeṣaraṃ/; K1 -śeṣaraṃ.
21 TO2 vyāghramanivasanaṃ; TO4 vyāgharacarmanivaśaraṃ; K1, BL2 -nivaśanaṃ•.
22 TO1, K1 catubhujaṃ.
23 B add. a comma. TO1 nānālakārabhūṣitaṃ/; TO2, TO3, TO4 and N1 add. /. K1 has a central dot and /. BL2 add. a central dot.
24 B, TO1, TO3, TO4, N1 dakṣiṇe kare; BL2 dakṣiṇakale.
25 B add. a comma. TO1 -dhala/; TO3, TO4, K1 and N1 add. /. TO2 add. //. BL2 add. a central dot.
26 BL2 vāme kare.
27 B add. a comma. TO1, TO3 and N1 add. /. TO2 padmamanivibhūṣitaṃ/; TO4 padmapaṇivibhūṣitaṃ/; K1, BL2 padmaṃmaṇivibhūṣitaṃ/.
28 TO1, TO2 and N1 add. /.
29 The rendering follows Tib. T3: rgya ba'i dbaṅ po kun gyi phyag rgya thugs kar gnas pa'o//. B sarvvarājendramudrā hṛdi saṃsthitaṃ; TO1 sarvvarājendramudrā hṛdi saṃsthitaṃ//; TO2, TO3 sarvvarājendramudrā hṛdi saṃsthitaṃ/; TO4, K1 sarvarājendramudrā hṛdi saṃsthitaṃ/; N1, BL2 sarvarājendramūdrā hṛdi saṃsthitaṃ/.
30 TO4 'haṅkāra.
31 B om. //. TO2, TO3, TO4, N1 kuryād.
32 K1 lokiteśvara •.
33 B, TO2, N1 /.

(2.3) tato jñānasattvam ākṛṣya[1] yathopadeśataḥ svamantreṇārghyapādyādikaṃ[2] dadyāt/[3] samājamudrayā[4] ekīkṛtyānena[5] mantreṇa [(6-]saha vinyaset/[-6)] oṃ suratavajra [(7-]alalalala hoḥ[-7)] samayas tvaṃ samayas tvaṃ samayam[8] aham/[9]

(2.4.1) yathopadeśato[10] 'bhiṣekakavacapaṭṭabandhādhimokṣaṇasamakālapūjāstutiñ[11] ca kṛtvā bhāvanāpūrvakaṃ[12] japaṃ kuryāt/[13]

(2.4.2) [(14-]svahṛdi candropari[-14)] ṣaḍakṣaraṃ pradīpamālām[15] iva gṛhāntaradyotinīṃ[16] paśyet/[17] mantraḥ/[18] oṃ maṇipadme hūṃ/[19] akṣaralakṣaṃ[20] japet/[21] tato dvitīyatṛtīyena[22] vigatakalmaṣo[23] bhavati[24] pañcānantaryakāriṇo 'pi koṭijāpena siddhyati/[25]

---

1 K1 and BL2 add. a central dot.
2 TO1 svamantrenārghādikaṃ; TO2, TO3, N1 svamantreṇārghapādyādikaṃ; TO4 svamaṃtrarārghapādyādikaṃ; K1 svamaṃtreṇārghapādyādikaṃ.
3 TO1 om. /.
4 TO4 sayāja-; K1, BL2 -mudrāyā.
5 TO2 ekīkṛtyāni; TO4 ekakṛtyānena; K1 ekīkṛtvānena; BL2 add. a central dot.
6 TO1 saha vineśyat//; TO2 savinyasyet/; TO3, K1, BL2 saha vinyaset//; TO4 savinyaset//.
7 TO1 aralalala hoḥ.
8 TO1, TO2, BL2 samayas tvaṃ; TO4 samayas tvaṃ meha//; K1 add. samayas tvaṃ. N1 samayas tvam.
9 TO1, TO3 maha/; TO4 //; K1 maham//; BL2 mahaṃ//.
10 TO4 yathāp-.
11 The rendering: -samakālapūjā- follows Tib. T3: dus thams cad du mchod pa daṅ/. B abhiṣekakavacapaṭṭabandhādhimokṣaṇasamatālapūjāstutiṃ; TO1 abhiṣekakavacapaṭū-bandhāṃtādhimokṣaṇasamatārapūjāstutiñ; TO2 abhiṣekakavacapaṭṭabandhādhimokṣaṇasamatālapūjāstutiñ; TO3 abhiṣekakavacapaṭṭabandhāntādhimokṣaṇasamatālapūjāstutiñ; TO4 abhiṣekakavacapaṭabaṃdhāntādhimokṣaṇasamatālapūjāstutiś; K1 'bhiṣekakavacapaṭṭa-bandhādhimokṣaṇasamatālapūjāstutiñ; N1 abhiṣekakavacapaṭabandhāntādhimokṣaṇasamatālapūjāstutiñ; BL2 'bhiṣekakavacapaṭṭabandhāntādhimokṣaṇe samatālapūjāstutiñ.
12 TO1 bhāvaṇā-.
13 TO1, TO3, K1, BL2 //.
14 TO1,TO3, TO4 svahṛdindropari.
15 TO1 -mārām.
16 TO1 -dyotinī; TO2 -dyotināṃ; TO3, TO4 -dyotinī; K1 -dyotanī; BL2 -dyotanīya.
17 TO1, TO2 paśyat//; K1, BL2 //.
18 B om. /. TO1, BL2 mantra//; TO2 mantraṃ//; TO4 mantraḥ//; K1 mantraḥ// //.
19 TO1, TO2, TO3, TO4, K1, N1, BL2 //.
20 TO1 -kṣa.
21 K1, BL2 //.
22 TO2 -tṛtīyana; K1 dvitīya/ tṛtīyena.
23 TO2 -kuṣo.
24 B add. a comma. TO1, TO2, TO3, TO4 and N1 add. /. K1 and BL2 add. //.
25 TO1, TO3, TO4, K1, N1, BL2 //.

(3) tata[1] utthātukāmo[2] 'rghādikaṃ[3] dattvā viśiṣṭāhaṅkāreṇa[4] viharet/[5] catuḥsandhyaṃ[6] japitvā kuśalamūlaṃ[7] pariṇamyābhipretasiddhaye[8] 'rdharātrau[9] jñānasattvaṃ visarjya[10] śatākṣaraṃ[11] coccārya[12] kāyavākcittarakṣāṃ[13] ca kṛtvā yathāsukhaṃ vihared[14] iti/[15]

(4) (16-yadi rogādiṃ nāśayitum icchati-16) tadā yathopadeśataḥ puṣya-nakṣatreṇāpatitagomayena[17] bhaṭṭārakasyāgrataś caturasraṃ maṇḍalakaṃ kuryāt/[18] abhipretaṣaḍakṣaravidarbhitam[19] aṣṭottaraśataṃ japet/[20] ṣaṇmāsena[21] sidhyati na (22-saṃśaya iti/-22)

//kāraṇḍavyūhāmnāyena racitaṃ sādhanaṃ samāptam//[23]

---

1 K1 tataḥ.
2 N1 utthoyu-.
3 B, N1 'rghyādikaṃ; TO1 'rghādin; TO3 arghādin; TO4 arghādikan.
4 TO2 visiṣṭā-; TO4 diśiṣṭāhaṃkāreṇa.
5 TO1, TO3 //; K1 vihare//.
6 TO2 catusaṃdhyaṃ.
7 TO2 add. /. K1 and BL2 add. a central dot.
8 TO1 pariṇamayābhijapreta-; TO3 pariṇāmyābhipretasiddhaye/; TO4 pariṇāmyābhi/ preta-; K1 pariṇāmyādibhiḥ preta-; BL2 pariṇamyādipreta-.
9 B ardharātrau.
10 TO1 and TO3 add. //. TO2 visayaṃ/; TO4 add. /. TO3, K1, BL2 visṛjya//; N1 visajya.
11 TO1,TO3, K1, BL2 -ra; TO2 -rañ; TO4 -raś.
12 TO4 cācārya; K1 yoccārya; BL2 yoccāryya.
13 TO1, TO3, TO4, K1, N1 kāyavākcittarakṣāñ; BL2 kāyavāgcittarakṣāñ.
14 TO2 viharet/.
15 TO1 itī/; TO2 om.; K1 //.
16 The rendering follows Tib. T3: gal te nad la sogs pa źi par 'dod na. B yadi rogādi nāśayituṃ icchati; TO1, TO3, TO4, N1 yadi rogādi nāśayitum icchati; TO2 yadi rogā nāśayitum icchati; K1 yadi rogādi nāśayatum icchati•; BL2 yadi rogādi nāśayantiṃ icchati•.
17 TO1 pūṣya-.
18 TO1, TO3, K1 //.
19 TO1, TO3, TO4, K1, N1, BL2 abhipretaṃ ṣaḍakṣaravidarbhitam.
20 TO4, K1, BL2 //.
21 TO3 illegible between ṣa- and -sena.
22 TO1, TO2 and N1 om. /. TO3 saṃśaya iti//; TO4 śansaya iti; K1 śaṃya sidhyati iti//; BL2 śaṃśaya: siddhyati iti//.
23 K1 add. //kārttikasya//. BL2 add. //kārttikāsya//.

## 4.3 Ṣaḍakṣarīlokeśvarasādhana (Bhatt. no. 11 āryaṢaḍakṣarīmahāvidyālokeśvarabhaṭṭārakopadeśaparamparāyātasādhanavidhiḥ)

(0) namaḥ[1] ṣaḍakṣarīlokeśvarāya/[2].

(1) samyak parahitodyuktamanasā[3] "lambya[4] dehinām/[5]
nihśeṣaduḥkhopaśamaṃ[6] satsukhe ca pratiṣṭhitam//[7]

(2.1) tanmanā[8] hṛdi sañcintya[9] bhāvayec[10] chubhradīdhitim/[11]
tatprabhābhiḥ[12] sphurantībhis[13] tanuṃ[14] svām[15] avabhāsayet//[16]

(2.2) viśramya[17] vidhivan[18] mantrī saṃhṛtya[19] sadvitarkitaḥ/[20]
sphuṭam[21] uccārayen[22] mamtraṃ[23] śvetadīdhitibhāsvaram//[24]
svanābhimaṇḍalenaivaṃ[25] praveśya hṛdi saṃharet/[26]
iti kurvan tridhā[27] dhyāyāt kāyavākcittaśodhanam//[28]
tatra svadehasaṃsthena[29] kāyādeḥ[30] śuddhim[31] ātmanaḥ/[32]

---

1 K1 nama.
2 TO1, TO2, TO3, TO4, K1, N1, BL2 //.
3 TO1 parahitodyurktamanasā; TO2 ārahitodyūktamanasā; K1, BL2 prarahitodyuktomanasā.
4 TO2 labo; K1 rambya; BL2 raṃbya.
5 K1, BL2 //.
6 TO1, TO3 -khopaśamanaṃ; K1, BL2 -khāpasamanaṃ; N1 -khopasamaṃ.
7 TO1, TO3 /.
8 TO2 tatmano; TO4 tanmaro; K1, N1, BL2 tanmano.
9 TO1 sacintya; K1 and BL2 add. a central dot.
10 TO2 bhāvayet; N1 bhāvatec.
11 TO1 -taṃ; TO3 chubhradīdhitaṃ/; TO2 subhradidhatiṃ/; TO4 chutradīdhitiḥ//; K1 chutradīdhitaṃ/; N1 chubhradīdhititiṃ/; BL2 -taṃ/.
12 TO1, TO3, TO4 -ātiḥ; K1 -ātis/; BL2 tatprabhāti.
13 TO2 spharantībhis; TO4 sulatībhis; K1, BL2 spharaṃtībhis.
14 K1, BL2 tanu.
15 TO2 svās.
16 TO4 avabhāmayet/; K1, BL2 abhāsayet//; N1 /.
17 TO4 viśuvya; K1 viśraṃmya (anusvāra insertion).
18 BL2 -vat.
19 TO2, TO3, TO4, N1 -tā; K1, BL2 -to.
20 TO1, TO3 and BL2 om. /. TO2, N1 sadvitakitaḥ/; TO4 //; K1 sahitarkitaḥ; BL2 sahitarkkitaḥ.
21 TO2 sphaṭam.
22 TO2, BL2 -yet.
23 K1 and BL2 add. a central dot.
24 TO2, TO3, K1, BL2 -tibhāsuraṃ//; TO4 -dīdhibhibhāsura//.
25 TO2, TO4 -lenainaṃ; TO3 -lelainaṃ; K1 -lenaiva •; N1 -nenaṃ; BL2 -naiva.
26 TO4, K1, BL2 //.
27 K1 tridhān.
28 TO1 and TO3 om. //. K1, BL2 a central dot.
29 TO1 svadehasasthena; K1 add. a central dot. BL2 svadehasasthenạ•.
30 TO4 kāyadaḥ.
31 K1, BL2 śuddham.
32 TO4, K1, BL2 //.

bahirgatena[1] mantreṇa[2] prāṇināṃ tu[3] vicintayet//[4]
(3.1) dṛṣṭoccāritamantrotthaṃ[5] purato devatātrayam/[6]
mantroccāraṇaṃ[7] saṃhārakramāt[8] pratyekam[9] ācaret//[10]
(3.2) vicitrapūjānirmāṇaṃ[11] tanniṣpādanam[12] eva ca/[13]
paripūriṃ[14] tataḥ[15] śuddhim[16] iṣṭārthe[17] pariṇāmanām//[18]
(3.3) mantrajāpaṃ[19] tataḥ kuryād[20] (21-vidhinā 'nte-21) japasya tu/[22]
pūjādiṃ[23] pūrvavat kṛtvā[24] devatāṃ[25] hṛdi saṃharet//[26]
samādhipratilambhādau[27] catuḥsandhyam[28] imaṃ vidhim/[29]
kurvaṃl[30] lakṣaṃ[31] japen[32] mantrī[33] vijaneṣu gṛhādiṣu//[34]
śvāsacintāṃ[35] vinā[36] kāryo[37] jāpaḥ[38] sphuraṇasaṃhṛtaiḥ/[39]

---

1 TO4 -tana.
2 K1 and BL2 add. a central dot.
3 K1 bhu.
4 TO1, TO3, K1, BL2 /.
5 TO2 -mantrortham; TO4 -mantrāttham; K1 and BL2 add. a central dot.
6 TO1 and TO3 om. /. TO4 devatāṃ trayaṃ.
7 B, TO1, TO3, TO4, K1, BL2 mantroccāraṇa.
8 TO1 sahārakramāt; K1, BL2 saṃhāra•kramāt.
9 TO1 patyekam.
10 TO1, TO3, K1, BL2 /.
11 TO1 -nirmmānaṃ; TO4 -niryyāṇaṃ; K1 and BL2 add. a central dot.
12 TO1, TO2, TO3, TO4, K1, BL2 tanniryyātanam; N1 tanniryātanam.
13 TO4 //.
14 TO1, TO3 paripūritan; TO2, TO4, K1, BL2 paripūritaṃ; N1 paripūri.
15 TO2 tatraḥ; K1, BL2 tantaḥ.
16 BL2 śuddhim•.
17 TO2 aṣṭārtne.
18 TO1 om. //. TO3, N1 /; K1 and BL2 have a central dot.
19 TO1, TO3, K1, BL2 mantrajāpa.
20 B kuryyāt; TO1, TO3 kuryāt; K1, BL2 kuryyāt•.
21 TO4 vidhināṃtre.
22 TO1, TO3, K1, BL2 //.
23 B, TO1, TO2, TO3, TO4, K1, N1, BL2 pūjādi.
24 K1 and BL2 add. a central dot.
25 TO1, K1, BL2 devatā.
26 TO1 saharet/; TO2, TO3, K1 /; BL2 om. //.
27 TO4 -labhādau; BL2 add. a central dot.
28 TO1 catusadhyam; TO3 catusandhyam.
29 TO1, TO3, K1, BL2 //; TO2 vidhau.
30 The rendering follows the Sandhi rule. B, TO3 kurvvan; TO1 pūrvvan; TO2 kurvvaṃ tu; TO4 kurvan; K1, BL2 kurvval; N1 pūrval.
31 TO1 lakṣa.
32 TO1, TO2, TO3, TO4, N1, BL2 japet.
33 K1 add. /. BL2 add. a central dot.
34 TO1, TO3, TO4 /.
35 TO1 śvāsacintā; TO2 svāsacintā.
36 TO1, K1, BL2 pinā.
37 TO1 kāyo; TO2 ryyo; TO4 kāryyā; K1 kāryyo•; BL2 add. a central dot.
38 B, TO1, TO2, TO3, TO4, K1, BL2 jāpa.
39 B, TO4 sphuraṇasaṃskṛtaiḥ/; TO1 sphuraṇaṃsatkṛtaiḥ; TO2 spharaṇasaṃhṛtaiḥ/; TO3 spharaṇasaṃskṛtaiḥ; K1 spharaṇasaṃskṛtaṃ; BL2 spharaṇasaṃskṛtaṃ/.

(4.1) pāpakṣayādau[1] sarvatra [(2-]caturasraṃ[3] ca maṇḍalam//[4-2)]
kārayitvā paṭādyasya[5] puro[6] dhyātvāthavā[7] vibhum/[8]
maṇḍalārcanam[9] arcāṃ[10] vā kṛtvā kruyād[11] amūn[12] vidhīn//[13]

(4.2) tatrāyaṃ devatākāropadeśaḥ//[14]
paryaṅkiṇaṃ[15] sitaṃ sākṣamālābjaṃ[16] sampuṭāñjalim/[17]
dṛṣṭvā vibhuṃ[18] tatpratimāṃ[19] devīṃ[20] vīrāsanāśritām//[21]
āryan[22] tu cintayet pītaṃ[23] vāme ratnacchaṭābhṛtam/[24]
riktasavyakaraṃ[25] ratnamauliṃ[26] vīrāsanānugam//[27]

//ity[28] āryaṣaḍakṣarīmahāvidyālokeśvarabhaṭṭārakopadeśaparamparāyātasādhanavidhiḥ//[29]

---

1 K1 -do.
2 K1 cature pañcamaṇḍalam/.
3 TO1, TO3, TO4, N1 caturasrañ.
4 TO1, TO3 /.
5 TO3 illegible between paṭā- and -sya. K1 parṣada asya; BL2 paṇa asya•.
6 TO2 purato.
7 TO4 dhyātvāthavādi.
8 TO1, TO3, BL2 //; TO4 bhuṃ/; K1 cituṃ//.
9 TO2 -na; K1, BL2 -caṇam.
10 TO1, TO3, TO4, K1, BL2 arthāṃ; TO2 sarvvāṃ; N1 arcām.
11 K1, BL2 kruyyānan.
12 K1 asūn; BL2 asūna.
13 TO4, N1 /; K1 vidhīna//; BL2 vidhī//.
14 B om. //. N1 /.
15 B, K1, BL2 paryyaṅkinaṃ.
16 TO3 -lākbja; TO4 -lākuṃ.
17 TO1 saṃpūṭāñjali; TO2 saṃpūṭāñjaliṃ/; TO4 sampūṭāñjaliḥ//; K1 and BL2 om. /.
18 TO1, TO3 vibhu; K1 vibhūna; BL2 vibhūta.
19 TO2 tatpratimā; K1 add. a central dot. BL2 tanpratimām•.
20 TO1, TO3 devīm; TO4 devin.
21 TO1, TO3, TO4, K1, N1, BL2 /.
22 B āryāṃ; TO3, BL2 āryān.
23 B, N1 pītāṃ; K1 and BL2 add. a central dot.
24 B -bhṛtām/; TO1, TO3, TO4 //; TO2 -bhūtaṃ; K1 -bhavaṃ; N1 -bhṛta; BL2 ratnacchadābhavaṃ/.
25 B riktasavyakarāṃ; TO1, TO3 raktasavyakaraṃ; K1 ratnasavyakaraṃ/; BL2 om.
26 TO1, TO3, TO4, N1 -lim; K1, BL2 -lī.
27 B vīrāsanānugām//; TO1, TO2, TO3, TO4 vibhuṃsanānugaṃ//; K1 vibhusanānugaṃ//; BL2 vibhusanānugaṃ//.
28 TO1, TO3, TO4 ity.
29 TO1, TO3 ācaryaṣaḍakṣarī-; TO2 ācāryyaṣaḍakṣarīmahāvidyālokeśvarabhaṭṭārakopadeśaparaparāyāta-; TO4 ācaryaṣaḍakṣarīmahāvidyālokeśvarabhaṭṭārakāyadeśaparamparāyātasādhanavidhi//; K1 ācāryyaṣaḍakṣarīmahāvidyālokeśvarabhaṭṭārakopadeśaparaṃparāyātasādhanaṃ vidhiḥ//.

## 4.4 Ṣaḍakṣarīlokeśvarasādhana (Bhatt. no. 12)

(1) kvacit[1] ṣaḍakṣarīsādhane bhagavān[2] samaṇipustakāṅkitapadmadharaḥ[3] maṇidharas[4] tu pustakarahitamaṇipadmadharaḥ[5] ṣaḍakṣarī[6] tu maṇirahitapustakapadmadharā/[7]

(2) pūjāmantraḥ/[8] oṃ lokeśvara puṣpaṃ pratīccha[9] svāhā[10] evaṃ[11] dhūpaṃ[12] dīpam[13] ityādi[14] bodhavyam/[15] anyadevatāyāṃ[16] tatsambodhanaṃ[17] kāryam/[18]

(3) jñānamaṇḍalākṛṣṭāv[19] ayaṃ[20] mantraḥ//[21] oṃ mahāsukha[22] vajrasattva jaḥ[23] hūṃ[24] vaṃ hoḥ[25] suratas tvaṃ alalalala hoḥ[26] aḥ aḥ aḥ aḥ//[27]

---

1 TO1, TO3, K1, BL2 iti.
2 TO4 bhavān; K1, BL2 bhagavan.
3 B add. a comma. TO1, TO2, TO3 sapustakāṅkitapadmadharaḥ/; K1, BL2 sapuṣṭakāṅkitapadmadharaḥ/; N1 add. /. TO4 sapustakākṣitapadmadharaḥ.
4 K1 maṇidharaṃ.
5 B add. a comma. TO1 pūstakarahitamaṇipadmadharaḥ/; TO2 and TO3 add. /. TO4 karahitamaṇipadmadharā/; K1, BL2 pustakaṃ rahitamaṇipadmadharaḥ; N1 pustaka/ rahitamaṇipadmadharaḥ/.
6 TO2, TO3 -rīn.
7 TO2 maṇiharitapustakapadmadharā//; K1 maṇidhara•rahita•maṇidharā/; TO1, TO3 //; BL2 maṇidhara•rahita•maṇidharā/.
8 B om. /. TO1, TO2, TO3 -rān tu//; TO4 -rās tu; K1 -ras tu/; N1 -rān/; BL2 -tra/.
9 TO1, TO2 praticcha.
10 TO1, TO2, TO3, TO4, K1 and BL2 add. //. N1 add. /.
11 TO1, TO3 eva; K1 tada; BL2 tadanu.
12 TO1, TO2, TO3, TO4, K1, BL2 dhūpa.
13 TO1, TO3, TO4, K1, BL2 dīpa.
14 TO1 naivedyā; TO3, K1 naivedyādi; BL2 naivyadyādi.
15 TO1, TO3, K1 //; TO2 om. /. BL2 vyeddhavyaṃ//.
16 TO2 alpadevatāyāṃ.
17 TO4 tatsambodharaṃ; K1 tatsarvvaṃ/ dhanaṃ; BL2 tatsarvvaṃ dhanaṃ.
18 TO4 kāryya; K1, BL2 //.
19 K1 -tav.
20 TO3 ayam.
21 B om. // and add. a comma. K1 om. //. N1 /.
22 TO4 -khe.
23 TO1 ja; TO3 jaṃ; TO4 om.
24 TO1 hūḥ.
25 K1 and BL2 add. //.
26 TO4, N1 ho.
27 B adds. [ṣaḍakṣarīsādhanam]. N1 om. //.

## 5.1 Siṃhanādalokeśvarasādhana (Bhatt. no. 17)

(0) namaḥ siṃhanādāya//[1]
dvibhujaikamukhaṃ śuklam[2] trinetraṃ[3] siṃhavāhanam/[4]
siṃhanādam[5] ahaṃ[6] vande[7] sarvavyādhiharaṃ[8] gurum//[9]

(1) ādau tāvan[10] mantrī[11] mukhaśaucādikaṃ[12] kṛtvā[13] mano 'nukūle[14] sthāne[15]
sukhāsanopaviṣṭaḥ//[16]

(2.1.1) śukla-akārapariṇataṃ[17] candramaṇḍalaṃ[18] tadupari[19] śuklahrīḥkāraṃ[20] hṛdi paśyet/[21]
tadraśmibhis[22] traidhātukam[23] avabhāsyākaniṣṭhabhuvanavartinaṃ[24] siṃhanādaṃ
sarvagurubuddhabodhisattvān ākṛṣya[25] purata[26] ākāśadeśe saṃsthāpya/[27]

---

1 B /.
2 K1 and BL2 add. a central dot.
3 K1 triṇotraṃ.
4 TO1 sihavāhānaṃ; TO4 siṃhavāhana; TO3, K1 and N1 om. /.
5 TO1 sihanādamaṃ; TO4 sihanādam.
6 TO1 om.
7 BL2 add. a central dot.
8 TO1 savvavyādhiharaṃ; TO4 -hara.
9 TO1 guru//; TO4 guru.
10 TO2, K1, BL2 tāvat.
11 TO1 mantri; BL2 add. a central dot.
12 TO1 mukhasaucādikaṃ.
13 K1 and BL2 add. a central dot.
14 TO1 'nukule; TO4 'nukula; K1, BL2 nukūla.
15 K1 and BL2 add. a central dot.
16 B om. //. TO2, N1 /; TO1 -nopaviṣṭa//; TO4 -naupaviṣṭaḥ//; K1 -noviṣṭaḥ//.
17 TO2, TO3, K1, N1 śukla-aṃkāra-; TO4 śukla-oṃkāra-; K1 add. a central dot. BL2 śukla-aṃkārapariṇataṃ•.
18 TO2 and N1 add. /.
19 TO1 -parī.
20 TO1, TO3, TO4, K1 śuklahrīkāraṃ; BL2 śukla•hrīḥkāraṃ.
21 TO1, TO2 paśyat; TO3, TO4, K1 and BL2 om. /.
22 K1 tadraśminābhis; BL2 tadraśmınābhi •.
23 TO1-dhatukaṃm; BL2 straidhātu-.
24 TO1, TO4 -bhuvanavarttina; TO3 -bhuvaṇavarttina; BL2 add. a central dot.
25 BL2 add. a central dot.
26 K1 -taḥ/, BL2 -taḥ.
27 B, K1, N1 and BL2 om. /. TO1 sasthāpya.

(2.1.2) tadanu[1] pūjāpāpadeśanādikaṃ kṛtvā[2] caturbrahmavihārān[3] vibhāvya/[4] oṃ[5] śūnyatājñānavajrasvabhāvāḥ[6] sarvadharmāḥ/[7] oṃ śūnyatājñānavajrasvabhāvātmako[8] 'ham[9] ity[10] anena[11] mantreṇa śūnyatām adhitiṣṭhet//[12]

(2.2) tataḥ[13] praṇidhānam[14] anusmṛtya[15] śuklapaṃkārapariṇataṃ[16] kamalaṃ[17] tadupari[18] śukla-akārapariṇataṃ[19] candramaṇḍalaṃ[20] tadupari śukla-āḥkārapariṇataṃ[21] śvetasiṃhaṃ/[22] tadupari[23] śukla-aṃkārapariṇataṃ[24] śvetapadmaṃ[25] tadvaraṭake[26] śuklahrīḥkāraṃ[27] sphuradraśmivisaraṃ/[28] etat sarvaṃ[29] pariṇamya[30] siṃhanādarūpam[31] ātmānaṃ[32] paśyet/[33] sarvāṅgaśuklaṃ[34] dvibhujam[35] ekamukhaṃ trinetraṃ[36] jaṭāmukuṭadharam[37]

---

1 BL2 add. a central dot.
2 K1 and BL2 add. a central dot.
3 TO1 catubrahma-.
4 B om. /. TO1,TO3, K1, BL2 //; TO2 catubrahma-.
5 B om.
6 TO1 śūnyatāṃ jñānavajasvabhātmako; TO3 śūnyatāṃ jñānavajasvabhāvātmako; TO4 śūnyatājñānavajrasvabhāvātmako; K1 śūnyatāṃ jñānavajrasvabhāvātmako haṃ; BL2 śūnyatāṃ jñānavajasvabhāvātmako haṃ.
7 B, TO2, TO3 and BL2 om. /. TO1 sarvvadharmmā; TO4 //.
8 TO1 -vajasvabhātmako; TO3, K1, BL2 śūnyatāṃ jñāna-.
9 TO2, TO4 and N1 add. /. TO1,TO3, K1 and BL2 add. //.
10 TO1 om.
11 TO1 itenena.
12 B, TO2, TO4 /; N1 om. //.
13 TO1 tata.
14 TO1, TO3, K1, BL2 praṇidhāna.
15 TO1 samayanusmṛtya; TO3, K1, BL2 samanusmṛtya.
16 TO1 śuklapaṃkāraparīnataṃ; TO2 śuklapaṃkāraparinataṃ; K1, BL2 paṃkārapariṇataṃ; N1 śukla-aṃkārapariṇataṃ.
17 TO1, TO3, TO4, K1, BL2 om.; TO2 and N1 add. /.
18 TO1, TO3, TO4, K1, BL2 om.
19 TO1, TO3, TO4, K1, BL2 om.; TO2, N1 śukla-aṃkārapariṇataṃ.
20 TO1, TO2, TO3, TO4, K1, N1 and BL2 add. /.
21 TO1, K1 śukla-ākārapariṇataṃ; TO2 śukla-āḥkārapariṇata; TO3 śuklaḥ āḥkārapariṇataṃ; N1 śukla•āḥkārapariṇataṃ; BL2 śukla •ākārapariṇataṃ.
22 B, TO1 and TO3 om. /. TO2 śvetasiṃha; K1, BL2 //.
23 BL2 add. a central dot.
24 TO2 śukla-aṃkārapariṇata śvetasiṃhanad upari śukla-aṃkārapariṇataṃ; K1 śuklaṃ akārapariṇataṃ; N1 śukla-oṃkārapariṇataṃ; BL2 śuklaṃ akārapariṇataṃ•.
25 TO1, TO2, TO3, TO4, K1, N1 and BL2 add. /.
26 BL2 add. a central dot.
27 TO1 -hrīkāraṃ.
28 B om. /.
29 TO1, TO2, sarvva; N1 sarvvam.
30 TO2 pariṇāmya; BL2 add. a central dot.
31 TO2 siṃhanādam.
32 TO1 ātmāna.
33 B om. /. TO1 paśyata//; TO2, TO4 paśyat/; TO3, K1, BL2 //.
34 K1 add. a central dot.
35 K1 and BL2 add. a central dot.
36 TO4 and N1 add. /. BL2 triṇetraṃ.
37 TO1 jatāmukuṭidhara; TO2 jaṭāmakuṭadharaṃ/; TO3, K1 jaṭāmakuṭidharaṃ; TO4 and N1 add. /. BL2 jaṭāmakuṭidharaṃ•.

amitābhālaṅkṛtaśirasaṃ[1] māhārājalīlayā sthitaṃ[2] siṃhāsane[3] vyāghracarmāmbaradharaṃ[4] sphuratpañcatathāgatam[5] aṃsalulitapañcacīram[6] ardhacandrālaṅkṛtaṃ/[7] vāmahastasthitaśuklapadmopari[8] sitakhaḍgaṃ[9] tatsamīpasthitaṃ[10] śuklapadmopari[11] nānāsugandhikusumaparipūrṇaśuklakaroṭakaṃ/[12] dakṣiṇe sitapadmopari[13] sitaphaṇiveṣṭitaṃ[14] sitatriśūladaṇḍaṃ/[15]

(2.3) evaṃbhūtaṃ[16] bhagavantaṃ dhyātvā[17] dhyānāt[18] khinno[19] mantrī mantraṃ[20] japet/[21] tatrāyaṃ[22] mantraḥ/[23] oṃ āḥ siṃhanāda[24] hūṃ phaṭ svāhā//[25]

---

1 TO1, TO3 amitābhalaṃkṛtaśiraṃ; TO4 apitābhālaṅkṛtaśirasa; K1, BL2 amitābhālaṃkṛtaśiraṃ•.
2 TO4 sthitaḥ; TO1 add. //. TO3, TO4 and N1 add. /. K1 sthita•; BL2 sthita.
3 TO1 sihāsanaṃ/; TO2, TO3, TO4, N1, BL2 siṃhāsanaṃ/; K1 siṃhāsanaṃ.
4 TO1-dhara; TO2, TO3, TO4, K1, N1 and BL2 add. /.
5 The rendering follows the Sandhi rule. B -gataṃ; TO1 spharatpañcatathāgatam/; TO2, TO3, TO4, K1, N1, BL2 -gataṃ/.
6 The rendering follows the Sandhi rule. B -raṃ; TO1 atsalulitapañcacīra/; TO2 apśūlūlitapañcacīraṃ; TO3 atsalulitapañcavīraṃ/; TO4 atsalulitapañcavīraṃ/; TO4 and N1 add. /. K1 atsalulitapaṃcavīram• ; BL2 atsalulitapañcavīram• .
7 B om. /. N1 -candraṅkitaṃ.
8 K1 and BL2 add. sthita.
9 TO2, TO3, TO4 and N1 add. /. BL2 khaḍgaṃ.
10 BL2 add. a central dot.
11 BL2 add. a central dot.
12 B om. /. TO4 -pūrṇakroṭakaṃ/; K1 nānāsugaṃdhīkusumaparipūrṇa •śuklakaroṭakaṃ/; BL2 -gandhīkusumaparipūrṇaṃ•śuklakaroṭakaṃ/.
13 TO1 -parī.
14 TO2 -niveṣṭitaṃ; TO4 om. N1 -niveṣṭita.
15 B om. /. TO4 sitaphatriśūladaṇḍaṃ.
16 TO1 -bhūta.
17 TO1, TO4 and N1 add. /. BL2 add. a central dot.
18 TO1 dhyānat.
19 BL2 add. a central dot.
20 TO1, TO4, N1 mantra.
21 K1, BL2 //.
22 TO1 tatrāya; BL2 tatreyaṃ.
23 B om. /. TO1, BL2 mantra//; TO2, TO3, TO4, K1 //.
24 K1, BL2 siṃhanādāya.
25 B, TO4 /.

(3.1) vidhir atra pratimākṛteḥ[1] paṭagatasya[2] vā[3] bhagavataḥ[4] purataḥ pratimaṇḍalam[5] ekavāradhāraṇyā/[6] tatreyaṃ[7] dhāraṇī/[8] namo ratnatrayāya[9] nama[10] āryāvalokiteśvarāya[11] bodhisattvāya[12] mahāsattvāya[13] mahākāruṇikāya/[14] tadyathā/[15] oṃ akaṭe vikaṭe[16] nikaṭe[17] kaṭaṃkaṭe[18] karoṭavīrye[19] svāhā/[20] apatitagomayam abhimantrya[21] aṣṭau maṇḍalakān[22] kuryāt/ pratimaṇḍalaṃ trayodaśavārān[23] āvartayan[24] dhāraṇīm[25] pratimaṇḍalamalitaśeṣagomayaṃ[26] dhāraṇyā[27] saptavārān abhimantrya[28] tena vyādhiṃ[29] pralepayet/[30]

(3.2) saptame divase[31] trayodaśe[32] divase[33] ekaviṃśatitame[34] vā[35] pañcānantaryakāriṇo 'pi sidhyanti/[36] (37-yadi na-37) sidhyanti/[38] tadā 'haṃ pañcānantaryakārī[39] syām//[40]

---

1 K1 -te.
2 TO3 paṭūgatasya.
3 BL2 add. a central dot.
4 TO1 bhagavantaḥ.
5 TO4 pratimaṇḍanam.
6 TO1, TO3 ekavārādhāraṇyā//; TO4 ekavārādhāraṇyā/; K1 ekavārādhāraṇyāḥ/; BL2 -yāḥ/.
7 TO1 tatrāyam; TO4 tatraiyaṃ; K1, BL2 tatrāyaṃ.
8 B om. /. TO2, TO3, K1 //.
9 TO1, TO3, K1 and BL2 add. /.
10 TO1 namo; TO2, K1, BL2 namaḥ.
11 K1 and BL2 add. /.
12 K1 and BL2 add. /.
13 TO4 om.; BL2 add. a central dot.
14 B, TO4 and N1 om. /. TO1, TO3 -karuṇīkāya/; TO2 -kārunikāya; K1, BL2 -kāruṇīkāya/.
15 TO4 //, B and N1 om. /.
16 K1 and BL2 add. a central dot.
17 TO1 trikaṭe kaṭe; TO2, TO3 and TO4 add. trikaṭe. K1 om.; BL2 trikaṭe•.
18 K1 and BL2 add. a central dot.
19 TO2, TO3 karoṭavīryya; TO4 roṭavīrya.
20 TO1, TO2, TO3, TO4, K1, N1, BL2 //.
21 K1 and BL2 add. a central dot.
22 TO1 -kā; BL2 add. a central dot.
23 TO2 vānān.
24 TO1 āvarttayen; TO2 āvarttayena.
25 TO1, K1 dhāraṇī; TO2, TO3, TO4 and N1 add. /. BL2 dhāraṇī/.
26 B, N1 pratimaṇḍalāmalitaśeṣagomayaṃ; TO3 pratimaṇḍalaṃ malitaśeṣagomayan; TO4 pratimaṇḍalam malitaśeṣagomaya; K1, BL2 pratimaṇḍalaṃ•malitaśeṣagamayan.
27 TO1, TO2, TO3, TO4, K1, N1, BL2 dhāraṇī.
28 TO1 bhimantrā.
29 TO1, K1, BL2 vyāpi; TO2, TO3, TO4 vyādhi.
30 B, TO2 and TO4 om. /. TO1, TO3, K1, BL2 //.
31 K1 and BL2 add. a central dot.
32 TO4 trayodaśa; N1 trayodaśame.
33 TO1 divaśe; K1 and BL2 add. a central dot.
34 TO1-viśatime; TO2, TO3, TO4, K1, N1, BL2 -viṃśatime.
35 TO4 cā; K1 and BL2 add. /.
36 B om. /. TO1, TO3, TO4 sidhyati; N1, TO2 sidhyati/; K1, BL2 sidhyati•.
37 K1, BL2 om.
38 B, TO1 om. /. TO2, TO3, TO4, N1 sidhyati; K1, BL2 om.
39 TO1 pañcānantaryakāri.
40 B, TO4 /; TO2 and N1 om. //.

//iti[1] siṃhanādasādhanaṃ[2] samāptam//[3]

(4) vidhāya sādhanaṃ dhanyaṃ[4] yad alābhi[5] śubhaṃ[6] mayā/[7]
siṃhanādasya nāthasya[8] nirvyādhiḥ[9] syāt tato[10] jagat//

//[11]kṛtir iyaṃ paṇḍitāvadhūtaśrīmadadvayavajrapādānām//[12]

---

1 B, TO1, TO3, TO4, K1, N1, BL2 om. iti.
2 TO1 siṃhanādasādhana; TO2 śrīsiṃhanādasādhanaṃ.
3 B /, TO1 -ptaḥ//.
4 TO1, TO3, TO4 dhanyāya; TO2, K1, N1, BL2 dhanyā.
5 TO1 arābhi.
6 TO1, TO3, TO4, N1 śubham.
7 TO1, K1 and BL2 om. /. TO4 //.
8 BL2 add. a central dot.
9 B, TO2, TO3, TO4, K1 nirvyādhi; TO1, BL2 nivyādi.
10 TO1 ta.
11 B /; TO2 and TO4 om. //.
12 TO2 paṇḍita avadhūta-; TO4 paṇḍitāvadhuta-; K1 paṇḍitāvadhūtaśrīmadvayavajrapādānāṃ//; BL2 paṇḍitā•vadhūtaśrīmadvayavajrapādānāṃ//.

## 5.2 Siṃhanādalokeśvarasādhana (Bhatt. no. 20)

(0) namaḥ[1] siṃhanādāya//[2]

(1) prathamaṃ mukhaśaucādikaṃ[3] kṛtvā[4] sukhāsanastho[5]

(2.1.1) yogī svahṛdi[6] sūryamaṇḍale[7] āḥkāraṃ[8] dṛṣṭvā[9] purato[10] gurubuddhādīn[11] ānīya[12] pāpadeśanādikaṃ[13] kuryāt/[14]

(2.1.2) tataḥ śūnyatām āmukhīkṛtyādhiṣṭhāya[15] ca[16] praṇidhim anusmaret//[17]

(2.2) tataḥ akārapariṇataṃ[18] hūṃkāraṃ[19] tatpariṇataṃ[20] candraṃ tasyopary[21] oṃkārapariṇataṃ[22] raktapadmaṃ/[23] tadupary[24] āḥkārapariṇataṃ[25] śvetasiṃhaṃ/[26] tasyopari candre[27] hrīḥkārasambhavaṃ[28] siṃhanādabhaṭṭārakaṃ[29] śvetaṃ[30] jaṭāmakuṭinaṃ[31] trinetraṃ[32] dvibhujaṃ[33] tapasviveśadharaṃ[34] mahārājalīlayā[35] sthitaṃ/[36] vāmahastādutthita-padmopari[37]

---

1 TO4 nama.
2 B /.
3 TO1, TO3 mukhacaucādikaṃ; TO4 mukhaśauvādikaṃ.
4 K1 and BL2 add. a central dot.
5 TO2 suhkāsastho; TO4 sukhāsanastha.
6 TO4 tvahṛdi.
7 TO1 sūyamaṇḍale.
8 TO1, TO3, TO4 ākāraṃ.
9 TO1 add. //. TO2, TO3, TO4 and N1 add. /. K1 and BL2 add. a central dot.
10 TO1 puraṭo; TO2 tato.
11 TO4 -dīnāṃ.
12 TO4 nīya; K1 and BL2 add. a central dot.
13 N1 -śādikaṃ.
14 TO4, K1, BL2 //.
15 TO1 mukhī-; K1, BL2 -ādhisthāya.
16 K1 and BL2 add. a central dot.
17 B, TO1, TO2, TO3, TO4, N1 /.
18 TO1 ākālaṃ pariṇataṃ; TO2 āḥkārapariṇataṃ; TO3, TO4, K1 ākārapariṇataṃ; N1 aṃkārapariṇataṃ.
19 B, N1 om.; K1, BL2 hūṃkāra.
20 B, N1 om.
21 The rendering follows the Sandhi rule. B, TO2, TO3, TO4, K1, N1 tasyopari; TO1 tasyopali; BL2 tasyopari•.
22 TO1, TO3, TO4 oṃkāraṃ pariṇataṃ; K1 candraṃ tasyopari oṃkārapariṇataṃ.
23 B, TO1, TO3, TO4 and N1 om. /.
24 The rendering follows the Sandhi rule. B, TO2, TO3, TO4, N1 tadupari; TO1 tadpariṇataṃ; K1, BL2 tadupari•.
25 TO1 om. TO2 āḥkārapariṇata; TO3, TO4, K1 ākārapariṇataṃ; BL2 ākārapariṇataṃ•.
26 B om. /. TO1 śvatasiṃhaṃ/; TO2 śvetasiha/; N1 -siṃhaṃ te/.
27 K1 and BL2 add. a central dot.
28 TO2 -sabhava; BL2 add. a central dot.
29 TO1 sihanādabhaṭṭārakaṃ; TO2 siṃhanādabhaṭṭāraka; TO4, K1, BL2 siṃhanādaṃ bhaṭṭārakaṃ.
30 TO2 -ta.
31 TO1, TO4 jaṭāmukuṭinaṃ; TO2 jaṭāmākuṭina; K1 and BL2 add. a central dot. N1 add. /.
32 TO1, TO2 -tra; K1, BL2 triṇetraṃ•.
33 TO1 -ja/; TO2, TO3, TO4 and N1 add. /. K1 and BL2 add. a central dot.
34 TO1 tapaśviveśa-; TO2 om.; TO4 tapaściveṇadharaṃ//; K1 tapaśvīśadharī/; N1 add. /. BL2 tapaśvīveśadharī/.
35 K1, BL2 mahātejalīlayā.
36 B om. /. TO4 //.
37 TO1 -padmopali; BL2 -utthita•padmopari.

jvaladūrdhvakhaḍgaṃ/[1] dakṣiṇe sitatriśūlaṃ[2] sitaphaṇiveṣṭitaṃ/[3] vāme nānāsugandhipuṣpaiḥ[4] pūrṇaṃ[5] śvetakapālam[6] amitābhamukuṭinaṃ[7] sphuratpañcatathāgataṃ[8] mahānirmāṇarūpiṇaṃ[9] dhyāyāt/[10]

(3) japamantraḥ/[11] oṃ āḥ hrīḥ siṃhanāda[12] hūṃ phaṭ[13] / iti[14] siṃhanādasādhanam//[15]

---

1 B om. /. BL2 //.
2 K1, BL2 -sitatriśūraṃ•.
3 B and K1 om. /. TO1 sitaphaṇīveṣṭitaṃ; TO4 //; K1 and BL2 have a central dot.
4 K1, N1 -puṣpai.
5 K1 pūrṇa; BL2 add. a central dot.
6 K1 and BL2 add. a central dot.
7 TO2 -makuṭinaṃ; N1 add. /.
8 TO1 sphulayatpañcatathāgataṃ; TO2 sphārayet pañcatathāgataṃ/; TO4 sphārayet pañcatathāgataṃ//; TO3, K1 sphūrayet pañcatathāgataṃ/; TO1, TO2 and N1 add. /. TO4 add. //. BL2 spharayet pañcatathāgataṃ/.
9 TO1 -māṇarūpīnaṃ; TO2 -mānarūpiṇaṃ; TO3 add. /. BL2 add. a central dot.
10 TO1, TO4, K1, BL2 //.
11 B om. /. TO1, K1 -tra//; TO2, TO4, N1, BL2 //.
12 TO1 sihanāda; TO2 -de; K1, BL2 siṃhanādāya.
13 B add. /. TO1, TO3, K1 and BL2 add. //.
14 N1 kāti?.
15 N1 -dhanaḥ//.

## 5.3 Siṃhanādānām dhāraṇī (Bhatt. no. 21)

(0) namo ratnatrayāya//[1]

(1) nama[2] āryāvalokiteśvarāya[3] (4-bodhisattvāya[5] mahāsattvāya[6] mahākāruṇikāya[7] tadyathā/[8] oṃ akaṭe[9] vikaṭe nikaṭe[10] kaṭaṃkaṭe[11] karoṭe[12] karoṭavīrye[13] svāhā//[14]

(2.1) eṣā[15] bhagavata āryāvalokiteśvarasya-4) purataḥ pratyūṣe[16] apatitagomayenāṣṭau[17] maṇḍalakān kṛtvā[18] pratimaṇḍalaṃ[19] trayodaśavārān[20] uccārayitavyā/[21] tataḥ saptavārān gomayaśeṣam abhimantrya vyādhim upalepayet/[22]

(2.2) sarvavyādhīn[23] upaśamayati/[24] yadi[25] saptame divase[26] trayodaśe vā[27] ekaviṃśatitame[28] vā[29] divase pañcānantaryakāriṇo 'pi na[30] sidhyanti/[31] tadāhaṃ[32] pañcānantaryakārī[33] syām iti[34] // siṃhanādānām[35] dhāraṇī samāptā//[36]

---

1 B, K1 /; TO1, TO3 and N1 om. //. BL2 a central dot.
2 TO1, TO2 namo; K1 namaḥ.
3 TO4 -rasya; K1 and BL2 add. a central dot.
4 TO4 om.
5 BL2 add. a central dot.
6 TO2 om.; BL2 add. a central dot.
7 TO1 mahākārunīkāya//; TO2 and N1 add. /. TO3 mahākāruṇīkāya/; K1, BL2 mahākāruṇīkāya//.
8 B and N1 om. /. TO1, K1, BL2 //.
9 TO1 akate; BL2 add. a central dot.
10 K1 and BL2 add. a central dot.
11 TO1, TO2, TO3, N1 kaṭaṅkaṭe; BL2 add. a central dot.
12 K1, BL2 karoṭake•.
13 B, TO1 karoṭavīrya; TO2 karoṭavīryya; K1 roṭavīryya; BL2 roṭavīryye.
14 B /.
15 TO2 eṣāṃ; K1 eṣa.
16 TO1, TO3, TO4 -yuṣe; K1 -yūṣa.
17 TO4 -mayanāṣṭaumaṇḍalakān; K1 -mayena aṣṭaumaṇḍalakān; BL2 -mayena•aṣṭau•maṇḍalakān.
18 TO1 akṛtvā; BL2 add. a central dot.
19 TO1 -la.
20 TO4 -śaṃ.
21 TO4 //; K1 and BL2 om. /.
22 B and N1 om. /. TO1, TO3, K1, BL2 //; TO4 -lapayet //.
23 TO1 sarvvavyāpīn; TO2, TO3 sarvvavyādhin; K1, N1, BL2 sarvvavyādhīm.
24 TO4, K1, BL2 upasamayati//; N1 upasamayati/.
25 N1 yade.
26 N1 divasī?.
27 K1 and BL2 add. a central dot.
28 TO1, TO2, TO4, BL2 -viṃśatime; TO3 -viṃśati.
29 K1 and BL2 add. a central dot.
30 K1, BL2 om.
31 B and TO4 om. /. TO1, TO2 siddhyati/; TO3, TO4, N1 sidhyati.
32 B tadā ahaṃ; TO1, TO3, TO4, K1 tadā.
33 TO1 -taryyakāri.
34 B add. /. TO1, TO3 and K1 add. //.
35 TO1, TO3, TO4, K1, N1, BL2 siṃhanādānāma; TO2 iti śrīsiṃhanādanām.
36 TO2 samāptaṃ//.

## 5.4 Siṃhanādalokeśvarasādhana (Bhatt. nos. 22, 23)

(0) oṃ[1] namaḥ[2] siṃhanādāya/[3]

(1) prathamaṃ[4] tāvan[5] mantri[6] mukhaśaucādikaṃ[7] kṛtvā[8] mṛduviṣṭare[9] upaviśya[10] sukhāsanasthaḥ[11]

(2.1.1) svahṛdi[12] candramaṇḍale sitahrīḥkāraṃ[13] dṛṣṭvā[14] tadraśmisamākṛṣṭān[15] purato[16] gurubuddhabodhisattvān dhyāyāt//[17]

(2.1.2) tadanu[18] pūjāpāpadeśanādikaṃ[19] kṛtvā[20] śūnyatām[21] vibhāvya/[22] oṃ śūnyatājñānavajrasvabhāvātmako[23] (24-'ham[25] ity[26] anenādhitiṣṭhet//[27]

(2.2) tato-24) jhaṭiti paṃkāreṇa[28] pariṇataṃ[29] raktapadmaṃ[30] tadupari[31] siṃkārapariṇataṃ[32] śvetasiṃhaṃ/[33] tasyopari[34] candre[35] hrīḥkārasambhavaṃ[36] siṃhanādalokeśvararūpam[37]

---

1 B, TO1, TO2, TO3, TO4, K1, N1, BL2 om.
2 TO1, TO2, TO3, TO4, K1, N1, BL2 om.
3 TO1, TO2, TO3, TO4, K1, N1, BL2 om.; BL1 //; K2 add. //.
4 TO2 prathaman; BL1 prathama.
5 TO2, BL1, BL2 tāvat.
6 K2 and BL2 add. a central dot.
7 TO2, K1, BL1 mukhasaucādikaṃ.
8 BL2 add. a central dot.
9 TO1, TO2, TO3, TO4, K1, N1, BL2 om.
10 TO1, TO2, TO3, TO4, K1, N1, BL2 om.; BL1 upaviśeṣe.
11 K2, BL1 -sane sthāḥ.
12 K2, BL1 -hṛdī; BL2 -hṛdīḥ.
13 TO2 -kāra; TO4 add. //. K2, BL1 hrīḥkāraṃ; N1 sita/ hrīḥkāraṃ.
14 TO2 add. /. K1 and BL2 add. a central dot.
15 TO2 tadaśmisamākṛṣṭān; K2, BL2 samākṛṣin •; BL1 tadraśmīsamākṛṣṭān.
16 TO4 puratā.
17 B, TO1, TO2, TO3, N1 /; BL1 a central dot.
18 TO4, BL1 -nū.
19 BL2 pūjā•pāpadeśanādikaṃ.
20 BL2 add. a central dot.
21 TO1, K2, BL1 śūnyatā; TO4 śūnyatām.
22 B and BL1 om. /. TO1, TO3, TO4, K1, BL2 //; K2 a central dot.
23 K1 śūnyatāṃ jñā-; K2 svabhāvaśuddhāḥ sarvadharmmā•svabhāvasudho haṃ paścā; BL1 svabhāvaśuddhāḥ sarvadharmmā svabhāvasudho haṃ paścā; BL2 śūnyatāṃ jñānavajasvabhāvātmako.
24 K2, BL1 om.
25 B 'haṃ; K2 haṃ.
26 TO1, TO3, K1, BL2 iti//.
27 B, K2, N1, BL1 /; TO2 anānādhitiṣṭhet/.
28 B, TO1, TO2, TO3, TO4, K2, BL1 paṃkāra.
29 TO1 paliṇataṃ; K1 add. a central dot. K2, BL1 parinatāṃ; BL2 paritaṃ•.
30 TO4 raktaṃ padmaṃ; K2, BL1 raktapadma; BL2 add. a central dot.
31 TO1, TO3, K1 tadpariṇataṃ; BL2 add. a central dot.
32 TO1, TO3, K1, BL2 om.; TO2 siṃhārapariṇataṃ; K2, BL1 sikārapariṇataṃ.
33 B, TO1, TO3 and K1 om. /. K2 svetasika; BL1 -sika; BL2 a central dot.
34 BL2 add. a central dot.
35 K2, BL1 candra.
36 BL2 add. a central dot.
37 TO1 -lokeśvarūpam; BL2 -lokeśvara •rūpam.

ātmānaṃ dhyāyāt/[1] śuklam amitābhajaṭāmukuṭinaṃ[2] trinetraṃ[3] dvibhujaṃ[4] tapasviveśadharaṃ[5] mahārājalīlayā[6] sthitaṃ/[7] vāmahastādutthitapadmopari[8] jvalatkhaḍgaṃ[9] dakṣiṇe sitatriśūlaṃ[10] sitaphaṇiveṣṭitaṃ[11] vāme[12] nānāsugandhipuṣpaiḥ[13] pūrṇaṃ[14] śvetakapālaṃ[15] sphuratpañcatathāgataṃ[16] mahānirmāṇarūpiṇaṃ[17] dhyāyāt//[18]

(2.3) japamantraḥ/[19] oṃ āḥ[20] hrīḥ[21] siṃhanāda[22] hūṃ phaṭ//[23]

(3.1) tadanantaraṃ[24] dhāraṇī[25] bhavati//[26] (27-namo ratnatrayāya[28] nama[29] āryāvalokiteśvarāya[30] bodhisattvāya[31] mahāsattvāya[32] mahākāruṇikāya//[33]

---

1 B om. /. TO4, K1, BL2 //; K2 a central dot.
2 TO2, K1 -jaṭāmakuṭinaṃ; TO4 -jaṭāmakūṭinaṃ/; K2, BL1 -jaṭāmakuṭinaṃ; BL2 -jaṭāmakuṭinaṃ•.
3 TO1 trinetra; TO2 and TO4 add. /. BL2 add. a central dot.
4 TO2, TO4 and N1 add. /. K1 and BL2 add. a central dot. K2, BL1 dvibhūja.
5 TO1, TO3, N1 tapaśviveśadharaṃ/; TO2 tapaśveveśadharaṃ/; TO4 tapaśviveṇadharaṃ//; K1 tapaśvīveśadharaṃ•; K2 tapaśviveṣadharaṃ; BL2 tapaśvīveśadharaṃ/.
6 TO1 mahārājalirayā/; TO2 saptajalīlayā.
7 B om. /. K2, BL1 a central dot.
8 TO1, TO3, TO4 -utthitapari; K1 -utthitepari; K2 vāme hastād-; BL1 -uṭhitapadmopari; BL2 -utthitopari.
9 TO1 jvaratkhaḍgaṃ; K1 -ga/; K2 -goṃ; TO2, TO3, TO4, N1 and BL2 add. /. BL1 jvalotkhaḍgaṃ.
10 TO1, K2, BL1 sitatriśūraṃ.
11 TO1 sitaphanivaṣṭitaṃ/; TO4 sitaphaṇiveṣṭitāṃ; TO2, TO3, N1 and BL2 add. /. K2 add. a central dot.
12 TO4 vārime; K2 vāmena; BL1 vāmeṇa.
13 K2 sugaṃdhīpuṣpaiḥ; BL1 illegible after sugandhīpu-.
14 TO1, K2, BL1 pūrṇa; TO3 illegible after pū-. N1 -pūṇa; BL2 pūrṇaḥ.
15 TO1 śvetakapāraṃ/; TO2 -la, TO2 om.; TO3, K1 and BL2 add. /. K2, BL1 sveta-.
16 TO2, TO4 spharatpañcatathāgataṃ/; TO1, TO3, K1, N1 and BL2 add. /. K2 -pañca•tathāgatāṃ.
17 TO1, TO2 -nirmmānarūpiṇa; K2 -nīryyānarūpaṃ; N1 -nirmmāṇaṃ rūpiṇa; BL1 -nirmmānarūpaṃ.
18 B dhyāyāt iti/; TO1, TO2 dhyāyāt iti//; TO4, N1 /; K2, BL1 dhyāyāt// iti.
19 B and BL1 om. /. TO1, TO3, K1, BL2 //; TO2, TO4 japyamaṃtraḥ//; K2 iti japyamaṃtra//; N1 japyamantraḥ/.
20 K2 ā.
21 K1, BL2 hrī.
22 TO2 siṃhanāde;.K1, BL2 siṃhanādāya.
23 B phaṭ/ //siṃhanādasādhanaṃ samāptam//; K2, BL1 phaṭ svāhā//.
24 K2 iti sādhana samuccaye siṃhanädalokeśvarasādhana ekonacatvāriṃsādhikaśatatamapaṭala//139//; N1 tadanatara; BL1 iti sādhanasamucayasiṃhanādalokeśvarasādhana ekoṇacatvāriṃśādhikaśatatamapaṭalaḥ// 139//.
25 K2, BL1 om.
26 B /, K1 has a central dot. K2, BL1 om.
27 K1 om.
28 TO2 /; K2 -yaḥ//; BL1 add. //. BL2 add. a central dot.
29 TO1, TO3, BL2 namaḥ; TO2, TO4, K2, BL1 namo.
30 K2 -lokṛtyeśvarāya; BL1 illegible between āryāvalokite- and -rāya. BL2 add. a central dot.
31 BL2 add. a central dot.
32 TO1 om.; BL2 add. a central dot.
33 B and TO4 om. //. TO2 /; TO1, TO3, K2, BL1 -kāriṇīkāya; N1 om. //. BL2 -kāriṇīkāya •.

tadyathā//[1] oṃ akaṭe[2] vikaṭe[3] nikaṭe[4] kaṭaṃkaṭe[5-27)] karoṭe[6] karoṭavīrye[7] svāhā//[8] ayaṃ[9] mantropacāraḥ//[10] bhagavato 'grataḥ[11] pratyūṣe[12] apatitagomayenāṣṭaumaṇḍalakān[13] kṛtvā[14] pratimaṇḍalake[15] trayodaśavārān[16] uccārayet/[17]

(3.2) gomayaśeṣaṃ[18] saptābhimantrya[19] vyādhim upalepayet/[20] sarvavyādhīn[21] upaśamayati/[22] yadi saptame[23] divase[24] trayodaśe[25] divase[26] ekaviṃśatitame[27] vā[28] divase[29] pañcānantaryakāriṇo[30] 'pi[31] na sidhyaty[32] ayaṃ[33] (34-tadā 'ham-34) eva[35] pañcānantaryakārī[36] bhaviṣyāmi/[37]

//siṃhanādasādhanam//[38]

---

1 B, TO4 and N1 om. //.
2 BL2 add. a central dot.
3 BL2 add. a central dot.
4 TO2, N1 kaṭaṅkaṭe; BL2 add. a central dot.
5 BL2 add. a central dot.
6 TO2 om.; TO4 karoṭi; K1, BL2 karokaṭe.
7 B, TO2 karoṭavīryya; K1, BL2 roṭavīryye; N1 karovīrye.
8 B /.
9 TO4 aya.
10 B om. //. K2, BL1 -ra•; N1 add. /.
11 K2 grata• ; BL1 grato.
12 K1, BL2 pratyūṣa•.
13 K1 apatitagomayanāṣṭaumaṇḍalakān; K2 apatitagomayenoṣṭamaṇḍala; N1 apatitagomayenāṣṭaumaṇḍalakān; BL1 apratitagomayanāṣṭamaṇḍala; BL2 apatita•gomayanāṣṭaumaṇḍalakān.
14 K2, BL1 om.; BL2 add. a central dot.
15 TO4 -maṇḍaleke; K1 add. a central dot. K2, BL1 om.; BL2 add. a central dot.
16 TO4 trayodavārān; K2, BL1 trayodaśaṃ vārān.
17 TO1, TO4, K1, BL2 //; N1 om. /. K2 uccārayat•; BL1 uccārayat//.
18 TO2 -ṣa; K2 gomayeśeṣaṃ.
19 TO1, TO2 saptabhimantrya; TO3 saptabhimaṃtrya; K2 saptābhirmatra; BL1 saptābhimantra.
20 B and K2 om. /. TO1, TO3, K1, BL2 //; BL1 uparepayat.
21 TO1, K2 -dhin; K1, BL2 -dhīm; BL1 -dhi.
22 TO2 upasamayati/; TO4 upaśamayaṃti/; K1, BL2 //; K2 upasamayeti•; BL1 upasamayat•.
23 TO2 same.
24 TO1 divaśā; BL2 add. a central dot.
25 TO2 -daśane; K2, BL1 -daśa; N1 add. me.
26 TO2 dise; K1 and BL2 add. a central dot.
27 TO1 ekaviśatitame; K1, BL2 ekaviṃśati; K2 ekaviṃśatime; BL1 ekaviṃśatitameva
28 TO1, TO3, K2 va; K1, BL2 om.
29 K2 dīvaśe•; BL1 di•; BL2 add. a central dot.
30 BL1 nantaryyakāriṇā.
31 K2 naṃtaryyekāriṇāpi; BL2 add. a central dot.
32 K2 sidhyet; BL1 syadhyabhy.
33 K1 eyaṃ; K2, BL1 ayan; TO1, TO2, TO3, TO4 and N1 add. /. BL2 add. //.
34 TO1 tadā ahaṃ; TO2, TO3, TO4, N1 tadā aham.
35 TO1 meva; K1 and BL2 add. a central dot. K2 yeva.
36 TO1 pacānantaryyakāli; K2 pañcānantaryyekāri.
37 TO1, TO2, TO4 and N1 om. /. TO3, K1, BL2 //; K2 bhaviṣyyati//; BL1 bhaviṣyati//.
38 B //siṃhanādadhāraṇī samāptā//; TO1, K1, BL2 //iti siṃhanādasādhanaṃ//; K2 // iti sādhanasamuccayasiṃhanādalokeśvarasādhanacatvāriṃsādhikaśatatamapaṭalaḥ //140//; BL1 // iti sādhanasamuccayasiṃhanādalokeśvarasādhanacatvāriṃsādhikaśatatamapaṭalā //140//.

## 5.5 Siṃhanādalokeśvarasādhana (Bhatt. no. 25)

(0) siṃhanādam ahaṃ[1] vande[2] sarvavyādhiharaṃ gurum/[3]
bhāvanāyogamātreṇa[4] mucyate[5] sarvakilbiṣāt//[6]

(1) prathamaṃ[7] tāvan[8] mukhaśaucādikaṃ[9] kṛtvā[10] śucivastraprāvṛtaḥ pavitrabhūmau sukhāsanopaviṣṭaḥ/[11]

(2.1.1) svahṛdi candre[12] hrīḥkāraṃ[13] vibhāvya[14] tena raśminākṛṣya[15] sarvatathāgatān pūjayitvā[16] pāpadeśanādikaṃ kuryāt//[17]

(2.1.2) tato maitrīkaruṇāmuditopekṣāś[18] ca[19] vibhāvya[20] svabhāvaśuddha-mantroccāraṇapūrvakaṃ[21] śūnyatāṃ[22] bhāvayet/[23] oṃ svabhāvaśuddhāḥ sarvadharmāḥ svabhāvaśuddho 'haṃ//[24] oṃ śūnyatājñānavajrasvabhāvātmako[25] 'ham[26] iti//[27]

(2.2) tadanantaraṃ[28] pratibhāsamātrakaṃ[29] svakāyam avalokya[30] raktarephapariṇataṃ[31] raktāṣṭadalapadmopary[32] hrīḥkārapariṇāmena[33] śvetasiṃhaṃ[34] tasyopari[35] pṛṣṭhacandre[36]

---

1 TO1 aha; TO3, TO4, N1 aham.
2 BL2 add. a central dot.
3 TO1 guru.
4 TO4 -yomātreṇa; BL2 add. a central dot.
5 TO1 mucyete.
6 TO1, TO3, K1, BL2 sarvvakilbiṣaḥ//; TO2 sarvvakilbīṣaiḥ/; TO4, N1 sarvakilbiṣaiḥ//.
7 TO1, TO3, N1 prathaman.
8 B, TO2, BL2 tāvat.
9 TO4 mukhaṇauvādikaṃ.
10 BL2 add. a central dot.
11 B, TO3, TO4, K1 and BL2 om. /. TO1 -ṭa.
12 K1 and BL2 add. a central dot.
13 TO1 hrīkāraṃ; TO2, N1 hrīḥkāram.
14 K1 and BL2 add. /.
15 BL2 add. a central dot.
16 BL2 add. a central dot.
17 B, TO1, TO2, TO3, TO4, N1 /.
18 TO1 -muditāpekṣāṃ; TO2, N1 -muditopekṣāñ; TO3, TO4, K1, BL2 -pekṣāṃ.
19 TO1, TO3 ca tu; K1, BL2 catur.
20 TO1, TO3, K1 and BL2 add. /.
21 K1 -śuddhāmantroccāraṇaḥ pūrvakaṃ; BL2 -śuddhāḥ mantroccāraṇaḥ pūrvakaṃ.
22 TO1 śūnyatā; K1 śūtāṃ.
23 B om. /. TO4, K1, BL2 //.
24 B and TO4 om. //. TO1, TO2, TO3, N1 /.
25 TO1 -bhātmako; TO3, TO4, K1, BL2 śūnyatāṃ jñāna-.
26 B 'haṃ.
27 B /.
28 B, TO2, TO4, N1 etadanantaraṃ; TO1 tadanantara; K1, BL2 tadanantaraṃ•.
29 TO2 pratisusam-.
30 TO4 avaloke; K1 and BL2 add. a central dot.
31 TO1, TO2, TO3, TO4, N1 -pariṇata; K1, BL2 -pariṇata•.
32 The rendering follows the Sandhi rule. B, TO2, N1, K1, BL2 -padmopari; TO1, TO3 raktaṣṭadalapadmopari; TO4 rektadalapadmopari.
33 TO1, K1 -meṇa; BL2 -meṇa •.
34 TO4 -siṃha; N1 -siṃhan.
35 K1 and BL2 add. a central dot.
36 TO1 -dreḥ; K1 -dra; BL2 pṛṣṭhaś candra.

hrīḥkāraṃ[1] saraśmikaṃ[2] tenaivākṛṣya[3] sarvatathāgatapraveśenātmānaṃ[4] siṃhanādalokeśvararūpaṃ[5] bhāvayet/[6] śvetavarṇaṃ[7] trinetraṃ[8] jaṭāmukuṭinaṃ[9] nirbhūṣaṇaṃ[10] vyāghracarmaprāvṛtaṃ[11] siṃhāsanasthaṃ[12] mahārājalīlaṃ[13] candrāsanaṃ[14] candraprabhaṃ bhāvayet/[15] dakṣiṇe sitaphaṇiveṣṭitaṃ[16] triśūlaṃ[17] śvetaṃ[18] vāme nānāsugandhikusumaparipūritapadmabhājanaṃ[19] vāmahastādutthapadmopari[20] jvalatkhaḍgaṃ[21] svakāye[22] pañcatathāgataṃ[23] sphurantaṃ[24] paśyet//[25]

(2.3) tato[26] hṛdbījenākṛṣya[27] jñānasattvaṃ[28] praveśayitvā tathāgatān[29] sphāryābhiṣiñced[30] ātmānaṃ[31] maulāv amitābhamudraṇaṃ[32] cintayet//[33]

---

1 1 and BL2 add. a central dot. N1 hrīkāraṃ.
2 K1 and BL2 add. a central dot.
3 TO4 tainaivākṛṣya; K1 and BL2 add. a central dot.
4 TO2 -praśenātmātmānaṃ; TO3 add. /. K1 -praveśyam ātmānaṃ; BL2 sarvatathāgata•praveśyam ātmānaṃ.
5 B siṃhanādaṃ lokeśvararūpaṃ.
6 B om. /. TO1, TO3, BL2 //; K1 paśyet//.
7 TO1, TO2 -ṇa; K1 śvetavarṇa•; N1 śvetavarṇan; BL2 add. a central dot.
8 TO2 -tra; BL2 add. a central dot.
9 TO2, TO4 -maku-; TO4 add. /. K1, BL2 jaṭāmakuṭinaṃ•.
10 TO1 nibhūṣanaṃ; TO2 add. /. K1 and BL2 add. a central dot.
11 TO4 -carmaprākṛtaṃ; TO2 add. /. K1 and BL2 add. a central dot.
12 TO1 sihāsa-; K1 and BL2 add. a central dot.
13 TO2 -līra; K1 and BL2 add. a central dot.
14 TO2 candrāsana; BL2 add. a central dot.
15 TO1, BL2 //; K1 ///.
16 K1 and BL2 add. a central dot.
17 TO1 triśūra.
18 B add. a comma. TO2, TO4 and N1 add. /. BL2 add. a central dot.
19 B add. a comma. TO1 -pūrītapadmabhājana; TO2 -kuśumaparipūritapadmabhājanaṃ/; TO3, TO4, N1 add. /. K1 -pūjitapadmabhājanaṃ//; BL2 add. //.
20 TO1, TO2, TO3, TO4 -utthaṃ padmopari; K1, BL2 -utthaṃ•padmopari; N1 -upasthitaṃ padmopari.
21 B add. a comma. TO1 jvaratkhaḍgaṃ/; TO2, TO3, TO4 and N1 add. /. K1 and BL2 add. //.
22 TO2, TO3, K1, BL2 svakāya.
23 TO2, K1 -tathāgata; BL2 -tathāgata•.
24 TO1 sphuranta; TO2 spharaṃtaṃ; N1 sphurantam; BL2 spharantaṃ•.
25 B, TO4, N1 /; TO1 paśyat//; TO2 paśyat/.
26 K1 tata; BL2 tataḥ.
27 TO1 hṛdbijen-; TO2 hṛdbījan-; K1, BL2 svahṛdbījenākṛṣya•.
28 N1 add. /.
29 K1 -tā.
30 TO1 -bhiṣeced; TO2 saṃsphāryyā-; TO4 -bhiṣiñcad.
31 BL2 add. a central dot.
32 K1, BL2 -mudrinaṃ; N1 -mudraṇañ.
33 B, TO2, N1 /.

(2.4) tato mantraṃ[1] japed[2] devatāmūrtinā/[3] tatrāyaṃ[4] mantraḥ/[5] oṃ āḥ hrīḥ[6] siṃhanāda[7] hūṃ[8] phaṭ svāhā//[9]

(3.1) tadanu sugandhādimaṇḍalaṃ kṛtvā[10] pūjārthaṃ[11] puṣpādikaṃ[12] ḍhaukayitvā[13] arcayet//[14] punar[15] mālāmantraṃ[16] japet/[17] oṃ[18] namo ratnatrayāya[19] nama[20] āryāvalokiteśvarāya[21] bodhisattvāya[22] mahāsattvāya[23] mahākāruṇikāya/[24] tadyathā/[25] oṃ akaṭe vikaṭe nikaṭe[26] kaṭaṅkaṭe karoṭe[27] karoṭavīrye[28] svāhā//[29]

(3.2) anena mantreṇa maṇḍalamṛttikāṃ[30] gṛhītvā[31] ekaviṃśativārān[32] āvartya[33] vyādhiṃ[34] pralepya svastho[35] bhavati/[36]

// iti[37] śrīsiṃhanādalokeśvarasādhanaṃ[38] samāptam//[39]

---

1 BL2 add. a central dot.
2 B, TO1 japet.
3 TO2 -murttinā/; K1, BL2 //.
4 TO1 tatrayaṃ; TO4 tatrāyam.
5 B om. /. TO2, TO4 //; K1 -ra //; BL2 mantraṃ//.
6 TO1, TO3, K1, BL2 hrī.
7 TO1 siṃhan[illegible] TO2 siṃhanādāya..
8 TO3 add. /. N1 add. //.
9 B /.
10 K1 add. a central dot.
11 TO1 pūjārtha; K1, BL2 pūjādi.
12 K1 and BL2 add. a central dot.
13 TO1,TO3, K1, BL2 ḍhauṣayitvā; TO4 ṭokayitvā.
14 B, TO2, TO4, N1 /; TO2 accayet/.
15 TO2 punas.
16 N1 mālāmantrañ.
17 TO1, TO3, K1, BL2 //.
18 TO2, TO3, K1, N1, BL2 om.
19 TO2 add. //.
20 TO2 namaḥ.
21 BL2 add. /.
22 BL2 add. a central dot.
23 BL2 add. a central dot.
24 TO1, TO3, TO4 and N1 om. /. K1, BL2 a central dot.
25 B, K1 and BL2 om. /. TO4 //.
26 TO1, TO3, K1 and BL2 add. kaṭe. TO2 and N1 add. trikaṭe.
27 K1 karokaṭe.
28 B karoṭavīryya; TO1, TO2, TO4 karoṭavīrya.
29 B /.
30 TO1, N1 -muttikāṃ; TO2 -murttikāṃ; TO3, TO4, K1 -mūrttikāṃ; BL2 -laṃ mūrttikāṃ.
31 BL2 add. a central dot.
32 TO1, TO2 ekaviśativārān.
33 TO1 āvattya; TO2, TO4 āvarttā; K1, BL2 āvātya.
34 TO1, TO2, TO3, K1, BL2 vyādhi.
35 TO1 svasthe; TO2 svastha; K1 svasthā.
36 TO1, TO3, TO4, K1, BL2 // //; TO2 and N1 om. /.
37 TO1, TO3, TO4, K1, N1 and BL2 om. //iti.
38 B, TO4, K1 siṃhanādalokeśvarasādhanaṃ; TO1, TO3, N1 siṃhanādalokeśvarasādhana; BL2 siṃhanādalokeśvarasādhanaṃ•.
39 N1 om.

## 6 Nīlakaṇṭhāryāvalokiteśvarasādhana (Bhatt. no. 39)

(0) namo lokanāthāya//[1]

(1) prathamaṃ[2] tāvat sādhakaḥ[3] prātar utthāya sukhāsane[4] sattvaparyaṅkenopaviśya[5]

(2.1.1) hṛdaye[6] prathamasvarapariṇatacandramaṇḍalopari[7] pītahrīḥkāraṃ[8] vibhāvya[9]

(2.1.2) tanmarīcisamūhair[10] bhagavantaṃ bhāvyamānam ānīya[11] tasmād eva bījāt[12] sphāritapuṣpadhūpādibhiḥ[13] saṃpūjya tasya purataḥ pāpadeśanādikaṃ[14] vidhāya[15] maitryādicaturbrahmavihārabhāvanāṃ[16] ca kuryāt/[17]

(2.1.3) tadanu[18] sabāhyābhyantaraṃ[19] vastu śūnyasvabhāvaṃ[20] vibhāvya/[21] oṃ svabhāvaśuddhāḥ[22] sarvadharmāḥ svabhāvaśuddho 'ham iti mantram āvartayet/[23]

(2.2) tadantaraṃ[24] nabhaḥpradeśe[25] prathamasvareṇa candramaṇḍalaṃ[26] tadupari[27] pītahrīḥkāraṃ[28] tenaiva raktapadmaṃ tadbījādhiṣṭhitaṃ[29] tat sarvaṃ[30] pariṇamya[31] bhagavantaṃ pītavarṇaṃ[32] ardhacandrāṅkitajaṭāmakuṭinaṃ[33] amitābhopalakṣitaśiraḥpradeśaṃ[34] raktapadmoparisthitaṃ[35] kṛṣṇasāraharinacarmaṇi[36]

---

1 B /.
2 TO2 -man.
3 TO1, TO3, TO4, BL2 -ka; TO2 -kaṃ.
4 TO4 -na.
5 TO2, TO3, K1, N1 -keṇo-; BL2 add. a central dot.
6 BL2 add. a central dot.
7 TO2 -candramalopari; K1 prathamasvarapariṇataṃ caṃdramaṇḍalopari; BL2 -pariṇataṃ•.
8 TO3, TO4, N1 -kāram; K1, BL2 pītaḥ hrīḥkāram.
9 K1 and BL2 add. //.
10 TO2 tat marīcisamūhai.
11 TO1, TO2, TO3, TO4, K1, N1 and BL2 add. /.
12 BL2 bījā.
13 TO1 sphāritapūṣpa-; K1 phari-; BL2 spharita•.
14 TO1 -denādi-.
15 K1 add. /.
16 TO2 -brahmavihāvanāñ; TO4 -nāñ.
17 K1, BL2 //.
18 N1 add. /.
19 TO3, TO4 -taram; BL2 add. a central dot.
20 TO1, TO3, K1, BL2 śūnyatāsva-.
21 B om. /. K1, BL2 -yaḥ//.
22 BL2 śubhāva-.
23 TO1 has a colon. TO3 and N1 om. /. K1, BL2 //.
24 TO4 tadanantaran.
25 TO4 -daiśe.
26 TO1, TO2, TO3, TO4 and N1 add. /. BL2 add. a central dot.
27 TO4 taduparī.
28 TO1, TO2, TO3, TO4, K1 and BL2 add. /.
29 K1 add. a central dot. BL2 tadbījādhisthitaṃ.
30 TO2, K1, BL2 sarvva; TO3, TO4 sarvvam.
31 K1 and BL2 add. a central dot.
32 TO2, N1 -ṇam; BL2 add. a central dot.
33 TO1 and TO3 add. /. TO2, K1, BL2 -makutīnaṃ/; N1 -mukuṭinaṃ/.
34 TO1 -parakṣitaśiraḥpradeśaṃ/; TO2 -śirapradeśaṃ/; TO3, K1, N1 and BL2 add. /.
35 K1 and BL2 add. a central dot.
36 BL2 add. a central dot.

vajraparyaṅkiṇaṃ[1] samādhimudropari[2] nānāratnaparipūrṇakapāladhāriṇaṃ[3] eṇeyacarmakṛtayajñopavītinaṃ[4] vyāghracarmāmbaradharaṃ[5] nirābharaṇaṃ[6] nīlakaṇṭhaṃ[7] nīlagulikāviśiṣṭakaṇṭhaṃ[8] pārśvadvaye[9] parasparābhisambaddha-pucchasamaṇiphaṇāviśiṣṭabhagavadavalokanaparordhvamukhakṛṣṇasarpa-dvayopalakṣitam[10] ātmānam evaṃ[11] vibhāvayet/[12]

(3) tato[13] mantraṃ[14] japet/[15] tatrāyaṃ[16] mantraḥ//[17] oṃ sphuliṅgāṭṭahāsa[18] kṣaḥ/[19] //ity[20] aparimitānuśaṃsaṃ[21] nīlakaṇṭhāryāvalokiteśvarasādhanaṃ[22] samāptam//[23]

---

1 B, TO1, K1 vajraparyyaṅkinaṃ; TO2 vajaparyyaṅkiṇaṃ/; TO3 vajaparyyaṅkinaṃ; TO4 and N1 add. /.
2 TO1, TO3, TO4, K1 -mudrā; BL2 -mudrā•.
3 TO1 nānāratnaparipūrṇadhāriṇaṃ/; TO2, TO3, TO4 and N1 add. /. K1 nānāratnaparipūrṇaṃ kapāriṇaṃ//; BL2 nānāratnaparipūrṇaṃ kapāladhāriṇaṃ.
4 TO1 eneyacarmmakṛtayajñopravitīnaṃ/; TO2, N1 eṇecarmmakṛtayajñopavītaṃ/; TO3 add. /. TO4 eneyacarmmakṛtayajñopavītaṃ/; K1 eṇayacarmmayajñopavītinaṃ/; BL2 eṇeyacarmmayajñopavītinaṃ/.
5 K1 add. /.
6 K1, BL2 nīlābharaṇaṃ.
7 TO1 nīrakaṇṭha; TO2 nīlakaṇṭha; K1 add. nīlābharaṇa. BL2 add. a central dot.
8 TO1 nīlagurīkāśiṣṭakaṇṭha; TO3 nīlagulikāśiṣṭakaṇṭhaṃ; K1 nīlagulikāviśiṣṭakaṃṭha; BL2 nīlagulikāśiṣṭakaṃṭha•.
9 TO2 illegible before -dvaye. TO3 pārśve dvaye.
10 TO1 -bhagvadavakaṇaparordhamukhakṛṣṇasarppadvayoparakṣitam; TO2 illegible between paraspa- and -saṃbaddhapucchasamaṇiphaṇāviśiṣṭabhagavalokanaparordhvamukhakṛṣṇasarppadvayopalakṣitam. TO4 parasparābhisambapucchasamaṇihaṇā-; K1 parasparābhisaṃbaṃdhapucchasamaṇiphaṇābhiviśiṣṭabhagavad-; BL2 parasparābhisaṃbandhapuccha•samaṇiphaṇābhiviśiṣṭa•bhagavadavalokana•parordhva-.
11 TO1 meva; N1 evam.
12 TO1, TO3, K1, BL2 //.
13 K1, BL2 om.
14 K1, BL2 om.
15 TO1, TO3, TO4 //; K1, BL2 om.
16 TO1, TO4 tatrāya.
17 B om. //. TO1, TO3 /; TO2 mantra/.
18 TO1 sphuligāṭṭahāsa; TO4 sphulaiṅgāṭṭahāsaṃ; N1 sphuliṅgāṭṭamahāsa; BL2 sphaligāṭṭahāsa.
19 TO1, TO3, K1, BL2 //; TO4 and N1 om. /.
20 TO2 ity.
21 TO2 illegible after aparimitānu-. K1 parimitānusaṃśaṃ; BL2 aparimitānusaṃśaṃ.
22 TO1 -na, TO2 illegible between nīlakaṇṭhā- and -valokiteśvarasādhanaṃ. K1 nīlakaṇṭhāvalokiteśvarasādhanaṃ; BL2 nīlakaṇṭhāvalokiteśvara-.
23 K1 add. //śrāvaṇasya//. BL2 add. śrāvaṇasya//.

## 7.1 Sarvakāmaprasādhanahālāhalaparitoṣaṇavajranāmasamādhiḥ (Bhatt. no. 9 )

(1) hrīḥkārajñānaniṣpanno[1] hālāhalo[2] mahadvapuḥ/[3]
trinetraṃ trimukhaṃ caiva[4] jaṭāmakuṭamaṇḍitam//[5]
ardhacandradharaṃ[6] devaṃ[7] kapālakṛtaśekharam/[8]
jinabimbajaṭāntaḥsthaṃ[9] sarvābharaṇabhūṣitam//[10]
sitāravindanirbhāsaṃ[11] śṛṅgārādirasānvitam/[12]
ṣaḍbhujaṃ hasitaṃ vaktraṃ[13] vyāghracarmasuvāsasam//[14]
dakṣiṇe[15] kare varadaṃ[16] dvitīye[17] cākṣamālikam/[18]
tṛtīye śaranartanaṃ[19] vāme padmavibhūṣitam//[20]
dvitīye[21] kucadharaṃ[22] caiva[23] tṛtīye[24] dhanur eva ca/[25]
dakṣiṇe triśūlaṃ[26] caiva[27] sarpeṇa[28] pariveṣṭitam//[29]
vāme pūrṇakapālaṃ[30] tu[31] puṣpair nānāsugandhibhiḥ/[32]

---

1 K1 hrīkārajñānaniṣpannaṃ•; BL2 -pannaṃ•.
2 TO2, N1 halāhalo; TO4 hāhalo; K1, BL2 halāhala.
3 TO1, TO3 and K1 om. /.
4 K1 and BL2 add. a central dot.
5 TO1, TO2, TO3 /; TO4 -ta//; N1 -jaṭāmukuṭaṃmaṇḍitaṃ//.
6 TO2 ardhacandradharan.
7 K1, BL2 deva•.
8 TO1 kapālakṛtaśekhaṃ/; TO2 om. /. K1 kapālakṛtaśeṣara; BL2 kapālakṛtaśeṣaraṃ/.
9 TO1, TO3 -jaṭāntasthaṃ; TO2 jinabimbaṃjaṭāntasthaṃ; TO4 -jaṭāṃtasthaṃ; K1 -jaṭāntasthai•; N1 -jaṭāntakasthaṃ; BL2 -tasthai•.
10 TO1, TO2, TO4 /.
11 TO4 sitāraviṃdanibhāsa; K1 and BL2 add. a central dot.
12 TO1 and TO3 om. /. TO4 sṛgārādirasānvitaṃ/.
13 K1 and BL2 add. a central dot.
14 TO1 -carmmasavāsasam; TO2 -carmmaśavāsanaṃ/; TO3 om. //. TO4 vyārdhacarmasaṃbāsasaṃ; K1 -carmmasavāsanaṃ•; N1 -carmmasavāsasaṃ//; BL2 -savāsanaṃ/.
15 TO2 -ṇa.
16 K1 and BL2 add. a central dot.
17 TO2 -ya.
18 TO3 //; K1 cāpamālikāṃ/; BL2 cāpamālikaṃ//.
19 TO2 sara-; TO4 śaraṃṇaraṃnarttaraṃ; K1 and BL2 add. a central dot.
20 TO1 padmabhūṣitaṃ; TO2 padmabhūṣitam/; TO3 padmavibhūṣita/; TO4 padmavibhūṣita//; K1, BL2 padmabhūṣitaḥ/; N1 padmabhūṣitaṃ/.
21 TO2, K1, BL2 -ya.
22 TO2 kucadharañ.
23 K1 add. a central dot.
24 TO2 -ya.
25 TO4 //.
26 TO2, N1 -lan.
27 TO1, TO3, K1, BL2 ca; TO2, TO4, N1 tu.
28 TO1 pappeṇa.
29 TO1, TO2, TO3, TO4, K1, BL2 /.
30 TO1 -pāran; TO3, N1 -lan; K1 pūrṇaṃ kapālan•; BL2 pūrṇaṃ kapālan.
31 BL2 add. a central dot.
32 TO1 and TO3 om. /. TO4 trānāsugaṃdhibhiḥ//.

raktapadmasthitaṃ[1] caiva[2] lalitākṣepasaṃsthitam//[3]
ratnācalaguhāntaḥsthaṃ[4] bhāvayed yogacintakaḥ/[5]
sphuradbuddhamayair[6] bimbair[7] vividhaiḥ[8] prātihāryakaiḥ//[9]
(2) sarvāhāraṃ[10] tu bhuñjāno[11] nirvikalpasamādhinā/[12]
antarjalpo[13] japen[14] mantrān[15] bhāvayet kramayogataḥ/[16]
(3) kṣipraṃ[17] ca prāpyate[18] bodhir anuttarasukhāvahā//[19]
//sarvakāmaprasādhanahālāhalaparitoṣaṇavajranāmasamādhiḥ//[20]

1 TO3, BL2 -padmaṃsthitaṃ; TO4 -sthita; K1 -padmaṃsthita.
2 K1 and BL2 add. a central dot.
3 TO1, TO3, N1 /; K1 a central dot.
4 TO1, TO2, TO3, N1 -guhāntasthaṃ; TO4 -guhāṃtasthaṃ; K1 add. a central dot. BL2 -guhāntasthaṃ•.
5 TO2 yogicintakaḥ/; TO4, K1, BL2 //.
6 TO1 yad?; TO4 -ya; BL2 spharadbhuddhamayar.
7 B bimbaiḥ; TO1 bimbai; TO3 bbimbai; K1 bimbai•; BL2 bbimbai•.
8 TO2 vividhiḥ.
9 TO2 prahihāryyakaiḥ/; TO3, K1, BL2 /; N1 prātihāryekaiḥ//.
10 TO1, TO3, K1, N1, BL2 -hāran.
11 TO4 bhujāro; K1, BL2 bhujāno•.
12 TO4 //; N1 -dhiḥ// nā/.
13 TO3, K1, BL2 antajalpo; TO4 aṃtajjapo.
14 TO2, BL2 japet; TO4 jape, K1 kṣapen.
15 K1 and BL2 add. a central dot.
16 TO1, TO2 and TO3 om. /. TO2, TO4 //.
17 TO2, TO3, N1 kṣiprañ; TO4 kṣipraś.
18 TO4 -ta.
19 TO1, TO3 sukhāmahā/; TO2, BL2 /; K1 om. //. TO4 sukhānahā.
20 B //sarvvakāmaprasādhanahālāhalaparitoṣaṇavajrānāmasamādhiḥ//; TO1 sarvvakāma-prasādhanahalāhalapratitoṣaṇavajronāsamādhiḥ//; TO2 sarvvakāmaprasādhanahalāhala-paritoṣanavajronāmasamādhiḥ//; TO3 sarvvakāmaprasādhanahalāhalaparitoṣaṇavajrānāmasamādhiḥ//; TO4 sarvakāmaprasādhanahalāhalaparitoṣaṇavajonāmasamādhiḥ//; K1 sarvakāmaprasādhana•halāhalapanitoṣanavajrānāmasamādhiḥ//; N1 sarvvakāmaprasādhana-halāhalaparitoṣaṇavajranāmasamādhiḥ//; BL2 sarvvakāmaprasādhana•halāhalapanitoṣaṇavajronāmasamādhiḥ//.

## 7.2 Hālāhalasādhana (Bhatt. no. 27)

(0) namo hālāhalāya/[1]
(1) [(2-]pūrvavac chūnyatāṃ[3-2)] paryantaṃ bhāvayitvā/[4]
(2) hrīḥkārabījaniṣpannaṃ[5] hālāhalaṃ[6] mahākṛpam/[7]
trinetraṃ trimukhaṃ[8] caiva[9] jaṭāmakuṭamaṇḍitam//[10]
prathamāsyaṃ sitaṃ[11] nīlaṃ[12] dakṣiṇaṃ[13] vāmalohitam/[14]
śaśāṅkārdhadharaṃ[15] mūrdhni[16] kapālakṛtaśekharam//[17]
jaṭāntaḥsthajinaṃ[18] samyak sarvābharaṇabhūṣitam/[19]
sitāravindanirbhāsaṃ[20] śṛṅgārarasasundaram//[21]
ṣaḍbhujaṃ smeravaktraṃ[22] ca vyāghracarmāmbarapriyam//[23]
varadaṃ dakṣiṇe pāṇau[24] dvitīye[25] cākṣamālinaṃ/[26]
tṛtīye[27] śaranartanaṃ[28] ca[29] vāme cāpadharaṃ[30] tathā/[31]
dvitīye[32] sitapadmaṃ[33] ca[34] tṛtīye[35] stanam eva ca//[36]

---

1 TO1, TO2, TO3 hārāhalāya//; TO4, K1, N1, BL2 //.
2 TO2 illegible between pūrvvava- and -nyatāparyyāntaṃ.
3 B, TO1, TO2, N1, M chūnyatā; TO4 chunyatā; BL2 -taṃ.
4 B, K1 and N1 om. /. BL2 //.
5 TO1, TO3, TO4 hrīkārabījaniṣpannaṃ; K1 -bījaniṣpanna; BL2 -bījaniṣpanna•.
6 TO1 hārāhala; TO2 hālāha; TO3, TO4, K1, BL2 -la.
7 TO1 mahakṛpaṃ//.
8 TO1 -kha; TO4 -mūkhaṃ.
9 TO1 cai; K1 and BL2 add. a central dot.
10 TO1, TO2, TO3, K1, BL2 /; N1 jaṭāmukuṭamaṇḍitaṃ/; TO4 -makūṭa-.
11 TO1 add. /. TO2, N1 sitan; TO3 sita/.
12 B nīla; TO1 nīra; BL2 add. /.
13 TO1 and TO3 add. /. K1, BL2 dakṣiṇe.
14 TO3 vāme lohitaṃ/.
15 TO1, TO3, K1 śaśāk-; TO2 śaśākordhadharaṃ; TO4 śaśāṅkordhadharaṃ.
16 BL2 add. a central dot.
17 TO1 kapārakṛtaśekharam; TO3 -kṛtaśeṣaram; K1 kapārakṛtaśeṣaraṃ/; BL2 kapārakṛtaśeṣaṃ/.
18 TO1 jatāntaḥsthajinaṃ; TO2, BL2 jaṭāntasthajinaṃ; K1 jaṭāntasthaṃ jinaṃ.
19 TO1 om. /. K1, BL2 //.
20 TO1 -nibhāsaṃ; TO2 -ninurbhāsa; K1 sitār vidanirbhāsaṃ•.
21 TO1, TO2, TO3, K1, BL2 /.
22 TO1 -vaktra; TO3, TO4, N1 -vaktrañ; K1 smeraṃ vaktraṃ.
23 TO1, TO2, TO3, TO4, BL2 /.
24 BL2 add. a central dot.
25 TO1, TO3 -ya.
26 B -mālikam/; N1 cakramālinaṃ/.
27 TO1 -ya; K1 -yaṃ.
28 TO2 śaranaṃ; TO4 śaranarttanam; K1 and BL2 add. a central dot. N1 śara/ narttanaṃ.
29 TO1, TO2, TO3, TO4, K1, N1, BL2, M om.
30 TO1, TO3 kṣeparan; TO2 kṣepadharan; TO4 kṣeparaṃ; K1 akṣadharaṃ; N1 cāpadharan; BL2 akṣadharan.
31 BL2 //.
32 TO4 -ya.
33 TO2, N1, BL2 sitapadmañ; TO4, K1 śitapadmañ.
34 K1 and BL2 add. a central dot.
35 TO2 -ya.
36 TO1, TO2, TO3, TO4, K1, N1, BL2 /.

vāmajānunā[1] (2-sitāṃ svābhadevīṃ-2) dadhānaṃ/[3] vāmena[4] kamaladharāṃ[5] dakṣiṇena bhujena[6] bhagavadāliṅganaparāṃ[7] kusumaśobhitajaṭākalāpāṃ/[8] dakṣiṇapārśve[9] sarpaveṣṭitaṃ[10] triśūlaṃ[11] vāmapārśve padmasthakapālaṃ[12] nānāsugandhikusumaiḥ[13] sampūrṇaṃ[14] raktapadmacandre līlākṣepasthitaṃ[15] vibhāvayed[16] bhagavantaṃ/[17]

(3) tato mantraṃ[18] japet/[19] oṃ vajradharma hrīḥ/[20]

// iti[21] hālāhalalokeśvarasādhanam samāptaṃ[22]//[23]

---

1 TO4 -nulā.
2 TO1, K1 sitābhadevī; TO3, TO4, M sitābhadevīṃ; N1 sitāṃ svābhadevī; BL2 sitābhadevī•; TO2 sitābhadevīn.
3 TO1 dadhāna; N1 daṃdhānaṃ/.
4 TO1 vāmeṇa; TO4 vāmaina.
5 TO1 kamaladharaṃ; TO3 kamalaṃ dharaṃ; TO4 and N1 add. /. K1, BL2 kalasaṃdharaṃ/.
6 TO2 bhuje.
7 TO1 add. /. TO2 varagavadāliṅganaparāṃ/; K1 -parā/; TO3 add. /. BL2 bhagavadāliṅgaṇaparāṃ/; N1 bhagavadā/ liṅganaparāṃ/.
8 TO2 kusumaso-; TO4 -jaṭaikalāyāṃ//; K1 -taṃ jaṭākapālā/; N1 om. /. BL2 -kalopo/.
9 TO1, TO3, M dakṣiṇe pārśve.
10 TO2 and K1 add. /.
11 B add. a comma. TO1, TO3, TO4, K1, N1 and BL2 add. /. TO2 illegible after tri-.
12 TO1, TO2, TO3, TO4, K1, BL2 -lan.
13 K1 -dhiḥ kusumaiḥ.
14 B add. a comma. TO1, K1 -ṇā//; TO2 and TO3 add. /. TO4 and BL2 add. //. N1 saṃpūrṇaṃ/.
15 TO1 lilākṣepasthitam; K1 nī-; N1 lī/ lākṣepasthitaṃ/; BL2 nīlākṣepaṃsthitaṃ.
16 B -yet; TO1, TO3, K1, BL2 -yet//; TO2 visvayed.
17 TO3, K1 and BL2 om. /.
18 TO4 mantrañ.
19 B om. /. TO1, TO3, TO4, K1 //.
20 TO1 and N1 om. /. TO3, K1, BL2 //.
21 TO2, TO4 iti.
22 B, TO1, TO2, TO3, TO4, N1 and M om.
23 K1 add. //pauṣasya//. BL2 add. pauṣasya//.

## 7.3 Hālāhalasādhana (Bhatt. no. 28)

(0) oṃ[1] namo hālāhalāya[2]

(1) siddhaṃ hālāhalaṃ[3] natvā[4] jagadvyādhivināśanam/[5]
mahāmāyāmayaṃ tasya vakṣyāmi[6] sādhanakramam//[7]

(2) tatrādau tāvan mantrī[8] kvacin mano 'nukūle pṛthivīpradeśe[9] sthitvā[10]

(3.1) ādyanutpannāḥ[11] sarvadharmāḥ[12] prakṛtiparinirvṛtā[13] māyāsvapnagandharvanagaropamā[14] ity adhimokṣeṇa[15] ādhyātmakam[16] evam ahaṃjñānam[17] adhiṣṭhāya[18] daśadiganantaparyantalokadhātuvyavasthitān[19] buddhabodhisattvavidyākrodhagaṇān[20] avalambya[21]

(3.2) oṃ (22-sarvavit pūra pūra-22) āvarta āvarta her ity[23] anena vividhapūjāmeghān (24-sphārayitvā manasābhyarcyābhāvena-24) praṇamya[25] dharaṇītalavinyastajānumaṇḍalo[26] hṛdi[27] kṛtāñjalir[28] evaṃ[29] brūyāt[30]

---

1 B om.
2 K2 halāhalāya//; BL1 halāhalāye//.
3 K1, BL1 halāhala.
4 K1 nnatvā.
5 K2 jagatpāpavināsanaṃ; BL1 jagatvyādhivināsanam.
6 K2 -mī.
7 K2 has a central dot.
8 K2 add. a central dot.
9 K2 -vī•pra-.
10 K2 add. a central dot. BL1 add. a colon.
11 K2 ādyanutpannā•.
12 BL1 sarvaḥ dharmmāḥ.
13 K2 -nivṛtā•; BL1 prakirtiparinivṛtāḥ.
14 K2 māyāsvapnagandharvva•nagaropamā•.
15 K2, BL1 api mokṣaṇa.
16 K2 -kam•.
17 K2 ahamnā•ram; BL1 ahasnānam.
18 K2 add. a central dot.
19 K2 daśadiganantā•paryaṃtalokadhātuvyavasthitān•; BL1 daśadiganantāp-.
20 K2, BL1 -bodhisatvaṃ vidyā-.
21 K2 add. a colon. BL1 add. a central dot.
22 K2 sarvvavin dhūra dhūra; BL1 sarvavin dhure dhure.
23 K2, BL1 īti.
24 K2 sphārayīmanasā•bhyarccābhāvena; BL1 sphārayimanasābhyarccābhāvena.
25 K2 add. a central dot.
26 K2 -jā•numaṇḍalo; BL1 -vīlestūjānu-.
27 BL1 hṛdī.
28 BL1 -līr.
29 K2, BL1 eva.
30 K2 kruyyāt; BL1 kruyyāt•.

(3.3) samanvāharantu[1] māṃ[2] buddhā bhagavanto[3] (4-bodhisattvā mahākṛpā vidyādevyā-4)
mahākrodhāḥ[5] sarvalokadhātuvyavasthitāḥ[6]
ābodhi śaraṇaṃ[7] yāmi[8] buddhaṃ dharmaṃ[9] gaṇottamam/[10]
(11-dadāmi tebhya ātmānaṃ-11) pratigṛhṇantu[12] nāyakāḥ//[13]

(3.4) anādim iti[14] saṃsāre saṃsaratā[15] mayāsmin[16] vā[17] janmani yat kāyavākyamanobhiḥ[18]
pāpakaṃ karma ratnatrayācāryāpādhyāyamātāpitābhikṣubhikṣuṇīsāmānyasattvānāṃ[19]
sāvadyābhyākhyānaṃ[20] saṃvartanīyaṃ[21] dāridryaṃ[22] saṃvartanīyaṃ[23] vyādhiṃ[24]
saṃvartanīyaṃ/[25] (26-athavā yat svataḥ-26) karma kṛtaṃ kāritam anumoditaṃ[27] ca tatsarvaṃ[28]
yuṣmākaṃ purastād[29] yadā sadyaḥ kṛtaṃ yac ca[30] tat sarvaṃ[31] animitta-
yogenānupalambhamānaḥ[32] pratideśayāmi/[33]

---

1 K2 samantāharantu.
2 K2, BL1 mā.
3 B bhagavantā; K2 add. a central dot.
4 K2 bodhisatvamahākṛpāvidyādevyo; BL1 bodhisatvo mahākṛpā•vidyādevyo.
5 K2, BL1 -dhā•.
6 K2 -dhātu•vyavasthitā•.
7 BL1 saraṇaṃ.
8 K2 add. a central dot.
9 K2 add. a central dot. BL1 dharmma.
10 K2 has a central dot.
11 K2 dadāmityabhyarātmā•naṃ; BL1 dadāmi tebhyar ātmānaṃ.
12 K2, BL1 pratigṛhnantu.
13 K2, BL1 -kā•.
14 K2 ati•; BL1 ati.
15 K2, BL1 sansaratā.
16 K2 mayāsmin•.
17 K2 svā.
18 K2 kāyavāgmanobhi•; BL1 kāyavāgmano-.
19 K2 ratnatrayo•pādhyāyamātāpitābhikṣu•ṇisāmānya-; BL1 ratnatrayocāryyopādhyāyo mātāpitabhikṣubhikṣuṇīsāmānya-.
20 BL1 sāvadyo 'bhy-.
21 K2 -ttaniyāṃ•; BL1 -ttanīyāṃ.
22 K2 dāridro; BL1 drāridro.
23 K2 -niyaṃ•; BL1 add. a central dot.
24 K2 vyāpi; BL1 vyāpī.
25 BL1 om. /.
26 K2 advāyutadasutaṃ; BL1 advāyudasutaṃ.
27 K2 anumoditañ; BL1 anumoditaṃñ (anusvāra insertion).
28 K2, BL1 tatsarva.
29 B, BL1 purastāt.
30 K2 and BL1 add. kṛtaṃ.
31 K2 sarvva; BL1 sarva.
32 K2 add. //.
33 K2 om. /.

(3.5) anantabhūyo[1] [(2-]'py evaṃ[-2)] kariṣyāmi/[3] yac[4] ca prathamacittotpādam[5] upādāya yāvad anuttarā samyaksambodhir yāvac[6] ca nirupādhiśeṣo[7] nirvāṇadhātur[8] atrāntare sarvabuddhabodhisattvavidyākrodhagaṇaśrāvakapratyekabuddhānāṃ[9] anyeṣāṃ[10] ca pṛthagjanānāṃ[11] kuśalamūlaṃ[12] tatsarvam anumodayāmi/[13]

(3.6) buddhapremas[14] tāvad[15] anumodanayā[16]
utpādayāmi[17] paramaṃ bodhicittam anuttaram/[18]
yathā traiyadhvikā[19] nāthāḥ sambodhau kṛtaniścayāḥ//[20]
sarvaṃ caitat kuśalamūlaṃ[21] pariṇāmayāmi/[22]

(3.7) samyaksambodhau samyaksambuddhavartitayā[23] pariṇāmanayā[24] tato vajrāñjalir[25] vibhāvya/[26] oṃ sarvatathāgatasaṃśitāḥ[27] sattvānāṃ sarvasiddhayaḥ[28] saṃpadyantāṃ[29] sarvatathāgatāś ca[30] māṃ adhitiṣṭhetām/[31] oṃ svabhāvaśuddhāḥ[32] sarvadharmāḥ svabhāvaśuddho 'ham iti[33] udīrayan[34] svaśirasi[35] muñcet/[36] ata eva svabhāvaśuddhāḥ[37]

---

1 K2, BL1 jānannabhūyo.
2 K2 pevaṃ; BL1 'pi avaṃ.
3 K2 has a central dot. BL1 -yami.
4 K2 ye.
5 K2 thamacittotpādam•.
6 K2 yā•va.
7 K2 nirūpadhiseṣe; BL1 nirupadhiseṣe.
8 K2 add. a central dot.
9 K2 -krodhaḥgaṇasrokakapratyakabuddhāṇāṃ; BL1 -krodhaḥgaṇaśrāvakapratyakabuddhānāṃ.
10 K2 anyaṣāñ; BL1 aneṣāñ.
11 K2, BL1 pṛthakaja-.
12 BL1 kuśalamulaṃ.
13 K2 has a central dot.
14 K2, BL1 -prasas.
15 K2, BL1 tāva.
16 K2 add. a central dot.
17 K2 -mī.
18 K2 and BL1 om. /.
19 K2 trayethikā; BL1 treyathikā.
20 K2 -yā•; BL1 om. //.
21 K2, BL1 -la.
22 K2 has a central dot.
23 K2 -ddha•va-.
24 K2 pariṇāmana.
25 K2 -li; BL1 -lī.
26 B om. /. K2 add. a central dot.
27 K2, BL1 -saṃsitā.
28 K2 -ye•.
29 BL1 -yatāṃ•.
30 K2 add. a central dot.
31 K2 api tiṣṭhatām•; BL1 api tiṣṭatām//.
32 K2, BL1 -ddhā.
33 K2 and BL1 add. a central dot.
34 K2 udirayan•; BL1 udirayan:
35 K2 -aśī.
36 K2 mucet•; BL1 mucet/.
37 K2 svabhāva•.

sarvadharmā vimokṣāt/[1] vighnopaśamo[2] bhavatīti[3] nātra sandehaḥ[4] kāryaḥ/[5]
proktavikalpaprabandhād[6] vighnānāṃ[7]

(4.1) tadanu svahṛccandre[8] akārodbhavahṛdayaṃ[9] sphuradamitamayūkhaṃ[10] vinyasya[11] sarvadharmanairātmyaṃ[12] bhāvayet/[13] tebhyaḥ svahṛdayākṣarebhyo[14] raśmimeghān[15] saṃsphārya tat sampaśyet[16] sthiracalān[17] sarvabhāvān/[18]

(4.2) hālāhalarūpaṃ[19] niṣpādya[20] vicintayed[21] atraivaṃ[22] praveśya[23] māyopamaṃ sakalaṃ[24] jagad ity avagacchan[25] ātmānaṃ[26] hālāhalarūpaṃ[27]
śaśāṅkakoṭisaṃsṛṣṭaṃ[28] jaṭāmakuṭadhāriṇam/[29]
sitāravindanirbhāsaṃ nīlakaṇṭhaṃ[30] trinetrakaṃ//[31]
mahāpannagasamuddhṛtaraktapadmopari[32] sthitam/[33]
ratnācalaguhāntaḥsthaṃ[34] vyāghracarmāmbarasuvāsasam//[35]
paryaṅkena[36] samādhisthaṃ[37] caturbhujavirājitam/[38]

---

1 B om. /.
2 K2 -pamo; BL1 -pamāṃ.
3 B bhavati iti.
4 K2, BL1 -haṃ.
5 K2 kāya•; BL1 kāyaḥ.
6 BL1 prākta•vi-.
7 B vighnān/.
8 K2 sva•hṛcandre.
9 K2 -ya; BL1 -vaṃ hṛdaya.
10 K2 phulad-; BL1 phalad-; BL1 add. /.
11 K2 add. •manasā•. BL1 vinyase manasā/.
12 K2, BL1 -ya.
13 K2 -yat•.
14 K2, BL1 svahṛdayo kṣarebhyo.
15 K2 raśmi•meghān.
16 K2 saparśāt•; BL1 sasparśāt//.
17 K2 sthilacatvān; BL1 sthiracatvān.
18 K2 sarvabhāvāt•.
19 K2, BL1 halāhalarūpa.
20 K2 niṣpanna•; BL1 niṣpanna.
21 The rendering follows the Sandhi rule. B, K2, BL1 vicintayet.
22 B, BL1 tatraivaṃ.
23 K2 add. a central dot. BL1 add. /.
24 K2 śakalaṃ.
25 K2 apaga-; BL1 apagacchann.
26 K2 nnātmānaṃ•.
27 K2, BL1 halāhalarūpaṃ.
28 K2 śaśāṅka•ko-.
29 K2 -dhārinam•; BL1 om. /.
30 K2, BL1 nīlakaṃṭha.
31 K2 and BL1 om. //.
32 K2 mahāpagasamudbhutarakta-; BL1 -samudbhūtarakta-.
33 K2 sthitaṃ•.
34 K2 ratnācarāṭanhāntastha•; BL1 ratnācaraguhāntastha/.
35 B vyāghracarmma(-āmbara-)suvāsasam; K2 and BL1 om. //.
36 K2 paryyaṃke•na•.
37 B samādhisthaṃ(sthitaṃ); K2 add. a central dot.
38 K2 caturabhūjavirājitam•; BL1 caturbhūja-; BL1 om. /.

kuṇḍikākṣadharaṃ[1] vīraṃ[2] amitābhakṛtaśekharam//[3]
triśūlam[4] ūrdhvakhaṭvāṅgaṃ[5] kulikābaddhayaṣṭikam/[6]
cintayet[7] tasya[8] vāmena[9] dakṣiṇena[10] kapālakam//[11]
kusumaparipūrṇaṃ[12] kulikaṃ[13] ca kṛtaphaṇaṃ[14] bhagavantam[15] avalokayantam/[16]
(4.3.0) tataḥ[17] pañcāṅgavinyāsaṃ[18] mudrābhir mantrasaṃhatābhiḥ[19] kuryāt/[20]
(4.3.1) uttānabhājo[21] karayor nibandhapārśve[22] cañcalatayā[23] śikhāyāḥ[24] parvadvitīyaṃ[25] khalu
saṃspṛśet/[26] nyasyeta[27] [(28-]tālau karapārśvataś[-28)] ca mūlamudreyam/[29]
asyā eva tu mudrāyās[30] tarjanyā viparītataḥ/[31]
veṣṭayitvā[32] ca tālābhyāṃ[33] avaṣṭabhya [(34-]śiro bhavet//[-34)]
imām eva[35] nyaset[36] mūrdhni viparītaprayogataḥ/[37]
śikhā[38] bhavati tasyaiva hālāhalaniṣevinaḥ//[39]

---

1 K2 -ṣapara•śu; BL1 -ṣaparaśu.
2 K2 add. a central dot.
3 K2 amṛtāmbhakṛtaśeṣaraṃ and a colon; BL1 amitābhakṛtaśeṣaraṃ/.
4 K2 triśūram.
5 K2 ūrdhna•khatvāṅga; BL1 ūrddhakhatvāṅga•.
6 K2 kulikā•baddhayesthikam•; BL1 -baddhayasthikam/.
7 K2 cintayat; BL1 cintaya.
8 K2 add. a central dot.
9 K2 vāmeṇa.
10 K2 add. a central dot. BL1 -ṇana.
11 K2 has a central dot. BL1 om. //.
12 K2 add. a central dot.
13 K2, BL1 -añ.
14 K2, BL1 kṛtahana.
15 K2 add. a central dot.
16 K2 -ta•; BL1 -yetam/.
17 K2 tata.
18 K2 pañcāṅga•vinyāsa.
19 K2 mmaṃtramahat; BL1 mmantramahatābhiḥ.
20 K2 abhikuryyāt•.
21 K2 -jā.
22 K2 nibandhe pārṣeva; BL1 nibandhepāṣeva.
23 K2 vaśyālatayā•; BL1 veśyālatayā.
24 K2 -yā•; BL1 śiṣāyāḥ.
25 BL1 -tiyaṃ.
26 K2 saspṛśyet•, BL1 //.
27 BL1 nyaseta.
28 K2 elokarapārśvataś; BL1 elākarapārśvataś.
29 K2 has a central dot.
30 BL1 mudrāyā.
31 K2 vīrītatā; BL1 virītataḥ.
32 K2 vestayitvā.
33 K2 add. a central dot.
34 K2 śiro bhavet•; BL1 śirodbhavet/.
35 BL1 meva.
36 K2 -se•; BL1 -se/.
37 K2 viparitā•prayoga; BL1 -ga.
38 BL1 sikhā.
39 K2 halāhala•niṣavina•; BL1 halāhalaniṣevinaḥ.

pṛthag[1] muṣṭidvayaṃ[2] baddhvā[3] madhyame[4] kṛtaśṛṅkhale/[5]
tāre[6] śūcī[7] ca tālau ca pārśvataḥ[8] kavaco bhavet/[9]
vikṣipya[10] tālatām eva kalpayed[11] astrakarmibhiḥ//[12]
tārā tarjanī[13] tālo 'ṅguṣṭhaḥ[14] dhārā 'nāmikā[15] madhyā śikhīti[16] paryāyaḥ/[17]

(4.3.2) athāsāṃ[18] mudrāṇāṃ mantrā bhavanti/[19] oṃ saḥ svāhā[20] hālāhalahṛdayaḥ/[21] oṃ jvalini[22] svāhā śiraḥ/[23] oṃ prajvālanadīpāya[24] svāhā[25] śikhā/[26] oṃ arghyāya[27] svāhā[28] kavacaḥ[29] sarvāṅge/[30] anantaśaktigarbhā[31] phaṭ/[32] astraṃ karadvaye/[33]

---

1 K2, BL1 pṛthak.
2 K2 muṣṭi•dva-.
3 K2 add. a central dot.
4 K2 -yeme.
5 K2 kṛta•śṛṅkhale•; BL1 śṛṅṣale/.
6 K2, BL1 tārera.
7 K2 add. a central dot.
8 K2 -ta•.
9 K2 has a central dot. BL1 om. /.
10 K2, BL1 -pe.
11 K2, BL1 kalpad.
12 K2 has a central dot. BL1 om. //.
13 B add. a comma.
14 B add. a comma.
15 B add. a comma.
16 BL1 śikhiti.
17 K2 paryāya•; BL1 paryāyaṃ.
18 K2 athāśāṃ.
19 K2 has a central dot and //.
20 K2 add. a colon and //. BL1 add. /.
21 K2 hālāhalahṛdaya •.
22 K2, BL1 jvalinī.
23 K2 and BL1 om. /.
24 K2 -ye.
25 K2 add. a central dot. BL1 add. /.
26 K2 -kha; BL1 -kha/.
27 K2 aghrāye; BL1 aghrāya.
28 K2 add. a central dot. BL1 add. //.
29 K2 -ca; BL1 -ca/.
30 K2, BL1 -ga.
31 K2 anantaṃ śaktigarbhā•; BL1 anantaṃ śaktigarbhā.
32 B om. /. K2 add. a central dot.
33 K2 om. /.

(4.4) tad eva svayam[1] evāhaṃ āryahālāhala[2] ity [(3-]ahaṅkāravān ātmānaṃ[-3)] hālāhalaṃ[4] bhāvayed[5] yāvat[6] khedo na jāyate/[7]

(4.5) [(8-]sati ca[-8)] khede[9] svahṛccandre svajvālahūṃkāraṃ[10] vinyasya[11] tanmayūkhāvabhāsini[12] ca paryanteṣu mantreṣu[13]
mantrākṣarāṇi[14] vinyasya[15] kuryāj[16] japaṃ[17] samāhitaḥ/[18]
hṛdayaṃ[19] vā japen[20] [(21-]mantraṃ mālāmantram athāpi[-21)] vā//[22] hṛnmantrakoṭijapte tu mālāyā[23] lakṣajāpayā/[24]
sarvathā tasya[25] sidhyanti[26] sampattivyāpayo[27] 'khilāḥ//[28]

(4.6) yāvad icchaṃ japaṃ kṛtvā[29] [(30-]bhāvanām api[-30)] śaktitaḥ/[31] kṣamayitvā[32] tato[33] nāthaṃ[34] preṣayet[35] mūlamudrayā//[36]

---

1 K2, BL1 -yem.
2 K2 āyahalāhala; BL1 māyahalāhala.
3 K2, BL1 ahaṃkāra cātmānaṃ.
4 K2, BL1 halāhalaṃ.
5 K2 add. a central dot.
6 K2 -vavat.
7 K2 has a central dot. BL1 om. /.
8 K2 satī ca khede•; BL1 sacita.
9 K2 add. a central dot.
10 K2 sajvāla-.
11 BL1 -se.
12 K2 vahāsīti; BL1 -khā ca hāsīti.
13 K2, BL1 om.
14 K2 maṃtra•kṣarāṇi; BL1 -ṇī.
15 K2 vicintya; BL1 vicinte.
16 The rendering follows the Sandhi rule. B kuryyāt; K2 and BL1 add. a central dot.
17 K2 -pa; BL1 jāpa.
18 K2 -ta•; BL1 -ta.
19 BL1 -yam.
20 K2 add. a central dot. BL1 -pet/.
21 K2 maṃtramālāmaṃtra yathāpi; BL1 mantramālāmantra yathāpi.
22 K2 has a central dot. BL1 /.
23 K2 māḥ lāyā.
24 K2 -yāḥ•.
25 K2 add. a central dot.
26 K2 -yeti; BL1 -yati.
27 B -vyādhayo; K2 -vyāpaya.
28 K2 has a colon. BL1 om. //.
29 K2 add. a central dot.
30 K2, BL1 bhāvanāpi.
31 K2 -ta•; BL1 om. /.
32 K2 kṣapayitvā.
33 BL1 tatvo.
34 K2 -tha; BL1 -thaḥ.
35 K2 preṣayat; BL1 prekhayit.
36 K2 has a central dot. BL1 om. //.

(5.1) atha paṭavidhānena bhagavantam ārādhayitum[1] icchati tadā paṭe[2] pūrvoktarūpaṃ[3] lakṣayed[4]
[(5-]ity ayaṃ[-5)] paṭavidhiḥ/[6]
dvitīyaṃ[7] khathyate[8]
suvarṇavarṇaṃ[9] yadi vā trinetraṃ
bhujadvayopetasunīlakaṇṭham/[10]
ratnācalasthaṃ[11] susamāhitaṃ[12] tanuṃ[13]
halāhalaṃ[14] piṅgalajaṭaṃ likhec[15] ca//[16]
ākrāntapādau[17] vasunīlarūpāv
ardhaṃgatoddaṇḍakṛtasvakāyau/[18]
pārśvadvaye[19] nātham[20] udīkṣamāṇau[21]
likhec[22] ca sarpau[23] purataḥ[24] kapālam//[25]
puṣpair[26] vicitraiḥ[27] paripūrṇam[28] etat
padadvayaṃ[29] hastadvayaṃ samantāt/[30]
[(31-]pramāṇam etat kathitaṃ jinena[-31)]
adhas tu jānusthitadhūpahasto[32]

---

1 K2 -yim; BL1 ālādhayīm.
2 K2, BL1 pate.
3 K2, BL1 -pa.
4 B lakṣayet.
5 K2 ity•eva; BL1 iteva.
6 K2 -dhi// //; BL1 // //.
7 K2 dvitīya; BL1 dvitiya.
8 K2 karppate; BL1 kappaṃta.
9 K2, BL1 -ṇa.
10 K2 bhūjadvayoppeṭasunīlakaṃṭha•; BL1 bhūjadvayoppetasunīlakaṇṭhaḥ.
11 K2, BL1 -stha.
12 K2, BL1 -tan.
13 K2, BL1 tava.
14 K2, BL1 halāhala.
15 K2 likhaṃñ (anusvāra insertion); BL1 liṣañ.
16 K2 om. //.
17 B ākrāntapādau (pucchau); K2 ākrāntapādau pucchau; BL1 ākrānta•pādau pucchau.
18 K2, BL1 -rūpārddhagatoddaṇḍakṛtasvakāyau: .
19 K2 -ya; BL1 -yo.
20 K2 -tha; BL1 -thas.
21 K2 sudīkṣamāno; BL1 udhiksamāno.
22 K2 likhac; BL1 liṣac.
23 K2, BL1 saṃghau.
24 K2 -ta•.
25 K2 has a central dot. BL1 /.
26 K2, BL1 puṣpai.
27 K2 -trai•.
28 BL1 -ṇamy; K2 add. a central dot.
29 K2 pataddhayaṃ; BL1 paṭa-.
30 K2, BL1 samantān•.
31 B (pramāṇam etat kathitaṃ jinena); K2 pramānam etat kathitaṃ jinena•; BL1 add. a central dot after jinena.
32 K2 -dhupahastā; BL1 -dhūpahastā.

niveśanīyaḥ[1] khalu[2] sādhako 'tra//[3]

(5.2.0) ato 'nyatamapaṭaṃ[4] prasārya[5] prātar evāpatitagomayena maṇḍalakaṃ kṛtvā mūlamudrayā[6] [(7-]mantrasahitayā āvāhayed abhinayena paṭākṛtau pañcāṅganyāsaṃ ca kuryāt pūrvoktavidhibhir eva mudrābhiḥ samantrasahitābhiḥ/

(5.2.1) tato mūlamudrayaiva[-7)] pañcopacāreṇa[8] mānasībhiś[9] ca pūjābhiḥ[10] sampūjya[11] bhagavantaṃ[12] sambodhayan[13] mudrām upadarśayet[14] kaniṣṭaśṛṃkhalā[15] [(16-]baṃdhitālā pṛṣṭhe[-16)] niveśitā/[17] [(18-]śikhādhārāvidhiḥ yau[-18)] tarjanyau[19] kṛtasūcakau/[20]

(5.2.2) oṃ visphuliṅgāṭṭahāsakeśari[21] iti[22] mantraḥ/[23]

(5.2.3) tataḥ pūrvoktarūpam ātmānaṃ[24] vicintayet/[25]

(6) tadrūparahito[26] vā[27] navasṛtaṃ[28] pūrvavat[29] mālāmantraṃ[30] trayodaśavārān uccārayet/[31]

---

1 K2 nivesanī•ya; BL1 nivyesanīyā.
2 BL1 ṣalu.
3 K2 and BL1 has a central dot.
4 K2, BL1 netamapaṭa.
5 K2 pasāryyā; BL1 prasāryā.
6 K2, BL1 -yauva.
7 K2, BL1 om.
8 K2, BL1 pañcāpacāreṇa.
9 BL1 māṇosībhiś.
10 K2 pūjābhi•.
11 K2 -yaḥ; BL1 add. a central dot.
12 BL1 -ta.
13 K2 sacodhayan; BL1 sabodhayan.
14 K2 upadarśayat•; BL1 add. //.
15 B kanyaśṛṅkhale(-lā) vā; BL1 kaniṣṭaśṛṃṣalā.
16 B sandhitārāpṛṣṭhe; K2 baṃdhitālā•pṛṣṭhe•.
17 B niveśetāṃ/; K2 and BL1 have a central dot.
18 K2, BL1 śikhādhārāvidhiyo.
19 BL1 tajjanyau.
20 K2 -sucakauḥ; BL1 -sucakau//.
21 BL1 -hāśakesar.
22 K2 ti.
23 K2 and BL1 om. /.
24 K2, BL1 -na.
25 K2 has a central dot. BL1 om. /.
26 K2 -pa•rahito.
27 K2 add. i?.
28 K2 navasṛta; BL1 -tau.
29 K2 -vata; BL1 pūrvokta.
30 K2 mālāmaṃtra•; BL1 -tra.
31 K2 has a central dot. BL1 //.

(7) maṇḍalakagomayena vyādhiṃ[1] pralepayet/[2] ṣaṇmāsaiḥ[3] sarvavyādhayaḥ[4] praśāmyanti/[5] athavā lakṣam ekaṃ japet/[6] sarvāśāparipūriṇo[7] 'tra na[8] kāryā[9] vicāraṇā/[10] tatrāryam[11] āryahālāhalahṛdayamantraḥ/[12] namaḥ sarvabuddhabodhisattvebhyo mahāpuruṣavṛṣabhebhyo[13] namaḥ āryāvalokiteśvara maheśvara mahāsthāmaprāpta[14] āryamaitreya samantabhadra āryavajrapāṇiprabhṛtibhyo[15] mahābodhisattvaprabhṛtibhyo[16] namskṛtvā bhagavann[17] āryāvalokiteśvara
(18-tava hṛdayam-18) āvartayiṣyāmi[19] sarvakāmaprasādhanam/[20]
adhṛṣyaṃ[21] sarvabhūtebhyo bhavamārgavināśanam//[22]
tadyathā/[23] he[24] bodhisattva priyabodhisattva[25] mahābodhisattva he hale[26] āryāvalokiteśvara[27] paramamaitracitta hitacitta[28] mahākāruṇika[29] kuru kuru mahāvidyeti[30] dhuru dhuru dharādhara calendrācala namas te 'stu hrīḥ sarvasattvābhayaprada[31] harihariharivāhanodbhava[32] bhavābhava[33] bhavānagha[34] kuru kuru (35-kuru kuru-35) (36-ghuru

---

1 K2, BL1 -dhī.
2 K2, BL1 //.
3 K2 -sai•; BL1 ṣan-.
4 K2 -ya•.
5 K2 -yati•; BL1 prasāmyanti•.
6 K2 and BL1 om. /.
7 BL1 sarvosāparipūriṇā.
8 K2, BL1 om.
9 BL1 kārya.
10 K2 -ṇāḥ; BL1 has a central dot.
11 K2 -yyem.
12 K2 āryya•halāhalahṛdaye mantra//; BL1 āryyahalāhalahṛdaye mantraḥ//.
13 BL1 mahāpuruṣabhebhyo.
14 K2 add. a central dot.
15 K2 āryya•vajrapāṇiprabhitibhyo•; BL1 -pāṇīprabhṛtībhyo.
16 K2 om.; BL1 -satvabhṛtibhyo.
17 K2, BL1 -vānn.
18 K2 tatvahṛdaye•; BL1 tatvahṛdaye.
19 K2 māvartayiṣyāmi•; BL1 māvarttayīṣyāmī.
20 K2 has a central dot. BL1 //.
21 K2 -ya•; BL1 -ye.
22 K2 has a central dot. BL1 -nāsanaṃ•.
23 K2 sayaṃthīdaṃ; BL1 saṃyathīdaṃ.
24 BL1 ha.
25 K2 priye-.
26 K2, BL1 hare.
27 BL1 -lokṛteśvara.
28 K2, BL1 om.
29 K2 and BL1 add. a central dot.
30 K2 -vipati•; BL1 -vipati.
31 BL1 add. a central dot.
32 BL1 harīharīharīvāha-.
33 K2 bhāva•bhava.
34 K2, BL1 -vānaya.
35 K2, BL1 turu turu.
36 BL1 dhuru dhuru.

ghuru[-36)] suru suru [(1-]muru muru[-1)] curu curu suprasāditāmalavimalamūrti[2] āryāvalokiteśvara[3] mahākāruṇika[4] [(5-]kṛṣṇājinadhara akṣadhara[-5)] daṇḍadhara jaṭāmakuṭāvalambita pralambadhara[6] mala mala kala kala cala cala tala tala nala nala [(7-]phala phala[-7)] [(8-]hulu hulu[-8)] hulula halāhala ho[9] bodhisattva[10] mahābodhisattva[11] namas te 'stu [(12-]hṛṃ hṛṃ hṛṃ[-12)] kuru kuru hṛdayam anusmara samayam anusmara jātim[13] anusmara[14] idaṃ me[15] kāryaṃ[16] kṛtamanorathaṃ[17] me[18] paripūraya[19] svāhā/[20] preṣaṇaṃ[21] ca sarvavad iti/[22]

(8) iti puṇyajanaḥ[23] sarvo[24] bhūyād hālāhala[25] iti/[26]
ahaṃ[27] ca mañjughoṣaḥ[28] syāṃ jagadāśāprapūrakaḥ//[29]
ābodhi mañjughoṣasya pādāmbujarajorasā/[30]
prajñāpālitanāmnāyaṃ[31] kathitaḥ padmabhṛdvidhiḥ//[32]
[(33-]// āryahālāhalasādhanaṃ samāptam//[-33)]

---

1 K2, BL1 om.
2 K2, BL1 -sādatām-.
3 K2 add. a central dot.
4 BL1 -ṇīka.
5 BL1 kṛṣṇāñjikanadhara rukṣadhara akṣaradhara.
6 B pralambaladhara; K2 add. a central dot. BL1 pralamyadhara•.
7 K2, BL1 hala hala.
8 BL1 hṛlu hṛlu.
9 K2, BL1 he.
10 K2 add. a central dot.
11 K2 mahābodhi•satva; BL1 om.
12 K2, BL1 hūṃ hūṃ hūṃ.
13 BL1 jātīm.
14 K2 add. a central dot.
15 K2 om.
16 K2 ekāryaṃ; BL1 -ya.
17 K2, BL1 kurumano-.
18 K2 ma; BL1 om.
19 K2 parīpūraye; BL1 aparīpūraya.
20 K2 has a central dot. BL1 // //.
21 K2 -ṇañ.
22 K2 has a central dot. BL1 //.
23 K2, BL1 -yājanaṃ.
24 K2 sarvva; BL1 sarvaṃ.
25 K2 has a central dot. BL1 hālāhalad.
26 K2 has a central dot. BL1 //.
27 K2, BL1 ahañ.
28 K2, BL1 -ṣa.
29 K2, BL1 -āsāprapūraka.
30 K2 -bhūjarajorasāḥ; BL1 -būjarajorasā//.
31 BL1 -tamāmnāyaṃ.
32 K2 padmabhūdvidhiḥ//; BL1 padmabhudvidhiḥ//.
33 K2 // iti sādhanasamucaye āryyahalāhalasādhanadvātriṃsatyadhikaśatatamapaṭala//132//; BL1 iti sādhanasamucaya āryyahalāhalasādhanadvātriṃsatyadhikaśatatamapaṭalaḥ //132//.

## 7.4 Hālāhalasādhana (Bhatt. no. 29)

(0) [(1-]oṃ namo halāhalāya[-1)]//[2]
natvā hālāhalaṃ[3] bhaktyā sarvāśāparipūrakaṃ/[4]
saṃkṣepād[5] ucyate[6] tasya sādhanaṃ karuṇātmanaḥ//[7]

(1.1) ādau[8] manohare[9] sthāne[10] sulipte[11] candanādinā/[12]
avatārya[13] paṭādisthaṃ[14] bhagavantaṃ pūjayed[15] iti//[16]
puṣpādiḍhaukanamantraḥ/[17] oṃ vajrapuṣpe hūṃ[18] oṃ vajradhūpe hūṃ[19] oṃ vajradīpe
hūṃ[20] ityādinā/[21] oṃ[22] sarvatathāgatapūjāmeghaprasarasamūhe[23] sphura[24] himaṃ[25]
gaganakaṃ[26] hūṃ[27] sarvapūjāḍhaukanamantraḥ/[28]

(1.2) prapūjya[29] puratas[30] tasya[31] niṣadya[32] ca[33] sukhāsane/[34]

---

1 B, TO1, TO2, TO3, TO4, K1, N1, BL2 om.
2 B om. //.
3 TO1, TO3, BL1 halāhalaṃ; TO4 halāhala; BL2 harāhalaṃ; K2 halāhalaṃ•.
4 TO1 sarvvāśāpalip-; TO4, K1 sarvāsā-; K2 sarvāsāparīpūrīkaṃ; BL1 sarvāsāparīpūrakaṃ•; BL2 sarvvāsā-.
5 TO1, TO2, sakṣepād; K2, BL1 -kṣapād.
6 K2 om.
7 K2 and BL1 om. //.
8 N1 add. /.
9 TO3, K1, BL2 -ra; K2 -rama; BL1 manonama.
10 K1 and BL2 add. a central dot.
11 K2, BL1 -ta.
12 TO4 //; K2 om. /. BL1 -no.
13 K2 avatāryye•.
14 K1 padādisthaṃ•; K2 patādistha; BL2 padādi-; BL1 patādi-.
15 TO1 pūjayad.
16 K2 and BL1 add. a central dot.
17 B om. /. TO1 -pūṣpādiḍhauśamantraḥ/; TO3 -ḍhauvaṇamantraḥ/; TO4, N1 //; K1 -ādidauṣanamaṃtra//; K2, BL1 -maṃtra//; BL2 -ḍhauṣanamantraḥ//.
18 B add. a comma. TO1 and N1 add. //. TO2, TO3, TO4, K1 and BL2 add. /. K2 add. a central dot.
19 B add. a comma. TO1, TO2, TO3, TO4, K1, N1 and BL2 add. /. K2 add. a central dot.
20 TO1, K1 and BL2 add. //. TO2, TO3 and N1 add. /.
21 TO1, TO4, N1 -di/; TO2 om. ityādinā/. TO3 -di; K1 iti; K2 -diṇā•; BL1 -diṇā; BL2 iti ādi.
22 TO1, TO3, TO4, K1, BL2 om.
23 K1 and BL2 add. a central dot.
24 TO1 sphurabhis; TO2, TO4, N1 sphara; K1, BL2 sphala; K2 sphūra.
25 TO1 om.; K2, BL1 hi.
26 TO3, BL2 gagaṇa-; K2, BL1 saṃgaga-.
27 TO1, TO3, TO4, K1, N1 and BL2 add. //. TO2 add. /. BL1 add. a central dot.
28 TO1 om. /. TO2, TO4, K1, BL2 //; TO3 -kanaṃ mantraḥ/; K2 -tra//; BL1 sarvapūjāḍhaukanamaṃtra//; N1 sarvva// pūjāḍhaukanamantraḥ//.
29 TO1 sapūjya; BL2 add. a central dot.
30 BL1 puras.
31 TO4 tusya; BL2 add. a central dot.
32 K2, BL1 niṣadā.
33 K2 and BL1 add. a central dot.
34 K1, BL2 -naṃ/; K2, BL1 sukhāne.

maitrīṃ[1] vibhāvya jagati[2] karuṇāṃ[3] ca mahākṛpaḥ//[4]
vinyasya[5] hṛdaye[6] mantraṃ[7] hrīḥkāraṃ[8] candrapṛṣṭhataḥ/[9]
paśyed[10] gaganam[11] āpūrṇaṃ[12] sambuddhais[13] tatsutaiḥ[14] sphuṭam//[15]
(1.3) hrīḥkārāṃśujapūjābhis[16] tān[17] prapūjya[18] gatabhramaḥ/[19]
deśanādyaṃ[20] tu[21] pāpāder[22] vidadhyāt[23] puṇyavṛddhaye//[24]
triratnaśaraṇādyagryaṃ[25] [(26-]mantram enam[-26)] udīrayet/[27]
sarvadharmāgranairātmyadyotakaṃ[28] karuṇāmanaḥ//[29]
oṃ svabhāvaśuddhāḥ[30] sarvadharmāḥ svabhāvaśuddho 'ham iti/[31]
mantrārtham āmukhīkurvan[32] sarvaṃ[33] vastu mahātmanā/[34]
grāhyagrāhakanirmuktaṃ[35] bhāvayej[36] jñānamātrakam//[37]

---

1 TO1, TO3, K1, K2, BL1, BL2 maitrī; TO2 maitrīm.
2 K1 and BL2 add. a central dot.
3 TO1, TO2, TO3, K1, K2, N1, BL2 -ṇāñ.
4 K2 -pa; BL1 om. //.
5 TO1 viśyane; K2 vinesya.
6 TO1, TO3, K1, BL2 hṛdayaṃ; TO2, K2 -ya.
7 K2, BL1 maṃtra; BL2 -tra; K1 add. a central dot.
8 TO1, K2 hrīkāra; TO2 -kāra; TO3 hrīkālaṃ; K1, BL2 hrīkāraṃ; BL1 hrīḥkāra.
9 K2 and BL1 om. /.
10 TO1, BL1 paśed; K1, BL2 paśyaṃ.
11 TO3, K1, BL2 gagaṇam; K2, BL1 gamaṇam.
12 K1 ārṇam; K2 āpura; BL1 āpūra; BL2 āṇḍaṃ?•.
13 B sambuddhaiḥ; TO1, TO3, K1, K2, BL1 saṃbuddhaiḥ; BL2 saṃbuddhais.
14 B, BL1 sannataiḥ; K1 tatsutai; K2, BL1 susubhaiḥ; BL2 tatsatai.
15 K1 sphutaṃ/; K2 sphuṭa; BL1 -ṭa•; BL2 /.
16 TO1 hrīkāraśuptapūjābhis; TO3, TO4 -śukapūjābhis; K1 hrīḥkārāṃśukapūjābhis; K2 hrīkārāṇḍaja-; BL1 hrīkārāguṇḍaja-; BL2 hrīkāraṃśukapūjābhis.
17 TO1 tan; K2, BL1 om.
18 TO1 apapūjya; K2 prapūjān//; BL1 prapūjāna//.
19 TO1 -ma/; TO3, K1, BL2 //; K2, BL1 satatramaḥ.
20 TO1 deśanāden; TO2 deśanāṃ; K1 deśanādis; K2 deśanāyanta; N1, BL1 deśanādyan; BL2 deśanādim.
21 K2 om.; BL1 na•.
22 TO1,TO3 pāpāde; TO2, K2, BL1 pāpādevī; K1, BL2 pāpāde•.
23 TO2, K2 dadhyāt; BL1 dhyāt•.
24 TO1 pūṇyavṛddhaye/; TO2 -yet/; TO3, BL2 /; K1 and K2 om. //. BL1 puṇye vṛddhaye.
25 TO1, TO2, TO3, K1, N1 -ādyagraṃ; TO4 -ṇāyagraṃ; K2 triśaraṇagamaṇādyagraṃ; BL1 trisaraṇādyagraṃ; BL2 -ādyagraṃ•.
26 TO1 mantrenam; TO3 illegible after mantra-. K1 om. enam. BL2 mantraṇam.
27 TO1 udirayet//; TO3, TO4, K1, BL2 //; K2, BL1 -yan•.
28 TO1 -dyatakaṃ; TO2 -nairātmmād-; TO4 sarvadharmāgre nai-; K2 -ka; BL1 -sarvvadharmmāgraṇairātme dyotaka; BL2 -ya•dyotakaṃ.
29 TO2 /; TO4, K1, BL2 karuṇāmalaḥ//; K2, BL1 -maṇaḥ.
30 K2 svabhāvasu•ddhāḥ; BL1 -śuddhā.
31 TO1, TO3, TO4, K1, K2, N1, BL2 //.
32 B -kurvvana; K1 and BL2 add. a central dot.
33 TO2 sarvva; TO4 sarvas; K1, N1, BL2 sarvvam; K2, BL1 sarva.
34 TO4 sadātmanā/; K2 and BL1 have a central dot.
35 TO1, TO3, TO4 grāhyagrāhyaka-; K2 -kavinir-; BL1 grāhegrāhakavinirmuktaṃ; BL2 grāhyagrāhyakanirmuktaṃ//.
36 The rendering follows the Sandhi rule. B, TO1, TO2, TO3, TO4, K1, N1, BL1, BL2 -yet; K2 -ye.
37 K2 and BL1 om. //.

pratyātmavedyaṃ[1] taṃ[2] dṛṣṭvā[3] hrīḥkāraṃ[4] śaśisaṃsthitam/[5]
tajjam[6] abjaṃ[7] sitaṃ[8] dhyāyāt[9] hrīḥkārānvitapuṣkaram//[10]
(2.1) tataḥ saṃsphārya[11] buddhaughaṃ[12] jagad[13] buddhaṃ[14] vidhāya ca/[15]
punaḥ[16] praveśya[17] tatraiva[18] bhūyād[19] dhālāhalaḥ[20] svayam//[21]
trimukhaḥ[22] ṣaḍbhujaḥ[23] śānto[24] ratnācalaguhāśrayaḥ/[25]
raktapadmasthite[26] candre[27] lalitākṣepasaṃsthitaḥ//[28]
sitapītamahānīlamūlavāmetarānanaḥ/[29]
vyāghracarmāmbaras[30] tryakṣaḥ[31] sarvābharaṇasundaraḥ//[32]
varadākṣaśarān[33] savye[34] vāme[35] satkāminīkucam/[36]

---

1 TO1, K2, BL1 -dya.
2 TO2, TO4 ta; K2, N1, BL1 tan.
3 K1 add. a central dot.
4 TO2, K2, BL1 -kāra.
5 TO1, TO3 and TO4 om. /. TO2 śaśisasthitam/; K2 śaśīsaṃsthitaṃ•; BL1 a central dot.
6 TO1 tarjjam; TO4 om.
7 TO2, K2, BL1, BL2 abja; TO4 om.; K1 ajja.
8 TO4 om.; BL1 sita.
9 TO1 and TO3 add. //. K1, BL2 a central dot.
10 TO1, TO3, K1, BL2 hrīkārānvitapuṣkaram//; TO2 illegible between hrīḥ- and -rāṃvitapuṣkaram//. K2 hrīḥkārāṃvitapuskaram•; BL1 -vītapuṣkaram.
11 BL1 sasphāryya.
12 K1 and BL2 add. central dot. K2, BL1 -gha.
13 TO2 jaga; BL1 jagaḥ.
14 K2, BL1 dhataṃ.
15 K1 om. /. K2 has a colon. BL1 and BL2 have a central dot.
16 TO1 puna.
17 TO4 pravairāya; K2, BL1 praveśa.
18 BL2 add. a central dot.
19 TO2 bhūyā; K1 add. dhātvā. BL2 dhyātvā.
20 The rendering follows the Sandhi rule. B, TO1, TO3, N1 hālāhalaḥ; TO2 harohalaḥ; TO4 hālāhaḥ; K1, BL2 halaḥ; K2 dhālāhala; BL1 dhālāhala.
21 TO1 /; TO2 soyaṃ//; TO4, K2 and BL1 om. //.
22 K1, K2, BL1 -khaṃ.
23 K1 -jaṃ; K2 khaḍbhujaṃ; BL1 khaḍbhūjaṃ.
24 TO4 -tau; K2, BL1 -tā; BL2 add. a central dot.
25 TO1, TO2, K1, BL2 ratnācaraguhāśrayaḥ/; TO4 //; K2 ratnācaragṛhāśrayeḥ; BL1 ratnācaragṛhāśraya•.
26 K1, BL2 -maḥ sthite; K2 -masite.
27 TO4 -dra; K1 and BL2 add. a central dot.
28 TO1, TO2, TO3, K1, BL2 /; K2 lalītākṣepasaṃsthitaṃ; BL1 lalitākṣepasaṃsthitaṃ
29 TO1 -nīravāmetasenanaḥ/; TO3 -nīlavāmetasenanaḥ/; TO2 sitapitamahānīra-; TO4 nīlacāmetasenanaḥ//; K1 -nīlāvāmatasenanuḥ/; K2 sītapītamahānīlamūlavāmetarānanaṃ; BL1 sitapītamahānīlamūlavāmetarānanaṃ; BL2 sitapītamahānīlā•vāmatasenanuḥ.
30 K2 -barās.
31 TO2 trākṣaḥ; K2 tryakṣa•.
32 TO1 and TO3 om. //. TO2, N1 /; K2 -dara; BL1 -bharanasundaraḥ.
33 TO4 -kṣarān; K2 -kṣamarānasa; BL1 varādākṣamarāna.
34 TO1, TO2, TO4 savyair; K1 savyeḥ; K2 save; BL2 add. a central dot.
35 TO1 vameḥ; TO2, TO3, TO4, K1, N1, BL2 vāmaiḥ.
36 K2 -kuca; BL1 -kuca•.

sitapadmaṃ[1] ca[2] kodaṇḍaṃ[3] bibhrāṇaṃ karapallavaiḥ//[4]
kapālaṃ[5] vāmato[6] nyasya[7] nānāpuṣpaiḥ prapūritam/[8]
viṣabhṛdveṣṭitaṃ[9] savye[10] triśūlaṃ[11] ca tathāmbuje//[12]
amitābhamaṇisaccūḍaḥ[13] kapālakṛtaśekharaḥ/[14]
śaśikhaṇḍayutottuṅgajaṭāmakuṭasañcayaḥ//[15]
vidhūtakalpanājālaḥ[16] sphuradbuddhaugharaśmikaḥ/[17]

(2.2) itthaṃ hālāhalo[18] bhūtvā[19] svahṛtkaṇṭhaśirahsu[20] ca//[21]
hūṃ[22] āḥ[23] oṃ[24] bhāvayec[25] candre[26] nīlāruṇasitān[27] kramāt/[28] hṛtkaṇṭhayos tathā madhye[29]
dhyeyo[30] hrīḥ[31] candrasaṃsthitaḥ//[32]

(2.3) tataḥ sthiracalān[33] sarvabhavān[34] bhāvayaṃs[35] tāṃs[36] tadākṛtīn/[37]

---

1 TO1, TO2, TO3, N1 -mañ; BL1 -ma; TO4 -maś; K2 -māṃ.
2 BL1 om.
3 TO2 kodaṇḍa; BL2 add. a central dot.
4 TO1, TO3 -vaḥ/; TO2 karallavaiḥ//; K1 kalapallavaḥ//; K2, BL1 kalapallavai; BL2 kalapallavaḥ//.
5 TO1, BL2 kapāraṃ; N1 kapālam.
6 N1 add. /.
7 K2 vinyasya; BL1 vinyasye.
8 TO4 prapuritaṃ/; K2 om. /. BL1 prapūrītaṃ.
9 TO2 vesthitaṃ; K2, BL1 viṣabhūdveṣitaṃ.
10 K2 save; BL1 savya; BL2 add. a central dot.
11 TO1 -śūraṃ; TO2, TO4, N1 -añ; K2, BL1 -sūrañ.
12 TO1, TO3, K1, BL2 /; TO4 -jai/; K2, BL1 -jai.
13 K2 -maṇimuktaṃ; BL1 -maṇimadbhūtaṃ.
14 TO1 kapārakṛśeṣaraḥ; TO3 -śeṣaraḥ; K1 -śeṣaraḥ//; K2 -śeṣaraṃ •; N1 //; BL1 -śeṣaraṃ//; BL2 -śeṣaraḥ/.
15 TO1 and TO3 om. //. TO2 /; TO4 -kuṭāsañcayaḥ/; K2 -yatoṭuṅga •jatāmakuṭasaṃcayaṃ; N1 -mukuṭasañcayaḥ/; BL1 śaśikhandayatotuṅga •jaṭāmakuṭasaṃcayaṃ; BL2 -saṃcayaḥ//.
16 TO1 -jaraḥ; TO2 -jāraḥ; BL1 vidhuta-; BL1 //.
17 TO2 spharadbuddhau-; TO2, TO4, N1 //; K1, BL2 pharad-; K2 spharaṇabuddhogharaśmikaḥ. BL1 sphuraṇabuddhaugharasmikaḥ.
18 TO1 hālahālā; K2, BL1 halāhalā.
19 BL2 add. a central dot.
20 TO1 -śīraḥsu; TO2 -ṭhasirase; K1, BL2 -śiraḥsūcaḥ; K2, BL1 svahṛkaṇṭhaḥ śiraḥśū.
21 TO1, TO3 /; K1, K2 and BL2 om. ca//. BL1 a central dot.
22 TO2 om.
23 K1 āṃ//; K2 ā, BL2 oṃ ā//.
24 TO2 hūṃ.
25 K1 svabhāvayac; BL1 -vaya.
26 K2, BL1 -dra; BL2 add. a central dot.
27 K2 -ṇaśitā; BL1 -sītān.
28 TO1, TO2, TO4, K1, K2, BL1 //; BL2 -ān//.
29 TO2 -yayā; BL1 -ya; BL2 madhya•yo.
30 TO2, BL2 om.; K2 dhyeyā; BL1 dhyayā.
31 TO1, TO2, TO3, TO4, K1, N1, BL2 hrīś.
32 TO1 candrasthitaḥ/; TO2, TO3 /; K1 caṃdrasaṃsthitaṃ//; K2 candrasaṃsthitaṃ; BL1 om. //. BL2 candrasaṃsthitaṃ//.
33 TO1 -carāṃ; K2, BL1 -calā; BL2 sthitacalāṃ.
34 B, TO1, TO2, TO3, TO4, K1, K2, N1, BL2 bhāvān.
35 TO4, K1 tāvayaṃs; K2 bhāvayen; BL1 bhāvayan; BL2 bhāvayaṃ•.
36 TO1 tāś; TO3, K1 tās; K2 ta; N1 tām; BL1 na; BL2 stās.
37 TO4 // and add. sarvān/. K2, BL1 -tiṃ; BL2 //.

[(1-]sarvāsat kalpanirmukto[-1)] japen[2] mantraṃ[3] samāhitaḥ//[4]
oṃ hālāhala[5] hrīḥ/[6]
antarjalpam atispaṣṭaṃ[7] na [(8-]drutaṃ na vilambitam/[-8)] yathāsukhaṃ[9] japam[10] kṛtvā[11]
visṛṣṭau pratipūjya[12] ca/[13]
saṃstutya[14] ca dṛḍhīkṛtya[15] samuccārya[16] śatākṣaram[17]//
[(18-]tatredaṃ śatākṣaram[-18)]
oṃ vajrasattva samayam[19] anupālaya[20] vajrasattvatvenopatiṣṭha[21] dṛḍho me bhava[22]
sutoṣyo me bhava[23] supoṣyo[24] me bhava[25] anurakto[26] me bhava[27] sarvasiddhiṃ[28] me
prayaccha[29] sarvakarmasu ca me cittaṃ[30] śreyaḥ[31] kuru[32] hūṃ hahahaha[33] hoḥ[34] bhagavan[35]
sarvatathāgatavajra mā me muñca[36] vajrībhava[37] mahāsamayasattva āḥ/[38]

---

1 K2 sarvāsaṃkalpanirmukto; BL1 sarvvāsaṃkalpanirmmukto.
2 TO1 japet.
3 TO1, TO4, K1, K2, BL2 mantra.
4 TO1, TO2 /, K1, BL2 // //; K2 -ta •; BL1 om. //.
5 TO1, TO2, TO3, TO4, K1, N1, BL2 halāhala.
6 TO1, TO3, TO4, N1 //; K1 hrī// //; K2 and BL1 om. /. BL2 // //.
7 TO1, TO3, TO4, K1 -ṭan; TO2 etispaṣṭhaṃ; K2 atīspaṣṭaṃ; BL2 -ṭan•.
8 TO1 viracitaṃ/; TO3 drutan na vilambitam; TO4 drutan na vilambitam //; K1, BL2 drutan na vilambitam/; K2 drutaṃ na viraṃbitaṃ•; BL1 drutaṃ na viraṃbitaṃ.
9 TO1 jath-; BL1 -suṣaṃ.
10 K2, BL1 japeṃ; BL2 add. a central dot.
11 BL2 add. a central dot.
12 K2, BL1 -pūji.
13 TO2, TO4, N1, BL1 //; K2 a central dot.
14 K2, BL1 -stubhya.
15 TO1, K2 dṛḍhikṛtya; BL1 -tye; BL2 add. a central dot.
16 TO1 samucārya; K2, BL1 muccāryya.
17 TO1 śaktaraṃ; K2, BL1 śatākṣaḥ.
18 TO1, TO2, TO3, TO4, K1, N1, BL2 om.; K2 tatraivaṃ śatākṣaram//; BL1 tatraivaṃ śatākṣaram•.
19 K2 -yem.
20 B add. a comma. TO1 -āraya; BL2 -ye •.
21 B add. a comma. TO2 -satvatenopa-; BL2 -paviṣṭha•; K2 vajrasatvatvenapaṭiṣṭa.
22 B add. a comma. K1 and BL2 add. a central dot.
23 B add. a comma. TO2 add. /. K1 and BL2 add. a central dot.
24 TO1, TO3, K1, BL2 -ṣo.
25 B add. a comma. K1, BL1 and BL2 add. a central dot.
26 TO1 anukto; K2 anurakṣyo; BL1 anurakṣyo •.
27 B add. a comma. K2 add. a central dot.
28 TO4 -siddhir; K1, K2, BL1 -siddhi.
29 B add. a comma. K2 prayeccha; BL1 prayaṃcha; BL2 add. a central dot.
30 TO4, K2, BL1 citta; BL2 add. a central dot.
31 K2 śraya.
32 B add. a comma.
33 BL2 hahaha.
34 TO1, TO3, TO4, K1, BL2 ho.
35 BL2 add. a central dot.
36 B add. a comma.
37 BL2 vajabhava.
38 TO1, TO4, K1, N1, BL2 //; K2 and BL1 om. /.

oṃ kṛto[1] vaḥ[2] sarvasattvārthaḥ[3] siddhir[4] dattā[5] yathānugā/[6] gacchadhvaṃ[7] buddhaviṣayaṃ[8] punar āgamanāya[9] ca//[10]
anena sañcodya[11] enaṃ[12] mantram uccārayet/[13] oṃ akāro[14] mukhaṃ[15] sarvadharmāṇām[16] ādyanutpannatvān[17] mur[18] iti/[19]
(3) dhyānāt samutthito[20] yogī[21] dānaṃ[22] dadyāt[23] svaśaktitaḥ/[24]
(4) rūpādikāmān[25] bhuñjāno[26] nirastāśeṣakalpanaḥ/[27]
prāpnoty[28] anuttarāṃ[29] bodhim[30] acirāt sādhakottamaḥ//[31]
likhitvā[32] sādhanaṃ prāptaṃ[33] yan[34] mayā[35] śubham[36] uttamam/[37] tena[38] kṛtsnaṃ[39] jagad bhūyād[40] acireṇa hālāhalaḥ//[41]

---

1 BL1 kṛtva.
2 K2 va.
3 K2 sarvatvārtha•.
4 TO1 siddhi; TO2, TO3, K1, K2, BL1, BL2 siddhiṃ.
5 TO1, TO3, TO4, K1, K2, BL1, BL2 datvā.
6 TO1, TO3, TO4, K1, K2 and BL1 om. /. BL2 a central dot.
7 K2 -dhoṃ•; BL1 -dhoṃ; BL2 gaccha tvaṃ.
8 TO4 -ya; K1, BL2 bodhiviṣayaṃ; K2 budhaviṣayaṃ.
9 TO1, TO3 -maṇāya; BL1 ogamanāya.
10 K2 om. //. BL1 has a central dot.
11 BL2 add. a central dot.
12 BL2 eva.
13 TO1, TO2, TO3, TO4, K1, N1, BL2 //; K2, BL1 -yan//.
14 TO4 -rā; K2 -ra.
15 TO1, TO3, K1, K2, BL2 mukha; BL1 muṣo.
16 K2 -ṇāṃm (anusvāra insertion).
17 The rendering follows TO2, TO4, N1, BL1 and BL2: ādyanutpannatvāt. The rendering follows the Sandhi rule. B, TO1, TO3 ādyam anutpannatvāt; K1 ādyanutpannatvā; K2 ādyaṃ anutpannatvāta.
18 K1 om.
19 TO1, TO3, TO4, K1, K2, N1, BL1 //; BL2 om. /.
20 BL1 samudhrito; BL2 sumutthito.
21 BL2 add. a central dot.
22 K2, BL1 -nan.
23 K2 dadhyāsya; BL1 dadyā.
24 TO1, N1 and BL1 om. /. TO4, K1, BL2 //; K2 śaktita•.
25 K2 add. a central dot. BL2 -māna.
26 K1 abhuṃjāno; K2, BL1 bhuñjamāno; BL2 add. a central dot.
27 TO1, TO3, TO4, K1, N1, BL2 //; K2 nirastāmeṣakalpana//; BL1 nirastām eva kalpanaḥ.
28 K2 -nobhy.
29 K2, BL1 -rā.
30 BL2 add. a central dot.
31 TO1 /; TO2 sārakottamaḥ; TO3 /; K2 om. //. BL1 -ma•.
32 TO2 nikh-; BL2 sikhitvā.
33 K2, BL1 -ta; BL2 add. a central dot.
34 K1, K2, BL1 jan; BL2 jat.
35 K2, BL1 mayo.
36 K2, BL1 subham.
37 TO4, K1, BL2 //; K2 om. /. BL1 -māṃ.
38 BL1 tyena.
39 TO4 tvaṃ?; K1, BL2 kṛtsna; K2 add. ena. BL1 kṛtsnena.
40 K2, BL1 -yod; BL2 add. a central dot.
41 TO1, TO3, K1, N1, BL2 halāhalaḥ//; TO4 halāhala; K2 hālāhalaṃ//; TO2 halāhalaḥ.

//hālāhalasādhanaṃ[1] (2-samāptam iti-2)//

1 TO1, TO2, TO3, K1, BL2 //halāhala-; TO4 //halāhalasādhadhaṃ; K2, N1, BL1 om.

2 TO1, TO2, TO3, TO4, N1 om.; K1 and BL2 om. iti. K2 iti sādhanasamuccaye halāhalasādhana caturtriṃśatyadhikaśatatamapaṭalaḥ//134//; BL1 iti sādhanasamucayahalāhalasādhana çaturtriṃśatyadhikasatatamapaṭala//134//.

## 8.1 Padmanarteśvaralokanāthasādhana (Bhatt. no. 30)

(1) pūrvoktavidhānena[1] viśvapadmacandre[2] raktahrīḥkārapariṇataṃ[3] padmanartteśvaram[4] ātmānaṃ bhāvayet//[5] sattvaparyaṅkaniṣaṇṇaṃ[6] dvibhujaikamukhaṃ[7] raktaṃ[8] sakalālaṅkāradharaṃ[9] amitābhamukuṭaṃ[10] vāmapārśve[11] pāṇḍaravāsinīsamāśliṣṭaṃ[12] āliṅganābhinayasthitavāmabhujena[13] raktapadmadharaṃ[14] nartanābhinayena[15] sūcīmudrayā[16] vikāśayadavaradakṣiṇakaram//[17]

(2) tata[18] oṃ kāyavākcittavajrasvabhāvātmako[19] 'ham[20] iti mantram[21] uccārayet/[22]

(3.0) tadanv aṣṭasu[23] dikṣv[24] aṣṭadevīṃ[25] cintayet/[26]

(3.1) tatrāṣṭadalaraktapadmapūrvapatre[27] vilokinī[28] śuklā[29] raktapadmadharā/[30]

(3.2) dakṣiṇapatre[31] tārā[32] haritā[33] palāśapadmadharā/[34]

---

1 BL2 add. a central dot.

2 TO1, TO3 -candrahrīḥkārapariṇataṃ padmanartteśvarapadmacandre; K1 add.hrīḥkārapariṇataṃ padmanṛtyeśvarapadmacaṃdre. BL2add. hrīḥkārapariṇataṃ•padmanṛtyeśvarapadmacandre.

3 TO1, TO2 hrīḥkāra-; TO4 raktaṃ hrīḥkāra-; BL2 add. a central dot.

4 TO4 padmanarttaśvaram; K1, BL2 padmanṛtyeśvaram.

5 B om. //. TO1, TO2, TO3, TO4 and N1 add. /.

6 TO2 add. /; TO3 satvaparyaṅka-; BL2 satvaparyaṃka-; TO4 sattvaparyaṅkaṃ; K1 sattvaparyaṅkaṃ niṣaṇaṃ; N1 sattvaparyaṅkaṃ niṣaṇṇaṃ/; BL2 add. a central dot.

7 TO4 and N1 add. /.

8 BL2 add. a central dot.

9 TO4 sakalālaṃkārodharaṃ; K1 add. a central dot. BL2 sakalālaṃ•raṃkāradharaṃ•

10 TO1 add. //. TO2, amitābhamakuṭaṃ/; TO3 amitābhamukuṭāṃ//; TO4 add. /. K1 amitābhamakuṭāṃ/; BL2 amitābhamakuṭāṃ//.

11 K1 vāmavārśve.

12 TO1 pāṇḍarāvāsinīsamāślitaṃ; TO2, TO3, TO4, N1 and BL2 add. /. K1, BL2 pāṇḍarāvāsinīsamāśliṣṭaṃ/.

13 TO1 āliṅgaṇābhinayasthitavāmabhūjena; K1 āliṅgaṇābhinayasthita•vāmabhujena; BL2 add. a central dot.

14 TO2, TO4, K1, N1 and BL2 add. /.

15 TO1 natanābhinayana; K1 and BL2 add. a central dot.

16 TO1 sūcimudrayo; TO2, TO4 sucīmudrayā; K1 sūcīmudrāyā.

17 B vikāśayadaparadakṣiṇakaram/; TO1, TO2 vikāsayadaparadakṣiṇakaram//; TO3 vikāśeyadaparadakṣiṇakaraṃ//; K1 vikāśaya•davaradakṣiṇakaram//.

18 B, TO2 tataḥ; K1, BL2 oṃ tata.

19 N1 -vajrāsvabhāvātmako.

20 The rendering follows the Sandhi rule. B 'haṃ.

21 TO2 mantra.

22 TO1, TO3, K1 //; TO2 ccārayet/.

23 K1, BL2 asta.

24 B, K1, BL2 dikṣu.

25 TO1 aṣṭadevi; TO2 aṣṭadeviś; TO3, K1, BL2 devī; TO4, N1 aṣṭadeviś.

26 TO1 cintayat//; TO3, TO4, K1, BL2 //.

27 TO1 tatrāṣṭadararaktapadmaūrvvapatre; TO2 -padmapūrvvapātre; K1, BL2 -padme pūrvvapatre.

28 K1 valokinī; BL2 add. a central dot.

29 TO1, TO2, TO3, TO4, K1, N1 and BL2 add. /.

30 B om. / and add. a semicolon. TO2 -padmadhara; TO3, TO4 -padma/.

31 TO1, TO3, K1, BL2 dakṣiṇe patre.

32 K1, N1 and BL2 add. /.

33 K1 add. /.

34 B om. / and add. a semicolon. TO2, TO3 palāsaṃpadmadharā/; N1 haritapalāśapadmadharā/; BL2 illegible before - dharā/.

(3.3) paścimadale[1] bhūriṇī[2] pītā[3] cakranīlotpaladharā/[4]
(3.4) uttaradale bhṛkuṭī śuklā[5] pītapadmadharā/[6]
(3.5) pūrvakoṇadale[7] padmavāsinī pītā[8] māñjiṣṭhapadmadharā/[9]
(3.6) [(10-]dakṣiṇakoṇadale[11] vajrapadmeśvarī[12] ākāśavarṇā[13] sitapadmadharā/[14]
(3.7) paścimakoṇadale[15] viśvapadmā[16] śuklā kṛṣṇapadmadharā/[17]
(3.8) uttarakoṇadale[18] viśvavajrā[19-10)] viśvavarṇā[20] viśvapadmadharā/[21]
(3.9) sarvā[22] etāḥ[23] sattvaparyaṅkiṇyo[24] dvibhujaikamukhāḥ[25] saumyāḥ/[26] karṇikāyāṃ[27] tu[28] bhagavān eva/[29]
(4) tato mantraṃ[30] japet/[31] oṃ hrīḥ padmanarteśvara[32] hūṃ/[33]
// padmanarteśvaralokanāthasādhanam[34] samāptam[35]//

---

1 K1 and BL2 add. a central dot.
2 TO2 bhūriṇi.
3 TO1, TO3, K1, N1 and BL2 add. /. TO2 pītābha.
4 B om. / and add. a semicolon. TO2 -nīlotparadharā/.
5 K1, N1, BL2 śukla.
6 B om. / and add. a semicolon. TO1 and TO3 add. //. K1, BL2 pītadharā/.
7 TO4 -dalai.
8 K1 and BL2 add. /.
9 B om. / and add. a semicolon. TO4 māṃjiṣṭha/ vajrā.
10 TO4 om.
11 N1 add. /. BL2 dakṣiṇe koṇadale.
12 K1 add. /. BL2 add. a central dot.
13 TO1 -varṇṇa.
14 B om. / and add. a semicolon. K1 and BL2 add. a central dot.
15 K1 paścimakoṇe; BL2 paścimakoṇe•.
16 TO1, TO2 -mo; K1 and BL2 add. a central dot.
17 B om. / and add. a semicolon. K1, BL2 kṛṣṇadharā•.
18 K1 uttarakoṇe dale•; BL2 add. a central dot.
19 N1 illegible after viśva-.
20 TO2 om.; K1 and BL2 add. a central dot. N1 illegible before -varṇā.
21 TO1, TO3 //.
22 TO1, TO3 sarvvāḥ.
23 TO1, TO3, K1, BL2 etā.
24 B sattvaparyyaṅkinyo; TO1, TO3 satvaparyaṅkinyo; TO2 paryyaṃkiṇo; N1 paryaṅkiṇyo; K1 satvaparyyakinyo•; BL2 satvaparyakinyo•.
25 TO4 add. /. K1 -mukhā; BL2 -mukha.
26 TO1, TO3, K1 and BL2 om. /. TO4 om.
27 K1 -yān.
28 K1 and BL2 add. a central dot.
29 TO1, TO3, K1, BL2 //.
30 N1 mantre.
31 B add. mantraḥ. TO1, TO3, TO4, K1, N1, BL2 //.
32 K1, BL2 padmanṛtyeśvara.
33 TO1, TO2, TO3, K1, BL2 //; TO4 and N1 om. /.
34 K1, BL2 // padmanṛtyeśvaralokeśvarasādhanaṃ.
35 B, TO1, TO2, TO3, TO4, K1, N1 om.; BL2 samāpta.

## 8.2 Padmanarteśvarasādhana (Bhatt. no. 31)

(0) namaḥ padmanarteśvarāya/[1]

(1) tatra viśvapadmopari candre raktahrīḥkārapariṇataṃ[2] padmanarteśvaraṃ raktavarṇam ekamukhaṃ jaṭāmukuṭinaṃ[3] trinetraṃ aṣṭabhujaṃ sarvālaṅkārabhūṣitaṃ sarpayajñopavītam ardhaparyaṅkena tāṇḍavaṃ[4] prathamabhujadvayena nṛtyābhinayaṃ[5] dvitīyadakṣiṇabhujena[6] hṛdi vikāśayantaṃ[7] sūcīmudrāṃ[8] vāmabhujena raktapadmaṃ[9] śirasi dhṛtaṃ tṛtīyabhujadvayena vajravaddaṇḍatriśūladharaṃ[10] caturthabhujadvayena akṣasūtrakuṇḍikādharaṃ aṣṭadevīparivṛtaṃ evaṃbhūtaṃ[11] padmanarteśvaralokanāthaṃ bhāvayet/[12]

(13-//padmanarteśvarasādhanam//-13)

---

1 TO2 //.
2 TO2 -parinataṃ.
3 TO2 jaṭāmakuṭinaṃ/.
4 B add. a comma. TO2 tāndavaṃ/.
5 TO2 add. /.
6 TO2 dvitiya-.
7 TO2 vikāśayaṃ.
8 TO2 sūcīmudrā.
9 TO2 raktapadma.
10 TO2 vajatridaṇḍītriśūradharaṃ.
11 TO2 evaṃbhūṣaṃ.
12 TO2 //.
13 TO2 oṃ.

## 8.3 Padmanarteśvarasādhana (Bhatt. no. 32)

(1) pūrvoktavidhānena[1] śūnyatābhāvanānantaram[2] viśvapadmasthacandropari[3] sitahrīḥkāraṃ vibhāvya//[4]

(2.1) tatpariṇāmena[5] padmanarteśvarāmnāyenāryāvalokiteśvarabhaṭṭārakam[6] ātmānaṃ vibhāvayet/[7] ekamukhaṃ aṣṭādaśabhujam[8] ardhaparyaṅkiṇaṃ[9] amitābhamakuṭamaṇḍitaṃ[10] sarvakarair[11] viśvapadmadhāriṇam//[12]

(2.2) yoginīvṛndaparivṛtaṃ[13] dakṣiṇavāmapārśvasthitatārāsudhanabhṛkuṭīhayagrīvaṃ[14] divyālaṃkālaṃ[15] vastrabhūṣaṇaṃ//[16]

(3) tato mantraṃ japet/[17] oṃ hrīḥ padmanarteśvara[18] hūṃ//[19]

(4) vyādhyādyupaśame[20] mahānuśaṃsaḥ/[21]
//iti[22] padmanarteśvarasādhanam[23] samāptaṃ[24]//

---

1 K1 and BL2 add. a central dot.
2 BL2 śūnyatābhāvanāntaraṃ•.
3 BL2 padmastha•candropari.
4 B, TO1, TO3 and TO4 om. //. TO2 and N1 add. /.
5 TO1, TO2 tatpariṇāmena.
6 K1 padmanṛtyeśvarāmnāya•āryyāva-; BL2 padmanṛtyeśvarāmnāya•nāryyāva-.
7 TO1, TO3, TO4, K1, BL2 //.
8 TO1 aṣṭādasabhujam; BL2 -bhuja•.
9 B arddhaparyyaṅkinaṃ; TO1 ardhaparyaṅkiṇa; K1 ardhaparyyaṃkinaṃ/. BL2 mardhaparyyaṃkitaṃ•.
10 B amitābhajaṭājūṭamaṇḍalaṃ and a comma; TO4, N1 amitābhajaṭājūṭamaṇḍalaṃ; TO1, TO3 amitābhajaṭājūṭamaṇḍalaṃ/; TO2 amitābhajaṭāmakuṭamaṇḍalaṃ/; K1 amitābhamakuṭamaṇḍalaṃ; BL2 add. /.
11 TO1 sarvvarai; TO3, K1, BL2 sarvvakarai.
12 B om. // and add. a comma. TO2, TO4 and N1 om. //. TO1, TO3, K1, BL2 /.
13 B add. a comma. TO1, TO3, K1, N1 and BL2 add. /.
14 B add. a comma. TO1 dakṣiṇavāmapārśve sthitārāsudhanabhṛkuṭīhayagrīvaṃ//; TO2 dakṣiṇavāmapārśve sthitatārāsudhanabhṛkuṭīhayagrīvaṃ/; TO3 add. //. TO4 dakṣiṇavāmapārśvasthitatārāsūdhanabhṛkuṭīhayagrīvaṃ/; K1, BL2 dakṣiṇavāmapārśve sthitārāsudhana•bhṛkuṭīhayagrīvau//; N1 add. /.
15 B, TO2, TO3, K1, N1, BL2 divyālaṅkāra; TO4 divyālaṃkora.
16 B, TO1, TO2, TO3, TO4, N1 /.
17 TO1, TO2, TO3, K1, BL2 //.
18 K1, BL2 padmanṛtyeśvara.
19 B /; K1, BL2 // //.
20 TO1 vyādhyādyapaśame.
21 TO1 mahānuśaṃsa//; TO2, TO3, K1, BL2 //; TO4 and N1 om. /.
22 TO4 iti.
23 TO1 padmanartteśvasādhanaṃ//; K1, BL2 padmanṛtyeśvarasādhanaṃ.
24 B, TO1, TO2, TO3, TO4, N1 om.; K1 and BL2 add. //caitramāsasya.

## 9.1 Harihariharivāhanodbhavalokeśvarasādhana (Bhatt. no. 33)

(1) pūrvoktavidhānena[1] śūnyatābhāvanānantaraṃ[2]
(2) sitahrīḥkāraniṣpannaṃ[3] harihariharivāhanodbhavaṃ[4] bhagavantam[5] āryāvalokiteśvaraṃ[6] sarvāṅgaśuklaṃ[7] jaṭāmakuṭinam[8] śāntaveśaṃ[9] dakṣiṇakareṇa[10] bhagavantaṃ[11] tathāgataṃ sākṣiṇaṃ[12] kurvantaṃ[13] dvitīyenākṣamālādhāriṇaṃ[14] tṛtīyena duḥkuhakaṃ[15] lokam[16] upadeśyantaṃ[17] vāmena[18] daṇḍadharaṃ[19] dvitīyena kṛṣṇājinadharaṃ[20] tṛtīyena kamaṇḍaludharaṃ[21] siṃhagaruḍaviṣṇuskandhasaṃsthitam[22] ātmānaṃ [(23-]bhāvayet// //[-23)]
(3) oṃ hrīḥ hūṃ[24] iti mantraṃ japet/[25]
//harihariharivāhanodbhavasādhanam[26] samāptaṃ[27]//

---

1 K1 add. a central dot.
2 N1 illegible between śūnyatābhā- and -nantaraṃ.
3 TO4 -kārainiṣpannaṃ; K1 sitahrīkāraniṣpannaṃ•; BL2 sitahrīkāraniṣpannaṃ•.
4 K1 add. a central dot.
5 TO1 -taṃm (anusvāra insertion); BL2 add. a central dot.
6 TO1 āyava-; TO2 -vara.
7 K1 sarvvāṅga•śuklaṃ•; BL2 add. a central dot.
8 TO2 illegible before -āmakuṭinam.
9 B add. a comma. TO2 śāntasave; K1 and BL2 add. a central dot.
10 K1 and BL2 add. a central dot.
11 TO1, TO3 -tan.
12 K1 śāntiṇam; BL2 śākṣiṇaṃ.
13 B add. a comma. K1 and BL2 add. /. N1 kurvvanta.
14 B dvitīyena akṣamālādhāriṇaṃ and a comma; TO1, TO3, TO4, BL2 dvitīyena varadadhāriṇaṃ/; TO2 dvitīyanākṣamālādhāriṇaṃ/; K1 dvitīyena varadadhāriṇī; N1 add. /.
15 BL2 -kuhaka.
16 BL2 loka.
17 B add. a comma. TO1, TO2 upadarśayantaṃ/; TO3 add. /. TO4 upadarśayet//; K1 saṃdarśayantaṃ; N1 upadaśayantaṃ/; BL2 saṃdarśayantaṃ//.
18 K1 māmena.
19 B add. a comma. TO1 śudadadha/; TO3 daṇḍadadhaṃ/.
20 B add. a comma. TO4, K1 and BL2 add. /.
21 B add. a comma. TO1, TO3 and TO4 add. //. TO2, K1 and N1 add. /. BL2 kamaṇḍarudharaṃ/.
22 TO2 siha-; K1, BL2 siṃhagaruḍaviṣṇuskandhasthitam.
23 B dhyātvā; TO1, TO2, TO3 dhyātvā//; TO4, N1 dhyātvā/.
24 TO2 add. /.
25 TO1, TO3 //; TO2, TO4, N1 and BL2 om. /.
26 TO1 //harihariharivāhanādbhavasādhanam.
27 B, TO1, TO2, TO3, TO4, N1 om.; K1 samāptam.

## 9.2 Hariharihariväahanodbhavalokeśvarasādhana (Bhatt. no. 34)

(1) ādau tāvan mantrī[1] sukhāsanāsīno[2] jagadabhyuddharaṇāśayaḥ[3] pāpa-deśanādikasaptavidhānuttarapūjāṃ[4] kṛtvā/[5]

(2.1) yaṃkāraniṣpannaṃ[6] vāyumaṇḍalaṃ[7] dhanvākāraṃ[8] nīlapatākāṅkitaṃ[9] tasyopari rephodbhavaṃ[10] raktavarṇam agnimaṇḍalaṃ[11] trikoṇaṃ[12] raktarephāṅkitaṃ[13] tadupari vaṃkāraparinispannaṃ[14] vāruṇamaṇḍalaṃ[15] vartulaṃ[16] śuklavarṇaṃ[17] śuklaghaṭamadhyāṅkitaṃ[18] tadupari laṃkārasambhavaṃ[19] mahendramaṇḍalaṃ[20] caturasraṃ pītavarṇaṃ pītatrisūcikavajracatuṣkoṇaśobhitaṃ[21]

(2.2) tadupari suṃkāraniṣpannaṃ[22] saptaratnamayaṃ[23] aṣṭāṅgaṃ[24] sumeruṃ[25] tasyopari paṃkārapariṇatam[26] viśvadalakamalaṃ[27] tasyopary[28] ātmānaṃ[29] vicintya//[30]

(2.3) oṃ hrīḥ hūṃ[31] krameṇa śirasi kaṇṭhe[32] hṛdi vinyasyātmānaṃ[33]

---

1 TO4 trī.
2 TO2 -sano; K1 and BL2 add. a central dot.
3 TO2, TO3, TO4, N1 add. /. K1, BL2 -raṇaṃ śayaḥ//.
4 TO1, K1 pāpadeśanādikaṃ sapta-; TO2 pāpadeśanādikaṃ sapha-; TO4 pāpadeśanādikasaptavidhānuttarapūjā; BL2 pāpadeśanādikaṃ•saptabhidhānuttarapūjāṃ.
5 B om. /. TO1 and TO3 add. //. K1 and BL2 add. a central dot.
6 TO2 -kāraṃ niṣ-; K1 and BL2 add. a central dot.
7 BL2 add. a central dot.
8 K1 and BL2 add. a central dot.
9 B add. a comma. TO1, TO3, N1 -ta; TO2 -kākitaṃ/; K1 nīlapaṭākāṅkitaṃ•; BL2 nīrapaṭākāṃkitaṃ•.
10 K1 -vaṃ •; BL2 add. a central dot.
11 B add. a comma. TO1, TO3, K1 and BL2 add. /.
12 K1 and BL2 add. a central dot.
13 B -rekhāṅkitaṃ; TO1, TO2 , TO3 and TO4 add. /. K1 and BL2 add. //. N1 -rekhāṅkitaṃ/.
14 TO2 vaṃkāraniṣpanna; K1 add. a central dot. N1 vaṃkāraniṣpannaṃ.
15 TO2 -la; TO3, K1 and BL2 add. /.
16 TO1 vatula; N1 om.
17 TO1, TO2 -ṇa; K1 add. a central dot. N1 add. /.
18 B śuklapatākāṅkitaṃ; TO1, TO3 śuklapatākāṅkitaṃ/; TO2 śuklaghaṭamadhyaṃkitaṃ/; TO4 add. //. K1 śuklapaṭāṅkitaṃ/; N1 add. /. BL2 śuklapaṭāṃkitaṃ/.
19 TO1 lakāra-; TO4 laṃkora-; K1 saṃkāra-; BL2 saṃkārasaṃbhavaṃ•.
20 TO4, N1 māhendra-; K1 add. a central dot. BL2 māhendramaṇḍalaṃ•.
21 TO1, TO2, TO3 pītatriśūkavajacatuṣkoṇaśobhitaṃ/; TO4 pītatriśūkavajracatuṅkoṇaṃ śobhitaṃ; K1 add. //. N1 pītatriśūkavajracatuḥkoṇaśobhitaṃ; BL2 pītatriśūcikavajacatuṣkoṇaṃ śobhitaṃ//.
22 TO1 sukāraniṣpannaṃ; TO2 vakāraniṣpanna vāruṇamaṇḍalavarttulaṃ śuklavarṇaśuklaghaṭamadhyāṅkitaṃ/ tadupari laṃkālasaṃbhavaṃ mahendramaṇḍalaṃ caturaśraṃ pītavarṇaṃ pītatriśūkavajacatuṣkoṇaśobhitaṃ/ tadupari suṃkāraniṣpanna; TO4, sūṃkāraniṣpannaṃ; K1, BL2 sūṃkāraniṣpannaṃ•.
23 K1 rapta-.
24 TO3, TO4 maṣṭāṅga; N1 aṣṭāśaṃ; BL2 -ga.
25 TO2 add. /. K1 and BL2 add. //.
26 K1 and BL2 add. a central dot.
27 TO1 viśvadara-; TO2 and N1 add. /.
28 The rendering follows the Sandhi rule. B, TO2, TO3, TO4, N1 tasyopari; TO1 -palim; K1, BL2 -parim.
29 TO3 mātmānaṃ; TO4 ātmāram.
30 B om. //. TO4 and N1 add. /.
31 K1, BL2 om.
32 K1 -ṭha.
33 TO2 -ātmā; K1 and BL2 add. /.

(2.4.1) anādikālasaṃcitakarmāvaraṇavigataṃ[1] harihariharivāhanodbhavaṃ[2] lokeśvaramūrtiṃ[3] suvarṇavarṇaraśmijvālākulaṃ[4] kumārarūpaṃ[5] vicintayen[6] mantrī/[7]

(2.4.2) paścāt svahṛdi puṇyajñānaviśuddhyā[8] candramaṇḍalaṃ[9] sūryamaṇḍalaṃ[10] ca[11] tatra[12] hrīḥkāravinirgataraśmijvālābhir[13] jñānasattvam ākṛṣya[14] vakṣyamāṇarūpaṃ[15] saṃpūjya[16] pūrvoktapūjābhiḥ[17] jñānasattvasamayasattvayor[18] ekīkaraṇād[19] bhagavantaṃ[20] harihariharivāhanodbhavaṃ[21] bhagavallokeśvaraṃ[22] sthiracittenātmānaṃ[23] vibhāvayet/[24]

(2.4.3) ṣaḍbhujaṃ[25] śuklavarṇaṃ[26] jaṭāmukuṭinaṃ[27] śāntaveśaṃ[28] dakṣiṇakareṇa[29] sambuddhaṃ[30] sākṣiṇaṃ[31] kurvantaṃ[32] dvitīyenākṣamālādharaṃ[33] tṛtīyena durgatisthitalokaṃ[34] śubham[35]

---

1 TO1 anādikālasacinta-; TO3 illegible after anādikālasaṃcitakarmāvaraṇavi-. K1 and BL2 add. a central dot. N1 anādikālasañcita-.
2 TO1 harihariharīvāha-; TO2 -bhava; TO3 -vāhadbhavaṃ; TO4 hariharivāhanodbhavaṃ; K1 add. a central dot.
3 TO1, TO2, TO3 -mūrtti; K1, BL2 -mūrtti•; N1 add. ra.
4 B suvarṇaratnaraśmijvālākulaṃ; TO1 -kura; K1 suvarṇavárṇaraśmijvārākulaṃ•; N1 suvarṇavarṇaṃ raśmi-; BL2 -raśmijvārākulaṃ•.
5 TO1 kumālarūpaṃ.
6 The rendering follows the Sandhi rule. B, TO2, TO4, N1 vicintayet; TO1, TO3 vicintayet/; K1 -tya//; BL2 -ya//.
7 TO1 mantri; TO2 mantro; K1, BL2 //.
8 K1 tulya-.
9 TO2 add. ca.
10 TO1 -la; TO2 om.; N1 -lañ.
11 TO1, TO3, TO4, K1 and BL2 add. /. TO2 om.
12 TO2, BL2 tataḥ.
13 TO1, TO3, K1, N1, BL2 -bhi.
14 K1 and BL2 add. a central dot.
15 TO1 vakṣyamānaṃ rūpaṃ; TO2 vakṣyamānarūpaṃ.
16 TO1 sapūjya; TO2 saṃpūjā; K1 and BL2 add. a central dot.
17 TO1 and N1 add. /. TO4 -bhi.
18 TO4 jñānasattvasamayatvayor; BL2 -sattva•yor.
19 The rendering follows the Sandhi rule. B, TO1, TO2, TO3, TO4, N1 -raṇāt; K1 -ruṇāt; BL2 -ruṇād.
20 BL2 add. a central dot.
21 TO2 -bhava; TO4 -nod; K1 and BL2 add. a central dot.
22 TO2, N1 lokeśvaraṃ; TO4 bhagavaṃt lokeśvaraṃ.
23 TO1 sthiracittenātmā; TO3 -mām.
24 B om. /. TO1 -ye//; TO3, K1 and BL2 add. //.
25 TO1 illegible after ṣaḍbhu-. BL2 -ja.
26 TO1 -varṇa; BL2 śuklaṃ varṇaṃ•.
27 TO3, TO4, K1 -makuṭinaṃ.
28 TO1 -veśa/; TO3 and TO4 add. /. N1 śāntāveśaṃ; BL2 add. a central dot.
29 TO2 dakṣiṇakareṇaṃ.
30 TO2 om.; K1, BL2 -buddha.
31 TO2 om.; BL2 śākṣiṇaṃ.
32 TO2, TO4 and N1 add. /. K1 and BL2 add. a central dot.
33 TO1, TO3, TO4, K1, N1 and BL2 add. /.
34 N1 -loka.
35 TO1, TO2, TO3, TO4, K1 and BL2 om.

upadeśayantaṃ[1] vāmena[2] daṇḍadharaṃ[3] dvitīyena[4] kṛṣṇājinadharaṃ[5] tṛtīyena[6] kamaṇḍaludharaṃ[7] bhagavantaṃ cintayet/[8]

(2.4.4) tatra viśuddhiḥ/[9] vāyvagnimaṇḍalābhyāṃ[10] hariḥ[11] vāruṇamaṇḍalena[12] garuḍaḥ[13] mahendramaṇḍalasumerubhyāṃ[14] harir iti viśuddhiḥ[15] satataṃ[16] bhāvayan[17] yogī[18] sarvasattvārthakaraṇasamartho[19] bhavati[20] sarvajanapriyo[21] bhavati[22] mahāprājño bhavati[23] nīrogo[24] nirupadravaś[25] ca dhanāḍhyo[26] bhavati[27] sarvaviṣakarmaṇi[28] mahāsamārtho[29] bhavati/[30]

(3) japamantraṃ[31] gurūpadeśato jñeyam/[32]

//harihariharivāhanodbhavalokeśvarasādhanam[33] samāptam[34]//

---

1 B add. a semicolon. TO1, K1, BL2 upadarśayantaṃ//; TO2 upadarśayaṃtaṃ/; TO3 and TO4 add. //. N1 add./.
2 BL2 add. //.
3 TO4, K1 and BL2 add. /.
4 TO1 dvitiyana; TO2 dvitīyeṇa.
5 TO2, TO3, K1, N1 and BL2 add. /. TO4 add. //.
6 TO2 -yeṇa; TO4 -ye.
7 TO1, TO3 and K1 add. /. BL2 kamaṇḍarudharaṃ/.
8 TO1, TO3, K1, BL2 //; TO2, N1 vicintayet/.
9 TO1 viśuddhi//; TO3, TO4 śuddhiḥ; K1, BL2 śuddhiḥ//.
10 TO2, TO3, N1 vāyu agni-; TO4 vāyumalābhyāṃ; K1, BL2 vāyum agni-.
11 B add. a comma. TO1 om.; TO2, TO3 and N1 add. /. TO4, K1 and BL2 add. //.
12 TO1 om.; TO4 vārumaṇḍalena.
13 B add. a comma. TO1 om.; TO2, TO3, TO4 and N1 add. /. K1 and BL2 add. //.
14 TO1 om.; TO4, BL2 māhendra-.
15 TO1, TO3, TO4, K1 and BL2 add. //. TO2 and N1 add. /.
16 TO2 satatra.
17 TO2 -yed; K1, BL2 -yet.
18 BL2 add. a central dot.
19 TO1, TO3 sarvasattvārthakaraṇam artho; TO2 sarvvasatvārthakaraṇasamatho; TO4 sarvasattvārthakaraṇam artho; K1, BL2 -kāraṇam artho; N1 -sattvātha-.
20 B add. a comma. TO1 bhava; TO2, TO3, TO4, K1, N1 and BL2 add. /.
21 TO4 sarvaja/ agni/ na priyo/.
22 B add. a comma. TO1, TO3, K1, N1 and BL2 add. /.
23 B add. a comma. TO3, K1, N1 and BL2 add. /.
24 K1 nīrogā.
25 BL2 nirūpa-.
26 TO4 dharādyo.
27 B add. a comma. TO1, TO3, K1 and BL2 add. //. TO2, TO4 and N1 add. /.
28 B, TO4, K1, N1 vaśaviṣakarmmaṇi; TO1, TO3, BL2 śavaviṣa-.
29 N1 mahāsamātho.
30 TO1, TO3, K1, BL2 //.
31 TO1 -tra.
32 TO1, TO3, K1, BL2 //; TO2 and N1 om. /. TO4 jñayaṃ//.
33 K1 harihariharivāhanodbhavalokyeśvarasādhanaṃ.
34 B, TO1, TO2, TO3, TO4, N1 om.; BL2 add. sapāpta//.

## 10.1 Trailokyavaśaṅkaralokeśvarasādhana (Bhatt. no. 35)

(1.1) prathamaṃ[1] tāvan[2] mano'nukūle sthāne[3] yogipaṭaṃ[4] prakāśya[5] tasyāgrato māhendramaṇḍalamadhye kuṅkumena[6] candramaṇḍalaṃ[7] kārayet//[8] oṃ vajrarekhe[9] hūṃ iti mantreṇa/[10]

(1.2) tadanu jaḥ[11] hūṃ vaṃ padmastha hor iti mantreṇāvāhanaṃ[12] kṛtvā[13] maṇḍalamadhye[14] trailokyavaśaṅkaralokeśvarabhaṭṭārakaṃ[15] pūjayed[16] anena[17] mantreṇa//[18] oṃ trailokyavaśaṅkarāya[19] vajrapuṣpe hūṃ pratīccha[20] svāhā/[21] tataḥ oṃ[22] munivajre[23] mur iti visarjya//[24]

---

1 TO1 prathama; TO2, K1, BL2 prathaman.
2 B, TO2, BL2 tāvat.
3 TO1 sthā; K1 add. /. BL2 add. a central dot.
4 TO1 paṭapraṭa; TO2 paṭaṃ; TO3, TO4, K1, N1, BL2 paṭa.
5 BL2 add. a central dot.
6 TO1 -ma; TO2, TO3, K1, BL2 kuṃkume; TO4 -maina.
7 TO2 -le.
8 B om. //. TO2 /.
9 K1 vajrarakṣa; BL2 vajarakṣa.
10 TO2, TO3, N1 and BL2 om. /. TO4 mantraiṇa; K1 mantre.
11 TO1 ja.
12 TO4 maṃtraṇāvāhanaṃ; K1 maṇavāhanaṃ; BL2 mantreṇa vāhanaṃ.
13 BL2 add. a central dot.
14 TO1 -ya; K1 and BL2 add. a central dot.
15 TO1 tailokyavasaṅkalalokeśvarabhaṭṭārakaṃ; TO2 tailokevaśaṃkarabhaṭṭārakaṃ; K1 add. a central dot. BL2 tailokyavaśaṅkara•lokeśvaraḅhaṭṭārakaṃ•.
16 TO1 pūjayeṭ; K1 pūjayet tad; BL2 add. tad.
17 TO1 danena; TO4 anana.
18 B om. //. K1, BL2 // //.
19 TO1 -kalāya; TO2 tailokya-; BL2 add. a central dot.
20 TO1, TO2, BL2 praticcha.
21 TO1, TO2, TO3, TO4, N1, BL2 //; K1 add. //pāśavajroparisthitanānānirmmāṇadhāribuddhabodhisattva-vajrayoginīdevādibhir abhiṣekaṃ vibhāvya/ śirasy āmitābhaṃ dhyāyāt/ tato hṛtsūryya hrīṃ hūṃ yīṃ iti jāpya•.
22 K1, BL2 om.
23 TO1 munīvajre.
24 B, TO4 and N1 om. //. TO1 vijasarjya/; TO2 sarjya; TO3 /; K1 visarjyaṃ//.

(2.1) svahṛdi rakta-āṃkāraṃ[1] vicintya tatpariṇāmena sūryaṃ[2] tadupari rakta-hrīḥkāraṃ[3] tadraśmisamākṛṣṭāmitābhatathāgataṃ[4] saṃpūjya[5] pāpadeśanādikaṃ kṛtvā trailokyaṃ[6] ca[7] vaśaṃ[8] vidhāya[9] raśmīn[10] svabīje[11] praveśya[12]

(2.2) tatpariṇāmena[13] jhaṭiti lokeśvaraṃ[14] sarvāṅgamahārāgaraktam ekamukhaṃ[15] dvibhujaṃ[16] trinetraṃ[17] jaṭāmakuṭamaṇḍitaṃ[18] vajrāṅkitapāśāṅkuśahastaṃ[19] raktapadme[20] vajraparyaṅkaniṣaṇṇaṃ[21] divyābharaṇavastravibhūṣitam[22] ātmānaṃ vicintya//[23]

(2.3) tribhuvanameṣadvayasthapāśavajroparisthitanānānirmāṇadhāribuddha-bodhisattvavajrayoginīdevādibhir[24] abhiṣekaṃ[25] vibhāvya[26] (27-śirasy amitābhaṃ-27) dhyāyāt//[28]

---

1 TO2 ākāraṃ; K1, BL2 āḥkāraṃ.
2 K1 add. a central dot.
3 TO1 rakta/ hrīḥkāraṃ.
4 TO2 tadaśmisamākṛṣṭāmibhābhatathāgataṃ; K1 tadraśmim ākṛṣṭāmitābhatathāgataṃ; BL2 tadraśmim ākṛṣṭāmitābhatathāgataṃ.
5 BL2 add. a central dot.
6 TO1, TO2 tailokyañ; TO3, K1, BL2 trailokya; TO4, N1 trailokyañ.
7 TO3, K1, BL2 om.
8 TO1 vasa; TO4 vaśam.
9 K1 and BL2 add. a central dot.
10 TO4 raśmin; K1, BL2 raśmī.
11 TO2 -ja.
12 K1 -yam •; BL2 -yaṃ.
13 K1 -meṇa•; BL2 add. a central dot.
14 BL2 add. a central dot.
15 BL2 add. a central dot.
16 K1 and BL2 add. a central dot.
17 BL2 add. a central dot.
18 TO1, TO2, TO3, K1 and BL2 add. /. TO4 add. //.
19 TO1, TO2, TO3 and BL2 add. /.
20 TO1, TO3, K1, BL2 -ma; TO4 -mai.
21 TO1 and N1 add. /. TO2 -kaṇiṣaṇṇaṃ; TO3 -kaniṣaṇṇa; K1 -kaniṣarṇa; BL2 -kaniṣaṇṇa•.
22 TO4 divyābharaṇavibhūṣitam; K1 -ṣit; BL2 -tām.
23 B, TO2, TO4 and N1 om. //. TO1, TO3 /; K1, BL2 // //.
24 TO1, TO3 tribhuvaṇameṣadvayastha-; TO2 tribhuvanameṣadvayasthapāsavajoparisthitanānāṇirmmāṇa-; TO4 -buddhabodhisattvavajrayoginīdevādi; K1 tribhunevadvayasthapāśa-vajroparisthitanānānirmmāṇadhāribuddhabodhisattvavajrayogiṇīdevādibhir; N1 illegible after -buddhabodhisattvavajrayoginī-. BL2 tribhuvanam eva dvayasthapāśavajrīparisthitanānā-nirmmāṇadhāribuddhabodhisattvavajayogiṇīdevādibhir.
25 TO4 tiraṣekaṃ; BL2 aṣekaṃ.
26 K1 and BL2 add. /.
27 TO1, TO2, TO3, K1, N1, BL2 śirasy āmitābhaṃ.
28 B /; TO1, TO2, TO3, K1, N1 and BL2 om. //.

(2.4) tato hṛtsūrye[1] hrīḥ[2] hūṃ yāṃ[3] iti jāpya[4] tryakṣaramantraṃ[5] dhyātvā oṃ śūnyatājñānavajrasvabhāvātmako[6] 'haṃ/[7] oṃ vajrātmakāḥ[8] sarvadharmā[9] vajrātmako 'ham[10] iti vajrātmakamantradvayaṃ[11] paṭhet/[12] evam abhyasyato[13] dhunanakampanādiguṇa[14] utpadyate//[15]

(2.5) tadanu[16] oṃ hrīḥ[17] āḥ[18] hāṃ hārīti[19] yakṣeśvari[20] svāhā[21] iti piṇḍaṃ[22] dadyāt/[23] oṃ āṃ kroṃ[24] hrīṃ sakalagaṇavīravīreśvarīṇāṃ[25] parikarair[26] a a avatara avatara avatarantu[27] daśadiglokapālā[28] imaṃ[29] baliṃ gṛhṇa gṛhṇa hūṃ svāhā[30] iti baliṃ[31] dattvā devatāyogena[32] vihared iti/[33]

(34-//sarahapādakṛtaṃ-34) oḍḍiyānakrameṇa[35] trailokyavaśaṅkaralokeśvarasādhanaṃ[36] samāptam//[37]

---

1 TO2, K1 -yya; TO4 hṛtsurya; BL2 hṛtsūrya.
2 TO3, TO4 hrī; K1, N1, BL2 hrīṃ.
3 TO2 yā; TO3 yī ?; TO4 yī; K1, N1, BL2 yīṃ.
4 BL2 add. //. K1 add. a central dot.
5 TO1 -tra.
6 TO4 -vajrabuddhabodhisattvaisva-.
7 B om. / and add. a comma. TO4 haḥ/; K1, BL2 //.
8 N1 vajranamekāḥ.
9 TO2, K1, BL2 -dharmmāḥ.
10 B 'haṃ.
11 TO4 -ya.
12 TO1, TO3, K1, BL2 //.
13 TO4 abhyasmatā.
14 BL2 dhunanampa-.
15 B, TO2, TO4, N1 /.
16 TO4 tetedanu.
17 K1, N1, BL2 hrīṃ.
18 TO4, K1 aḥ.
19 TO2 hāriti; K1, BL2 hāritī.
20 B -rī.
21 TO1, TO3 and N1 add. /. TO2, K1 and BL2 add. //.
22 TO1, TO3 piṇḍīn; N1 piṇḍīn/.
23 TO4 , K1, BL2 //.
24 TO4 hrīṃ.
25 TO2 -gana-; K1, BL2 sakaragaṇavīreśvarīṇāṃ.
26 B parikarai; TO1, TO3, TO4, K1, N1, BL2 parikaraiḥ; TO2 parikaraḥ; The rendering follows the Sandhi rule.
27 K1 avataraṃ•; BL2 add. a central dot.
28 TO4 daśadiśloka-; BL2 add. a central dot.
29 B, N1 idaṃ.
30 TO1, TO3, TO4 and BL2 add. //.
31 TO1, TO3, TO4, N1 balin.
32 TO2 -geṇa; BL2 -yoge.
33 TO2, K1, BL2 //.
34 TO1, TO2, TO3, TO4 , K1, N1, BL2 om.
35 TO1, BL2 oḍyānakrameṇa; TO2 oḍyānakameṇa; TO3, BL2 oḍyāyanakrameṇa; TO4 oṃghrāyanakrameṇa; K1 vadyāyanakrameṇas; N1 oḍyayanakrameṇa.
36 TO1 tailokevasaṅkaralokeśvarasādhanaṃ sarahapādakṛtaṃ; TO2 trailokāvaśaṅkaralokeśvarasādhanaṃ; TO3, TO4, K1, N1 and BL2 add. sarahapādakṛtaṃ.
37 TO1 samāptaṃḥ// (anusvāra insertion); TO2 //sarahapādakṛtasamāptaṃ//; K1 add. //jyeṣṭhamāsasya//; BL2 add. jyeṣṭhamāsasya//.

## 10.2 Trailokyavaśaṅkaralokeśvarasādhana (Bhatt. no. 36)

(0) oṃ[1] [(2-]namo lokanāthāya/[-2)]

(1.1) prathamaṃ[3] tāvan[4] mano'nukūle[5] sthāne[6] [(7-]yogī paṭaṃ[-7)] prakāśya[8] tasyāgrato[9] māhendramaṇḍalamadhye[10] kuṅkumena[11] candramaṇḍalaṃ[12] racayet/[13] anena mantreṇa[14] oṃ vajrarekhe[15] hūṃ//[16]

(1.2) jaḥ[17] hūṃ vaṃ padmastha hoḥ[18] anena mantreṇāvāhanaṃ kṛtvā[19] maṇḍalamadhye[20] trailokyavaśaṅkaralokeśvarabhaṭṭārakaṃ[21] pūjayet/[22] anena mantreṇa[23] oṃ[24] trailokyavaśaṅkarāya[25] vajrapuṣpe[26] hūṃ pratīccha[27] svāhā/[28] pūjāmaṃtram[29] idaṃ[30] oṃ munivajre[31] muḥ[32] visarjanamantro[33] 'yam//[34]

---

1 B, TO1, TO2, TO3, TO4, K1, N1, BL2 om.
2 TO1, TO2, TO3, TO4, K1, N1, BL2 om.; K2 lokaṇāthāye//.
3 TO1, K1 prathama; TO2 prathaman.
4 B, K2 and BL1 add. mantrī. TO1, TO2, BL2 tāvat.
5 TO1 nure.
6 BL1 -naṃ.
7 B yogipaṭaṃ; TO2 paṭaṃ.
8 K2 prakāsya; BL1 prakāse; BL2 add. a central dot.
9 TO1 taśy agrato.
10 TO1, TO2 -ya; BL2 add. a central dot.
11 TO1 kuṃkamena; K2 -meṇa; BL2 kuṃkumeṇa.
12 TO2 -la; K2, BL1 maṇḍalaṃ.
13 B and TO3 om. /. TO4 rayet//; K1, BL2 //. K2, BL1 kārayat•.
14 TO1, TO2, TO3 and N1 add. /. TO4 -traiṇa/; K1 and BL2 add. //. K2 and BL1 add. a central dot.
15 K1, K2, BL2 vajralekhe; BL1 vajraleṣe.
16 B, TO1, TO2, TO3, K1, N1, BL2 /; K2 and BL1 om. /.
17 K2 ja.
18 TO1, TO3, N1 and BL2 add. /. TO2, TO4 and K1 add. //. K2 ho.
19 BL2 add. a central dot.
20 K2 -ya; BL2 add. a central dot.
21 TO1 -roke-; TO3, TO4, K1, BL2 trailokyavaśaṃkaraṃ loke-; N1 trailokyavaśaṅkaraṃ loke-; K2 trailokyavasaṅkaralokeśvarabhaṭṭārakam; BL1 trailokevasaṃkara-.
22 B om. /. K1, K2, BL1 and BL2 add. //.
23 TO1 -tre/; TO2, TO3 and N1 add. /. TO4 maṃtraiṇa/; K1, K2 and BL2 add. //. BL1 add. a central dot.
24 BL1 om.
25 K2 -vasaṃkalāye; BL1 -kevasaṃaka-.
26 TO4 vapuṣpe.
27 TO1, TO2, K2, BL1 praticcha.
28 TO4, K1, K2, N1, BL2 //.
29 B, TO1, TO2, TO3, TO4, K1, N1, BL2 om.
30 B, TO1, TO2, TO3, TO4, K1, N1, BL2 om.; K2 and BL1 add. a central dot.
31 TO2 -vajra; K2 munīvajre; BL1 muṇivajre.
32 TO1 muni; TO2 and N1 add. /. TO3, K1, BL2 muni/; TO4 muni//; K2 mu•.
33 TO1 -trāyaṃ; TO3 -trāyam/; TO4 visarjjanamaitrauyaṃ/; K2 -tra//; BL1 -traḥ.
34 B, BL2 /; TO1, TO3, TO4, K2, BL1 om.; K1 yaṃ/; BL2 yaṃ.

(2.1) paścāt[1] svahṛdy[2] āṃkāraṃ[3] cintayet/[4] taṃ[5] pariṇamya[6] sūryamaṇḍalaṃ[7] niṣpadyate/[8] tasyopari[9] śaktibījaṃ[10] bālāruṇasamaprabhaṃ[11] draṣṭavyam/[12]

(2.2) etasya raśmibhir[13] amitābhaṃ[14] pūjayitvā[15] pāpadeśanāpuṇyānumodanāṃ[16] triśaraṇagamaṇaṃ[17] bodhicittotpādanaṃ[18] kṛtvā[19] punaḥ[20] śarīre praviśanti//[21]

(2.3) etat sarvaṃ[22] pariṇamya[23] jhaṭiti padmoparisthaṃ[24] (25- vajraparyaṅkaṃ[26] vikasitatrinetraṃ[27] jaṭāmakuṭadhāriṇaṃ[28] raktavarṇaṃ[29] vajrāṅkitapāśāṅkuśahastaṃ/[30]

(2.4) tribhuvanameṣadvaye[31] pāśabaddhavajropari[32] sthitā -25) nānānirmāṇadhāriṇyo[33] vajrayoginyo[34] 'bhiṣekaṃ[35] prayacchanti[36] tathā bodhisattvā[37] nānābharaṇayuktāḥ[38] pūjāṃ[39]

---

1 K2, BL1 paścā.
2 The rendering follows the Sandhi rule. B, TO1, TO2, TO3, TO4, K1, BL1, BL2 svahṛdi; K2 hṛdī.
3 K1, BL2 ākāraṃ; K2 aḍkāraṃ; N1 āṃraṃ; BL1 aṃkāraṃ.
4 TO2 vicintayet/; K1 viciṃtayet//; K2 and BL1 have a central dot. BL2 vicintayet//.
5 BL1 tam; BL2 tat.
6 K1, BL2 -ṇāmena; K2 parīṇ-.
7 TO4 -lan; K2 sūryye maṇḍalaṃ.
8 K1, BL2 //; K2 -dyatya; BL1 om. /.
9 K2 -rī.
10 TO2, BL1 -bīja; K2 śaktībīja; BL2 add. a central dot.
11 TO1 bārāluṇa-; TO2 vāruṇasamaprabha; K2 bāruṇa-; N1 -prabha; BL1 bārāruṇa-.
12 TO1, TO3, BL2 //; TO2 -ya/; K1 -ya//; K2 and BL1 have a central dot.
13 TO4 raśmaibhir; K2 rāsmibhir.
14 TO2 -bha; K2 and BL1 add. tathāgataṃ.
15 BL2 add. a central dot.
16 B, TO1, TO2, TO4, K1, N1, BL2 pāpadeśanādikaṃ; TO3 pāpaṃ deśanādikaṃ; BL1 pāpadeśanāpunyānumodanā
17 B, TO1, TO2, TO3, TO4, K1, N1, BL2 om.; BL1 -śarana-.
18 B , TO1, TO2, TO3, TO4, K1, N1, BL2 om.; BL1 bodhicitot-.
19 BL1 add. danaṃ. K2 and BL2 add. a central dot.
20 TO2, K2 puna.
21 B praviśantaṃ; TO2 pravisanti/; TO4 /; K2 pravīśanti//; BL1 praviśeṃti•; BL2 praviśati//.
22 TO2, K1, BL2 sarvva; TO4 sarvam; K2, N1, BL1 sarvvam.
23 TO2 pariṇāmya; K2 parīnamya; BL1 parīṇamya.
24 TO2 paristhaṃ; K2 -paristhītā.
25 K2 om.
26 B, BL1 -paryyaṅkinaṃ; TO1 -paryaṃkam; TO2, TO4 -paryyaṅka; K1 -paryyaṃkaṃ; BL2 add. a central dot.
27 TO1 -tra; TO2 sita-; BL2 vikasita•trinetraṃ.
28 TO1, TO3, K1 and BL2 add. /. TO4 jāṃṭāmakuṭadhāriṇaṃ/; N1 -makuṭedhāriṇaṃ/.
29 TO3, TO4 -ṇam; BL1 -ṇa.
30 B, TO1, TO3, TO4 and BL2 om. /. BL1 add. a central dot.
31 TO1, TO2 -ya; K1 tribhuvanaṃ meṣadvayo; BL1 tribhuvaṇameṣadvayam; BL2 tribhuvanaṃ meṣadvaye.
32 TO1, TO2, K1 pāśabaddhe tasyopari; BL2 pāśabaddhe•tasyopari; TO3 pāśebaddhe tasyopari; TO4 pāśabaddhai tasyopari; BL1 ābaddha-.
33 TO2 -ānadha-; K1 and BL2 add. a central dot. K2, BL1 -yā.
34 TO2 -nirmmānadhār-; K2 -gīn mā; BL1 -gin mā.
35 K2 -ka; BL1 abhiṣeka.
36 B add. a comma. TO1, TO2, TO3, TO4 and N1 add. /. K1 and BL2 add. //. K2 and BL1 add. a central dot .
37 K2 add. a central dot.
38 K2 add. -tā•. BL1 -bharanayuktā.
39 TO2 pūjāṅ; BL1 pūjā.

kurvanti//[1] vidyādharahariharahiraṇyagarbhanānāyoginīgaṇā[2] nṛtyavādyādikaṃ[3] nānābhūtagaṇādinānānaraśiraḥkapālamālāvṛtaṃ[4] tathā nānācchatracāmarādikaṃ[5] paśyet/[6] etādṛśe[7] samaye[8] amitābhas[9] tathāgataḥ[10] śirasi draṣṭavyaḥ/[11] īdṛśam[12] ātmānaṃ[13] vicintayet//[14]

(2.5) paścān[15] nābher[16] upari sūryamaṇḍalaṃ[17] raśmimayaṃ vicintya[18] tasyopari[19] vāme śaktibījaṃ[20] hṛdi[21] krodhabījaṃ[22] āḥkārasvarabhūṣitaṃ[23] iti[24] bhaṭṭārakasya[25] (26-hṛdaye bhāvyamantraḥ//-26)

(2.6) etat[27] sarvaṃ[28] dhyātvā[29] vajrātmakamantroccāraṇaṃ[30] kṛtvā[31] vajrātmakaṃ cintayet/[32] oṃ śūnyatājñānavajrasvabhāvātmako[33] 'haṃ/[34] iti[35] vajrātmakamantraḥ//[36]

---

1 B om. // and add. a comma. TO2, TO3, TO4, N1 /; BL1 add. a central dot. K2 om. //.
2 TO1 -yoginigaṇā; TO2 -gabhanānāyoginīganān; K1 vidyādhara•hariharihiraṇyagarbha •nānāyogiṇīgaṇā; BL1 -hīraṇegarbha-; BL2 vidyādhara•hariharihiraṇyagarbha•nānāyoginīgaṇā.
3 B add. [kurvvanti]. TO2 vādyādikaṃ; K1 nṛtyaṃ vādyādikaṃ; K2 nṛtyāvādyādikaṃ; BL2 nṛtyaṃ vādyādikaṃ•.
4 TO1 -kapāramārāvṛtaṃ/; TO2 nānānaraśiraḥkapālamālāvṛtaṃ/; TO3 and TO4 add. /. K1, BL2 nānābhūtagaṇādi•nānānaraśiraḥkapālamālāvṛtaṃ//; K2 nānābhūtagaṇādinānānaraśirakapāramālāvṛtaṃ; N1 nānābhūtagaṇādinānāraśiraḥkapālamālāvṛtaṃ/; BL1 nānābhūtagaṇādinānānarasirakapālamālāvṛtaṃ.
5 TO4, BL1 nānāchatracāmarādikaṃ.
6 TO1, TO3, K1, BL2 //; K2 has a colon. BL1 has a central dot.
7 K2 tat sadṛśya; BL1 tat sadṛśe.
8 K2, BL1 samaya.
9 BL1 amitāṃbha.
10 BL1 -ta.
11 TO1, K1, BL2 //; TO2 -yāḥ/; TO4 praṣṭavyaḥ//; K2, BL1 -ya.
12 TO2 īdṛśa; BL1 idṛsam.
13 TO2 tmānaṃ.
14 B, TO2, TO3, TO4, N1, K2 /; BL1 has a central dot.
15 BL1 paścā.
16 K2 -bhel; BL1 ṇābher.
17 K1, BL2 -araṃ.
18 K1 and BL2 add. //.
19 K2 -rī.
20 TO1 and TO3 add. /. TO2 -bijaṃ; K2 śaktībījaṃ; BL2 add. a central dot.
21 K2, BL1 -dī.
22 K2 kroḍhabījaḥ; BL1 kroḍhabījaṃ.
23 TO2 and N1 add. /. K1, BL2 -kāraṃ sva-; K2 ākāsvarabhūṣitaṃ•; BL1 āḥkārāsvara-.
24 TO1 i.
25 B, TO1, TO2, TO3, TO4, K1, N1, BL2 om.; K2 bhaktārakasya.
26 B bhāvyamantraḥ/; TO1, TO3, K1, BL2 bhāvyamantraḥ//; BL1 hṛdayabhāvyamaṃtraḥ/.
27 BL2 eta.
28 BL1 sarvvan.
29 BL2 add. a central dot.
30 TO1 -ṇa; TO4 vajrātmakaṃ mantroccāraṇaṃ.
31 BL2 add. a central dot.
32 TO2 -ye/; TO4, K2, BL1, BL2 //; K1 viciṃtayet//.
33 TO1 śūnyatājñānavajasvabhātmako; TO3 śūnyatāṃ jñāna-.
34 B om. /. K1, K2, BL2 //; BL1 add. a central dot.
35 TO1, TO2, TO3, TO4, K1, N1, BL2 om.
36 B, TO2, N1 /; BL1 -tra//.

(2.7) etac cābhyāsayogena[1] dhunanakampanāveśanaṃ[2] kṛtvā[3] advaitajñānam[4] utpadyate/[5] sa[6] yogī[7] dviradavad[8] garjati[9] madirāmatta[10] iva[11] pañcavarṇaṃ[12] viharati/[13] yadi[14] pañcavarṇaṃ[15] na[16] viharati/[17] tadā tasya[18] dehe dhunanakampanāveśanādikaṃ[19] na tiṣṭhati/[20] evaṃ[21] pratītyaiva[22] pañcavarṇaṃ[23] vihartavyaṃ[24] tena[25] siddhiḥ syāt/[26] siddhe[27] sati[28] paradehe dhunanakampanāveśanaṃ[29] kṛtvā[30] rāgadveṣādikaṃ[31] niṣedhayati/[32] yathā

---

1 K2 -yāṃsa-; BL2 add. a central dot.
2 TO1 dhūtanakampanāvaśaṃ; TO2 dhunanakaṃpanāveśaṃ; TO3 dhutanakampanāveśaṃ; TO4 dhutarakampanāveśaṃ; K1 dhunanakaṃpanādeśaṃ; K2 dhunanakaṃpanāvesaraṃ; N1 dhunanakampanāveśaṃ; BL1 na kaṃpanāvesaraṃ; BL2 dhunanakampanādeśaṃ.
3 K1 add. a central dot. K2 add. a central dot.
4 TO1 advainam; N1 tādvaitajñānam.
5 TO4, K1, BL2 //; K2 has a central dot and //. BL1 has a central dot.
6 K2 and BL1 add. ca.
7 TO1 yogi.
8 The rendering follows the Sandhi rule. B, TO2, TO4, K2, N1 dviradavat; TO1, TO3 dviradavat/. K1, BL2 dviradavat//.
9 B add. a comma. TO1, TO2, TO3, TO4, K1, N1, BL2 om.; K2 add. a central dot .
10 BL1 madīrāmatta.
11 K2, BL1 om.
12 K1, N1 -ṇa; K2 pacivarṇa; BL1 pacīvarṇa.
13 TO4, K1, BL2 //; K2 viharatī •; N1 om. /. BL1 a central dot.
14 TO2 yadī.
15 TO2, TO4 -ṇan; K1 paṃcavarṇa; N1 -ṇam.
16 TO4 om.
17 TO2 and TO4 om. /. K2 and BL1 have a central dot.
18 K2 tasye; BL1 ta.
19 TO1 dhūtanakaṃpanāveśanādikaṃ; TO2, TO4, N1 dhunanakampanāveśanādikan; TO3 dhutanakaṃpanāveśanādikaṃ; K2 dhunanakaṃpanādhyeṣanādvaitajñānādikaṃ; BL1 dhunanakaṃpanādheṣaṇādvaitajñānādikaṃ.
20 TO1, TO3, K1, BL2 //; K2, N1 and BL1 om. /.
21 TO4 evam.
22 TO1, TO2, BL2 pratitya; TO3, TO4, N1, BL1 pratītya.
23 TO1, K1, K2, BL1 -ṇa.
24 The rendering follows the Sandhi rule. B viharttavyam; TO1, TO3 viharet/; TO2, TO4, N1 viharet; K1 viharet//; K2 viharatavyam; BL1 viharatavyaṃ •; BL2 viharat//.
25 K2 etyena.
26 TO1, TO2, TO3, TO4, N1 and BL1 om. /. K1, K2 and BL2 have a central dot.
27 TO1 sīddhe.
28 K1, K2, BL1 and BL2 add. a central dot.
29 TO1 dhūtanakaṃpanāveśanaṃ; TO3 dhutanakaṃpanāveṣanaṃ; K2 dhunanakaṃpanādveṣaṇaṃ; BL1 dhunanakaṃparādheṣaṇaṃ.
30 K1, K2 and BL2 add. a central dot.
31 TO2 -dvekhādika.
32 TO2, TO4, N1 and BL1 om. /. K1, BL2 //; K2 -yeti•.

siddhirasena[1] viddhaṃ[2] tāmraṃ[3] kṛṣṇatāṃ[4] tyajati[5] tathā[6] śarīram[7] evādvaitarasena[8] viddhaṃ[9] rāgadveṣādikaṃ tyajati//[10]

(2.8) hrīḥ[11] hūṃ yāṃ[12] japyamantraḥ/[13] oṃ hrīḥ[14] aḥ[15] hāṃ[16] hārīti[17] yakṣeśvari[18] svāhā[19] hārītīmantraḥ//[20] oṃ āṃ[21] kroṃ hrīṃ sakalagaṇavīravīreśvarīṇāṃ[22] parikarair[23] a a avatara[24] avatara[25] avatarantu[26] daśadiglokapālā[27] imaṃ[28] baliṃ[29] gṛhṇa gṛhṇa hūṃ svāhā[30] balimantraḥ/[31]

//iti[32] sarahapādāvatārita[33] oḍḍiyānavinirgatatrailokyavaśaṅkaralokeśvarasādhanaṃ[34] samāptam//[35]

---

1 TO3, N1 siddharasena; K2 sirasena; BL1 siddhir asya na; BL2 add. a central dot.
2 BL2 viddha.
3 TO2 tāṃra; K1, BL2 tāmlam.
4 BL1 -ṇāṃ.
5 TO1, TO4 and N1 add. /. K1, BL2 tyajeti//; K2 add. a central dot. BL1 tyaṃjati.
6 K1, BL2 yathā.
7 TO2, K1 sarīram.
8 K2 -ṇa.
9 K1, K2, BL1 viddha.
10 B, TO2, TO4 /; TO1 syati//; K2, N1 and BL1 om. //.
11 TO1, TO2, TO3, TO4, K1, BL2 hūṃ; K2 hrī.
12 TO1, TO3, K1, N1 and BL2 add. //. TO2 add. /. K2 yā; BL1 ā.
13 TO3, TO4, K1, BL2 //; K2 jāpyamaṃtraḥ •//; BL1 jāpyamantraḥ.
14 TO1, TO3, TO4, K1, N1 hrīṃ; K2 om.; BL1 āṃ; BL2 hrī.
15 K2 aṃ?; BL1 om.
16 TO1, TO2, TO3, TO4, K1, K2, N1, BL1, BL2 om.
17 K1, BL2 hāritī; K2, BL1 -tī.
18 B, K2, BL1 yakṣeśvarī.
19 TO1, TO2, TO3, TO4, K1 and BL2 add. //. K2 and BL1 add. a colon and //.
20 B hārītimantraḥ/; TO1, TO3 hārītimantraḥ//; TO4 hārītīmantra//; K1 hāritimantraḥ//; BL2 hāritimantraḥ// //.
21 BL1 om.
22 TO1 -viravīreśvarīṇāṃ; K1 sakaraga-; K2 sakalagaṇavīreśvarī-; BL1 -vairaśvarīṇāṃ; BL2 add. a central dot.
23 B, TO1, TO2, TO3, TO4, K1, BL2 parikaraiḥ; K2, N1, BL1 -kare.
24 BL1 ava•tara.
25 BL1 tara.
26 K1 and BL2 add. a central dot.
27 TO4 -lo; K2, BL1 -lāṃ.
28 B, TO1, TO2, TO3, TO4, K2, BL1 idaṃ.
29 TO4 bali.
30 TO1, TO2, TO3, TO4, K1, K2, N1, BL1 and BL2 add. //.
31 TO1, TO3, TO4, K1, N1, BL1, BL2 //; K2 balīmaṃtraḥ; BL2 om. /.
32 TO1, TO2, TO3, K1 and N1 om. //iti. TO4, BL2 //; BL1 iti.
33 K1 vatārita; BL2 add. a central dot.
34 TO1 oḍiyānavinirgatatrailokya-; TO4 vaḍiyānavinirggatatrailokyavaśaṃkaralokeśvarasādhana; K1 vaḍiyānavinirggatatrailokyavaśaṅkaralokyeśvarasādhanaṃ// // jyeṣṭhasyaiva//; K2 uḍiyānavinirgata// // iti sādhanasamucaye sarahapādāvatārīta uḍiyānavinirggatatrailokevaśaṃkaralokyaśvarasādhana ṣatriṃsatyedhikaśatatama paṭala//136; N1 uḍḍiyāṇavinirgatatrailokyavaśaṃkaralokeśvarasādhanaṃ; BL1 uḍiyānavinirggatataḥ// iti sādhanasamuccayasarahapādāvatārīta uḍiyānavinirggatatrailokyavasaṃkaralokyaśvarasādhana ṣatriṃśatyadhikaśatatamapatala//136//; BL2 oḍiyānavinirggatatrailokyavaśaṃkaralokeśvarasādhanaṃ// jyeṣṭhasyaiva//.
35 TO1, TO2, TO3, TO4, K1, N1, BL1, BL2 om.

## 10.3 Trailokavaśaṅkaralokeśvarasādhana (Trailokavaśaṅkarāmnāyabhugmalokeśvarasādhana)

(0) namo lokanāthāya//

(1.1) praṇipatya lokanāthaṃ lokahitaṃ buddhabodhim anavadyaṃ/[1] sugatasutajinajanakāñ[2]
[(3-]citram tat sādhanaṃ[-3)] vakṣye/[4]

(1.2) utthāya[5] śaśihṛtsaroruhaṃ[6] vidhau[7] mohāndhakārāpahaṃ hrīḥkāraspharadaṃśujālajaṭilaṃ[8]
paṅkajarāgāruṇaṃ/[9]

(2.1) saṃvīkṣya[10] trimokṣarūpam[11] amalaṃ vaktrādiśaucaṃ[12] sudhīḥ kṛtvā
prāg vidadhītakopajavān[13] sthānātmayogāvanaṃ/
yatrāṅga[14] saṃkuṅkumapaṅkaliptaṃ
sugandhipuṣpaprakarāvakīrṇaṃ/[15]
dhyānālayaṃ ramyatamaṃ praviśya
mṛdvāsane[16] tuṅgatare[17] nyāsīdet//[18]

(2.2) [(19-]tato 'grataḥ[-19)][(20-]kuṅkumaraktacandanaiḥ[21] pralipya sanmaṇḍalakaṃ[-20)] savartulaṃ[22]
[(23-]vikīrya raktaiḥ kusumaiś ca tan navair[-23)] japet[24] svamantreṇa [(25-]sad arpabhājanaṃ/[-25)]

---

1 N2 om. /.

2 The rendering follows Tib. T3: bde gśegs sras daṅ rgyal ba'i yab ñid daṅ//. K1, BL2, N2 sugatasutañjinajanakaṃ.

3 The rendering follows Tib. T3: ṅo mtshar can gyi sgrub thabs. K1, BL2, N2 citran tatsādhanaṃ.

4 N2 -yo.

5 K1, BL2, N2 utthāyā.

6 K1, N2 -ha.

7 N2 vidyā.

8 K1 hrīḥkāradaṃśujālajaṭilaṃ; N2 hrīkāraspharadaṃśujālajaṭilaṃ.

9 N2 paṅkejarāgāruṇaṃ/.

10 The rendering follows Tib. T3: yaṅ dag bsam źiṅ. K1, BL2, N2 samvīkṣa.

11 K1, N2 trivimokṣarūpam.

12 The rendering follows Tib. T3: źal sogs bsaṅ. K1, BL2, N2 vaktrādisaucaṃ

13 K1 -kopajayat; BL2 -kopajapan.

14 The rendering is probably a misprint for yatrāṅgaṃ.

15 K1 sugandhipuṣpaprakarāvakīrṇa/; N2 om. /.

16 N2 mṛdvālana.

17 N2 tuṅgataramya.

18 The rendering follows Tib. T3: rab tu 'dug byas te/. K1, BL2 nyaśīdet//; N2 has dots after mya- instead of the rendering.

19 N2 has dots before -aina instead of the rendering.

20 N2 has dots between kuṅkuma- and -la/ instead of the rendering.

21 N2 -candaneḥ.

22 K1 sarvatula/.

23 The rendering follows Tib. T3: me tog dmar po so ma gcal du bkram. K1 vikīrya raktaiḥ kusumaiḥ ca tan navai; BL2 vikīrya raktaiḥ kusumaiś ca tan navai; N2 vakārya raktaḥ kusumaḥ ca tan na.

24 N2 vajrapet.

25 BL2 sad arpabhyajanaṃ/; N2 has dots between sad a- and -bhāṃjana// instead of the rendering.

(3) dṛṣṭvā tato nabhasi sarvajinān[1] saputrān mantrī[2] tu[3] sarvajagaduddharaśokadakṣān/[4]
(5-pūjāvidhīn bahuvidhān nijabījajātāns-5) tebhyaḥ samāhitamano vidadhītabuddhyā//[6]
tatas teṣām agrato 'vasthitam
avanatakāyaṃ jānupatitaṃ
baddhāñjalim[7] ātmānam[8] adhimucya
pāpadeśanādikam iti kuryāt//[9]
diśāmi pāpāny akhilāni bhītaḥ pāpād aśeṣād[10] vid api viraktaṃ[11] śubhāni sarvāṇi[12]
anumodayāmi tāny agrabodhau pariṇāmayāmi//[13] prayāmi ratnatritayaṃ parāyanaṃ dadāmi
buddhebhya (14-idaṃ svadehaṃ/-14)
(15-dadhā vau-15) hṛdayaṃ jagadhite[16] karomi buddhapratipad[17] āśrayaṃ/[18]
(4) (19-duḥkhādūraṃ samabhivīkṣya jagat samastaṃ-19) tasmiṃ kṛpāṃs[20] mahatīṃ[21]
pravibhāvya mantrī/[22] śūnyatām[23] vibhāvya nikṣilaṃ[24] jagad[25] upābham[26] ātmānas[27] apy
amalam advaitaṃ[28] prapaśyet//[29] tataḥ/[30] oṃ svabhāvaśuddhāḥ sarvadharmāḥ

---

1 K1 sarvaninān.
2 K1, N2 mantras; BL2 mantraṃs.
3 K1, N2 ta.
4 N2 sarvajanaduṣṭaraṇyavavdakṣān/.
5 The rendering follows Tib.T3: mchod pa'i cho ga rnam maṅ raṅ gi sa bon bskyed//. K1 pūjādhidhīn bahuvidhān nijabījajātāns; N2 pūjāvidhi •bahuvidhān nijabījajātāns; BL2 pūjāvidhin bahuvidhān nijabījajātāns.
6 BL2, N2 // //.
7 K1 baddhāñjani.
8 K1 mānam.
9 K1 /; N2 om. //.
10 N2 aṣeṣād.
11 N2 add. /.
12 K1 sarvāni.
13 N2 parināmayāmi•.
14 The rendering follows Tib. T3: bdag gis lus 'di. K1 idaṃ kadevaraṃ/. BL2 idaṃ kadevanaṃ/; N2 idaṃ kadevare.
15 The rendering is possibly a misprint for dadau vai. BL2 dadāvau.
16 BL2 jagadhita.
17 The rendering follows the Sandhi rule. K1, N2 -pratipat; BL2 -pratipatyam.
18 K1 samāśrayaṃ/; N2 samāśrayaṃ//.
19 The rendering follows Tib. T3: 'gro ba mtha' dag sdug bsṅal gyis mnar yaṅ dag blta//. K1 duḥkhāduraṃ samabhivīkṣajagat samastaṃ; BL2 duḥkhāduraṃ samabhivīkṣajagan samastaṃ; N2 duḥkhāt tu rasam abhivīkṣajagan samastaṃ.
20 N2 kṛpāṃ su.
21 BL2 mahatī; N2 mahatāṃ.
22 N2 //.
23 K1, N2 śūnyaṃ.
24 The rendering follows Tib. T3: ma lus. K1, N2 nikṣiraṃ; BL2 nikṣira.
25 K1 jagada.
26 BL2 adupābham; N2 upābham•.
27 The rendering is possibly a misprint for ātmānam.
28 The rendering follows Tib. T3: gñis med. K1, BL2 N2 advitayaṃ.
29 The rendering follows Tib. T3: rab tu blta bar bya/. K1 prasaśet//; BL2 praśasyet//; N2 praśaśet.
30 N2 om. /.

svabhāvaśuddho 'haṃ// oṃ[1] śūnyatājñānavajasvabhāvātmako[2] 'haṃ/[3] ity anena[4] tad adhitiṣthet//

(5.1) tataḥ purastāt spharadaṃśujālaṃ [(5-]hrīḥkāraṃ mūrdhni palāśavarṇaṃ tatsambhavaṃ pūrṇaśaśaṅkabimbaṃ paśyet//[-5)] laṣadhrīḥkṛtidīptamadhye/[6] tasyopary[7] hrīḥkṛticaṃdrarociṣaṃ[8] rociḥ paridyotitasarvadigmukhaṃ/ madhyasthitahrīḥkṛtirocir[9] jvalaṃ saṃcintayed[10] dhvastatāmasaṃ/[11] tasyopariṣṭhān nijajātavikāsitaṃ[12] paṃkeruham[13] arkavarṇaṃ/[14] hrīḥkārasaṃśobhitamadhye[15] samvibhāvayituṃ[16] gatamānasaḥ san/[17]

(5.2) tataḥ svabījānikhilān[18] munīndrān[19] visphārya[(20-]saṃhṛtya ca tān kṛtān/[-20)] bījāṅkasūryendubindujātam[21] ātmānap[22] īkṣaṇajanādhināthaṃ/[23] padmendūparisaṃsthitaṃ[24] samāpadaṃ[25] lālityaṃ[26] nīlānvitaṃ[27] vidyud-vidrumasaṃnibhaṃ[28] bhramaharaṃ[29] prosphullapadmānanaṃ/[30]

---

1 N2 om.

2 The rendering is probably a misprint for śūnyatājñānavajrasvabhāvātmako. K1 śūnyatājñānavajasvabhātmako.

3 N2 om. /.

4 N2 enena.

5 The rendering follows Tib. T3: pa la śa'i me tog lta bu'i hrīḥ yig bsam// des byuṅ zla ba gaṅ ba'i gzugs bltas la//. K1 hrīḥkāra mūrdhnī kṣapalāgavarṇaṃ tatsambhavaṃ pūrṇaśaśaṅkabimbaṃ paśyet//; BL2 hrīḥkāra mūrdhni kṣapalāgavarṇaṃ tatsambhavaṃ pūrṇaśaśaṅkabimbaṃ paśyet; N2 hrīḥkāra mūdhnī kṣapalāgavarṇaṃ tatsambhava pūrṇaśaśaṅkabimbaṃ paśyel.

6 The rendering is probably a misprint for lasaddhrīḥkṛtidīptamadhye/. K1 laṣaddhrīḥkṛtidīptamadhya/; N2 laṣadhrīḥ/ kṛtidīptamadhya//.

7 The rendering follows the Sandhi rule. K1, BL2, N2 tasyopari.

8 The rendering is probably a misprint for hrīḥkṛticaṃdrarociṣāṃ. BL2 hrīḥkṛticaṃdrociṣaṃ; N2 hrīkṛticandrociṣaṃ.

9 BL2 madhye sthitahrīḥkṛtirocir; N2 madhyasthitadīḥkatirociru.

10 BL2 cintayet; N2 cintaye.

11 N2 om. /.

12 N2 nijajātavikāsiṃ taṃ.

13 N2 karuham.

14 N2 arkavarṇa//.

15 K1 -saṃsobhitamadhya; N2 -saṃsojitamadhya.

16 BL2 samvibhāvayantaṃ; N2 samvibhāvayetuṃ.

17 N2 sana/.

18 N2 svabijānikhilam.

19 N2 indrā.

20 N2 saṃsthābhāvanāna kṛtona.

21 K1 bījāṅkasūryandujabindujātam; BL2 bījāṅkasūryendujabindujātam; N2 bījāṅkasūryyabhujabindujātam

22 The rendering is probably a misprint for ātmānam. K1 ātmānay; N2 ātmānāṃ.

23 K1 īkṣatajanādhināthaṃ/; N2 yīkṣetajanāḥ vinathā.

24 K1, BL2 padmenduparisaṃsthitaṃ; N2 padmenduparisasthita.

25 The rendering follows Tib. T3: mñam pa'i zabs kyis yaṅ dag bźugs//. K1, BL2 samapadaṃ; N2 sapada.

26 The rendering follows Tib. T3: rol źiṅ. K1, BL2 lānitya; N2 // tatya.

27 N2 -ta•.

28 K1, BL2 -sannibhaṃ; N2 has dots between vedya- and -drunasannibha instead of the rendering.

29 N2 -hara.

30 The rendering is possibly a misprint for proḍhaphullapadmānanaṃ/. K1 prāsphullapadmānanaṃ/; N2 prāsphullapadmānana.

nīlāmbhojaviśālanetrayugalaṃ[1] subhrūlatālaṅkṛtaṃ[2] muktādāmavibhūṣitāsurajaṭāṃ[3]
divyāmbarālaṅkṛtaṃ/[4] prodyataraktamarīcijālajaṭilaiḥ[5] satvārthasamāpādanaṃ[6] vibhrāṇaṃ
[(7-]pravikāsipadmam aruṇaṃ[-7)] vāmena hastalaśan/[8] sarvākāravaraprasācaturaṃ[9]
savyadāṣṇāsanāsad[10] ratnābharaṇam[11] prasannamanasaṃ[12] lokeśvaraṃ bhāsvaraṃ/[13]

(5.3) tato hṛdambhoruhacandrabimbe
hrīḥkāram udīkṣya[14] prabhāparītaṃ/[15]
hṛtkaṇṭhaśīrṣendutaleṣv[16] hūṃ-āḥ-
oṃ-kāram[17] [(18-]uddīdhitim āśu paśyet//[18)]

(5.4) tato vidikṣu prasamīkṣya[19] padmān[20]
bandhūkavarṇāś caturapraphullān/
tadūrdhvataḥ śītarucīn saṃpūrṇaṃ
vibhāvayet[21] kuṅkumasamprakāśān/[22]
tataḥ [(23-]svahṛdmantramarīciṃ[24] vaktrān[25]
niścārya[26-23)] candrāntarāyatātmāna[27]
veśat[28] teṣu tadūrdhvato[29] 'rkās[30]

---

1 N2 nālāmbhājāvaśāṃlanetrayugala.
2 K1, N2 subhrulatālaṅkṛtaṃ.
3 The rendering follows Tib. T3: ral pa mdzes śiṅ mu tig chun pos rnam rgyan. K1 muktāhāmavibhūmitāsurajatān; BL2, N2 muktādāmavibhūmitāsurajatān.
4 N2 divyāmbarālakṛtaṃ/.
5 K1, BL2 prādyatarakta-.
6 The rendering follows Tib. T3: phun tshogs sems can don//. K1 satvārthasamāpādakaṃ; BL2 satvārthasampādakaṃ; N2 has dots between satvārthasaṃ- and -kaṃ instead of the rendering.
7 The rendering follows Tib. T3: padma dmar po rnam par rgyas pa. K1, BL2 pravikāsipadmam aruṇa; N2 pravikāśipadmam aruṇa.
8 The rendering is probably a misprint for hastalasan/. K1, BL2 hastalaśat/.
9 The rendering is probably a misprint for sarvākāravaraprasādaturaṃ. N2 -prasādacaturaṃ.
10 The rendering is probably a misprint for savyadakṣiṇasanasad. BL2 savyadāṣṇāsatāsad; N2 has dots between sa-, -dablā- and -sanāsad instead of the rendering.
11 N2 has dots after ra- .
12 N2 has dots before -manasaṃ.
13 The rendering follows Tib. T3: 'od rab gsal. K1, BL2 bhāśvaraṃ/; N2 bhāśvaraṃ//.
14 The rendering follows Tib. T3: ñe bar bsam. K1, BL2, udvīkṣa; N2 udīkṣa.
15 N2 prabhāprarītaṃ/.
16 The rendering follows Tib. T3: zla ba'i steṅ rnams su and the Sandhi rule. K1, BL2, N2 hṛtkaṇṭhaśīrṣendutareṣu.
17 N2 kāra.
18 N2 has dots.
19 The rendering follows Tib. T3: yaṅ dag blta//. K1, BL2, N2 prasamīkṣa.
20 K1 padmāna.
21 BL2 vibhāvayen; N2 vibhāvaye.
22 N2 śuṅkumasamprakāṇāla/.
23 The rendering follows Tib. T3: raṅ sñiṅ sṅags kyi 'od zer ni źal nas ṅes 'thon. K1, BL2 svahṛtmantramarīci vaktrān niścārya.
24 N2 has dots.
25 N2 has dots.
26 N2 has dots before -ścārya.
27 The rendering is probably a misprint for candrāntarāyātātmānaṃ. N2 candrācaturoyatātmā//.
28 The rendering is probably a misprint for veśan. N2 navenuśa.
29 K1 tadūdhvato; BL2 taddūdhvato.
30 The rendering is probably a misprint for 'rkān.

tathaiva vidhvastaghanāndhakārān/[1]
āgneyakoṇādigatārkasaṃsthaṃ[2]
bījāsu[3] śuklāsitaraktapītaṃ/[4]
lāṃ[5] māṃ tataḥ pāṃ atha tāṃ catuskaṃ[6]
[(7-]candrārkasaṃyogabhavaṃ prapaśyet//[-7)]

(5.5) tato mṛgākāryakarmabījajātāḥ[8] paśyed[9] yathā svāsanagāś[10] ca[11] tāmraḥ/[12]
devī vicitrābharaṇāmbarāgrāḥ savibhramāratnakṛtāvatansaḥ/[13] āgneyapadme[14] hi
madhyāsti[15] locanā[16] kundenduvarṇā[17] dvibhujā manoramā/[18] nairtyapadme[19] hi madhyāsti[20]
māmakīṃ[21] śnigdhendranīlāpratimāṃ[22] kṛpāvatī/[23] vāyavyapadme[24] hi madhyāsti[25] pāṇḍalā
sarojarārkanibhā muditānvitā/[26] aiṣāpadme[27] hi[28] madhyāsti[29] tārāṃ[30] [(31-]suvarṇavarṇaṃ[32]
susamāṃ[33] vibhāvayet// etās tu[-31)] jānupatitā viyugalāyatākṣāḥ[34] pīnonnatastanayugās[35]

---

1 N2 om. /.
2 N2 has dots after āgneyako-.
3 N2 has dots.
4 N2 has dots before -satarakṣapītaṃ/ instead of the rendering.
5 N2 lā.
6 The rendering is probably a misprint for catuṣkaṃ.
7 The rendering follows Tib. T3: zla ba ñi ma yaṅ dag sbyor ba bsam. K1 candrārkkasaṃyogabhva prapaśyet/; N2 candrārkasaṃyogabhava prapaśyet/; BL2 candrārkasaṃyogabhava prapaśyet//.
8 K1 mṛgākāryakamabījajātāḥ; N2 mṛgākāryakavījātāḥ.
9 The rendering follows Tib. T3: blta. K1, BL2 paśye; N2 punya.
10 N2 has dots.
11 N2 has dots.
12 The rendering is probably a misprint for tāmrāḥ/. N2 tamūḥ.
13 N2 //.
14 K1 āgneye padme.
15 The rendering is probably a misprint for madhye 'sti.
16 N2 has dots after loca-.
17 BL2 kundenduvarṇa; N2 has dots.
18 N2 om. /.
19 N2 naittapadme.
20 The rendering is probably a misprint for madhye 'sti.
21 N2 has dots.
22 The rendering is probably a misprint for snigdhendranīlapratimāṃ. N2 snigdhendranīlapatimāṅ.
23 N2 -ti/.
24 N2 has dots between naitta- and -me instead of the rendering.
25 The rendering is probably a misprint for madhye 'sti.
26 N2 //.
27 N2 has dots before -ṣāpadma instead of the rendering.
28 N2 has dots.
29 The rendering is probably a misprint for madhye 'sti. N2 madhyāṣi.
30 BL2, N2 tarāṃ.
31 N2 has dots.
32 K1, BL2 suvarṇavarṇā.
33 K1, BL2 susamā.
34 N2 has dots before -paritāviyagalāyatākṣāḥ instead of the rendering.
35 The rendering follows Tib. T3: nu ma zuṅ dag mtho. K1, BL2 pinonnahastanayugās; N2 has dots after pīnottadastanayugā- instead of the rendering.

tanmadhyarāgāḥ/[1] līlānvitā[2] [(3-]gurunita svadarāvarāṅgī[-3)] baddhāṃjalīḥ[4] [(5-]smayavatīḥ
kuṭilasukeśāḥ//[6]
(5.6) tataḥ[-5)] svahṛdmantramayūkhamālākṛṣṭaṃ[7] [(8-]sthitam vīkṣya purokṛtaṃ[-8)]
rīkṣaśrījñānacakram[9] vidhivat[10] suvateyadeyā[11] kurvīn[12] niveśanādīn/[13]
(5.7) tataḥ svam ātmān[14] [(15-]carīścakumbhe niṣiñcitājñānajalābhipūrṇaḥ/[-15)] dṛṣṭvā
jinātmakajalaprajātān vagīśvarān[16] sarvaśiraḥsu[17] paśyet/
(5.8) atha svahṛdbījamarīcikājātair[18] devīgaṇai vyāptasamastanāyakaiḥ/[19]
anekapūjāspharaṇair[20] vicitrai[21] dhyāyāt svacakram paripūjamānaṃ/
(5.9) atho hṛdindādharaṇaiḥ[22] supūrṇaviveṣṭitaṃ raktakalākalāpaiḥ/[23]
[(24-(25-]suraktam oṃ hūṃ[-25)] hṛdi[26] madhyasamsthaṃ vilokayej[27] jvalam ātmabījaṃ[28-24)]
visphārya rasmīn[29] varṇavṛndān lākṣāruṇair[30] avabhāsya lokaṃ/[31]

---

1 N2 has dots before -namadhyarāgāḥ instead of the rendering.
2 N2 has dots between lī- and -vitā.
3 The rendering is probably a misprint for guruhitā svadarāvarāṅgī. N2 has dots between gu- and -ta svadarāvarāṅga instead of the rendering.
4 N2 vidhāñjalā.
5 N2 has dots.
6 BL2, N2 kuṭilāsukeśāḥ//.
7 The rendering follows the Sandhi rule. K1, BL2 svahṛtmantramayūkhamālākṛṣṭaṃ; N2 has dots before -matarakhamālākṛṣṭam instead of the rendering.
8 The rendering follows Tib. T3: mdun gyi bar snaṅ la ni bźugs par. K1 sthitam vīkṣa puroktarīkṣaśrījñānacakram; BL2 tam vīkṣa puroktarīkṣaśrījñānacakram; N2 sthitan vīdā prarātra.
9 The rendering is probably a misprint for vīkṣaśrījñānacakram. N2 has dots after rīkṣa- .
10 N2 has dots.
11 K1 savateyadayā; N2 has dots before -deyā.
12 The rendering follows the Sandhi rule. K1 add. /. BL2 kurvīt; N2 kurvāt.
13 N2 om. /.
14 The rendering is possibly a misprint for ātmānaṃ. N2 has dots after ātmā- .
15 The rendering is possibly a misprint for carīścakumbhaniṣiktajñānajalābhipūrṇaṃ/. K1 carīścakumbhe niṣiñcitājñānajalābhipūrṇaiḥ/; N2 has dots before and after -danī-, and before niṣiñcitājñānajalābhipūrṇaiḥ instead of the rendering.
16 N2 has dots after vāgā- instead of the rendering.
17 N2 has dots after vīśvara- instead of the rendering.
18 BL2 syahṛd-; N2 svahṛdbījamarīcitājātai.
19 N2 has dots before and after -nā-, and before -bhastanāyakaiḥ/ instead of the rendering.
20 BL2 anekapūjaspharaṇair; N2 has dots between anekapū- and -spharaṇai instead of the rendering.
21 N2 vicitre.
22 K1 hṛdindāvaraṇai; N2 hṛdindādharaṇai.
23 N2 has dots between raktakalā- and -paiḥ.
24 N2 has dots before and after -kṛti-, and before and after -tadī- instead of the rendering.
25 The rendering follows Tib. T3: śin tu dmar po'i oṃ hūṃ yi ge. K1, BL2, N2 raktamo hūṃ.
26 K1, BL2 hṛti.
27 The rendering follows the Sandhi rule. K1, BL2, N2 vilokayed.
28 K1 add. /.
29 K1, BL2 rasmīnan; N2 add. tu.
30 N2 rākṣāruṇair.
31 K1 //; N2 lokāṃ/.

gṛhītasambuddhaviśuddhabodhā[1] tatraiva mantrī[2] pratisaṃharet[3] san/ [(4-]saṃsphārya saṃhāravidhīn punaḥ[-4)] punas tathaiva[5] kuryād akhinnamānasaḥ/[6] tābhyāṃ [(7-]bhavet khedacāryas tadā[-7)] mantraṃ[8] japed unmukha[9] cakrayuktitaḥ/ pratidivasaṃ[10] pratisaṃdhyāṃ[11] [(12-]kuryād japabhāvanā ime[-12)] yatnāt/

(5.10) yadi vā svasyāvasare yāvat[13] pratyakṣam ābhāti pratisaṃdhyaṃ[14] pariśuddhatryakṣaramantrair[15] adhiṣṭhite vidhivat/[16]

(6.1) sarvebhyo[17] bhūtebhyo[18] dadyād balim[19] [(20-]abhijapan mantrī/[-20)]

(6.2) tataḥ utthātuvāñchana[21] [(22-]kuryāt[23] praṇidhānam ekapadaṃ/[24-22)] atha vā śrīnāgārjunapādādikṛtābhyudgatābhiḥ[25]// // śrītrailokavaśaṅkarapadam[26] amala[27] śāśvataṃ[28] labheyāhaṃ[29] [(30-]puṇyenānena jagat tad eva saṃprāpayeyaṃ amalaṃ[31]//[-30)]

(6.3) uccāryo[32] oṃ hūṃ iti hṛdbīje[33] [(34-]saṃharec caturdevīṃ/[-34)]

---

1 The rendering is probably a misprint for gṛhītasambuddhaviśuddhabodhān. N2 has dots between gṛhītam bu- and -vaśuddhabodhā instead of the rendering.
2 N2 has dots after mantr-.
3 The rendering follows Tib. T3: bsdus ba. K1, BL2 pratisaṃkaret; N2 has dots before and after -ti-
4 N2 has dots.
5 N2 tathava.
6 N2 -nabhaḥ/.
7 The rendering follows Tib. T3: ṅal ba cher gaṅ gi tshe//. K1, BL2, N2 bhavet khedadracārya tadā.
8 K1 mantrañ.
9 The rendering is probably a misprint for unmukhaḥ.
10 N2 pratidivam.
11 The rendering follows Tib. T3: thun mtshams la. K1 pratisaṃdhyā; BL2 pratisandhyā; N2 has dots after saṇyaṃ- instead of the rendering.
12 The rendering is probably a misprint for kuryāj japabhāvanām imās. N2 has dots.
13 K1 yāva.
14 K1 pratisandhyaṃ; BL2 pratisandhya.
15 N2 pariśuddhatrākṣaramantrer.
16 K1 and N2 om. /.
17 N2 sarve yo.
18 N2 has dots before -tebhyo.
19 N2 bali.
20 N2 has dots.
21 The rendering is probably a misprint for utthātuvāñchanaḥ. N2 utthātuvāṃcana.
22 The rendering follows Tib. T3: tshigs bcad gcig pa'i smon la gdab//. K1 kuryā praṇidhānam ekapadan/; BL2 kuryā praṇidhānam ekapadyan.
23 N2 has dots.
24 N2 ekapadyan/.
25 The rendering follows Tib. T3: dpal ldan klu grub źabs// la sogs kyis mdzad mṅon 'phags kyis. K1 -kṛtābhigadyābhi; BL2 -kṛtābhimadyābhiḥ// //; N2 -kṛtābhigayogiḥ.
26 N2 has dots between śrītrailoka- and -śaṅkarapadam.
27 The rendering is probably a misprint for amalaṃ.
28 The rendering follows Tib. T3: myur du. K1, BL2 sāsvataṃ; N2 gāsvata.
29 K1, BL2 labhayāhaṃ/.
30 N2 has dots between pu-, -vajra-, -devaṇaṃ prāpaye- and -raṃ// instead of the rendering.
31 K1, BL2 maraṃ.
32 The rendering is probably a misprint for uccārya.
33 K1, BL2 dbīja.
34 The rendering follows Tib. T3: lha mo bźi bsdu. K1 sihare caturdevīḥ/; BL2 illegible between sihare- and -devīḥ/. N2 has dots between si- and -dadevīḥ/ instead of the rendering.

(6.4) utthāya[1] [(2-]sarvakṛtyaṃ[3] kurvan[4] vividhākāryaṃ ca[5] caturthasandhyāsamaya[6] tathaiva kiṃ tv asti kaściñ[-2)] ca [(7-]viśeṣa eṣaḥ/[-7)] jñānaṃ samutsṛjya[8] dhiyā svacakre[9] saṃhṛtya[10]
[(11-]sarvaṃ[12] tadvat/[13]
sandhyāvaśāne[14-11)] [(15-]paramārthacittam
samāmukhīkṛtya[-15)] śvāpī[16] mantrī/
prabhātakāle[17] praṇidhānaśaktyā[18]
prabuddha utthāya tathaiva kuryāt//

(7.1) yaḥ[19] sarvathā dhyāyana[20] trailokanāthan[21]
tasya pranasyanti[22] mahābhayāni/[23]
nāgendratoyāśanirākṣasādi-
hiraṇyaretoripubandhanebhyaḥ/[24]
lokeśvaraṃ paśyati yaḥ svadehaṃ[25]
tatāpagacchanti[26] jarārujādyāḥ[27]
dāridradurbhāgyaṃ[28] nṛpādipīḍā[29]
akālakālaṃ[30] prabhavaś ca[31] mṛtyuḥ/

---

1 N2 has dots between u- and -ya.
2 N2 has dots between sarvatavāṅka-, -vividhā- and -vaṣṭika instead of the rendering.
3 The rendering follows Tib. T3: bya ba thams cad bya//. K1 sarvakṛtyaṅ; BL2 sarvakṛtya.
4 BL2, N2 kurvana.
5 The rendering follows Tib. T3: daṅ. K1 vā; BL2; N2 cā.
6 The rendering is probably misprint for caturthasandhyāsamaye.
7 BL2 viśeṣaḥ/.
8 K1 samutsṛja; N2 saṃutsṛju.
9 K1 svacakra.
10 N2 has dots after saṃh- .
11 N2 has dots.
12 The rendering follows Tib. T3: ma lus. K1 śebimbidadhī; BL2 śebimbidadhīta.
13 K1 tadvata/.
14 The rendering is probably a misprint for saṃdhyāvasāne.
15 The rendering follows Tib. T3: lhag ma don dam sems ñid ni// yaṅ dag mṅon du byas nas. K1, BL2 paramārthacitta samāmukhīkṛtya; N2 has dots before -rāthadhisatī and after mukhā- instead of the rendering.
16 The rendering is probably a misprint for śvasī. N2 has dots.
17 N2 prabhāgakābhā.
18 N2 pranidhānaśaktyā.
19 N2 ya.
20 The rendering is probably a misprint for dhyāyan.
21 The rendering is probably a misprint for trailokanāthaṃ.
22 The rendering is probably a misprint for pranaśyanti.
23 N2 //.
24 The rendering: -rākṣasādi- follows Tib. T3: srin po. K1 nāgendratoyāśanirākṣamādi - hiraṇyaretoripubandharebhyaḥ/; BL2 nāgendratoyāśanirākṣamau hi hiraṇyaretoripubandharebhyaḥ/; N2 nāgendratoyāśanirākṣamādihiraṇyaretoripubandhanebhyaḥ.
25 BL2 svadeha.
26 K1, BL2 tatopagacchanti.
27 K1 rārujādyāḥ; BL2 rārujādyāḥ/.
28 The rendering follows Tib. T3: dbul daṅ skal ṅan. K1, N2 dāridradaurbhāgya; BL2 dāridradorbhāgya.
29 BL2, N2 nṛpādipītā.
30 K1 akālaṃ kālaṃ.
31 N2 ya.

anādimadhyāṃ[1] bhavasantato yat[2]
kāyena vācā manasā ca pāpaṃ/
mohanhatan[3] tasya tad (4-eti nāśaṃ-4)
yo lokanāthaṃ smarati praśāntaṃ/[5]
(7.2) sadādaraṃ[6] dhyāyati yo jane
saṃjānāti[7] sarvāni ca vāmanāni//[8]
adṛṣṭapūrvāś ca kulākalāpān[9]
aṣṭānyādīṃl[10] labhate guṇāś ca/
(7.3) (11-yo bhāvanaḥ lokavaśaṅkarasya-11)
māsāṣaḍaṣṭāv[12] atha saṃvipatte/[13]
(14-tasyānnapānāsanapadmabhūmi-
dravyās varādyāḥ-14) prabhavanti nūnaṃ/[15]
(7.4) (16-yo mantrajāpaṃ vitanoti samyak
saḥ sarvadoṣān sahasā tyajati/-16)
(17-guṇāś ca-17) sarve samupāśrayante[18]
tasmāt[19] japen[20] mantram akhinnacittaḥ/

---

1 BL2, N2 anādimadhyām.
2 K1 yata.
3 The rendering is possibly a misprint for mohahataṃ.
4 The rendering follows Tib. T3: źi. K1, BL2, N2 aiti nāsa.
5 K1, N2 prasāntaṃ/.
6 The rendering follows Tib. T3: rtag tu gus pas. K1, BL2, N2 sadādaran.
7 The rendering follows Tib. T3: śes. K1, BL2 śañjānāti; N2 has dots before -nāti.
8 The rendering follows Tib. T3: chuṅ ṅu. K1, BL2 vāṃ mayāni//; N2 vāmayāni//.
9 N2 kalākalāpān.
10 The rendering follows Tib. T3: la sogs yon tan brgyad rnams. K1, BL2, N2 aṣṭāṇimādīl.
11 The rendering follows Tib. T3: gaṅ gis 'jig rten dbaṅ phyug sgom byed na/. K1, BL2, N2 yo bhāvanā lokavaśaṅkarasya.
12 The rendering is probably a misprint for māsaṣaḍaṣṭāv.
13 K1 -patteḥ/; N2 om. /.
14 The rendering is possibly a misprint for -dravyavarādyāḥ. BL2 tasyānnapānāsanasadmabhūmidravyās varādyāḥ; N2 tasyānnapānāsanasadmabhamidravyā varādyāḥ.
15 N2 om. /.
16 The rendering follows Tib. T3: gaṅ gi sṅags ni yaṅ dag bzlas byas na// ñes pa daṅ bcas thams cad spoṅ bar 'gyur//. K1 yo mantrajāpa vidanoti samyak tat sarvadoṣāḥ sahasā tyajanti/; BL2 yo mantrajāpa vidanoti samyak te sarvadoṣāḥ sahasā tyajati; N2 yo mantrajāpa vidanoti samyak tat sarvadoṣāḥ sahasāṃ tyajanti.
17 BL2 guṇāṇya.
18 K1, N2 samuśrayante.
19 The rendering follows Tib. T3: de phyir. K1 tasya; BL2 tasyā; N2 tasmā.
20 The rendering follows the Sandhi rule. K1, BL2, N2 japet.

(8) trailokavaśaṃkarasya[1] guṇino lokeśvarasya sphuṭakṛtvā[2] sādhanam indudhāmavana[3] [(4-]puṇyaṃ mayāvāpya/[-4)] tenāśeṣajagatkṛpāparavaśaṃ[5] pradhvastacetastamo bhūtvā sarvajagadvasaṅkarapādayāpa[6] iva[7] śāśvataṃ//
samāptam idaṃ śrītrailokavaśaṅkarāmnāyabhugmalokeśvarasādhanaṃ//
kṛtir iyam ācāryapaṇḍitaśrīśūnyasamādhivajrapādānām iti//

---

1 N2 trailokavasaṅkarasya.
2 The rendering is probably a misprint for sphuṭīkṛtvā. K1, BL2 sphaṭakṛtvā; N2 sphuṭakṛtvā.
3 The rendering is probably a misprint for indudhāmavanaṃ. K1, N2 indudhāmavena.
4 The rendering follows Tib. T3: bdag gis . . . gaṅ źig bsod nams stobs kyis ni//. K1, BL2 puṇyamayāvāyitayan/; N2 puṇyamayāvāyiyan/.
5 The rendering follows Tib. T3: de yis 'gro ba ma lus sñiṅ rje gźan dbaṅ. K1 tenāśeṣajātakṛṣāparavaśaṃ; BL2, N2 tenāśeṣajāgaṅkṛṣāparavaśaṃ.
6 The rendering follows Tib. T3: 'gro ba thams cad dbaṅ du byed pa'i go 'phaṅ thob ciṅ. K1 jagadvasaṅkarapadayāyā; BL2 -padayopā; N2 -pādayāpā.
7 BL2, N2 ivaṃ.

# 11 Raktalokeśvarasādhana (Bhatt. no. 37)

(0) oṃ[1] namo[2] lokeśvarāya/[3]

(1) oṃ[4] ciṭi[5] cinaṭi[6] vikloli[7] vikloli[8] amukaṃ sadhanaparivāraṃ[9] me vaśam[10] ānaya[11] svāhā/[12] pūrvasevāyutaṃ[13] japtvā[14] paścāt[15] sādhanam ārabhet/[16]

(2) dakṣinottarapārśve[17] tārābhṛkuṭīdevīdvayasahitaṃ[18] āryāvalokiteśvarabhaṭṭārakaṃ[19] raktavarṇaṃ[20] raktamālyāmbarānulepanaṃ[21] pāśāṅkuśadhanurbāṇadharaṃ[22] caturbhujaṃ[23] śṛṅgāraikarasaṃ[24] raktakusumācitāśokataror[25] (26-adhastād[27] avasthitam-26) ātmānaṃ[28] vicintayet[29] trisandhyam/[30]

---

1 B, TO1, TO2, TO3, TO4, K1, N1, BL2 om.
2 BL1 namaḥ.
3 TO1, TO3, TO4, N1, BL1, BL2 //; TO2, K1 lokanāthāya//; K2 -yaḥ/.
4 K2 om.
5 K2, BL1 citi.
6 TO4 cirati; K1, K2, BL1, BL2 cinati.
7 TO1 -lori; TO4, K1, K2, BL1, BL2 om.
8 K2, BL1 ciloli.
9 TO1, TO3 -vāram; TO4 sadharaparivāram; BL1, BL2 sādhana-.
10 K1 vaṇam; K2, BL1 om.
11 K2, BL1 samānaye.
12 TO1, TO2, TO3, TO4, N1, BL1, BL2 //; K1 // //; K2 om. /.
13 TO1 -sevāśavāśataṃ; TO3, TO4, K1, BL2 -sevā śataṃ; K2 -sevyā ayūtaṃ; N1 -sevā ayutaṃ; BL1 -yā amukaṃ.
14 B, TO2, TO3, TO4, N1 japtā; TO1 japtāya; K2, BL1 japtāt; BL2 add. a central dot.
15 TO2 paścā.
16 TO1, TO3, K1, K2 //; TO2 āracet/; BL1 has a central dot.
17 K2 dakṣinapārśve; BL1 dakṣiṇapārśve.
18 TO1 -ṭidevidvaya-; K1 tārā•bhṛkuṭīdvayadevīsahītaṃ•; K2 -dvaye sahītaṃ; N1 add. /. BL1 -dvaye sahītaḥ; BL2 tārā•bhṛkuṭīdvayadevīsahītaṃ•.
19 TO1, TO3 -varaṃ bha-; K2 -lokṛteśvara-.
20 TO1, BL1 -ṇa; BL2 add. a central dot.
21 TO1 -nurepanaṃ; TO2 raktam mālyā-; K2 raktamālāmba-; BL1 raktamālāmbarānulepanaṃ; BL2 add. a central dot.
22 TO1 pāśāṅkuśadhanurbbāna; TO2, TO3, BL2 pāśāṅkuśadhanurbbāṇa; TO4 pāśāṃkuśadhanurbāṇa; K1 pāśāṅkuśadhanurbāṇa; K2, BL1 pāśāṅkuśadhanurbbāṇadhara; N1 pāśāṃkuśadhanurbbāṇadhara.
23 TO1, TO2, TO3, N1 and BL2 add. /. K1 -jaḥ.
24 TO4 and N1 add. /. K2 śṛṃkharaikarasaṃ•; BL1 add. a central dot.
25 B raktaṃ kusumavatāśokataror; TO1 raktasukumāritāśokataro; TO3, TO4 raktaṃ sukumāritāśokataro; K1 raktakusumāritāśokatalo; K2 raktakusumāvatāsokataro; N1 raktakusumāritāśokataror; BL1 raktaṃ kusumāvatāsokataro; BL2 raktakusumāritāśokatalo.
26 TO2 adhastāvasthitaṃ.
27 TO1 dhastad; TO3, TO4, K1, BL2 dhastād; K2, BL1 'dhastātad.
28 TO2 om.
29 TO1 cintayet; TO3, TO4 cintaye; K1 ciṃtaya; K2 add. a central dot. BL1 vicintayat; BL2 vicintaya.
30 TO1, TO3, K1, BL2 //; K2 and BL1 om. /.

(3) lavaṇāhutīnām[1] aṣṭottaraśataṃ[2] juhūyāt/[3] saptāhāt[4] striyaṃ[5] puruṣaṃ[6] vā vaśam ānayati[7] trisaptāhān[8] mahāpuruṣam/[9] lavaṇasahitena[10] madanena[11] puttalikāṃ[12] sādhayitvā[13] pratikṛtiṃ[14] caturaṅgulapramāṇāṃ[15] kṛtvā[16] nirdhūme[17] khadirāṅgāre[18] mantram[19] uccārayan[20] trisandhyaṃ[21] tāpayed[22] yasya nāmnā sa[23] vaśo[24] bhavati/[25] vajrodakabhāvitalavaṇaṃ[26] parijapyāṣṭottaraśatavāraṃ[27] yasya pradīyate[28] sa bhakṣitamātreṇa[29] vaśo[30] bhavati/[31]
(32-//raktalokeśvarasādhanaṃ samāptam//33-32)

---

1 B, N1 lavaṇāhutīnāṃ; TO1 -naṃ; TO4 lavarāhūtīnāṃ; K1 lavanāhutināṃ; K2 lavanām āhutīnām; BL1 lavanām āhutināṃ; BL2 lavanāhutīnāṃ.
2 K2, BL1 apy etaraśata.
3 TO4, K2, BL1, BL2 //; K1 juhyāt//; K2 juhuyāt//.
4 TO1 saptat; TO3 saptāt; K1, BL2 saptā; K2, BL1 saptāhā.
5 K2 strīyam.
6 TO4 puruṣan.
7 B add. a comma. TO1, TO2, TO3, TO4 and N1 add. /. K1 and BL2 add. //. K2 ārayatiḥ; BL1 add. a central dot.
8 TO2 -hāt; K1, BL2 triśap-; K2, BL1 -hā.
9 K2 om.; BL1 purṣam; BL2 has a central dot.
10 TO1 ravana-; TO3, K1 lavana-; K2, BL1 lavanasahitaṃ na; BL2 lavanasahitena•.
11 TO1, TO3, BL2 madena.
12 TO1, TO3, BL2 puttikāṃ; K1 putrikāṃ; K2 puttarikāṃ; BL1 putarikāṃ.
13 K1 and BL2 add. a central dot.
14 TO1, TO3, TO4, K1, BL2, K2 -ti.
15 TO1 catulaṅula-; TO2 catulāṅgula-; K1, BL2 -pramānaṃ; K2 caturāṅgunaṃ pramāṇaṃ•; N1 -māṇaṃ; BL1 caturaṅgurapramāṇaṃ.
16 BL2 add. a central dot.
17 TO4, K1, BL2 -ma.
18 TO4 -gāra; K1 and K2 add. a central dot.
19 BL1 mutram.
20 K1 -yana; K2 -yet//; BL1 -yet; BL2 add. a central dot.
21 K2 add. a central dot.
22 The rendering follows the Sandhi rule. B tāpayet; TO1, TO2, TO3, TO4, K1 and N1 add. /. K2, BL1 om.; BL2 add. //.
23 TO2 sarva.
24 TO2 so.
25 K2 and BL1 have a central dot.
26 TO1 -tavaśaṃ; TO2 -bhāvilivaṇaṃ; K1, K2, BL1, BL2 -vanaṃ.
27 K1, BL2 parijapyā aṣṭottaraśatavāraṃ; K2 palijapyāstotaravāranataṃ; BL1 palijapyāṣṭottaravāraṃ ṇataṃ.
28 TO1, TO3 dīyate/; TO2, TO4, K2, N1 dīyate; K1, BL2 dīyate//.
29 BL1 -bhaktitamātre.
30 N1 vaśaśo.
31 TO1, TO3, K1, BL1, BL2 //; K2 // //; TO2, TO4 and N1 om. /.
32 K2 iti sādhanasamuccaye•raktalokeśvarasādhana aṣṭatriṃsatyadhikaśatatamapaṭalaḥ //138//; BL1 iti sādhanasamuccaye raktalokeśvarasādhana aṣṭatriṃśatyadhikaśatatamapaṭala //138//.
33 K1 add. //āṣāḍhasya//. BL2 add. āṣāḍhasya//.

## 12 Lokeśvarasya vaśyādhikāravidhi (Bhatt. no. 38)

(1) pūrvoktavidhānena[1] tathaiva śūnyatānantaraṃ raktahrīḥkārajaraktapadmaṃ[2]

(2) tanmadhye[3] rakta-āḥkārapariṇatam[4] āryāvalokiteśvaraṃ raktavarṇaṃ jaṭāmakuṭadharam[5] amitābhagarbhajaṭāmakuṭadharaṃ[6] vāmakaragṛhītaraktapadmaṃ[7] tac[8] ca dakṣiṇakareṇa[9] vikāśayantaṃ vividhālaṅkāravastravibhūṣitam[10] ātmānaṃ niṣpādya//[11]

(3) svahṛdaye hrīḥkārajaraktapadmadaleṣu[12] ṣoḍaśasvarapariṇatarūpān śubhrabhramarān cintayet/[13] tataḥ sādhyahṛdaye[14] 'pi pūrvavat padmaṃ[15] vicintya[16] svahṛdisthapadmāt[17] svavajramārgeṇa bhramarān[18] niḥsārya[19] oṃ bhramarāḥ[20] sādhyahṛdi padmāmṛtam[21] ākarṣaya[22] jaḥ[23] iti mantreṇa sādhyavajre[24] praveśya[25] tatpadmasthāmṛtaṃ bhramarair[26] ākṛṣya tān punar api tadvajreṇa niṣkāsya[27] svavajramārgeṇa tatraiva praveśya[28] taccittāmṛtamadhubindumudgiratas[29] tān paśyed[30] iti//[31]

(4) mantraḥ[32] oṃ hūṃ/[33]

---

1 BL2 add. a central dot.
2 TO2 -kārarakta-; K1 raktaḥhrīkāra-; BL2 ktaḥhrīkārajaraktapadmaṃ•.
3 TO1, TO3 -dhya; TO2, BL2 tat madhye.
4 TO1 rakta-ākārīṇatam; TO3, TO4 rakta-ākāra-; K1, BL2 rakta-āḥkāraṃ pari-.
5 B (jaṭāmakuṭadharaṃ); TO1, TO3, TO4, K1 jaṭāmakuṭadharaṃ; N1 jaṭāmukuṭadharam; BL2 jaṭāmakuṭadharaṃ•.
6 TO1 -makūdharaṃ/; TO2, TO3, K1 and BL2 add. /. N1 -mukuṭadharaṃ.
7 TO1 -gṛhita-; K1 and BL2 add. /.
8 B tat.
9 TO2 dakṣiṇa; BL2 dakṣiṇe kareṇa.
10 TO1 vividhālakāra-; TO2 illegible between vividhāraṃ- and -stravibhūtam. BL2 -vastra •vibhūṣitam.
11 B, TO2 and TO4 om. //. TO1, TO3 /; N1 nimmārya/.
12 TO1 -dareṣu; K1 add. a central dot.
13 TO1, TO3, K1, BL2 //.
14 TO2 hrye.
15 BL2 add. a central dot.
16 BL2 add. //.
17 TO1, TO3 and TO4 add. /. K1 and BL2 add. //.
18 TO4 -manān; BL2 bhrarān.
19 TO1, TO3 nirmmāya; TO2 nirmmāryya śvayo//; TO4 nirmmārya/; K1, BL2 nirmmāya//; N1 nissārya/.
20 TO1 -malāḥ.
21 BL2 padmo/ mṛtam.
22 TO2 ākaṣaya; TO4 ākarṣadhva; K1 add. a central dot.
23 TO1, TO2, TO3, K1, N1, BL2 ja.
24 TO4 -vajrai.
25 BL2 add. a central dot.
26 BL2 -marer.
27 TO4 niṣkrāsya.
28 TO1 pravyeśya.
29 TO1 tacittā-; TO2 -bindumudbhir atas; K1, BL2 -bindumaṃgiratas.
30 K1 puṇyad.
31 B, TO2 /.
32 TO1, TO4, K1, N1 and BL2 add. //. TO2 add. /.
33 B om. /. TO4, K1, N1, BL2 //.

(5) tāvad bhāvayed avicchedaṃ[1] yāvad dināni sapta/[2] sādhyaṃ[3] ca pādayoḥ[4] patantaṃ[5] dhyāyād[6] iti/[7]
//lokeśvarasya vaśyādhikāravidhiḥ//[8]

---

1 TO1, TO3, TO4 -dyaṃ; K1 -dyaṃ/; BL2 add. a central dot.
2 TO4 saptā; K1 om. /. BL2 //.
3 TO1, TO2, TO3, K1, N1, BL2 -yañ; TO4 sādhyaś.
4 TO2 -yā.
5 TO1 paṭhataṃ; TO2 patanta; TO3, TO4 paṭhataṃ taṃ; K1, BL2 patitaṃ taṃ.
6 N1 dhyāyed.
7 TO1, TO3, K1, BL2 //; TO2, TO4 and N1 om. /.
8 TO1 -dhi//; TO2 vasyā-.

## 13 Māyājālakramāryāvalokiteśvarasādhana (Bhatt. no. 40)

(1) pūrvoktavidhānena śūnyatābhāvanānantaram[1]

(2.1) ākāśe[2] rephodbhavasūryasthahūṃkārajaviśvavajrapariṇataṃ[3] vajraprākāraṃ[4] vajrapañjaraṃ[5] ca vibhāvya/[6] tanmadhye[7] ghoraśmaśānaṃ[8] tasya ca madhye[9] raktāṣṭadalakamalaṃ[10]

(2.2) tanmadhye[11] ca nīlahrīḥkārasambhavaṃ[12] bhagavantam āryāvalokiteśvaraṃ[13] kṛṣṇavarṇaṃ[14] pratyālīḍhasthaṃ[15] sūryamaṇḍalasthitaṃ[16] pañcamukhaṃ trinetraṃ dvādaśabhujaṃ[17] sitaraktadakṣiṇamukhadvayaṃ[18] tathāpītaharitavāmamukhadvayaṃ[19] dakṣiṇabhujaiḥ[20] ḍamarukhaṭvāṅgāṅkuśapāśavajraśaradharaṃ[21] vāmabhujais[22] tarjanīkapālaraktakamalamaṇicakracāpadharaṃ[23] daṃṣṭrākarālasakalavadanaṃ[24] ṣaṇmudropetaṃ[25] sārdramuṇḍamālālaṅkṛtaśarīraṃ[26] nagnaṃ sarvāṅgasundaram ātmānaṃ jhaṭiti pratyākalaya[27]

---

1 TO2 -bhav-; K1 -tarām; BL2 śunātābhāvanānantarām.
2 TO1 and TO3 add. /.
3 TO2 illegible after rephodbhavasūryya-, and before and after -javi-. TO4 -ta; BL2 hūṃkāraviśvavajapariṇataṃ •.
4 TO2 illegible before -raṃ. TO4 vajapākāram; K1 vajraprākāra; BL2 vajaprakāra.
5 TO1, TO3 vajapaṃjalaṃ; TO2, TO4 vajapañjarañ; K1 paṃjalaṃ; BL2 paṃjalañ.
6 B and N1 om. /. K1, BL2 //.
7 TO2, TO3 -ya.
8 TO1, TO2, TO3, TO4, K1, N1 ghoraṃ śma-; BL2 ghoraṃ•śmaśānaṃ•.
9 TO4 -ya.
10 TO2 add. /. K1 raktā •aṣṭadala; BL2 add. a central dot.
11 TO1, TO3 -ya.
12 TO1, TO3 nīlaḥ hrīḥ-; TO2 nīra-; K1 nīlaṃ •hrīḥ-; BL2 nīlaṃ•hrīḥkālasaṃbhavaṃ•.
13 BL2 add. a central dot.
14 B kṛṣṇaṃ; TO2 kṛṣṇa.
15 TO1, TO3, K1, BL2 -stha; TO2 illegible.
16 TO1, TO3, K1, N1 and BL2 add. /. TO2 illegible before -taṃ. TO4 -maṇḍalaṃ sthitaḥ/.
17 TO2 and TO4 add. /. BL2 add. a central dot.
18 TO1, TO2, TO3, K1, N1 and BL2 add. /. TO4 -dakṣiṇadvayaṃ/.
19 TO1, TO3, TO4 and N1 add. /. TO2 -pita-; K1 add. ///. BL2 tathā •pītaharitavāmamukhadvayaṃ//.
20 TO1, TO2, TO3, K1 -bhujai; TO4, N1 -bhujair; BL2 -bhujai•.
21 TO1, TO3, TO4, K1, N1 and BL2 add. /. TO2 ḍamarukhaṭvāṅgapāśāṅkuśavajaśaradharaṃ/;
22 K1 -jair.
23 TO1, TO3, TO4 and N1 add. /. TO2 tarjjanīkapālaraktakamaramaṇicakracāpadharaṃ/; K1 tarjaṇīkapākaraktakamalamaṇicakracāpadharaṃ/; BL2 tarjjaṇīkapāla •raktakamaramaṇicakracāpadharaṃ/.
24 TO1, TO3 daṃṣṭrākalāla-; TO2 daṃṣṭrakarālasakarālavadanaṃ; TO3, TO4 and N1 add. /. K1, BL2 draṣṭākalālasakalavadanaṃ//.
25 TO1, TO3 and N1 add. /. TO2 -mudropabhūṣitaṃ/; TO4 -tāḥ/; K1 and BL2 add. //.
26 TO1, TO2, TO3 sārdhamuṇḍamālālaṃkṛtaśarīraṃ/; TO4 sārddhamuṇḍamālālaṃkṛtaśarīraṃ/; K1 sārddhamamaṇḍalālaṃkṛtaśarīraṃ/; N1 add. /. BL2 sārddhamaṇḍalālaṃkṛtaśarīraṃ/.
27 TO2 pratyākalaṃpya; TO3, TO4, K1, BL2 pratyākanayya.

(3) hṛccandre[1] (2-hrīḥkāramadhye vartinam//-2) oṃ āḥ hūṃ[3] munivaravajre[4] hrīṃ[5] hūṃ[6] jaḥ[7] iti[8] mantram[9] akṣasūtrākāraṃ[10] japet/[11] pañcānantaryakāriṇo[12] 'pi lakṣajāpāt[13] sidhyati/[14] (15-//māyājālakramāryāvalokiteśvarasādhanam//[16]-15)

1 TO1 -draḥ; TO3 -dreḥ; K1, BL2 -dra.
2 B hrīḥkāramadhyavarttī; TO1, TO3 hrīḥkāramadhyavartta; TO2, TO4 hrīḥkāramadhyavartti; N1 hrīḥkāramadhyavarttiṃ.
3 TO1, TO3, TO4, K1 and N1 add. iti. BL2 add. //iti//.
4 TO2 om.; K1 munivajra; BL2 munivaja.
5 TO1, TO2, TO3, K1, BL2 om.
6 TO2 om.
7 TO2 om.; K1 and BL2 add. //.
8 BL2 add. //.
9 TO3 mantra; K1 mantraḥ//; N1 makṣatram.
10 TO1, TO2 -kāra.
11 TO1, TO3, K1, BL2 //; TO4 om. /.
12 TO1 pañcānantaryakāliṇo.
13 TO1 lajāpāt; TO4 -pā.
14 TO1, TO2, TO4 and N1 om. /. TO3, K1, BL2 //.
15 TO1 //māyājārakramāryāvalokiteśvarasādhanaṃ//.
16 BL2 add. bhādrapadasya•//.

## 14 Sopacāramāṣamukhadhāraṇī (Bhatt. no. 41)

(1) nama[1] āryāvalokiteśvarāya[2] bodhisattvāya[3] mahāsattvāya[4] mahākāruṇikāya[5] tadyathā[6] oṃ
cala[7] cala[8] cili[9] cili[10] culu culu kulu[11] kulu[12] mulu[13] mulu[14] hūṃ hūṃ [(15-]hūṃ hūṃ phaṭ
phaṭ[-15)] phaṭ phaṭ padmahaste[16] svāhā/[17] dine dine pañcavārān trisandhyam[18] uccārayet/[19]
gardabho[20] 'pi granthaśatatrayaṃ[21] gṛhṇāti/[22] [(23-]padmahastādhāraṇīyam// //[24-23)]

(2.1) nama[25] āryāvalokiteśvarāya[26] bodhisattvāya[27] mahāsattvāya[28] mahākāruṇikāya[29] tadyathā[30]
oṃ dharaṇīdhare[31] dharādhare[32] bhadre[33] subhadre[34] svāhā/[35]

---

1 TO1, TO2, TO3 namaḥ; K1, BL2 namo.
2 K1 add. //. BL2 add. a central dot.
3 BL2 add. a central dot.
4 BL2 add. a central dot.
5 TO1 -ruṇikāya; TO2 add. /. K1 -runīkāya//; BL2 add. a central dot.
6 TO1 and TO2 add. /. K1 and BL2 add. //.
7 TO1 cara.
8 TO1 cara.
9 TO2 ciri.
10 TO2 ciri.
11 TO1, K1, BL2 huru; TO2, M hulu; TO3 dulu?; TO4 hūlu.
12 TO2, M hulu; TO3 dulu?; TO4 hūlu; K1, BL2 huru.
13 BL2 muru.
14 BL2 muru.
15 TO2 om.
16 BL2 -hasto.
17 TO2, TO4, K1, N1, BL2 //.
18 TO1 triśadhyam; TO2 trisandham.
19 TO4, K1, BL2 //.
20 TO1 gadabho; TO3, TO4, K1 gadarbho.
21 TO1 graṃṭhaśatatraṃ; TO2 illegible after granthaśata-.
22 TO1, TO2 //; TO3, TO4, K1, N1, BL2 gṛhnāti//.
23 B padmahastā dhāraṇīyam/; TO1 padmahastadhāraṇī//; TO2 padmahasto dhāraṇī// //; TO3 padmahastādhāraṇī//; TO4 padmahastādhāraṇī/; K1, BL2 padmahastādhāraṇī// //; M: padmahastadhāraṇī// //.
24 N1 //.
25 TO1, TO2, K1, BL2, M namaḥ.
26 BL2 add. a central dot.
27 BL2 add. a central dot.
28 BL2 add. a central dot.
29 TO1, TO3 -ṇīkāya; K1 -ṇīkāya//; BL2 add. //.
30 K1 and BL2 add. //.
31 K1, BL2 -ṇidhare•; N1 add. /.
32 N1 add. /. BL2 add. a central dot.
33 K1 add. /.
34 TO2 illegible after su-.
35 TO1, TO2, TO3, TO4, K1, N1, BL2 //.

(2.2) somagrahe[1] sūryagrahe vā[2] pañcagavyena[3] prakṣālya[4] aṣṭottaraśatamāṣān[5] mukhe prakṣipya[6] tāvaj japed[7] yāvan[8] na[9] mukto[10] bhavati/[11] lokanāthasya paṭapratimāyā[12] agrato bhūtvā[13] ghṛtena pradīpaṃ prajvālya[14] candanena[15] apatitagomayena vā[16] maṇḍalakaṃ[17] kṛtvā[18] (19-śucim ācāram-19) uttarasādhakaṃ[20] dvāre[21] sthāpayitvā[22] svayaṃ[23] candrasūryam apaśyan[24] pūrvasevāyutaṃ[25] japtvā[26] brahmacaryeṇa[27] sādhayet/[28]

(2.3) aśrutāny api[29] śāstrāṇi vetti[30] tatkṣaṇāt/[31]
śrutāni[32] na kṣayaṃ yānti[33] dhāraṇībalabhāvataḥ/[34]
yasya mūrdhni[35] pradīyante[36] cūrṇīkṛtya[37] ca pādayoḥ//[38]
sa sarvo vaśatāṃ[39] yāti[40] yāvac candradivākarau/[41]

---

1 K1 and BL2 add. a central dot.
2 TO1, TO3, TO4 and BL2 add. /. TO2 illegible.
3 TO1, TO4 -yana; TO2 illegible before -gavyena.
4 TO2 pakṣālya; K1 and BL2 add. a central dot.
5 TO1, TO3, TO4, K1 -śatavārān; TO2 -śatmāsān; BL2 -śatavārān•.
6 BL2 add. a central dot.
7 B japet.
8 TO2 -vat.
9 TO2 om.
10 TO2 sukto na.
11 TO1 bhavanti//; TO3, TO4 //.
12 TO1 paṭatimāyā; TO4 paṃṭa-.
13 TO1, TO3, K1, BL2 bhūto.
14 K1 and BL2 add. a central dot.
15 TO3, TO4 candranena.
16 BL2 add. a central dot.
17 TO1 maṇḍala; TO2 maṇḍakaṃ?; K1, BL2 maṇḍalaṃ.
18 TO2 and TO4 add. /. N1 add. //. BL2 add. a central dot.
19 B, TO4, N1 śucisācāram; TO2 sucisācāram.
20 TO1 uttarasākaṃ; TO4 -sādhanaṃ.
21 B dvāri.
22 TO1, TO3, K1 and BL2 add. /. TO2 add. / munivara vajre hrīḥ jaḥ hūṃ/. N1 add. //.
23 TO4 -yaś.
24 TO1, TO3, TO4, K1, N1 and BL2 add. /.
25 The rendering follows the Sandhi rule. B pūrvvasevāyuta; TO1, TO2, TO3, N1, BL2 pūrvvasevā ayutaṃ; TO4, K1 pūrvasevā ayutaṃ.
26 K1 and BL2 add. a central dot.
27 TO1 brahmacayeṇa; TO4 brahmacaryaṇa; BL2 brahmacaryyena.
28 TO1, TO3, K1, BL2 //.
29 TO1, TO3, K1, BL2 ati.
30 N1 illegible after ve-.
31 TO1, TO2, TO3, TO4 bhakṣaṇāt/; K1, BL2 bhakṣaṇāt//; N1 illegible before -kṣaṇāt/.
32 TO2 illegible before -ni.
33 BL2 add. a central dot.
34 TO1 and TO3 om. /. TO2 dhāraṇibarabhā-; TO4 //.
35 TO2 illegible before -ddhni.
36 BL2 add. a central dot.
37 TO1 cūṇīkṛtya; TO4 cūrṇāṃ kṛtya; K1, BL2 cūrṇikṛtya.
38 TO1 and TO3 om. //. TO2, TO4, N1 /.
39 TO4 -tā; K1, BL2 vasatāṃ.
40 TO2 yānti; K1 and BL2 add. //.
41 TO1, TO3, TO4, K1, N1, BL2 //.

rogās tasya na jāyante[1] ḍākinīgrahataskarāḥ//[2]
lepanāt sarvavyādhīnāṃ[3] śāntir[4] bhavati nityaśaḥ/[5]

(2.4) hrīḥkārabījasambhūtaṃ[6] lokanāthaṃ vibhāvya ca//[7]
dvibhujaṃ[8] varadaṃ savye[9] vāme padmadharaṃ[10] sitam/[11] jaṭāntaḥsthāmitābhaṃ[12] ca[13]
viśvābjacandrasaṃsthitam/[14]
vajraparyaṅkiṇaṃ[15] nāthaṃ[16] bhāvayed[17] vidhivad[18] vudhaḥ//[19]
//sopacāramāṣamukhadhāraṇī[20] samāptā//[21]

---

1 TO2 jātante.
2 TO1, TO2 -hastaskarāḥ/; TO3, N1 /; TO4 -hastaskarāḥ//.
3 TO1 -dhinā; TO4 -dhināṃ; BL2 add. a central dot.
4 TO1, BL2 śānti.
5 TO1, TO3, BL2 nityasaḥ/; TO2 nityasaḥ//; TO4, K1 //.
6 BL2 add. a central dot.
7 TO1, TO2, TO3, TO4 /.
8 TO2 dvībhujaṃ.
9 K1 -ya; BL2 -ya•.
10 TO1 -dhara.
11 TO1, K1, BL2 sitāṃ; TO2, TO4, N1 //.
12 TO1 jaṭāntasthamitābha; TO2 jaṭāntasthāmitābhañ; TO3 jaṭāntasthāmi-; TO4 jaṭāṃtasthāmitābhaś; K1 jaṭāṃtasthāmitābhañ; N1 -bhañ; BL2 jaṭāṃtasthāmitābhañ.
13 TO4 add. mitābhaṃ ca.
14 TO1 -candrasasthitam; TO3 om. /. TO4 //.
15 B, TO1 vajraparyyaṅkinaṃ; TO2 vajaparyaṃkiṇaṃ; TO3, M vajraparyaṅkinaṃ; K1 vajraparyyaṃkinaṃ; BL2 -yaṃninaṃ.
16 TO1, TO3 nātha; BL2 add. a central dot.
17 TO1 bhāvāyad.
18 B bidhivad.
19 TO2 /; N1 om. //.
20 B sopacāramāṣamukhā dhāraṇī; TO3, TO4, N1 sopacāramāṣamukhādhāraṇī; TO2 somacāramāṣamukhadhāraṇī; K1 sopacāramādhamukhādhāraṇī; BL2 sopacārasādhamukhādhāraṇī.
21 TO1 -tāḥ; TO2 -aṃ.

## 15 Sugatisandarśanalokeśvarasādhana (Bhatt. no. 42)

(1) oṃ pūrvoktavidhānena śūnyatābhāvanānantaraṃ

(2) śuklahrīḥkārodbhavaṃ sugatisandarśanalokeśvarabhaṭṭārakaṃ śuklavarṇaṃ ṣaḍbhujaṃ varadābhayākṣamālādharaṃ dakṣiṇe vāme padmakuṇḍītridaṇḍī[dharaṃ] ca ratnābharaṇabhūṣitaṃ vratasūtradhāriṇaṃ jaṭāmukuṭaṃ padmopari candramaṇḍalasthitaṃ saumyarūpaṃ bhāvayet/

(3) tasya jāpamantro 'yaṃ oṃ hrīḥ svāhā/
//iti sugatisandarśanalokeśvarsādhanam//

## 16 Pretasantarpitalokeśvarasādhana (Bhatt. no. 43)

(1) iti śūnyatābhāvanānantaraṃ

(2) śvetahrīḥkārodbhavaṃ jaṭāmukuṭinaṃ ṣaḍbhujaṃ prathamabhujadvayena varadau dvitīyabhujadvayena ratnapustakau tṛtīyabhujadvayena akṣamālātridaṇḍikaṃ sarvālaṅkārabhūṣitaṃ vrata(akṣa)sūtradhāriṇaṃ saumyamūrtiṃ padmopari candramaṇḍale sthitaṃ śvetavarṇaṃ vibhāvayet/

(3) mantraś ca tathaiva/
//pretasantarpitalokeśvarsādhanam//

## 17 Sukhāvatīlokeśvaradhyānaṃ//

mūlamukhaṃ śaraccandragauraṃ[1] dakṣiṇamukhaṃ haritavarṇaṃ[2] vāmamukhaṃ raktavarṇaṃ[3] paṃcacīraśeṣaraṃ[4] jaṭāmitābhaśobhitaṃ[5] mayūrapicchābhavastrābharaṇam pītavarṇayā ekavadanayā dakṣiṇavaradakarayā[6] vāmābhayakarayā[7] vāmākasthayā[8] svaśaktyā virājitaṃ dakṣiṇaprathamakare jvālāmālāṃkitakhaḍgadharaṃ[9] vāmaprathamakare kamaladharaṃ dakṣiṇavāmayor dvitīye śaraśarāsanadharaṃ[10] tṛtīyayo dakṣiṇavāmayor[11] vajrāṃkitaparaśupāśadharaṃ[12] caturthayor dakṣiṇavāmayor[13] varadavāmāṃkasthaśaktyāliṃganavātakarpaṭāṃkitatriśūladharaṃ[14] dakṣiṇavāmayor[15] paṃcamayor dharmacakramudrādharaṃ viśvapadmopari vidhumaṇḍale saṃsthaṃ saumyarūpaṃ sukhāvatīvyūhākhyaṃ lokeśvaraṃ sukhāvāptaye bhāvayet//[16]

---

1 BL2 saracandragauraṃ.
2 BL2 add. a central dot.
3 BL2 add. a central dot.
4 The rendering is probably a misprint for paṃcacīraśekharaṃ. BL2 paṃcacīrakaśeparaṃ?.
5 BL2 add. a central dot.
6 BL2 -varadakayā.
7 The rendering follows the Sandhi rule. K1 vāma abhayakarayā; BL2 vāma abhayakareyā.
8 BL2 vāmāṃkasthyā.
9 BL2 dvālāmālāṃkitakhaḍgadharaṃ.
10 BL2 śaraśarāsanadhanaṃ.
11 BL2 dakṣavāmayor.
12 BL2 add. a central dot.
13 BL2 dakṣavāmayor.
14 BL2 illegible between varadavāmāṃkasthaśa- and -liṃganavātakarpaṭāṃkitatriśūladharaṃ.
15 BL2 dakṣavāmayor.
16 BL2 bhāvayeha// //.

# Tibetan Texts

## List of Tibetan Translations

The Tibetan translations are based on the Sanskrit versions which include different numbers of *sādhanas.* We can distinguish the four kinds of sādhana collections in the *Tanjur* of the Tibetan Tripiṭaka: (1) *sGrub thabs brgya rtsa* (*sGrub thabs brgya daṅ lṅa bcu*), (2) *sGrub thabs brgya rtsa,* (3) *sGrub thabs rgya mtsho* (*sGrub thabs kun las btus* pa), (4) *lHa so so na tshogs kyi sgrub thabs* [Bühnemann 1994: 11-13]. Among these, the correlation between the Tibetan translations (1), (2), (3) and the Sanskrit versions have been clarified by several researchers. But no Sanskrit manuscript correlated with (4) has been found yet [Bühnemann 1994: 22].

Thomas [1905] points out that (1) is the Tibetan translation of the Sanskrit manuscript preserved at the University of Cambridge Add. 1686, and (3) is the translation of the Sanskrit manuscripts preserved at the University of Cambridge, Add. 1593 and 1648. Bühnemann [1994: 22, 31-36] suggests that (2) is the Tibetan translation of the Sanskrit manuscript preserved at the China Library of Nationalities, Beijing (Manuscript 140).

Yoshizaki [1979] clarified the correlation between the Tibetan translations (1), (2), (3) and the four Sanskrit manuscripts preserved at Tokyo University, nos. 451-454. Yoshizaki [1979] and Tsukamoto, Matsunaga, Isoda [1989: 385-485] showed the correlation between the Tibetan translations (1), (2), (3) and the Sanskrit texts in the Bhattacharyya edition. Bühnemann [1994] clarified the correlation between (2) and the Sanskrit manuscript preserved at the China Library of Nationalities, Beijing (Manuscript 140).

On the other hand, Meisezahl [1980: 136-157] edited the Tibetan translations of nos. 3, 7.2, 14 on the list. His edition is based on the Peking edition, the sDe dge edition and the Co ne edition.

In editing the Tibetan translations, the Peking edition, the sDe dge edition and the Taipei edition are used. In order to denote the above-mentioned Tibetan translations and editions, the following abbreviations are used in the list of Tibetan translations and the footnotes of the texts.

- B: Bhattacharyya edition.
- P: The Peking edition, Vols. 79, 80, Tokyo-Kyoto: Suzuki Foundation.
- D: The Ningma edition of the sDe-dge bKa'-gyur and bsTan-'gyur sponsored by the Head Lama of the Tibetan Nyingma Meditation Center, Vols. 61, 62, Oakland: Dharma Publishing, 1981.
- TP: The Taipei edition, Vols. 31, 32, SMC Publishing INC.
- T1: (1) *sGrub thabs brgya rtsa* translated by Pa tshab Tshul khrims rgyal mtshan (P 3964-4126, D 3143-3304, TP 3147-3308).
- T2: (2) *sGrub thabs brgya rtsa* translated by Ba ri ba (P 4127-4220, D 3306-3399, TP 3311-3404).
- T3: (3) *sGrub thabs rgya mtsho* translated by Grags pa rgyal mtshan (P 4221-4466, D 3400-3644, TP 3405-3649).
- M: [Meisezahl 1980: 136-157]

The following list shows the Tibetan translations corresponding to the Sanskrit texts. The text numbers (1.1, 1.2...) on the list are identical to the numbers of the Sanskrit texts. The Tibetan translations corresponding to the text numbers are indicated by the numbers of the Peking edition, the sDe dge edition and the Taipei edition.

A dotted line on the list means the absence of the corresponding sādhana. The Tibetan translations of Sugatisandarśanalokeśvarasādhana (no. 15 on the list) and Pretasantarpitalokeśvarasādhana (no. 16) are not included in the Tanjur.

1 Lokanāthasādhana

| no. | B no. | editions | T1 | T2 | T3 |
|---|---|---|---|---|---|
| 1.1 | 8 | P | ---- | ---- | 4228 |
| | | D | ---- | ---- | 3407 |
| | | TP | ---- | ---- | 3412 |
| 1.2 | 18 | P | ---- | ---- | 4236 |
| | | D | ---- | ---- | 3415 |
| | | TP | ---- | ---- | 3420 |
| 1.3 | 19 | P | ---- | ---- | 4237 |
| | | D | ---- | ---- | 3416 |
| | | TP | ---- | ---- | 3421 |

2 Khasarpaṇalokeśvarasādhana

| no. | B no. | editions | T1 | T2 | T3 |
|---|---|---|---|---|---|
| 2.1 | 13 | P | 3974 | ---- | 4230 |
| | | D | 3153 | ---- | 3409 |
| | | TP | 3157 | ---- | 3414 |
| 2.2 | 14 | P | 3975 | ---- | 4231 |
| | | D | 3154 | ---- | 3410 |
| | | TP | 3158 | ---- | 3415 |
| 2.3 | 15 | P | ---- | ---- | 4232 |
| | | D | ---- | ---- | 3411 |
| | | TP | ---- | ---- | 3416 |
| 2.4 | 16 | P | ---- | 4152 | ---- |
| | | D | ---- | 3331 | ---- |
| | | TP | ---- | 3336 | ---- |
| 2.5 | 24 | P | ---- | ---- | 4233 |
| | | D | ---- | ---- | 3412 |
| | | TP | ---- | ---- | 3417 |
| 2.6 | 26 | P | ---- | ---- | 4234 |
| | | D | ---- | ---- | 3413 |
| | | TP | ---- | ---- | 3418 |

3Vajradharmasya sādhanopāyikā

| no. | B no. | editions | T1 | T2 | T3 |
|---|---|---|---|---|---|
| 3 | 10 | P | ---- | ---- | 4243 |
| | | D | ---- | ---- | 3422 |
| | | TP | ---- | ---- | 3427 |

4 Ṣaḍakṣarīlokeśvarasādhana

| no. | B no. | editions | T1 | T2 | T3 | T4 | T5 |
|---|---|---|---|---|---|---|---|
| 4.1 | 6 | P | 3971 | 4153 | 4226 | 3674 | 4839 |
| | | D | 3150 | 3332 | 3405 | 2853 | ---- |
| | | TP | 3154 | 3337 | 3410 | 2859 | ---- |
| 4.2 | 7 | P | ---- | ---- | 4227 | | |
| | | D | ---- | ---- | 3406 | | |
| | | TP | ---- | ---- | 3411 | | |
| 4.3 | 11 | P | 3972 | ---- | 4229 | | |
| | | D | 3151 | ---- | 3408 | | |
| | | TP | 3155 | ---- | 3413 | | |
| 4.4 | 12 | P | 3973 | ---- | 4229 | | |
| | | D | 3152 | ---- | 3408 | | |
| | | TP | 3156 | ---- | 3413 | | |

* The translations: T4 and T5 are included in the Tanjur separately from T1, T2 and T3.

5 Siṃhanādalokeśvarasādhana and Siṃhanādadhāraṇī

| no. | B no. | editions | T1 | T2 | T3 |
|---|---|---|---|---|---|
| 5.1 | 17 | P | ---- | ---- | 4235 |
| | | D | ---- | ---- | 3414 |
| | | TP | ---- | ---- | 3419 |
| 5.2 | 20 | P | 3976 | ---- | 4238 |
| | | D | 3155 | ---- | 3417 |
| | | TP | 3159 | ---- | 3422 |
| 5.3 | 21 | P | 3977 | ---- | 4238 |
| | | D | 3156 | ---- | 3417 |
| | | TP | 3160 | ---- | 3422 |
| 5.4 | 22,23 | P | 3978 | 4150 | 4239 |
| | | D | 3157 | 3329 | 3418 |
| | | TP | 3161 | 3334 | 3423 |
| 5.5 | 25 | P | ---- | ---- | 4240 |
| | | D | ---- | ---- | 3419 |
| | | TP | ---- | ---- | 3424 |

6 Nīlakaṇṭhāryāvalokiteśvarasādhana

| no. | B no. | editions | T1 | T2 | T3 |
|---|---|---|---|---|---|
| 6 | 39 | P | ---- | ---- | 4252 |
| | | D | ---- | ---- | 3431 |
| | | TP | ---- | ---- | 3436 |

7 Hālāhalalokeśvarasādhana

| no. | B no. | editions | T1 | T2 | T3 |
|---|---|---|---|---|---|
| 7.1 | 28 | P | ---- | ---- | 4243 |
| | | D | ---- | ---- | 3422 |
| | | TP | ---- | ---- | 3427 |
| 7.2 | 27 | P | 3979 | 4155* | 4241 |
| | | D | 3158 | 3334* | 3420 |
| | | TP | 3162 | 3339 | 3425 |

*According to Meisezahl [1980:140-141], these are translations of the Sanskrit text 7.2. But it is not literally translated into Tibetan.

| no. | B no. | editions | T1 | T2 | T3 |
|---|---|---|---|---|---|
| 7.3 | 28 | P | ---- | ---- | ---- |
| | | D | ---- | ---- | ---- |
| | | TP | ---- | ---- | ---- |
| 7.4 | 29 | P | 3980 | 4151 | 4242 |
| | | D | 3159 | 3330 | 3421 |
| | | TP | 3163 | 3335 | 3426 |

8 Padmanarteśvaralokanāthasādhana

| no. | B no. | editions | T1 | T2 | T3 |
|---|---|---|---|---|---|
| 8.1 | 30 | P | 3981 | 4156 | 4244 |
| | | D | 3160 | 3335 | 3423 |
| | | TP | 3164 | 3340 | 3428 |
| 8.2 | 31 | P | ---- | ---- | ---- |
| | | D | ---- | ---- | ---- |
| | | TP | ---- | ---- | ---- |
| 8.3 | 32 | P | 3982 | ---- | 4245 |
| | | D | 3161 | ---- | 3424 |
| | | TP | 3165 | ---- | 3429 |

9 Harihariharivāhanodbhavalokeśvarasādhana

| no. | B no. | editions | T1 | T2 | T3 |
|---|---|---|---|---|---|
| 9.1 | 33 | P | 3983 | ---- | 4246 |
| | | D | 3162 | ---- | 3425 |
| | | TP | 3166 | ---- | 3430 |
| 9.2 | 34 | P | 3984 | 4154 | 4247 |
| | | D | 3163 | 3333 | 3426 |
| | | TP | 3167 | 3338 | 3431 |

10 Trailokyavaśaṅkaralokeśvarasādhana

| no. | B no. | editions | T1 | T2 | T3 |
|---|---|---|---|---|---|
| 10.1 | 35 | P | 3985 | ---- | 4248 |
| | | D | 3164 | ---- | 3427 |
| | | TP | 3168 | ---- | 3432 |
| 10.2 | 36 | P | 3986 | 4192 | 4249 |
| | | D | 3165 | 3371 | 3428 |
| | | TP | 3169 | 3376 | 3433 |
| 10.3 | --- | P | ---- | ---- | 4257 |
| | | D | ---- | ---- | 3436 |
| | | TP | ---- | ---- | 3441 |

11 Raktalokeśvarasādhana

| no. | B no. | editions | T1 | T2 | T3 |
|---|---|---|---|---|---|
| 11 | 37 | P | 3987 | ---- | 4250 |
| | | D | 3166 | ---- | 3429 |
| | | TP | 3170 | ---- | 3434 |

12 Lokeśvarasya vaśyādhikāravidhi

| no. | B no. | editions | T1 | T2 | T3 |
|---|---|---|---|---|---|
| 12 | 38 | P | ---- | ---- | 4251 |
| | | D | ---- | ---- | 3430 |
| | | TP | ---- | ---- | 3435 |

13 Māyājālakramāryāvalokiteśvarasādhana

| no. | B no. | editions | T1 | T2 | T3 |
|---|---|---|---|---|---|
| 13 | 40 | P | 3988 | 4220 | 4253 |
| | | D | 3167 | 3399 | 3432 |
| | | TP | 3171 | 3404 | 3437 |

14 Sopacāramāṣamukhadhāraṇī

| no. | B no. | editions | T1 | T2 | T3 |
|---|---|---|---|---|---|
| 14 | 41 | P | ---- | ---- | 4254/4255 |
| | | D | ---- | ---- | 3433/3434 |
| | | TP | ---- | ---- | 3438/3439 |

## 1.1 (T3) Lokanāthasādhana

(1- 'jig rten mgon po'i sgrub thabs bźugs so//-1) rgya gar skad du/ lo ka nā tha sā dha naṃ/ bod skad du/'jig rten mgon po'i sgrub thabs/

(0) jig rten mgon po la phyag 'tshal lo//

(1) 'dir sṅon gyi cho gas zla ba'i dkyil 'khor la mdun pa'i[2] gsum pa'i sa bon bcu gsum[3] gnon pa/ zla ba'i thig les rnam par brgyan pa/

(2) de rnams yoṅs su gyur pa las dpal ldan 'jig rten mgon po źi ba ral pa'i cod pan 'chaṅ ba/ sku zla ba bźin du dri ma med pa/ rgyan thams cad kyis brgyan pa/ phyag g'yon na padma bsnams pa/ g'yas pa mchog sbyin pa[4]/

(3) phyag gñis khu tshur bciṅs nas guṅ mo padma kha ma bye[5] blta bu/ padma daṅ zla ba'i gdan la bźugs par bsgom par bya'o//
'di'i phyag rgyas rgyas gdab par bya'o/

(4) oṃ ma ṇi padme hūṃ źes pa yi ge 'bum du bzlas pas sdig pa (6- thams cad -6) dag par 'gyur ro// gñis daṅ gsum gyis rmi lam du mthoṅ bar 'gyur ro// bya[7] ba bzlas na mtshams[8] (9- med pa lṅa byas -9) pas kyaṅ 'grub par 'gyur ro//

dpal ldan 'jig rten mgon po'i sgrub thabs rdzogs so//

---

1 TP om.
2 P om.
3 D add. pas.
4 P om.
5 D byed?, TP add. ba.
6 P om.
7 D, TP bye.
8 P mcham.
9 P om.

## 1.2 (T3) Lokanāthasādhana

rgya gar skad du/ lo ka nā tha sā dha ṇaṃ/ bod skad du/ 'jig rten mgon po'i sgrub thabs/

(0) 'jig rten mgon po la phyag 'tshal lo//
(1) rnal 'byor rim pa sṅon ma bźin//
'jig rten mgon po zla ba'i 'od//
hrīḥ[1] yi yi ge las byuṅ ba'i//
ral pa'i cod pan gyis brgyan pa//
ral pa'i mthar gnas rdo rje chos//
nad rnams ma lus 'joms byed pa//
phyag g'yas mchog sbyin de bźin du//
g'yon pa na ni padma bsnams//
rol pa'i stobs kyis yaṅ dag bźugs//
źi ba chen po 'od raṅ 'bar//
(2.1) mchog sbyin utpa la phyag na bsnams//
źi ba'i sgrol ma g'yas phyogs bźugs//
(2.2) de nas rta mgrin g'yon phyogs na//
phyag 'tshal ba daṅ dbyug pa'i phyag//
drag chen sku mdog damr po ste//
stag gi pags pa'i na bza' dgyes//
de bźi cho ga yaṅ dag ldan//
(5) jig rten mgon po rab bsgoms na//
ñon moṅs dri ma kun las 'das//
yid kyis[2] śiṅ rta gaṅ bar 'gyur//
(6) 'dir sṅags ni// oṃ hrīḥ źes so//

'jig rten mgon po'i sgrub thabs rdzogs so//

---

1 D hrī.
2 D, TP kyi.

## 1.3 (T3) Lokanāthasādhana

//rgya gar skad du/ lo ke śwa ra sā dha naṃ/ bod skad du/ 'jig rten dbaṅ phyug gi sgrub thabs/

(0) 'phags pa spyan ras gzigs dbaṅ phyug la phyag 'tshal lo//

(1) lāṃ gi sa bon las[1] dag pa'i mthar thug pa (2-thams cad-2) cho ga sṅon[3] ma bźin du bya'o//

(2) de las lām[4] yoṅs su gyur pas las 'jig rten mgon po zla[5] ba'i 'od zer lta bu 'bar źiṅ rgyan thams cad kyis brgyan pa/ ral pa'i cod pan can/ padma daṅ/ zla[6] ba la skyil mo kruṅ gis bźugs pa/ phyag g'yon[7] padma bsnams śiṅ/ g'yas mchog sbyin pa bsgom par bya'o//

(3) dam tshig gi phyag rgya ni khu tshur gñis bciṅs nas guṅ mo dag padma kha 'bus pa'i rnam par sbyar[8] bar bya'o/

(4) oṃ ṇa ṇi padme hūṃ źes pa ni bzlas pa'i sṅags so//

'jig rten dbaṅ phyug gi sgrub thabs rdzogs so //

---

1 D and TP add. yaṅ.
2 P om.
3 D illegible between s- and -on.
4 P laṃ.
5 D illegible.
6 D illegible.
7 D and TP add. na.
8 TP skyar.

## 2.1 (T1) Khasarpaṇalokeśvarasādhana

rgya gar skad du/ (1-kha sarpa-1) ṇa sā dha naṃ/ bod skad du/ bde ba 'byuṅ ba'i sgrub thabs/

(0) (2-kha sarpa-2) ṇa la phyag 'tshal lo/

(1) re źig daṅ por sṅags pas bde ba'i stan la ñe bar gnas śiṅ gdoṅ pa'i gtsaṅ sbra la sogs pa byas pas//

(2.1.1) gtsaṅ źiṅ dben pa'i phyogs su raṅ gi sñiṅ gar yi ge a las zla ba'i dkyil 'khor rnam par bsgom par bya ba'o// de'i steṅ du yi ge hrīḥ dkar po'o//

(2.1.2) de'i 'od zer gyis bsdul[3] la mdun gyi nam mkha' la bla ma daṅ/ saṅs rgyas daṅ/ byaṅ chub[4] sems dpa' la sogs pa sbyan draṅs la/ sñiṅ ga'i sa bon gyi 'od zer las byuṅ ba'i mchod pa'i sprin gyis legs par mchod ciṅ/ sdig pa bśags pa la sogs pa daṅ/ tshaṅs pa'i gnas bźi bsgoms pa yaṅ bya ste/

(2.1.3) de nas stoṅ pa ñid bsgom par bya źiṅ oṃ stoṅ pa ñid kyi ye śes rdo rje'i raṅ bźin gyi bdag ni ṅa yin no// śes bya ba 'dis kyaṅ[5] byin gyis brlab par bya ba'o//

(2.2) de'i rjes la sṅar bźin du yi ge hrīḥ rnam par bsgoms la nam mkha'i dkyil nas[6] spros źiṅ bsdu bar yaṅ byas la// de las ṅes par byuṅ ba'i 'jig rten dbaṅ phyug tu bdag ñid bsgom par bya ste/ dkar po 'od zer bye ba 'phro ba ral pa daṅ/ dbu rgyan daṅ ldan pa/ snaṅ ba mtha' yas kyis sbyi bor mtshan pa/ rgyan thams cad kyis brgyan pa/ bźin 'dzum pa/ skyil kruṅ phyed pas padma daṅ zla ba'i gdan la bźugs pa/ g'yas pas mchog sbyin pa/ g'yon pas padma bsnams pa'o//

(2.3) g'yas kyi phyogs na 'phags ma sgrol ma daṅ/ gźon nu nor bzaṅs gñis so// g'yon gyi phyogs na khro gñer[7] can daṅ/ rta mgrin gñis so//

(2.4) de nas mgo bo la yi ge oṃ/ mgrin par yi ge āḥ sñiṅ gar yi ge hūṃ/ 'di dag rnams legs par bsams la/ ji srid du skyo bar ma gyur gyi bar du gnas par bya'o//

(3) skyo ba daṅ sṅags bzlas par bya'o// de la sṅags ni 'di yin te/ oṃ hrīḥ swāhā/ bya ba'o//

(8-kha sarpa ṇa'i-8) sgrub thabs rdzogs so// // paṇḍi ta chen po ratna a[9] ka ra gu pta'i źal sṅa nas/ dge sloṅ tshul khrims rgyal mtshan gyis bsgyur ba'o//

---

1 D, TP kharsa pa.
2 D, TP kharsa pa.
3 TP bskul.
4 D illegible.
5 D, TP om.
6 D, TP na.
7 P ñer.
8 D, TP kharsa pa ṇi'i.
9 TP ā.

## 2.1 (T3) Khasarpaṇalokeśvarasādhana

rgya gar skad du/ ā rya (1-kha sarpa ṇa-1) lo ke śva ra sā dha naṃ/ bod skad du/ 'phags pa (2-kha sarpa ṇa-2) 'jig rten dbaṅ phyug gi sgrub thabs/

(0) 'phags pa spyan ras gzigs dbaṅ phyug la phyag 'tshal lo//

(1) daṅ por[3] re źig sṅags pas stan bde ba la 'dug ste/ źal bsaṅ ba la sogs pa byas źiṅ/

(2.1.1) sbyaṅs nas raṅ gi sñiṅ gar a yig las zla ba'i dkyil 'khor bsgom par bya'o// de'i steṅ du hrīḥ yig dkar po/

(2.1.2) de'i 'od zer gyis mdun gyi nam mkha'i mthil du bla ma daṅ/ saṅs rgyas daṅ/ byaṅ chub sems dpa' la sogs pa rnams spyan draṅs nas/ sñiṅ ga'i sa bon gyi 'od zer las byuṅ ba'i mchod pa'i sprin tshogs rnams kyis yaṅ dag par mchod nas/ sdig pa bśags pa la sogs pa byas nas tshaṅs pa'i gnas bźi bsgom par bya'o//

(2.1.3) de nas stoṅ pa ñid du bsgoms te/ oṃ śū nya tā dzñā na bdzra swa bhā wa ātma ko 'haṃ/ źes pas byin gyis brlab par bya'o//

(2.2) de nas sṅon bźin du hrīḥ yig rnam par bsgoms nas/ nam mkha'i mthil du spro ba daṅ bsdu ba'i rim pas// de las byuṅ ba'i 'jig rten dbaṅ phyug gi bdag ñid bsgom par bya ste/ 'od zer dkar po bye ba daṅ ldan pa ral pa'i cod pan can/ 'od dpag tu med pas dbu brgyan pa/ rgyan thams cad kyis brgyan pa/ padma daṅ zla ba'i gdan la skyil kruṅ phyed pas bźugs pa/ phyag g'yas pa mchog sbyin/ g'yon pa padma bsnams pa'o//

(2.3) g'yas phyogs logs na 'phags ma sgrol ma daṅ/ nor bzaṅs gźon nu gñis so// g'yon gyi logs na khro gñer can daṅ rta mgrin gñis so//

(2.4) de nas bcom ldan 'das kyi spyi bor oṃ yig/ mgrin par āḥ yig/ sñiṅ gar hūṃ yig bsgoms la ji srid mi skyo ba'i[4] du'o//

(3) skyo na sṅags bzlas par bya ste/ de la sṅags ni 'di'o// oṃ hrīḥ swāhā

źes pa ni 'phags pa 'jig rten dbaṅ phyug (5-kha sarpa ṇa'i-5) sgrub thabs[6]// slob dpon rñogs pa med pas mdzad pa rdzogs so//

---

1 D, TP kharsa pā ṇi.

2 D, TP kharsa pā ṇi.

3 TP po.

4 D and TP add. bar.

5 D kharsa pā ni'i, TP kharsa pā ṇi.

6 D add. so.

## 2.2 (T1) Khasarpaṇalokeśvarasādhana

rgya gar skad du/ kharsa[1] pa ṇa sā dha naṃ/ bod skad du/ bde ba 'byuṅ ba'i sgrub thabs/

(0) bcom ldan 'das bde ba thams cad 'byuṅ bar mdzad pa la phyag 'tshal lo//

(1) mṅon 'dod 'bras spyi[2] dpag bsam ljon
śiṅ[3] dpal ni kun nas ñer rgyas pa'i/
bde bar gśegs tshul lam chen rnams ni
śin tu bde mdzad ded dpon pa/
srid źi mñam par dgoṅs pa dṅos po'i
raṅ bźin ma lus thams cad kyis[4]/
skye dgu'i chad pa 'di ni phyag na
padma 'di yis źi gyur cig//

(2) sṅa mor gdoṅ sogs legs bkrus la//
dben pa'i gnas su cho ga yis[5]//

(3.1) sñiṅ ga'i sa bon spro bya ba//
padma'i stan la legs[6] gnas[7] pa'i//
zla rgyas steṅ du rab 'bar ba[8]//
sa bon raṅ gi sñiṅ gar bsgom//

(3.2) 'od des legs par bskul byas la//
yaṅ dag spyan draṅs mkha' dbyiṅs mdun//
dpal ldan [(9-]kha sar[-9)] pa ṇa mgon[10]//
bla ma saṅs rgyas rgyam tsho[11] sras//
mchod sprin rnam pa sna tshogs pa//
sa bon de las byuṅ bas mchod//

(3.3.0) de nas mṅon par phyag[12] byas la[13]//
sdig pa bśags la [(14-]sogs pa'o[-14)]//

---

1 P khar sa.
2 D, TP ster.
3 D źin.
4 D, TD kyi.
5 TP yi.
6 P le gla.
7 P illegible before -nas.
8 P bar.
9 D, TP kharsa.
10 D illegible.
11 P illegible.
12 D phyag.
13 P pa.
14 P gsol ba'o.

(3.3.1) blo 'khor ba thog ma med pa nas// 'khor ba gaṅ yin par bdag gis mi dge ba bgyis pa 'am/ bgyid du stsal[1] 'am/ gźan bgyid pa[2] la[3] gyur par[4] rjes su yi raṅ bar bgyis pa/ de dag thams cad bcom ldan 'das kyi spyan sṅar bdag gis bśags par bgyi'o//

(3.3.2) rdzogs pa'i saṅs rgyas daṅ/ saṅs rgyas kyi sras daṅ/ 'phags pa rnams daṅ gźan dag rnams kyis byas pa'i dge ba gaṅ yin pa la yaṅ rjes su yi raṅ ṅo//
bdag gis de dag ma lus pa[5] rdzogs pa'i byaṅ chub tu yaṅ dag par yoṅs[6] su
(7-bskyad par-7) bgyi'o//

(3.3.3) thugs rje'i raṅ[8] bźin bla med pa'i[9]/
saṅs rgyas la ni bdag skyabs mchi//
chos kyi raṅ bźin gyis[10] med pa'i //
chos rnams thams cad ro gcig pa'o//

(3.3.4) rab dga' la sogs sar źugs pa'i//
byaṅ chub sems tshogs la de bźin/
mya ṅan las (11-'das par-11) bźed pa'i saṅs rgyas la yaṅ gźan la phan pa'i don du riṅ bar bźugs par bdag gsol ba 'debs so/

(3.3.5) sgrib[12] pa thams cad[13] rtsad[14] nas gcod par byed pa'i rgyur gyur pa byaṅ chub kyi sems bdag gis bskyed par bgyi'o//

(3.3.6) sras daṅ bcas pa'i bde bar gśegs pa'i lam la bdag gis bsam pa rnam par dag pas legs par bstan[15] par bgyi'o//

(3.4) de nas cig[16] (17-daṅ du ma daṅ-17) bral ba'i phyir na/ g'yo ba daṅ/ mi g'yo ba'i 'jig rten[18] 'di dag ñid ma lus pa yaṅ stoṅ pa'o źes rnam par bsams la/ oṃ stoṅ pa ñid kyi ye śes kyi rdo rje'i raṅ bźin bdag ñid ni ṅa yin no źes bya bas stoṅ pa ñid byin gyis brlab par bya'o// byin gyis brlabs la chos 'di dag thams cad ni raṅ bźin gyis rnam par dag pa yin la de bźin du ṅa yaṅ yin no źes kun tu bltas la/ oṃ chos thams cad raṅ bźin gyis rnam par dag pas bdag kyaṅ raṅ bźin gyis dag pa'o/ źes brjod par bya ba'o//

(4.1) de nas ni bsgom (19-pa po-19) rnam par śes pa'i bdag ñid tsham du gyur pa las sṅon gyi smon lam gyi[20] legs par bskul bas yi ge paṃ[21] yoṅs su gyur pa las kha dog sna tshogs pa'i

---

1 D add. ba.
2 D, TP par.
3 D, TP om.
4 D, TP pa la.
5 D, TP om.
6 D illegible after yoṅ-.
7 D, TP skyad par.
8 D, TP bdag.
9 D pa'o.
10 D, TP gos.
11 P 'da' bar.
12 P sgreb.
13 D illegible.
14 P om.
15 P brten; D bsten.
16 D gcig.
17 D, TP om.
18 TP rtan.
19 D, TP pa'o//.
20 D gyis.
21 D add. las.

padma'o// a las skyes pa'i zla ba'i dkyil 'khor rgyas śiṅ dri ma med pa'o// de'i steṅ du śin tu 'od 'bar gyur ba'i yi ge hrīḥ ste[1]/ nam mkha'i dkyil gaṅ ba daṅ/ spro ba'i tshogs kyis khyab par rnam par bsgoms la/ de dag yoṅs su gyur pa las raṅ gi sa bon gyis[2] yu ba'i sñiṅ po la rgyan du byas śiṅ kha bye ba'i padma sṅon du blta'o// de nas de dag kun yoṅs su gyur nas bdag ñid bcom ldan 'das su bsgom par bya ste/ goṅ[3] ltar 'od bye ba kun nas 'phro bas sku śin tu dkar ba dbu rgyan[4] daṅ ldan źiṅ ral pa ni braṅ khar te/ snaṅ ba mtha' yas kyi[5] dbu rgyan pa/ sna tshogs padma las byuṅ ba'i zla ba'i dkyil 'khor la phyed kruṅ gyis bźugs pa/ sku rgyan thams cad daṅ ldan źiṅ źal mdzum pa lo brgyad gñis kyi tshod du gyur pa ste/ phyag g'yas pas mchog sbyin pa/ phyag g'yon pas yu ba daṅ ldan pa'i padma bsnams śiṅ/ phyag smad[6] pa de'i 'og na bdud rtsi'i rgyun mdog śiṅ tu dkar ba 'thuṅ bar byed pas tshim pa med par kha gyen du gdaṅs śiṅ gsus pa che ba śin tu riṅ bar gyur pa ñe bar gnas pa'i yi dwags[7] khab[8] lta bu'i kha tshim par mdzad do// ri bo po ṭa la'i naṅ na bźugs pa dpal daṅ ldan pa thugs rjes brlan par gyur pa'i kun tu gzigs pas sgeg[9] pa'i ñams daṅ ldan pas kun nas legs par ston[10] par byed pa/ śiṅ tu (11-źi ba-11) sna tshogs pa'i mtshan rnams kyis brgyan pa'o//

(4.2.0) de'i mdun na sgrol ma'o// g'yas zur[12] na gźon nu nor bzaṅs so//

(4.2.1) de la sgrol ma ni ljaṅ gu phyag g'yon pas yu ba daṅ bcas pa'i utpa la bzuṅ nas phyag g'yas pas kha 'byed par mdzad pa/ rgyan sna tshogs daṅ ldan pa/ śiṅ tu gźon śiṅ laṅ tsho la bab[13] pa sta[14] zur legs par lteṅ[15] pa'o//

(4.2.2) nor bzaṅs gźon nu yaṅ mchan khuṅ g'yon pa na po ti bcug ciṅ thal mo kha sbyar ba gser gyi 'od kun tu snaṅ ba/ gźon nu'i gzugs su gnas pa rgyan rnams thams cad daṅ ldan pa'o//

(4.2.3) nub tu ni khro gñer can no// byaṅ du ni rta grin no// de la khro gñer can ni phyag bźi ma gser gyi 'od daṅ ldan pa ral pa'i thor tshugs can/ (16-phyag g'yon pa dag gis dbyu gu rtse gsum daṅ sbyi blugs bsnams pa/-16) phyag g'yas pa dag gis phyag 'tshal ba'i staṅs daṅ phreṅ ba 'dzin pa spyan gsum ma'o//

(4.2.4) rta mgrin mdog dmar ba boṅ thuṅ[17] gsus pa che ba skra ser po gyi na du 'bar ba sbrul gyi ga śa can/ sma ra śin tu ser ba kha'i sgo nas khrag yoṅs su 'dzig[18] pa spyan gsum dmar źiṅ

---

1 D, TP om.
2 D, TP gyi.
3 P gaṅ.
4 TP brgyan.
5 D kyis.
6 D smid.
7 P, D dags.
8 D om.
9 D illegible.
10 D bstan; TP bsten.
11 D gzan pa; TP gźon pa.
12 TP zuṅ.
13 D babs.
14 D, TP lta.
15 D, TP bsten.
16 D, TP om.
17 P add. ba.
18 D 'dzag.

zlum pa khro gñer daṅ smin ma śin tu bsdus pa stag gi pags pa'i śam thabs can dbyug tho daṅ ldan pa phyag g'yas pa phyag 'tshal ba'i staṅs stobs[1] so//

(4.2.5) de dag ñid thams cad kyaṅ raṅ gi gtso bo'i źal la spyan lta bar byed pa/ ji ltar mdzes par gnas pa[2] bsam par bya ba'o//

(4.3) (3-de nas raṅ gi sñiṅ gar zla ba'i dkyil 'khor gyi steṅ du yi ge hrīḥ rnam par bsams la/ de las kyaṅ rnam pa sna tshogs pa'i 'od zer kun tu spros śiṅ/ khams gsum yoṅs su bkaṅ bas sems can rnams thams cad kyaṅ 'jig rten dbaṅ phyug gi go 'phaṅ la rab tu bkod de/-3) 'od zer de dag slar yaṅ sa bon gyi[4] yi ge de ñid la legs par (5-gźug pa-5) bya ba'o//[6] slar yaṅ de dag spros pa ñid kyis ye śes sems dpa' spyan draṅs la dam tshig sems dpa' daṅ chu daṅ 'o ma bźin du lhan cig gcig tu gyur pa'i ṅo bor bsgom par bya'o//

(4.4) de nas sku daṅ gsuṅ daṅ thugs rnam par dag pa ni rim pa ji lta ba bźin du mgo bo la yi ge oṃ dkar po mgrin par yi ge (7-āḥ dmar-7) po/ sñiṅ gar yi ge hūṃ nag po rnams bsam par bya'o// 'di dag gis kyaṅ sems can gyi phuṅ po ma lus pa'i ñon moṅs pa[8] tshogs thog ma med pa nas 'byuṅ ba rnams rnam par 'jig[9] par byed pa mtha' yas pa'i sgom[10] pa 'di ni nus pa ji lta ba bźin du gsal bar bya ba'o//

(5) gsal daṅ 'dzin daṅ śes rab daṅ//
bskal bzaṅs nad med phun tshogs rnams//
bsgom pa'i sbyor bas thob pa yin//
rtsod ldan la ni mṅon du yaṅ//

(6) bsgoms pas skyo na sṅags sems rtse gcig pas bzlas so// de la sṅags ni 'di yin te/ oṃ hrīḥ swāhā/ yi ge 'di dag rnams kyaṅ stoṅ ka'i zla ba dri ma med pa'i phreṅ ba ñid kyis 'od 'bar źiṅ 'od zer du ma 'phro bar byad pa'o// bzlas pas skyo na yaṅ bsod nams yoṅs su bsdos la laṅs te lha'i ṅa gyal gyis bgrod pas ji ltar[11] bde[12] bar[13] rgyi[14] bar[15] bya ba'o//

(7) dpal ldan 'jig rten dbaṅ phyug gi/
sgrub thabs cho ga bźin byas pas/
bsod nams bdag la legs byuṅ gaṅ/
des de'i go 'phaṅ skyes thob śog/

---

1 D, TP thabs.
2 D, TP par 'od.
3 D, TP om.
4 D, TP om.
5 D zugs par.
6 D and TP add. de nas raṅ gi sñiṅ gar zla ba'i dkyil 'khor gyi steṅ du yi ge hrīḥ rnam par bsams la/ de las kyaṅ rnam pa sna tshogs pa'i 'od zer kun tu spros śiṅ/ khams gsum yoṅs su bkaṅ bas sems can rnams thams cad kyaṅ 'jig rten dbaṅ phyug gi go 'phaṅ la rab tu bkod de/.
7 D illegible.
8 D, TP pa'i.
9 D, TP 'jigs.
10 D bsgom.
11 D, TP om.
12 TP bed.
13 D, TP ba'i.
14 P rgyu.
15 D, TP ba.

(1-kha sar-1) pa ṇa źes bya ba'i sgrub thabs rdzogs so// //padma 'byuṅ gnas blo gros kyi źal sṅa nas mdzad pa'o// paṇḍi ta a bha yā[2] ka ra'i źal sṅa nas/ dge sloṅ tshul khrims rgyal tshan[3] gyis bsgyur ba'o//

---

1 D, TP kharsa.
2 P ya.
3 D mtshan.

## 2.2 (T3) Khasarpaṇalokeśvarasādhana

rgya gar skad du/ (1-kha sarpa ṇa-1) sā dha naṃ/ bod skad du (2-kha sarpa ṇa'i-2) sgrub thabs/

(0) (3-kha sarpa ṇa'i-3) phyag 'tshal lo//
(1) mṅon 'dod 'bras ster 'od gsal dpal gyi dpag bsam śiṅ//
bde gśegs tshul gyis[4] lam chen 'jug nas ded dpon mdzad//
srid źi'i dṅos[5] mñam dṅos po kun gyi ṅo bo ñid//
de 'dir chu skyes phyag gis 'gro rnams sdigs pa źi mdzad do//
(2) sṅa bar kha sogs dag byas nas//
'jam źiṅ yaṅs pa'i stan la 'dug//
bdag ñid dben par cho ga 'dis//
(3.1) sñiṅ gar zla ba'i sa bon 'od//
raṅ gi sñiṅ gar bsgom par bya//
(3.2) zla ba gaṅ ba'i 'od zer 'phro//
de yi 'od zer rtse mos bskul//
yaṅ dag gdan draṅs nam[6] mkha la 'phags//
dpal mgon (7-kha sa rpa ṇi-7) daṅ//
bla ma saṅs rgyas de sras tshogs//
mchod spyin sa bon las byuṅ ba'i//
sna tshogs rnams kyis mchod par bya//
(3.3.0) de nas mṅon par phyag 'tshal[8] źiṅ//
sdig pa bźags pa la sogs bya//
(3.3.1) gaṅ źig śin tu thogs ma med pa nas// 'khor bar 'khor ba'i tshe bdag gis mi dge[9] ba bgyis pa daṅ// (10-bgyid du-10) stsal ba daṅ/ bgyid[11] pa la rjes su yi raṅ ba de thams cad bcom ldan 'das kyi mdun[12] bdag gis bśags par bgyi'o[13]//
(3.3.2) rdzogs[14] saṅs rgyas sras daṅ 'phags// gźan yaṅ gaṅ źig dge mdzad pa// des[15] ṅes par rjes yi[16] raṅ/ yaṅ dag rdzogs pa'i byaṅ chub bsṅo//
(3.3.3) sñiṅ rje'i raṅ bźin mchog gyur pa'i//
saṅs rgyas la ni skyabs su mchi//

---

1 D, TP kharsa pā ṇi.
2 D, TP kharsa pā ṇi'i.
3 D kharsa pā ṇi'i; TP kharsa pā ṇi la.
4 D, TP gyi:
5 D ṅos.
6 D, TP om.
7 D, TP kharsa pā ṇi.
8 P illegible before -l.
9 P dga.
10 D bgyi daṅ.
11 D, TP bgyis.
12 P add. du.
13 P gyi'o.
14 P add. saṅs.
15 D de la.
16 P ya.

chos kun rgyun mi 'chad par ni//
gcig tu dga' gzugs chos daṅ ni//
(3.3.4) rab dga' la sogs sa la bźugs//
byaṅ chub sems pa'i tshogs de bźin/
mya ṅan 'da' bar bźed rnams la//
saṅs rgyas gźan la phan pa'i phyir//
yun riṅ rnams su bźugs par yaṅ//
bdag gis gsol ba gdab par bgyi//
(3.3.5) sgrib pa thams cad rtsad nas zad byed pa'i//
rgyur gyur byaṅ chub sems ni bdag gis bskyed//
(3.3.6) bde gśegs sras daṅ bcas pa'i lam la yaṅ//
rnam dag bsam pas yaṅ dag bsten par bgyi//
(3.4) g'yo daṅ mi g'yo'i 'gro 'di ma lus rnams//
gcig daṅ du bral stoṅ pa ñid ces bsam//
oṃ śūnya tā dzñā na bdzra swa bhā wa[1] ātma ko 'haṃ[2]/ źes pas stoṅ pa ñid byin gyis brlab par bya//
byin brlabs raṅ bźin rnam par dag pa 'dis//
chos kun de bźin bdag med blta bar bya//
oṃ swa bhā wa[3] śu ddhaḥ[4] sarba dharmāḥ swa bhā wa[5] śuddho 'haṃ[6]/ źes brjod par bya'o//
(4.1) de nas bdag ñid rnam par śes pa tsam du bsgoms nas/ sṅon gyi smon lam gyis bskul nas baṃ yig yoṅs su gyur pa las sna tshogs chu skyes la oṃ yig las skyes pa'i zla ba gaṅ[7] ba'i dkyil 'khor dri ma med pa de'i steṅ du hrīḥ yig śin tu 'od gsal źiṅ 'od zer gyi tshogs 'phro bas nam kha'i khams[8] khyab pa rnam par bsgom par bya'o// de yoṅs su gyur pa las raṅ gi sa bon ze[9] 'bru daṅ/ sdoṅ bus brgyan pa'i chu skyes kha bus[10] pa blta bar bya'o// 'dir de rnams thams cad yoṅs su gyur pa las bdag ñid bcom ldan 'das su bsgom pa[11] bya'o// bsil zer bye ba'i 'od kyis dkar ba'i sku'i dbu la ral pa'i cod pan daṅ/ 'od dpag tu med pas brgyan pa/ sna tshogs padma daṅ zla ba'i dkyil 'khor la skyil kruṅ phyed pas bźugs pa/ sku la rgyan thams cad kyis brgyan pa/ źal 'dzum źiṅ lo brgyad gñis lon pa lta bu phyag g'yas pa mchog sbyin/ phyag g'yon na sdoṅ bu daṅ bcas pa'i chu skyes bsnams pa/ phyag nas bdud rtsi'i rgyun 'bab pa la sred pa can rnams preta[12] 'og nas steṅ du kha gdaṅs śiṅ/ lto ba che źiṅ śin tu riṅ ba kha dog gnag pa khab kyi kha can rnams tshim par mdzad pa dpal ldan gru 'jin gyi ri la bźugs pa/ sñiṅ rje'i snum mdaṅs daṅ ldan źiṅ sgegs pa'i ñams daṅ ldan pa/ śin tu źi ba rgyan sna tshogs pas brgyan pa/

---

1 P ba.
2 P haṃ.
3 P ba.
4 P ddha.
5 P ba.
6 P haṃ.
7 TP graṅ.
8 D illegible.
9 D zeu.
10 D'bus.
11 D par.
12 P om.

(4.2.0) de'i mdun du sgrol ma/ g'yas phyogs logs na nor bzaṅ gźon nu'o/

(4.2.1) de la sgrol ma ljaṅ gu/ phyag g'yon pa na sdoṅ bu daṅ bcas pa'i utpa la bsnams pa/ phyag g'yas pa mchog sbyin brkaṅ ba/ sna tshogs pa'i rgyan gyis brgyan pa/ laṅ tsho dar la nu ma rgyas pa'o//

(4.2.2) nor bzaṅs gźon nu thal mo sbyar źiṅ gser mdog ltar gsal ba/ bźon nu'i tshul 'dzin pa/ phyag g'yon na[1] po ti daṅ bcas śiṅ rgyan thams cad daṅ ldan pa'o//

(4.2.3) rgyab na khro gñer can no// g'yon na rta mgrin no// de la khro gñer can phyag bźi pa gser mdog lta bu/ ral pa'i tshogs daṅ ldan pa/ phyag g'yon na dbyug gu rtse gsum daṅ spyi blugs bsnams pa/ phyag g'yas phyag 'tshal ba'i tshul daṅ/ bgraṅ phreṅ bsnams pa/ spyan gsum daṅ ldan pa/[2]

(4.2.4) rta mgrin ni sku mdog dmar po thuṅ źiṅ lto 'phyaṅ ba/ skra dmar ser gyen du [(3-]'bar ba[-3)]/ sbrul gyi ser la khar byas pa[4]/ sma ra ser pos źal gyi dkyil 'khor brgyan pa/ spyan gsum dmar źiṅ zlum pa/ smin mtshams su khro gñer bsdus pa/ stag[5] gi pags[6] pa'i na bza' can/ dbyug[7] pa'i mtshan ma daṅ ldan źiṅ phyag g'yas pa phyag 'tshal ba'i tshul daṅ ldan pa'o//

(4.2.5) de nams thams cad raṅ gi gtso bo'i źal nas bskul źiṅ lta[8] ba ji ltar mdzes pas[9] bźugs par bsgom par bya'o//

(4.3) de nas raṅ gi sñiṅ ga'i sa bon las zla ba'i dkyil 'khor gyi steṅ du hrīḥ yig rnam par bsgom par bya'o// de nas[10] 'od zer rnam pa sna tshogs pa 'phros te/ khams gsum kheṅs na[11] sems can thams cad 'jig rten dbaṅ phyug gi go 'phaṅ la bkod nas slar yaṅ de bźin du 'od zer sa bon gyi yi ge la gźug par bya'o// yaṅ de'i 'od kyis ye śes sems dpa' spyan draṅs la/ dam tshig sems dpa' daṅ lhan cig tu 'o ma daṅ chu 'dres pa bźin du gzugs gcig tu bsgom par bya'o[12]//

(4.4) de nas lus ṅag yid gsum rnam par dag pa'i phyir rim pa ji lta bźin du spyi bor oṃ yig dkar po// mgrin par āḥ yig dmar po// sñiṅ gar hūṃ yig nag po bsgom par bya'o// 'dir yaṅ rgyun mi 'chad[13] par 'od zer gyi dra ba mtha' yas pa byuṅ ste/ sems can gyi phuṅ[14] po ma lus pa'i sdig pa yaṅ dag par 'joms pa bsgom par bya źiṅ ji ltar nus par spro ba bya'o//

(5) mkhas śiṅ 'dzin pa'i śes rab daṅ//
bskal bzaṅ nad[15] med phun sum tshogs//
bsgom pa'i sbyor bas thob 'gyur te//
brtson 'grus ldan pas mṅon sum byed//

---

1 TP om.
2 TP pa'o//.
3 D illegible.
4 P ba.
5 P sta ga.
6 P lpags.
7 D illegible between db– and -g.
8 D, TP blta.
9 D, TP pa.
10 TP bas.
11 D, TP nas.
12 D illegible.
13 P chad.
14 D illegible before -uṅ.
15 D add. med.

(6) bsgom pas ṅal na sems rtse gcig pas sṅags bzlas par bya'o// de la sṅags ni 'di'o// oṃ hrīḥ swāhā/ (1-'di yi-1) kha dog ston ka'i skar ma'i phreṅ ba dri med ltar// rab tu 'od gsal dpag tu med pa'i 'od zer 'phro ba can// bzlas pas skyo bar gyur na bsod nams yoṅs su bsṅos nas ldaṅ// lha'i[2] ṅa rgyal daṅ bcas ci bde bar ni gnas par bya/

(7) dpal ldan 'jig rten dbaṅ phyug gis[3]/
sgrub thabs cho ga[4] byas pa'i[5]/
bdag gi[6] bsod nams gaṅ bsags des//
'gro rnams de yi gnas thob śog/

po ta la'i (7-kha sar pa ṇi'i-7) sgrub thabs/ slob dbon padma 'byuṅ gnas blo gros źabs kyis mdzad pa rdzogs so//

---

1 D di'i.
2 TP lha yi.
3 D gi.
4 D and TP add. 'di.
5 P pa yi; TP pa'o.
6 D, TP gis.
7 D, TP kharsa pā ṇi'i.

## 2.3 (T3) Khasarpaṇalokeśvarasādhana

rgya gar skad du/ śrī [(1-]kha sarpa ṇi[-1)] sā dha naṃ/ bod skad du/ dpal [(2-]kha sarpa ṇi'i[-2)] sgrub thabs/

(0) dpal ldan [(3-]kha sarpa[-3)] ṇi la phyag 'tshal lo//

(1) 'dir dge bsñen dge byed ces bya ba dge ba'i las la brtson źiṅ sñiṅ rje daṅ ldan pa źig yod par grags pa des/ po ta la ker 'gro bar brtsams te chas nas khā ḍi maṇḍal [(4-]kha sarpa ṇi[-4)] źes grags pa'i groṅ źig yod par bsdad pa na/ der bcom ldan 'das 'phags pa 'jig rten dbaṅ phyug gis gnaṅ ba byin te/ khyod raṅ ma 'gro bar 'dir rnam par snaṅ mdzad mṅon par byaṅ chub pa'i rgyud kyi rgyal po'i rim pas ṅa'i sku gcig gyis daṅ/ de sems can thams cad kyi don chen por 'gyur ro źes gsuṅs nas/ de nas des bcom ldan 'das kyi sku gcig myur du bźeṅs so źes thos so//

(2) de la bcom ldan 'das bsgrub pa'i phyir lta ba phun sum tshogs na dge sloṅ mchog gi tshul khrims ñams kyaṅ bla'i[5]/ lta ba ñams pa ni de lta ma yin no/ 'dir [(6-]de la re[-6)] źig chos thams cad bdag med par rnam par bltas nas rnam par rtog pa mtha' dag spaṅs te/ brtse ba'i bsam pas kye ma sems can 'di rnams ñon moṅs pa la sogs pa'i las kyi bar du gcod pa[7] sdug bsṅal ba ste/ de la skye ba daṅ/ rgyas pa daṅ/ nad daṅ[8]/ ṅal[9] 'chi ba'i sdug bsṅal rnams kyis śin tu mnar ba daṅ ldan pa'i sems can rnams dpag tu med pa'i sdug bsṅal bar gyur pa rnams la de'i phyir bdag ñid 'dzig rten dbaṅ phyug sgrubs te/ de rnams kyi sdug bsṅal thams cad bsal źiṅ/ thams cad mkhyen pa'i ye śes la dgod par bya'o/ źes dam bcas nas/

(3.1) raṅ gi sñiṅ gar paṃ yig las skyes pa'i padma 'dab ma stoṅ gi lte ba'i dbus su a yig las skyes pa'i zla ba'i dkyil 'khor gyi steṅ du oṃ hāṃ suṃ bhriṃ haṃ źes pa'i sa bon lṅa bkod la/

(3.2) de rnams kyi 'od zer gyis yaṅ dag par bskul źiṅ bla ma daṅ/ saṅs rgyas daṅ/ byaṅ chub sems dpa' rnams gdan draṅs te/ mdun gyi nam mkha'i mthil du bźugs nas phyag daṅ/ mchod pa daṅ/ sdig pa bśags pa daṅ/ gsum la skyabs su 'gro ba la sogs pa mchod pa rnams pa bdun nam bcu gcig byas te/ byams pa daṅ/ sñiṅ rje daṅ/ dga' ba daṅ/ btaṅ sñoms te tshaṅs pa'i gnas bźi bsgom par bya'o//

(3.3) de nas oṃ śū nya tā dzñā na bdzra swa bhā ba[10] ātma ko 'haṃ[11] źes brjod pas stoṅ pa ñid byaṅ chub tu byas bcom ldan 'das sbyan ras gzigs dbaṅ phyug gi rnal 'byor du bdag ñid byas te/

(4) de yaṅ stoṅ ka'i zla ba bźin du dkar źiṅ ral pa'i cod pan can[12] 'od dpag med kyis[13] dbul brgyan ciṅ/ rgyan thams cad kyis brgyan pa/ rin po che daṅ/ seṅ ge'i gdan gyi steṅ na

---

1 D, TP kharsa pā ṇi.
2 D, TP kharsa pā ṇi'i.
3 D, TP kharsa pā ṇi.
4 D, TP kharsa pā ṇi.
5 D sla'i.
6 P re.
7 D, TP pas.
8 P om.
9 D, TP om.
10 D, TP wa.
11 P ham.
12 D, TP om.
13 D, TP kyi.

padma 'dab ma stoṅ la ral[1] pa'i tshul gyis bźugs pa/ źal gcig phyag gñis pa/ g'yon na[2] padma bsnams pa/ g'yas na bdud rtsi'i chu rgyun 'bab pa'i mchog sbyin pa'o//

(5.1) mdun na sgrol ma sems dpa'i skyil kruṅ gis bźugs pa/ gser sṅon po'i mdog lta bu dkar źiṅ mkhregs la mtho ba/ rgyan thams cad kyis brgyan pa/ phyag gñis na utpa la sdoṅ bu daṅ bcas pa bsnams śiṅ spyan gyis gzigs pa'o//

(5.2) de'i rjes su nor bzaṅs gźon nu gser 'bar ba blta bu'i rin po'i che'i rgyan daṅ/ rin po che'i cod pan can/ phyag[3] g'yon na ka pā[4] li bsnams śiṅ thal mo sbyar ba'o//

(5.3) de'i rjes su[5] khro gñer can ral pa'i cod pan can[6] steṅ[7] brdzes pas[8] brgyan pa/ gser 'bar ba[9] lta bu na bza' dmar po yoṅs su bsnams pa/ phyag g'yas pa phyag 'tshal pa'i tshul du byas pa/ gźan na bgraṅ pheṅ 'dzin pa/ g'yon pa dag gis dbyug gu rtse[10] gsum daṅ/ ril pa spyin[11] blugs bsnams pa/

(5.4) de'i rje su rta mgrin dbu skra[12] dmar ser gyen du 'bar ba/ sku mdog dmar po klu'i rgyan daṅ ldan pa/ lho ba 'phyaṅ źiṅ stag gi pags pa'i na bza' bsnams pa[13]/ phyag na dbyug pa bsnams pa/

(5.5) de bźin du lha'i bdag ñid bcom ldan 'das 'khor daṅ bcas par[14] bsgom par bya'o//

(6.1) de nas maṇḍal byas te chog 'dis mchod par bya'o// de nas daṅ po maṇḍal byas nas bsruṅ ba bya ste/ oṃ maṇi dha ri bdzri ṇi ma hā pra ti sa re ra kṣa ra kṣa maṃ hūṃ[15] phaṭ swāhā/ oṃ bdzra re khe hūṃ/ maṇḍal gyi sṅags so//

(6.2) oṃ a ga tstsha bha ga bān[16] maṇḍal la ka siṃ hā sa ne/ oṃ āḥ źes pa'i sṅags brjod nas gsol ba gdab par bya ste/

(6.3) maṇḍal gyi dbus su seṅ ge'i gdan gyi steṅ du padma 'dab ma stoṅ la bźugs pa/ lha'i bdag ñid mchod par bya'o// de la mchod pa'i sṅags ni oṃ bdzra puṣpe hūṃ/ oṃ bdzra dhūpe hūṃ/ oṃ bdzra gandhe hūṃ/ oṃ bdzra ā[17] hā re hūṃ/ mchod ciṅ bstod de sṅags bzlas par bya'o// oṃ sarba ta thā ga ta pū[18] dza me[19] gha pra sarā mū he hūṃ/ mchod pa byin gyis brlabs pa'i sṅags so// oṃ ā tāṃ hūṃ[20] bhriṃ haṃ phaṭ swāhā/ oṃ sarba ta thā ga ta pū dza

---

1 D, TP rol.
2 D, TP om.
3 D, TP mtshan.
4 P pa.
5 P om.
6 D, TP om.
7 D and TP add. du.
8 P illegible before -s.
9 P om.
10 P, D rtsa.
11 TP spyi.
12 D illegible.
13 P om.
14 P, TP pa.
15 P om.
16 D, TP wān.
17 P a.
18 P pu.
19 TP ma.
20 TP om.

la li ta na mi [(1-]ti ra[-1)] na mā mi bha ga bān[2] taṃ dzaḥ hūṃ baṃ hoḥ pra ti tstsha ku [(3-]su ma añdza lin[-3)] nā thā hoḥ[4] źes pa ni phyag 'tshal ba'i sṅags so//

(6.4) oṃ muḥ swāhā/ źes pa ni gśegs su gsol pa'i sṅags so//

(6.5) oṃ kha kha khā hi khā hi/ grihna grihna grihna[5]/ du sarba bhū ti kā imaṃ ba liṃ swāhā/ źes pa ni gtor ma'i sṅags so//

(6.6) de nas mchod pa rtsom pa'i dus su de bźin du brjod nas sems sbyaṅ bar bya'o// gaṅ yaṅ spyod pa ṅan pa rnams/ bdag gis spaṅ źiṅ saṅs rgyas daṅ/ byaṅ chub sems[6] dpa'i bslab pa rnams la bslab bo[7]// bdag gis ji srid nus pas mchod pa bsgrub bo// gaṅ yaṅ mi bya ba ni de yaṅ 'dod chags las skyes pa daṅ/ źe sdaṅ las skyes pa daṅ/ gti mug las skyes pa'i mi dge ba'i rtsa ba rnams so// 'dir thams cad de bźin du[8] 'dod chags daṅ/ źe sdaṅ daṅ/ gti mug gi bsam pa can rnams daṅ/ de bźin du 'dod chags las skyes pa'i dge ba'i rtsa ba ni klu'i rgyal po dga' bo [(9-]dag go[-9)]/ źe sdaṅ las skyes pa ni ra[10] ma[11] ṇo/ gti mug las skyes pa ni gnod sbyin rnam thos sras so// de'i phyir 'dod chags daṅ źe sdaṅ daṅ/ gti mug la sògs pa yoṅs su spaṅs nas sems sbyaṅs te/ thams cad de bźin du sñiṅ rje'i sems kyi raṅ bźin gyis sbyin pa la sogs pa'i dge ba'i rtsa ba rnams bya'o//

slob dpon dge byed kyis mdzad pa'i [(12-]kha sarpa ṇi'i[-12)] sgrub thabs rdzogs so//

---

1 D re ta; TP rai ta.
2 D, TP wān.
3 P ru mā ñdza lin; TP su ma añdza lan.
4 D, TP ho.
5 D, TP om.
6 TP sams.
7 D, TP po.
8 D and TP add. sems can.
9 P, TP daṅ ñe dga' bo dag go/.
10 D illegible.
11 P ba.
12 D, TP kharsa pā ṇi'i.

## 2.4 (T2) Khasarpaṇalokeśvarasādhana

rgya gar skad du/ [(1-]kha sarpa ṇā[-1)] sādha naṃ/ bod skad du/ [(2-]ka sarpa ṇa'i[-2)] sgrub pa'i thabs/

(0) 'phags pa spyan ras gzigs dbaṅ phyug la phyag 'tshal lo//

(1) daṅ por re źig sṅags[3] pas gdan bde ba la ñe bar 'dug nas/

(2.1.1) raṅ gi sñiṅ gar a las zla ba'i dkyil 'khor ro/

(2.1.2) de la yi ge hrīḥ mdog dkar ba bltas[4] te/ de las byuṅ bar gyur pa'i 'od kyis[5] mdun du bla ma daṅ/ saṅs rgyas daṅ/ byaṅ chub sems dpa' rnams lta[6] bar bya'o/ de nas sñiṅ ga'i sa bon gyi 'od kyis yaṅ dag par mchod de/ sdig pa bśags pa la sogs pa byas nas/

(2.1.3) oṃ swa bhā ba[7] śuddha[8] sarba dha rmaḥ[9] swa bhā ba[10] śu ddho 'haṃ[11]/ źes bya bas bdag ñid stoṅ pa ñid du dmigs par bya ste/

(2.2.1) sṅon du btan pa'i hrīḥ yig las spro ba daṅ bsdu pa'i[12] rim pas spyan ras gzigs kyi bdag ñid du bsgom par bya'o// yan lag thams cad kyi mdog dkar ba/ ral pa'i cod pan gyis brgyan pa/ 'od dpag med pas[13] dbu la 'chiṅ ba/ rgyan thams cad kyis brgyan pa/ skyil kruṅ phyed pas bźugs pa/ phyag g'yas pas mchog spyin pa[14]/ g'yon pas padma 'dzin pa/ padma daṅ zla ba'i gdan la gnas pa'o//

(2.2.2) g'yas kyi logs na sgrol ma daṅ/ nor bzaṅs gñis so// g'yon pa'i logs na khro gñer can daṅ rta mgrin gñis so//

(2.2.3) bcom ldan 'das kyi spyi bor zla ba la oṃ mo[15]/ mgrin par āḥ/ sñiṅ gar hūṃ/ de ltar bsgom pa go bar bya'o/

(3) rnal 'byor pa bsam gtan gyis ṅal na bzlas pa bya'o/ sṅags 'di yin te/ oṃ hrīḥ swahā/

[(16-]kha sarpa ṇa'i[-16)] sgrub thabs rdzogs so// // paṇḍi ta don yod rdo rje daṅ/ khams pa lo tsā[17] ba dge sloṅ ba ris bsgyur ba'o//

---

1 D khar sa pā ṇi.
2 D khar sa pā ṇi'i.
3 P sdigs.
4 P ltas.
5 P kyi.
6 D blta.
7 D wa.
8 D śuddhaḥ.
9 D rmāḥ.
10 D wa.
11 D haṃ.
12 P ba'i.
13 D pa.
14 P om.
15 D om.
16 D khar sa pā ṇi'i.
17 P tstsha.

## 2.5 (T3) Khasarpaṇalokeśvarasādhana

rgya gar skad du/ ārya [(1-]kha sarpa ṇi[-1)] sā dha naṃ// bod skad du/ 'phags pa mkha spyod kyi sgrub thabs/

(0) 'phags pa mkha' spyod la phyag 'tshal lo//

(1) sdug bsṅal can gyi mgon gyur pa'i/
mgon po mkha' spyod la phyag 'tshal//
de yi sgrub thabs bsdus pa las//
cuṅ zad rgyas par bri bar bya/

(2) daṅ por[2] re źig sṅags pas[3] rkoṅ pa daṅ/ lag pa la sogs pa[4] chus bkrus śiṅ mchog tu gtsaṅ bar byas nas ri phug skye bos dben par gnas te/ kha bsaṅ bar bya'o/ kha cig ṅas yid daṅ mthun pa'i gnas su 'jam źiṅ yaṅs pa'i gdan la ñe bar 'dug nas/

(3.1) raṅ gi sñiṅ gar dbyaṅs yig daṅ po yoṅs su gyur pa las zla ba'i dkyil 'khor yid kyis bsam par bya ste/ de'i dbus su ston ka'i zla ba brgya'i 'od zer gyi phreṅ ba rab tu 'bar ba'i hrīḥ yig gi sa bon blta bar bya'o//

(3.2) de nas yaṅ hrīḥ yig gi sa bon las 'phros te/ 'gro ba rnams kyi[5] ma rig pa'i mun pa 'joms par byed ciṅ 'od zer gyi lcags kyu'i rnams par 'phros te/ phyogs bcu mtha' yas pa'i 'jig rten gyi khams na bźugs pa rnams thams cad snaṅ bar mdzad nas/ de na bźugs pa'i yaṅ graṅs med dpag tu med pa'i bla ma daṅ/ saṅs rgyas daṅ/ byaṅ chub sems dpa' rnams spyan draṅs nas mdun gyi nam mkha' la bźugs par bya'o//

(3.3.0) phyi nas de rnams nam mkha'i phyogs su 'khod ciṅ/ mchog gi sñiṅ rje daṅ ldan pa'i bla ma daṅ/ saṅs rgyas daṅ/ byaṅ chub sems dpa' rnams la me tog daṅ/ spos daṅ/ mar me daṅ/ dri daṅ/ phreṅ ba daṅ/ byug pa daṅ/ [(6-]phye ma[-6)] daṅ/ na bza' daṅ/ gdugs daṅ/ rgyal mtshan daṅ / dril bu daṅ/ ba dan la sogs pa śin tu phul du byuṅ ba'i mchod pa'i rnam pas mchod ciṅ/ sdig pa bśags pa bya'o//

(3.3.1) gaṅ źig skye ba 'di[7] daṅ/ skye ba gźan rnams su thogs ma daṅ tha ma med pa'i 'khor ba nas 'khor ba'i skye gnas rnams su bdag gi lus daṅ ṅag daṅ yid kyis[8] kyaṅ[9] sdig pa'i[10] las ci bgyis pa daṅ/ bgyid du stsal[11] ba daṅ/ rjes su yi raṅ bar bgyis pa de rnams thams cad 'jig rten gsum gyi mgon po bcom ldan 'das spro ba chen po rnams daṅ/ bla ma daṅ/ saṅs rgyas daṅ/ byaṅ chub sems dpa' rnams kyi spyan sṅar so sor bśags par bgyi'o// cho ga 'dis so sor bśags śiṅ slar yaṅ mi byed pa'i sdom pa 'dzin ciṅ bsod nams la rjes su yi raṅ bar bya ste/

(3.3.2) rdzogs pa'i saṅs rgyas daṅ/ raṅ rgyal daṅ/ ñan thos rnams daṅ/ byaṅ chub sems dpa' rnams daṅ/ gaṅ źig 'jig rten gsum na mchis pa'i dge ba thams cad la rjes su yi raṅ ṅo//

---

1 D kharsa pā ṇi.
2 D, TP po.
3 P pa.
4 P om.
5 D, TP kyis.
6 P phyes.
7 P illegible.
8 P kyi.
9 P om.
10 P ba'i.
11 The rendering is probably a misprint for stsol.

(3.3.3) de'i rje su dkon mchog gsum la skyabs su 'gro bar bya ste/ rkaṅ gñis rnams kyi mchog saṅs rgyas la skyabs su mchi'o// 'dod chags daṅ bral ba rnams kyi mchog chos la skyabs su mchi'o// tshogs rnams kyi mchog/ dge 'dun la skyabs su mchi'o//

(3.3.4) phyi nas lam la[1] bsten[2] pa ni rdzogs pa'i saṅs rgyas kyis gsuṅs pa'i lam la[3] bdag gi bsten gyi gźan ni ma yin no//

(3.3.5) de nas gsol ba gdab par bya ste/ saṅs rgyas bcom ldan 'das rnams daṅ de'i sras byaṅ chub sems dpa' chen po rnams kyaṅ yoṅs su mya ṅan las mi 'da' źiṅ 'khor ba ma stoṅs kyi bar du sems can gyi don mdzad du gsol/

(3.3.6) de'i rjes su bskul ma gdab par bya ste/ rnam pa de bźin du bcom ldan 'das de bźin gśegs pa rnams kyis bla na med pa'i chos gsuṅ bźin bstan pas gaṅ gis myur du sems can rnams 'khor ba'i rgya mtsho gtiṅ mtha' med pa las bsgral[4] du gsol/

(3.3.7) gsol ba btab pa'i rjes su[5] de nas bsod nams yoṅs su bsṅo bar bya'o/ bla na[6] med pa'i mchod pa rnam pa bdun gyis mchod nas gaṅ de bźin du dge ba'i rtsa ba bskyed pa rnams de bźin du bdag gis rdzogs pa'i byaṅ chub tu yoṅs su bsṅo bar bgyi'o// yaṅ na bsdus nas bla na med pa'i mchod pa rnam pa bdun gsuṅs te/ tshigs su bcad pa 'di bklag par bya'o/

(3.3.8) lus daṅ ṅag daṅ yid kyis gaṅ bgyis pa'i//
sdig rnams rgyal ba rnams kyi spyan sṅar bśags//
'jig rten gsum gyi dge ba thams cad la//
rab tu dga' bas rtag tu rjes yi raṅ//
dkon mchog gsum la rtag tu bdag skyabs mchi//
rgyal ba'i gsuṅ la skyabs śiṅ bsten par bgyi//
ji srid srid pa brtan gyur de srid du//
skye dgu'i yab rnams mya ṅan mi 'da' źiṅ//
'dir[7] yaṅ rtag tu sems can don mdzad ciṅ//
saṅs rgyas sras bcas de rnams bźugs su gsol//
the tshom mthar byed ji lta ba yi chos//
kye kye mthu chen khyod kyis bstan du gsol//
'khor ba'i rgya mtshor 'gro rnams lhan cig der[8]//
gaṅ gis pha rol 'gro źiṅ bde bsags pa//
bsod nams rab tu gaṅ bsags 'di kun kyaṅ//
rdzogs pa'i byaṅ chub bdag gis bsṅo bar bgyi//
rgyal ba rnams daṅ de yi sras//
dag daṅ 'gro[9] ba'i bla ma la//
bdag gis dṅos po thams cad ni//
thams cad du ni dbul bar bgyi//

---

1 P om.
2 D brten; TP brtan.
3 P om.
4 P sgral.
5 P om.
6 D, TP om.
7 P 'di.
8 TP de.
9 P 'bro.

źes pa 'dis mchod pa rnam pa bdun gyis mchod nas/ oṃ āḥ hūṃ muḥ źes pas gśegs su gsol lo[1]//

(3.4) de nas chad med pa bźi ni byams pa daṅ/ sñiṅ rje daṅ/ dga' ba daṅ/ btaṅ sñoms kyi mtshan ñid rnams ni 'og nas 'chad par 'gyur ba'i rim pas bsgom par bya'o// de la 'dir byams pa[2] ni sems can thams cad la[3] śin tu phan par byad ciṅ/ bu gcig pa ltar mñes gśin pa'i mtshan ñid can no// sñiṅ rje ni ci 'dra na/ gtiṅ mtha' med pa'i 'khor ba'i rgya mtsho'i naṅ tu lhuṅ pa'i mtha' yas pa'i sems can gyi khams bdag gis yaṅ dag par gdon par 'dod pa'i bsam pa can no// yaṅ dga' ba ni ci 'dra na/ khams gsum na gnas pa'i sems can rnams kyaṅ gaṅ źig legs par spyod pa de rnams la de'i loṅs sbyod kyi dbaṅ phyug la sogs pa rnams la sems dga' ba'o// gaṅ 'dir btaṅ[4] sñoms ni khoṅ khro ba daṅ/ rjes su brtse ba dag ṅes par bciṅs śiṅ phan pa daṅ/ gnod par byed pa spaṅs nas sems can rnams la mchog tu phan par spyod pa ste/

(3.5) tshad med pa bźi bsgom[5] źiṅ/ de nas chos thams cad kyi raṅ bźin yoṅs su dag par bsam par bya'o// chos thams cad 'di bźin du raṅ bźin ṅo bo ñid med ciṅ yoṅs su dag pa'o źes pa la sogs pa mṅon du bya'o// di bźin du chos thams cad raṅ bźin yoṅs su dag ciṅ/ oṃ swa bhā ba[6] śuddhaḥ[7] sarba dha rmāḥ[8] swa bhā ba[9] śuddho 'haṃ[10] źes pa 'dis brtan par bya'o// chos thams cad raṅ bźin yoṅs su dag pa la gsar du sgrib par mi 'gyur ro źe na/ bden te/ gźan 'dir 'gyur ba daṅ mi 'gyur ba de bźin du gaṅ las 'gyur ba ni 'khor ba'i rgyu 'dod chags la sogs pa'i dri ma sna thogs pa'i phyir slar yaṅ chos thams cad kyis[11] ji ltar med par 'gyur na/ khad par du 'phags pa'i lam bsgom pa des 'gog ste/ de'i phyir bcom ldan 'das kyis 'gog pa mṅon du bya źes so// de'i phyir na chos thams cad raṅ bźin gyis yoṅs su dag pa źes bya ba la sogs pa'i tshig las bskyed pa bźin no/ 'dir maṅ po smras pas ci źig bya//

(3.6) chos thams cad kyi raṅ bźin yoṅs su dag pa mṅon du bya ba'i phyir/ chos thams cad stoṅ pa ñid do źes bsgom par bya'o// de la 'dir stoṅ pa ñid ni yid tsam gyis de bźin du 'dir de daṅ de'i rnam pas bdag ñid snaṅ źiṅ so sor gsal bar bya ste/ dper na rmi lam bźin no/ phyi rol tu yid kyis[12] gzuṅ ba med de yid kyis so// gzuṅ ba'i dṅos po med na 'dzin pa'i yid kyaṅ med do// de'i phyir chos thams cad kyaṅ yid kyi raṅ bźin no// de rnams kyi gzuṅ ba daṅ 'dzin pa la sogs pa'i rtog pa'i spros pa mtha' dag ji sñed pa/ don dam pa stoṅ pa ñid kyi de kho na ñid do// 'di'i don gñis su med pa'i snaṅ btsam gyi bdag ñid du g'yo ba daṅ/ mi g'yo ba'i 'gro ba thams cad bsam par bya'o// 'dir de bźin du stoṅ pa ñid ni/ oṃ śū nya tā dzñā na bdzraṃ[13] swa bhā ba[14] ātma ko 'haṃ[15]/ źes pa'i sṅags 'dis byin gyis brlab par bya'o//

---

1 D, TP om.
2 D, TP pas.
3 P om.
4 P gtaṅ.
5 D, TP sgom.
6 D, TP wa.
7 P śuddha.
8 P rmā.
9 D, TP wa.
10 P haṃ.
11 P kyi.
12 P kyi.
13 P, TP bdzra.
14 D, TP wa.
15 P haṃ.

(4.1) [(1-]ri dwags kyis mtshan pa'i dri ma[-1)] daṅ bral ba'i mtshan mor byed pa'i dkyil 'khor gyi steṅ du śin tu dkar źiṅ dkar ba'i hrīḥ yig gi sa bon las bcom ldan 'das dpal ldan mkha' la gśegs pa'i 'jig rten dbaṅ phyug ston ka'i zla ba dri ma med pa'i dkyil 'khor brgya śar ba ltar śin tu dkar ba'i sku can mchog tu sgeg pa'i ñams 'bar źiṅ yid du 'oṅ ba/ rin po che sna tshogs pa la sogs pas brgyan ciṅ rnam par spras ba'i[2] sku mṅa' ba/ ral pa'i cod pan 'dzin pa/ padma dkar po rgyas pa'i spyan mṅa' ba/ bcom ldan 'das 'od dpag tu med pa rgyal ba'i rin po ches dbu rnam par mdzes pa/ gaṅs kyi[3] bye ma'i chus bkrus pa bźin dkar ba'i na bza' sku la bsnams pa/ śiṅ rta'i 'khor lo'i tshad tsam pa'i śin tu yid du 'oṅ ba'i chu[4] skyes dkar po'i steṅ na gnas pa'i [(5-]ri dwags kyi mtshan ma daṅ bral ba'i[-5)] zla ba'i dkyil 'khor gyi gdan la skyil kruṅ phyed pas bźugs pa/ phyag g'yas pa mchog sbyin// g'yon pa yid 'phrog pa'i padma dkar po kha 'bus pa bsnams pa/ de lta bur gyur pa'i bcom ldan 'das kyi skur bdag ñid bskyed ciṅ bsgom par bya'o//

(4.2) bcom ldan 'das kyi g'yas phyogs su[6] logs su 'phags ma sgrol ma daṅ nor bzaṅs so// g'yon phyogs logs su khro gñer can daṅ rta mgrin bsgom par bya'o źes so//

(4.3) mgo bor dri ma med pa'i zla ba'i dkyil 'khor gyi steṅ du oṃ yig go// de'i rjes su mgrin par dri ma med pa'i zla ba'i dkyil 'khor gyi steṅ du āḥ yig go/ sñiṅ gar dri ma med pa'i [(7-]ku mu da'i[-7)] gñen gyi dkyil 'khor gyi steṅ du hūṃ yig blta bar bya'o// de'i rim pa 'dis ji srid 'dod kyi bar de srid bsgom par bya'o//

(4.4.1) de'i rjes la de bźin du dam tshig sems dpa'i gzugs kyis bcom ldan 'das 'jig rten mgon po'i thugs kar [(8-]ri dwags kyi mtshan ma[-8)] daṅ bral źiṅ dri ma med pa'i ri boṅ 'dzin pa'i dkyil 'khor gyi steṅ du smin drug gi zla ba 'am/ kun da'i mdog lta bu'i hrīḥ yig gi sa bon las skyes pa'i 'od zer khor yug gi mthar thug par 'phros te/ 'jig rten gsum gyi mi śes pa'i mun pa bcom par gyur nas/ thog ma med pa nas yaṅ dag par bsgrub pa'i bcom ldan 'das ye śes sems dpa'i sku śin tu riṅ po nas nam mkha'i phyogs su gdan draṅs śiṅ bkug ste/ de bźin du bcom ldan 'das mdun du[9] nam mkha'i phyogs su bźugs nas rin po che sna tshogs pas spras pa'i gser gyi snod du dri bzaṅs kyi chu daṅ/ dri źim po'i me tog bcug ste/ des de bźin du gdan draṅs pa'i ye śes sems dpa'i sku bcom ldan 'das 'jig rten mgon po'i źabs la mchod yon phul nas/ de'i rjes su lha'i me tog daṅ/ spos daṅ/ mar me daṅ/ źal zas daṅ/ dri daṅ/ phreṅ ba daṅ/ byug pa daṅ/ phye ma daṅ/ na bza' daṅ/ gdugs daṅ/ rgyal mtshan daṅ/ dril bu daṅ/ ba dan la sogs pa rnams kyis phyi daṅ/ gsaṅ ba'i mchod pa daṅ/ phyi rol gyi sna tshogs pa'i rim pas de bźin du bcom ldan 'das ye śes sems dpa'i bdag ñid la mchod par bya'o// slar yaṅ mṅon par mchod ciṅ bstod nas dzaḥ hūṃ baṃ hoḥ śes pa'i yi ge bźi po 'di'i phyag rgya blta bar bya'o//

---

1 The rendering follows Sanskrit: kalāṅkāṅka-. P, D, TP ri dags kyis mtshan pa'i dri ma.
2 D, TP pa'i.
3 P illegible.
4 D illegible.
5 The rendering follows Sanskrit: niṣkalaṅka-. P, D, TP ri dags kyi mtshan ma daṅ bral ba'i.
6 D, TP om.
7 The rendering follows Sanskrit: -kumuda-. P, D, TP ku mu ta'i.
8 The rendering follows Sanskrit: -kalāṅkāṅka-. P, D, TP ri dags kyi mtshan ma.
9 D, TP gyi.

(4.4.2) cuṅ zad thal mo gug por sbyar nas guṅ mo rtse mor byas te/ sor mo'i lhag ma rnams cuṅ zad khab sdus śiṅ/ (1-kha mdun du-1) byas te/ cuṅ zad ma reg par gzuṅ[2] bar bya'o// mthe bo daṅ mdzub mo dag (3-bsñen nas gnas-3) śiṅ chu skyes kha bye ba'i phyag rgya'o//

(4.4.3) phyag rgya 'dis de bźin du gdan draṅs nas bcom ldan 'das ye śes sems dpa'i mtshan ñid yoṅs su mñes par[4] byas nas/ yaṅ dam tshig[5] sems dpa'i gzugs la bcom ldan 'das naṅ du bsgom par bya'o// oṃ āḥ hūṃ/ źes pa 'dis gñis su med pa 'di dag ñid lhag par mos par bya'o//

(4.5) de'i rjes la (6-ri dwags kyi mtshan ma-6) daṅ bral ba'i (7-zla ba'i-7) dkyil 'khor gyi dbus su thim źiṅ dri ma med pa'i rtsa'i[8] dbaṅ po'i dkyil 'khor brgya'i 'od zer gyi tshogs 'bar ba'i hrīḥ yig gi[9] sa bon las rnam par 'phros[10] nas graṅs med gźal du med pa'i bcom ldan 'das dpal (11-kha sarpa ṇi-11) 'jig rten dbaṅ phyug rje btsun phyogs bcu nas byon źiṅ dpag tu med pa'i 'jig rten gyi[12] khams kyi nam mkha' la bźugs nas/ yaṅ de na gnas pa'i sems can rnams la gser daṅ/ rin po che daṅ/ mu tig daṅ/ mu men daṅ/ byu[13] ru daṅ/ baiḍūrya daṅ/ indra ṇī la la sogs pa'i rin po che'i char phab nas/ dbul ba la sogs pa'i sdug bsṅal bcom źiṅ/ bla na med pa'i dpal[14] 'byor la bkod nas/ bdag med pa la sogs pa'i chos gsuṅs pas bdud rtsi'i rgyun[15] bab pa des yaṅ dag par tshim par byas nas/ slar yaṅ rgyun mi 'chad[16] par sna tshogs pa'i rab tu byed pas/ gźan gyi don mdzad nas 'gro ba rnams kyaṅ bcom ldan 'das 'jig rten dbaṅ phyug gi gzugs su bskyed nas/ de la yaṅ bsil zer byed pa'i dkyil 'khor gyi dbus su śel daṅ/ nor bu'i 'od zer phreṅ ba lta bu'i hrīḥ[17] yig gi sa bon bkod nas/ de bźin du bcom ldan 'das naṅ du yaṅ dag par źugs par gyur te/ de lta bu la sogs pa spro ba daṅ bsdu ba'i rim pas ji srid ṅal bar ma gyur pa de srid du bsgom par bya'o//

(5) de nas yaṅ bsgoms[18] pas ṅal na sṅags[19] bzlas par bya'o// de la sṅags ni 'di'o// oṃ hrīḥ[20] swāhā/ sṅags gaṅ bcom ldan 'das 'jig rten mgon po'i sñiṅ po thun moṅ ma yin pa'i mthu daṅ ldan pa de dag gis de bźin du sṅags kyi rgyal po ste/ tham cad kyis de bźin du rgyal ba mchog rnams kyis mṅon par mchod pas bkur sti daṅ phyag bya'o źes so// tiṅ ṅe 'dzin las laṅs nas 'gro ba rnams 'jig rten dbaṅ phyug gi skur blta[21] źiṅ/ de'i ṅa rgyal byas nas ji ltar 'dod pa bźin gnas par bya'o źes so//

---

1 The rendering follows Sanskrit: sammukham. P, D, TP kha mdon du.
2 P bzuṅ.
3 D, TP ñe bar gnas.
4 P, TP om.
5 D chag.
6 The rendering follows Sanskrit: kalaṅkapaṭala-. P, D, TP ri dags kyi mtshan ma.
7 P om.
8 P rtse'i.
9 P om.
10 P 'phos.
11 D, TP kharsa pā ṇi.
12 P gya.
13 D byi.
14 P nal.
15 P illegible before -n.
16 P chad.
17 P hrī.
18 P bsgom.
19 TP spags.
20 P hrī.
21 P lta.

(6) cho ga 'dis bcom ldan 'das maṅ du bsgoms na/[1] ral gril sogs pa'i dṅos grub mtha' dag mṅon du byed ciṅ źabs kyi druṅ du yaṅ dag par 'byuṅ źiṅ 'jug na/ gźan dṅos grub phra mo smos ci dgos te/ ṅes par 'byuṅ ṅo// gaṅ źig skye bos dben pa'i nags tshal daṅ/ dur khrod daṅ/ ri'i phug rnams su gnas nas bcom ldan (2-'das bsgom pa-2) de rnams kyis yun mi riṅ bar de bźin du 'dir ṅes par bcom ldan 'das mṅon du byed de/ bcom ldan 'das raṅ ñid kyis de rnams kyi dbugs 'byin pa daṅ rab tu dbugs 'byin pa la sogs pa ster bar mdzad do// (3-ṅes źugs maṅ po ster bar mdzad do/-3) (4-ṅes par źugs na-4) maṅ po smras pas ci źig bya/ mchog tu śin tu rñed par dka' ba'i saṅs rgyas ñid kyaṅ de rnams kyi lag pa'i mthil na/ rag chuṅ gi 'bras bu bźag pa bźin du 'gyur ro źes so//

(7) dpal ldan mkha' spyod 'jig rten mgon//
mchog gi sgrub thabs byas pa yis//
bsod nams gaṅ bsags de yis ni/
'jig rten thub pa'i druṅ 'gro śog/

dpal ldan mkha' spyod 'jig rten dbaṅ phyug gi sgrub thabs cuṅ zad rgyas par mdzad pa/ a nu pa ma ra kṣi tas mdzad pa rdzogs so//

---

1 D illegible.
2 D illegible; TP 'das sgom pa.
3 D, TP om.
4 P ṅes źugs.

## 2.6 (T3) Khasarpaṇalokeśvarasādhana

rgya gar skad du/ śrī [(1-]kha sarpa ṇa[-1)] sā dha naṃ/ bod skad du/ dpal ldan mkha' sbyod kyi sgrub thabs/

(0) dpal ldan mkha' spyod la phyag 'thsal lo/

(1) daṅ po re źig sṅags pas stan bde ba la ñe bar 'dug ste/

(2.1.1) raṅ gi sñiṅ gar paṃ yig yoṅs su gyur pa las padma 'dab ma brgyad pa/ de'i steṅ du a yig yoṅs su gyur pa las zla ba'i dkyil 'khor/ de'i steṅ du hrīḥ yig las 'od zer bltas te/ 'od zer des 'og min gyi sa la bźugs[2] te/ 'jig rten dbaṅ phyug gdan draṅs nas mdun gyi nam mkha'i mthil du bltas te

(2.1.2) dig pa bśags pa la sogs[3] bya'o// 'di lta ste sdig pa bśags pa daṅ/ bsod nams la rjes su yi raṅ ba daṅ/ bsod nams yoṅs su bsṅo ba daṅ/ gsum la skyabs su 'gro ba daṅ/ bdag ñid dbul ba daṅ/ gsol ba 'debs pa daṅ/ byaṅ chub tu sems bskyed par byas nas tshaṅs pa'i gnas bźi bsgom par bya ste/ byams pa daṅ/ sñiṅ rje daṅ/ dga' ba daṅ/ btaṅ sñams so//

(2.1.3) de nas stoṅ pa ñid bsgom par bya'o// oṃ śūnya tā dzñāna bdzra swa bhā ba[4] ā tma ko 'haṃ[5]/ źes pas

(2.2) raṅ gi lus gzugs[6] brñan daṅ 'dra bar bltas la/ sñiṅ ga'i[7] dbus su paṃ yig las skyes pa'i padma 'dab ma brgyad pa/ de'i steṅ du ā[8] yig las zla ba'i dkyil 'khor/ de'i steṅ du hrīḥ yig dmar po'i 'od zer[9] gyis de bźin gśegs pa rnams bkug ciṅ bcug nas bdag ñid 'jig rten dbaṅ phyug gi gzugs su bsgom par bya ste/ sku mdog dkar po ral pa'i cod pan can// phyag g'yas pa mchog sbyin/ cig śos na padma dkar po bsnams pa/ skyil kruṅ phyed pas bźugs śiṅ rgyan thams cad kyis rnam par brgyan pa/ 'od dpag tu med pa'i cod pan can mtshan sum cu rtsa gñis daṅ ldan pa/ dpe byad bzaṅ po brgyad cus spras pa/ zla ba'i gdan la zla ba'i 'od lta bu'i bdag ñid rnam par bsgom par bya'o//

(2.3) de'i g'yas su 'phags ma sgrol ma daṅ nor bzaṅs/ g'yon du khro gñer can daṅ/ rta mgrin/

(2.4) śar du rnam par snaṅ mdzad/ lhor rin chen 'byuṅ ldan/ nub tu 'od dpag med/ byaṅ du don yod grub pa rnams so//

(2.5) mer spyan ma/ bden bral du mā ma kī/ klu du gos dkar mo/ dpal[10] ldan du rdo rje dbyiṅs kyi dbaṅ phyug ma rnams so//

(3) de nas sñiṅ ga'i sa bon gyi 'od zer gyis ye śes sems dpa' dgug ciṅ rab tu gźug par bya'o//

(4) mig la sogs pa byin gyis brlabs śiṅ/ lus daṅ ṅag daṅ/ yid byin gyis rlabs nas/ dbaṅ bskur ba źu bar bya'o// ji ltar 'khruṅs tsam ñid nas ni// de bźin gśegs rnams khrus gsol ba/ lha yi chu bo dag pa yi[11]// de bźin bdag kyaṅ khrus mdzad gsol/ oṃ sarba ta thā ga ta a bhi ṣe ka ta sa ma ya śrī ye hūṃ phaṭ swāhā/

---

1 D kharsa pā ṇa.
2 D, TP źugs.
3 D and TP add. pa.
4 D, TP wa.
5 P haṃ.
6 D and TP add. su.
7 P gi.
8 D, TP a.
9 TP zar.
10 D, TP dpaṅ.
11 D, TP yis.

(5) spyan ma la sogs pa'i lha mo bcu yaṅ dag par spros nas mchod pa dań bstod pa byas te/ sṅags bzlas par bya'o/ de la ṅags ni 'di'o/ oṃ hrīḥ swāhā/ źes so//

dpal ldan mkha' sbyod kyi sgrub thabs rdzogs so//

## 3 (T3) Vajradharmasya sādhanopāyikā

(1) sñiṅ gar hrīḥ yig zla steṅ dgod//
chos rnams bdag med bsgom byas la//
de las 'od zer dmar po ni//
yaṅ dag 'phro ba mkha' mñam de//
'jig rten dbaṅ phyug rnam (1-par blta-1)//
brtan daṅ g'yo ba'i 'gro ba rnams//
yaṅ dag byaṅ chub sems dpa'i don//
bskyed ciṅ sñiṅ gar rab tu źugs//
de la hrīḥ yig gźan 'jug pas//
skad cig gis ni ye śes sbyor//
(2) de la kha dog dkar daṅ dmar//
padma rā ga'i raṅ bźin 'od//
saṅs rgyas lṅa yi cod pan can//
rab tu dgyes pa'i spyan rgyas pa//
phyag g'yon na[2] padma sdoṅ bur bcas//
'dab ma bcu drug pa dag bsnams//
de la phyag g'yas kyis kyaṅ ni//
padma rgyas pa thugs kar 'dzin//
rma bya'i steṅ du zla ba yi//
dkyil 'khor dbus su ñe bar bźugs//
sems dpa'i skyil kruṅ kun nas 'khyil//
sgeg[3] pa'i ñams daṅ bcas śiṅ brten[4]//
las chen mchod rten naṅ gnas pa'i//
gźal yas khaṅ gi spyod lam can//
rtag tu rdo rje'i chos mchog ni//
bsgom byas byaṅ chub thob par 'gyur//
(3) bsgoms pas ṅal na sñiṅ gar zla ba la sṅags bkoṅ la phreṅ ba'i rnam pa bźin du mi g'yo ba'i sems kyis bzlas par bya'o// de la bzlas pa'i sṅags ni 'di'o// oṃ bdzra dha rmā hrīḥ źes so//
rdo rje chos kyi sgrub thabs cho ga bsdus pa rdzogs so//

---

1 P ba ltar.
2 D, TP om.
3 TP sgog.
4 D, TP bsten.

## 4.1 (T1) āryaṢaḍakṣarīmahāvidyāsādhana

rgya gar skad [(1-]du/ ṣa ḍa[-1)] kṣa ra sā dha na/ bod skyad du/ yi ge drug pa'i sgrub thabs/

(1.1) daṅ por re źig sṅags pas bde ba'i stan la ñe bar gnas te/ gdoṅ pa'i gtsaṅ sbra[2] la sogs pa byas la/

(2.1.1) raṅ ñid kyi sñiṅ ga'i zla ba la gnas pa'i yi ge hrīḥ dkar po las rnam par 'phros pa'i 'od zer gyis/ bla ma daṅ saṅs[3] rgyas daṅ byaṅ chub sems dpa rnams mdun du bltas bas[4]/ legs par mchod ciṅ gsum la skyabs su 'gro ba la sogs pa rnams bya ste/ dkon mchog gsum la bdag skyabs[5] mchi/ źes bya ba la sogs pas so//

(2.1.2) ji srid du sems can du bsdu par bya bas bsdus par gyur ba[6]/ sgo ṅa las skyes pa daṅ/ mṅal las skyes pa daṅ/ drod gśer las skyes pa daṅ/ brdzus[7] te skyes pa daṅ/ gzugs can daṅ/ gzugs can ma yin pa daṅ/ 'du śes yod pa daṅ/ 'du śes med pa daṅ/ 'du śes yod pa yaṅ ma yin 'du śes med pa yaṅ ma yin pa ste/ ji srid du gaṅ 'ga' źig sems can gyi khams su gdags par bya bas btags[8] par gyur pa rnams/ thams cad kyaṅ bdag gis phuṅ po lhag ma med pa'i mya ṅan las 'das pa'i dbyiṅs su legs par dgod par bya'o//

(2.1.3) de nas oṃ raṅ bźin gyis rnam par dag pas chos thams cad raṅ bźin gyis rnam par dag pa ni bdag yin no źes bya ba lan gsum brjod par bya ba'o// de'i rjes thogs su gtoṅ pa ñid yud tsam cig dmigs par bya'o//

(2.1.4) de'i rjes thogs la sñiṅ gar padma dkar po'i steṅ du zla ba'i dkyil 'khor ro// de'i steṅ du hrīḥ dkar po'i rnam pa'o// de las[9] 'od zer 'bum phrag du ma kun nas 'phros par bsgoms la/ des sems can rnams kyi yaṅ thog ma med pa'i dus nas bsags pa'i 'dod chags la sogs pa'i ñon moṅs pa'i tshogs rnams lhag ma ma lus par rnam par sbyaṅs te/ slar yaṅ de ñid la gźug par bya'o//

(2.2.1) de yoṅs su gyur pa las bdag ñid 'jig rten dbaṅ phyug gi gzugs su bsgom par bya ste/ rgyan thams cad kyis brgyan pa sku mdog dkar po phyag bźi'i g'yon pas padma 'dziṅ pa/ g'yas pas[10] 'phreṅ ba 'dzin pa phyag gźan dag gñis kyis [(11-]thugs kar thal mo kha sbyar[-11)] nas gnas pa'o//

(2.2.2) phyag daṅ sku mdog de lta bu daṅ ldan pa dag gis nor bu 'dzin pa[12]/ g'yas phyogs na padma gźan gyi steṅ na gnas pa'o// g'yon phyogs na de kho na[13] du yi ge drug gi rig ma chen mo padma gźan la gnas pa'o//

---

1 D illegible.
2 TP sgra.
3 D illegible after saṅ-.
4 D, P pas.
5 D phyag.
6 P pa.
7 TP rdzus.
8 P brtags.
9 D, TP la.
10 D, TP pa.
11 D illegible.
12 P om.
13 D add. bźin.

(2.3.1) de'i rjes la/ oṃ rdo rje sems dpa' bde [(1-]ba chen po dzaḥ[-1)] hūṃ baṃ ho/ dpa' bo khyod a la la la la hoḥ aḥ aḥ aḥ aḥ źes bya ba byin gyis rlobs par byed pa'i sṅags kyi rgyal po brjod par bya'o//

(2.3.2) de ltar bsgoms la de nas saṅs rgyas thams cad kyi sñiṅ por gyur pa yid bźin gyi nor bur brtag par bya ba'i gsaṅ sṅags kyi rgyal po 'di[2] bdag ñid 'jig rten dbaṅ phyug gi sñiṅ ga'i zla ba'i dkyil khor la kha dog dkar po phreṅ ba'i rnam par kha nas phyir byuṅ nas lte khuṅ du legs par 'jug pa 'khor lo[3] 'khor ba'i tshul du mtshan ma med pa'i rnal 'byor gyis blta bar bya ba'o// de ltar 'das[4] pa byas nas/ g'yo ba daṅ gźug[5] pa la sogs pa thob[6] ste/ dad pa daṅ sñiṅ rje daṅ ldan źiṅ bla ma la gus pa'i rnal 'byor ba[7] ni dus riṅ po mi thogs pa ni[8] 'grub par 'gyur ro// oṃ ma ṇi padme hūṃ/ bzlas pa'i sṅags so//

(3) de nas laṅs pa'i dus na ni sṅags kyi rgyal po 'di brjod nas[9] laṅs par bya ste/ oṃ bdzras satwa[10] sa ma ya/ ma nu pā la ya/ bdzra satwa twe[11] no pa ti ṣṭha/ dri ḍho me bha ba/ su toṣyo me bha ba/ su po ṣyo me bha ba/ a nu ra kto me bha ba/ sarba sidhi mme pra ya tstsha sarba karma su tsa me [(12-]tsha taṃ śrī[-12)] yaṃ/ ku ru hūṃ ha ha ha ha hoḥ/ bha ga bān sarba ta thā ga ta bdzra mā me muñtsa bdzra bhā ba ma hā sa ma ya bdzra[13] satwa āḥ de skad brjod la ji ltar bde bar rgyu bar bya ba'o//

'phags pa yi ge drug pa rig pa chen mo'i sgrub thabs rdzogs so// // dge sloṅ tshul khrims rgyal mtshan gyis bsgyur ba'o//

---

1 D illegible.
2 D illegible.
3 TP add. ltar.
4 TP bzlas.
5 D illegible between g- and -ug.
6 D, TP 'thob.
7 TP pa.
8 D, TP na.
9 P la.
10 D illegible.
11 P te.
12 D tsha taṃ śri; TP tshi ttaṃ śri.
13 D, TP om.

## 4.1 (T2) āryaṢaḍakṣarīmahāvidyāsādhana

rgya gar skad du/ ā rya a ba lo ki te[1] śwa ra sya ṣa ḍa kṣa ra sā dha naṃ/ bod skad du/ 'phags pa spyan ras gzigs dbaṅ phyug gi yi ge drug ma'i[2] sgrub[3] thabs/

(0) 'jig rten mgon po la phyag 'tshal lo//

(1.1) daṅ po re źig sṅags pas bde ba'i gdan la 'dug ste// kha dag pa la sogs pa byas nas

(2.1.1) saṅs rgyas la sogs pa bltas te yaṅ dag par mchod nas/ gsum la skyabs su 'gro ba byas[4]/ dkon mchog gsum la skyabs su 'chi[5]/ źes bya ba la sogs pa bya'o//

(2.1.2) ji srid sems can thams cad kyi graṅs su gtogs pa/ sgo ṅa las skyes pa 'am/ mṅal las skyes pa 'am/ brdzas[6] te skyes pa daṅ[7]/ drod gśer las skyas pa 'am/ gzugs can nam/ gzugs med pa 'am/ 'du śes can nam/ 'du śes med pa 'am/ yod min med min gyi 'du śes la sogs pa ji srid sems can gyi khams su gtogs pa brjod pa de thams cad bdag gis phuṅ po lhag ma med pa'i mya ṅan las 'das pa'i dbyiṅs su gźag par bya'o//

(2.1.3) de nas oṃ swa bhā ba[8] śuddhaḥ sarba dha rmāḥ swa bhā ba śu ddho 'haṃ[9]/ źes bya ba lan gsum brjod la/ yud tsham gyis stoṅ pa ñid du bsgom par bya'o//

(2.1.4) de nas raṅ gi sñiṅ gar padma dkar po'i steṅ du zla ba'i dkyil 'khor/ de'i steṅ du hrīḥ dkar po/ de nas[10] 'od zer brgya stoṅ phrag maṅ po byuṅ bar bsams la/ sems can thams cad kyis thog ma med pa'i dus nas bsags pa'i 'dod chags la sogs pa ñon moṅs pa'i tshogs khams gsum du rtog[11] pa dag par byas nas/ yi ge de ñid raṅ gi sñiṅ gar bcug pas/

(2.2.1) de yoṅs su gyur pa las bdag ñid 'jig rten dbaṅ phyug gi gzugs/ rgyan thams cad kyis brgyan pa/ sku mdogs dkar ba/ phyag bźi pa/ ral pa'i cod pan 'chaṅ ba/ g'yon pa padma bsnams pa/ g'yas kyi[12] bgraṅ phreṅ 'dzin pa/ phyi ma'i phyag gñis kyis[13] sñiṅ gar thal mo sbyor[14] źiṅ 'dzin pa/ 'od dpag tu med pa'i ral pa'i dbu rgyan can no//

(2.2.2) g'yas phyogs su nor bu 'dzin pa/ de daṅ 'dra ba'i mdog daṅ phyag daṅ mtshan ma can te/ (15-dri ba'i-15) phyag gis thal mo sbyar ba'o// g'yon phyogs su yi ge drug pa'i (16-rig pa 'jig-16) rten dbaṅ phyug daṅ 'dra ba'i sku mdog daṅ phyag mtshan bsgom par bya'o//

(2.3.1) de nas oṃ ma hā su kha bdzra satwa dzaḥ hūṃ baṃ hoḥ su ra ta stwaṃ a la la la la hoḥ[17]/ aḥ aḥ aḥ aḥ źes bya ba'i byin gyis brlab pa'i sṅags brjod par bya'o//

---

1 TP ta.
2 TP pa'i.
3 D and TP add. pa'i.
4 TP add. nas.
5 TP mchi.
6 D, TP rdzus.
7 D, TP 'am.
8 D, TP wa.
9 P haṃ.
10 D, TP las.
11 D, TP gtogs.
12 D, TP kyis.
13 P om.
14 D sbyar.
15 TP phyi ma'i.
16 D illegible.
17 D, TP ho.

(2.3.2) de ltar bsgoms nas 'jig rten mgon po'i thugs kar zla ba'i skyil 'khor la phreṅ ba'i rnam pa lta bu'i dkar po źal nas byuṅ ste/ lte bar 'jug ciṅ 'khor lo 'khor ba'i sbyor bas saṅs rgyas thams cad kyi sñiṅ po yid bźin gyi[1] nor bu rtog pa sṅags kyi rgyal po 'di bzlas par bya'o// de nas 'khor źiṅ 'jug pa la sogs pa thob nas/ dad pa daṅ sñiṅ rje daṅ ldan pa bla ma la gus pa'i rnal 'byor pas dus mi riṅ bar 'grub par 'gyur ro// oṃ ma ṇi padme hūṃ źes bya ba'i sṅags bzlas par bya'o//

(3) de nas ldaṅ ba'i dus su sṅags 'di brjod de gnas par bya'o// oṃ bdzra satwa sa ma ya/ ma nu pā la ya/ bdzra sa twa te[2] no pa ti ṣṭha dri ḍḍho me bha ba/ su to ṣya me bha ba/ su po ṣyo me bha ba[3]/ a nu ra kto me bha ba[4]/ sarba siddhi me[5] pra ya tstsha sarba karmā[6] su tsa me ci ttaṃ śre[7] yaḥ ku ru hūṃ/ ha ha ha ha hoḥ bha ga bān sarba ta thā ga ta bdzra mā[8] me mu ñdza[9] bdzrā bha ba ma hā sa ma ya satwa aḥ[10] źes bya[11] brjod la ji ltar bde bas gnas par bya'o/

yi ge drug pa'i sgrub thabs/ dpal lhan cig skyes pa'i rol pas mdzad pa rdzogs so// paṇḍi ta don yod rdo rje daṅ/ khams pa lo tstsha ba dge sloṅ ba ris bsgyur ba'o//

---

1 P gyis.
2 D twe.
3 P baḥ.
4 P baḥ.
5 D, TP mme.
6 TP karma.
7 P śri.
8 P ma.
9 TP ñtsa.
10 TP āḥ.
11 D, TP om.

## 4.1 (T3) āryaṢaḍakṣarīmahāvidyāsādhana

rgya gar skad du/ ā rya ṣa ḍa kṣa rī ma hā bidya sā dha naṃ[1]/ bod skad du/ 'phags pa yi ge drug pa[2] rig pa chen po'i sgrub thabs/

(0) 'jig rten mgon po la phyag 'tshal lo//

(1.1) daṅ por re źig sṅags pas stan bde ba la 'dug ste/ kha bsaṅ ba la sogs pa byas nas

(2.1.1) raṅ gi sñiṅ gar zla ba la gnas pa'i hrīḥ yig dkar po las 'od zer 'phros nas bla ma daṅ/ saṅs rgyas daṅ/ byaṅ chub sems dpa' rnams mdun du bltas te yaṅ dag par mchod nas gsum la skyabs su 'gro ba la sogs pa bya ba ni/ dkon mchog gsum la bdag skyabs mchi// źes bya ba la sogs pas

(2.1.2) ji srid sems can rnams daṅ/ sems can gyi khoṅs su gtogs śiṅ bsdus pa rnams[3]/ sgo ṅa las skyes pa daṅ/ mṅal las skyes pa daṅ/ drod gśer las skyes pa daṅ/ rdzus te skyes pa daṅ/ gzugs can daṅ/ gzugs med pa daṅ/ 'du śes can daṅ/ 'du śes med pa daṅ/ 'du śes yod min med min daṅ/ gaṅ yaṅ cuṅ zad sems can gyi khams[4] su gtogs śiṅ bgraṅ ba de dag thams cad bdag gis phuṅ po lhag ma med pa'i mya ṅan las 'das pa'i dbyiṅs su gźag par bya'o//

(2.1.3) de nas oṃ swa bhā ba[5] śuddhaḥ sarba dharmāḥ swabhā ba[6] śuddho 'haṃ[7]/ źes lan gsum brjod par bya'o// de'i rjes su skad cig gis stoṅ par dmigs śiṅ/

(2.1.4) de nas raṅ gi sñiṅ gar padma dkar po'i steṅ du zla ba'i skyil khor/ de'i steṅ du hrīḥ[8] dkar po/ de la 'od zer brgya stoṅ dpag tu med pa 'byuṅ bar bsams la/ sems can thams cad kyi dus thog ma med pa nas bsags pa'i 'dod chags la sogs pa'i ñon moṅs pa'i tshogs ma lus pa rnam par dag par byas nas/ slar yaṅ de ñid la de bźin du źugs nas

(2.2.1) gaṅ de ñid yoṅs su gyur pa las bdag ñid 'jig rten dbaṅ phyug gi sku/ rgyan thams cad kyis brgyan pa/ sku mdog dkar po phyag bźi pa g'yon na[9] padma bsnams pa[10]/ g'yas na bgraṅ phreṅ[11] bsnams pa/ phyag gźan gñis thugs kar thal mo sbyar ba/ 'od dpag med kyi ral pa'i cod dpan can bsgom par bya'o//

(2.2.2) g'yas phyogs su nor bu 'dzin pa de daṅ sku mdog phyag mtshan mtshuṅs pa padma'i naṅ gi steṅ du gnas pa'o// de bźin du g'yon du padma gźan gyi steṅ du yi ge drug ma'i rig[12] mchen mo 'jig rten dbaṅ phyug daṅ 'dra ba'i sku mdog daṅ phyag mtshan bsgom par bya'o//

---

1 P na.
2 TP ma.
3 P om.
4 D, TP khoṅs.
5 D, TP wa.
6 D, TP wa.
7 P haṃ.
8 D and TP add. yig.
9 D, TP om.
10 P om.
11 P 'phreṅ.
12 D and TP add. byed.

(2.3.1) de nas oṃ ma hā su kha bdzra sa twaḥ[1] dzaḥ hūṃ baṃ hoḥ su ra ta stwa[2]/ a la la la[3] ho/ aḥ aḥ aḥ āḥ[4] źes bya ba'i[5] byin gyis brlab[6] pa'i sṅags kyi rgyal po brjod par bya'o//

(2.3.2) de bźin du bsgoms nas/ de nas 'jig rten dbaṅ phyug gi[7] thugs kar zla ba'i dkyil khor gyi rnam pa la bgraṅ phreṅ gi rnam pa lta bu kha[8] dog dkar po źal nas byuṅ[9] ste/ lte bar 'jug ciṅ 'khor lo ltar 'khor ba'i sbyor bas/ saṅs rgyas thams cad kyi sñiṅ po rtog pa'i sṅags kyi rgyal po yid bźin gyi nor bu 'di mtshams med pa'i sbyor[10] ba[11] lta[12] źiṅ de nas bzlas pa bya'o// de nas 'khor źiṅ 'dzag pa la sogs pa thob nas dad pa[13] daṅ/ sñiṅ rje daṅ ldan źiṅ bla ma la gus pa'i rnal 'byor bas dus[14] mi riṅ bas dṅos grub tu 'gyur ro// oṃ ma ṇi padme hūṃ źes bya ba'i sṅags bzlas par bya'o//

(3) de nas ldaṅ ba'i dus su sṅags kyi rgyal po 'di brjod nas ldaṅ bar bya'o// oṃ bdzra satwa sa ma ya/ ma nu pā la ya/ bdzra satwa twe no pa ti ṣṭha dri ḍho me bha ba/ su toṣyo me bha ba/ su po ṣyo me bha ba/ a nu ra kto me bha ba/ sarba siddhi me[15] pra yatstsha/ sarba karmā[16] su tsa me/ tsi (17-taṃ śrī-17) yaḥ ku ru hūṃ/ ha ha ha ha hoḥ/ bha ga wān[18] sarba ta thā ga ta bdzra mā me muñtsa bdzraṃ bha ba ma hā sa ma ya satwa āḥ źes brjod nas ci bder gnas par bya'o//

yi ge drug ma'i sgrub thabs/ dpal lhan cig skyes pa'i rol pas mdzad pa rdzogs so//

---

1 D twa.
2 D stwaṃ/.
3 D add. la.
4 P ā.
5 TP bas.
6 D, TP brlabs.
7 D om.
8 P illegible.
9 TP phyuṅ.
10 P illegible after sbyo-.
11 D, TP bas.
12 D, TP blta.
13 P pas.
14 P om.
15 D, TP mme.
16 D, TP karma.
17 D, TP ttaṃ śre.
18 P bā na.

## 4.1 (T4) āryaṢaḍakṣarīmahāvidyāsādhana

(1-'phag pa yi ge drug ma'i sgrub pa'i thabs źugs so-1)// rgya gar skad du/ ā rya ṣa ḍa kṣa ra sā dha naṃ/ bod skad du/ 'phag pa yi ge drug pa'i sgrub pa'i[2] thabs/

(0) 'jig rten mgon po la phyag 'tshal lo//

(1.1) daṅ por re źig sṅags pas gdoṅ bkrus nas stan bde ba la 'dug ste//

(2.1.1) saṅs rgyas la sogs pa[3] bsams la/ skyabs su 'gro ba la sogs pa bya'o// bdag ni dkon mchog gsum la skyabs su soṅ ba yin no// źes mos par[4] byas nas/

(2.1.2) sems can ji sñed sems can du bsdus[5] pas yaṅ dag par bsdus la/ sgo ṅa las skyes pa 'am/ mṅal las skyes pa 'am/ drod gśer las skyes pa 'am/ rdzus te skyes pa 'am/ gzugs can nam/ gzugs can ma yin pa 'am/ 'du śes can nam/ 'du śes med pa 'am/ 'du śes med 'du śes med min te/ ji srid du sems can ni khams gsum de[6] btags[7] pas/ btags pa de dag thams cad bdag ñid kyis phuṅ po lhag ma med pa'i dbyiṅs su dgod par bya'o śes bsam/

(2.1.3) de nas oṃ swa bhā ba bi śuddhaḥ sarba dharma[8] swa bhā ba bi śuddho 'haṃ[9]/ de nas stoṅ pa ñid du bsdu pas bsdus pa[10] tsham gyis bsgoms la/

(2.1.4) de'i 'og tu raṅ gi sñiṅ gar zla ba'i dkyil 'khor/ de'i steṅ du yi ge hrīḥ las 'od zer brgya stoṅ 'byuṅ bar bsgoms te/ yaṅ de ñid kyis thog ma med pa nas bsags pa'i 'dod chags la sogs pa'i ñon moṅs pa ma lus pa mtha' dag rnam par dag par byas nas bdag ñid kyi sñiṅ gar bźugs pa las/

(2.2.1) bdag ñid 'jig rten dbaṅ phyug gi sku rgyan thams cad kyis brgyan pa/ sku mdog dkar po phyag bźi pa g'yas na bgraṅ phreṅ g'yon na padma bsnams pa/ gźan gñis kyis thugs kar thal mo sbyar ba'o//

(2.2.2) g'yas su nor bu 'dzin pa sku mdog daṅ phyag la sogs pa yaṅ de daṅ dra'o// g'yon du 'bru drug pa'i rig sṅags[11] chen mo phyag bźi pa ston ka'i sprin lta bu'o//

(2.3.1) de nas oṃ mahā su[12] ka bdzra satwa/ dza hūṃ baṃ hoḥ[13] su ra ta staṃ[14]/ a la la la la ho/ a a a a źes bya bas byin gyis brlabs pa'i sṅags kyi rgyal po brjod par bya'o//

(2.3.2) de ltar bsgoms nas de'i 'og tu 'jig rten dbaṅ phyug gi thugs kar zla ba'i dkyil 'khor la phreṅ ba 'dra ba dkar po źal nas byuṅ źiṅ lte bar[15] byugs te 'khor lo 'khor ba'i tshul gyis saṅs rgyas thams cad kyi yid bźin[16] nor bu'i rtog pa'i sṅags kyi rgyal po 'di mtshan ma med pa'i

---

1 D, TP om.
2 D, TP om.
3 D, TP par.
4 P pa.
5 D, TP bsdu.
6 P du.
7 D gdags.
8 D dharmāḥ.
9 P haṃ.
10 P om.
11 D, TP pa.
12 D pu.
13 P ho.
14 TP stwaṃ.
15 P par.
16 D add. gyi.

tshul gyis bzlas par bya'o// de nas lus g'yo ba daṅ bcas [(1-]par gyur pa[-1)] la sogs par gyur ba'i[2] rnal 'byor pa dad pa daṅ sñiṅ rje daṅ/ bla ma la gus pa daṅ ldan pa[3] ni riṅ po mi thogs par 'grub par 'gyur ro// oṃ ma ṇi padme hūṃ źes de ltar bzla'o//

(3) de nas ldaṅ ba'i dus su sṅags 'di brjod pa'o// oṃ bdzra satwa sa ma ya/ ma nu pā la ya/ bdra satwa twe no pa tiṣṭha/ dri ḍho me bha ba/ su toṣyo me bha ba/ a nu rakto me bha ba/ su poṣyo me bha ba/ sarba siddhi me pra yatstsha/ sarba karma su tsa me/ ci ttaṃ śreyaḥ ku ru hūṃ ha ha ha ha hoḥ/ bha ga ban[4]/ bdzra mā me muñtsa/ bdzri[5] bha ba[6]/ mahā sa ma ya satwa āḥ de ltar bzlas nas ci bde bar gnas par bya'o//

yi ge drug pa'i grub thabs rdzogs so// // slob dpon chen po pū dza bdzras mdzad pa'o// // rgya gar gyi mkhan po chen po dī paṃ ka ra śrī dzñā na daṅ/ lo tsa ba dge sloṅ śākya blo gros kyis bsgyur ba'o//

---

1 D, TP pa.
2 D, TP pa'i.
3 D, TP pas.
4 D illegible between wān- and -tathāgata.TP wān sarba tathā ga ta.
5 TP bdzrī.
6 TP ga.

## 4.1 (T5) āryaṢaḍakṣarīmahāvidyāsādhana

rgya gar skad du/ ā rya ṣa ḍa kṣa ra sā dha naṃ/ bod skad du/ 'phag pa yi ge drug pa'i sgrub pa'i thabs/

(0) 'jig rten mgon po la phyag 'tshal lo//

(1.1) daṅ por re źig sṅags pas gdoṅ bkrus nas stan bde ba la 'dug ste/

(2.1.1) saṅs rgyas la sogs pa bsams la skyabs su 'gro ba la sogs pa bya'o/ bdag ni dkon mchog gsum la skyabs su soṅ ba yin no// źes mos par byas la/

(2.1.2) sems can ji sñed bsdus bas yaṅ dag par bsdus pa sgoṅ las skyes pa 'am/ mṅal las skyes pa 'am/ drod bśer las skyes pa 'am/ brdzus te skyes pa 'am/ gzugs can nam/ gzugs can ma yin pa 'am/ 'du śes can nam/ 'du śes med pa 'am/ 'du śes yod min med min te/ ji srid du can sems can rnam gyi khams su rtogs pa de dag thams cad/ bdag gis phuṅ po lhag ma med pa'i dbyiṅs su dgod par bya'o// źes bsams la/

(2.1.3) de nas oṃ swa bhā wa śuddha sarba dhar ma swa bhā wa śuddho 'haṃ/ de ltar stoṅ ka ñid du bsdus tsham gyis bsgoms la/

(2.1.4) de'i 'og tu raṅ gi sñiṅ gar zla ba'i dkyil 'khor/ de'i steṅ du yi ge hrīḥ las 'od zer brgya stoṅ du ma 'bsgoms te/ yaṅ de ñid kyis thog ma med pa nas bsags pa'i 'dod chags la sogs pa ñon moṅs pa ma lus pa thams cad rnam par dag par byas nas bdag ñid sñiṅ gar bźugs pa las/

(2.2.1) bdag ñid 'jig rten dbaṅ phyug gi sku rgyan thams cad kyis brgyan pa/ sku mdog dkar po źal gcigs phyag bźi pa/ g'yas na phreṅ ba/ g'yon pa na padma bsnams pa/ phyag gñis kyis thugs kar thal mo sbyar ba'o//

(2.2.2) g'yas su nor bu 'dzin pa sku mdog phyag mtshan la sogs pa de daṅ dra/ g'yon du daṅ po 'bru drug ma rig sṅags chen mo phyag bźi ma ston ka'i sprin lta bu'o//

(2.3.1) oṃ mahā su kha bdzra satwa/ a la la hoḥ aḥ aḥ aḥ aḥ źes bya bas byin gyis brlabs pa'i sṅags kyi rgyal po 'di brjod par bya'o//

(2.3.2) de ltar bsgoms nas de'i 'og tu 'jig rten dbaṅ phyug gi thugs ka'i zla ba'i dkyil 'khor las sphreṅ ba 'dra ba skor/ źal nas phyuṅ źiṅ lte bar źugs te 'khor lo'i tshul gyis saṅs rgyas thams cad kyi thabs yid bźin gyi nor bu lta bu rtog pa sṅags kyi rgyal po 'di mtshan ma med pa'i tshul gyis zla par bya'o/ de nas lus g'yo ba daṅ bcas par gyur pa la sogs par gyur ba'i rnal 'byor pa dad pa daṅ/ sñiṅ rje daṅ/ bla ma la gus pa daṅ ldan pas ni riṅ por ma thogs par 'gyur ro// oṃ ma ṇi padme hūṃ źes de ltar bzlas so//

(3) de nas ldaṅ ba'i dus su yaṅ sṅags brdzod par bya'o/ yi ge brgya pa brjod par bya'o/ de ltar bzlas nas ci bder gnas par bya'o//

yi ge drug pa'i grub thabs slob nor bu 'dzin pa'i sñiṅ po dpon chen po dpal mar me mdzad kyis mdzad pa rdzogs so// jo bo rje lha gcig gis dpal gyi yer par mdzad//

## 4.2 (T3) Kāraṇḍavyūhāmnāyena racitaṃ sādhanaṃ

rgya gar skad du/ ṣa ḍa kṣa ra sā dha naṃ/ bod skad du/ yi ge drug ma'i[1] sgrub thabs/

(0) 'phags pa spyan ras gzigs dbaṅ phyug la phyag 'tshal lo//

(1.1) mgon po padma'i rigs las byuṅ//
thams cad mkhyen pa'i cod pan can//
nad rnams thams cad źi ba'i phyir//
phyag 'tshal[2] nas ni sgrub thabs brtsam//
daṅ por re re[3] źig dṅos grub slob dpon gyi rjes su 'jug pas/ de'i phyir thams cad du bsgom[4] pa daṅ/ bla ma'i mchod pa la brtson par bya ste// bla ma yoṅs su mñes pas thams cad du las rnams 'grub par 'gyur źiṅ dkyil 'khor rab tu źugs pas dṅos grub thob par yaṅ 'gyur te/ raṅ gi dam tshig daṅ sdom pa bsruṅs pas ṅes par dṅos grub thob bo//

(1.2) sṅon du kha bsaṅ ba la sogs pa byas nas lha khaṅ du rje btsun gyi thaṅ[5] sku la sogs pa bkram nas

(2.1.1) raṅ gi thugs kar daṅ po'i yi ge las zla ba'i dkyil 'khor/ de'i steṅ du brgyad pa'i bźi pa'i sa bon la bdun pa'i gñis pa'i gdan daṅ/ daṅ po'i bźi pas brgyan ciṅ// bcu drug pa daṅ yaṅ dag par ldan pa kha dog dkar źiṅ yid du 'oṅ ba'o//

(2.1.2) de las sna tshogs pa'i 'od zer 'phros te/ 'od zer de rnams kyi tshogs las[6] bla ma rdzogs pa'i saṅs rgyas kyi skur bsgoms nas mchod pa daṅ/ phyag daṅ bstod pa bya ste/ sṅags 'dis so/ oṃ bdzra pu ṣpe hūṃ/ oṃ bdzra dhū pe hūṃ/ oṃ bdzra dī pe hūṃ/ oṃ bdzra gandhe hūṃ / oṃ bdzra nai [(7-]be dya[-7)] hūṃ źes so//

(2.1.3) de nas/
dkon mchog gsum la bdag skyabs mchi//
sdig pa thams cad so sor bśags//
'gro ba'i dge la rjes yi raṅ//
saṅs rgyas byaṅ chub yid kyis gzuṅ//
saṅs rgyas chos daṅ tshogs mchog la//
byaṅ chub bar du bdag skyabs mchi//
raṅ gźan de[8] ñid[9] rab bsgrub phyir//
byaṅ chub sems ni bdag gis bskyed//
byaṅ chub mchog tu sems bskyed nas//
sems can thams cad mgron[10] du gñer//
mṅon 'dod byaṅ chub mchog spyad bas[11]//
'gro la phan phyir saṅs rgyas śog//

---

1 TP pa'i.
2 D, TP btsal.
3 D om.
4 P sgom.
5 P khaṅ.
6 P la.
7 D, TP bi dye.
8 TP don.
9 D illegible; TP ni.
10 P 'gron.
11 TP pas.

(2.1.4) smon pa sṅon du 'gro bas chos thams cad bdag med par bsgom par bya'o// oṃ śū nya tā dzñā na bdzra swa (1-bhā wa-1) ā tma ko 'haṃ[2] źes so//
sa bon sgyu ma'i dper byas nas//
khams gsum pa ni ma lus pa//
blta źiṅ reg nas de bźin du//
ji ltar thams cad sgyu ma bźin//
thams cad de bźin dmigs med pas//
'gro ba gnas pa rtag tu grol//
des na[3] thog[4] ma med pa'i dus nas rnam rtog ṅan pa'i sa bon las byuṅ ba'i raṅ bźin las grol bar byas te/ oṃ swa bhā ba[5] śu ddhaḥ sarba dha rmāḥ[6] swa bhā[7] ba[8] śu ddho 'haṃ[9]/

(2.2) de nas sṅon du gsuṅs pa'i sa bon yoṅs su gyur pa las padma'o// de'i steṅ du hrīḥ yig de thams cad yoṅs su gyur pa las dpal ldan 'jig rten mgon po rdo rje daṅ/ padma'i sñiṅ po la zla ba'i steṅ du rdo rje skyil kruṅ gis[10] bźugs pa/ ri boṅ 'dzin pa'i 'od zer lta bu/ kunda daṅ zla ba'i kha dog 'bar ba las/ ral pa'i cod pan can źi źiṅ 'od dpag tu med pas dbu brgyan pa/ stag gi pags pa'i śam thabs bsnams pa/ phyag bźi pa sna tshogs pa'i[11] rgyan gyis brgyan pa/ phyag g'yas na bgraṅ phreṅ[12] bsnams pa/ phyag g'yon na padma daṅ nor bus rnam par brgyan pa/ phyag gñis thal mo sbyar ba/ rgyal ba'i dbaṅ po kun gyi phyag rgya[13] thugs kar gnas pa'o// de nas ṅa rgyal bsgom par bya ste/ bdag ñid 'jig rten dbaṅ phyug go// źes so//

(2.3) de nas ji ltar ñe bar brtan[14] pas ye śes sems dpa' spyan draṅs te/ raṅ gi sṅags kyis mchod yon daṅ/ źabs bsil la sogs pa phul te/ phyag rgya bsdus nas gcig du byas te/ sṅags 'dis lhan cig tu dgod do// oṃ su ra ta stwaṃ/ bdzrā[15] a la la la la hoḥ[16]/ sa ma ya stwaṃ/ sa ma ya stwaṃ/ sa ma ya stwaṃ/ a haṃ źes so//

(2.4.1) ji ltar ñe bar bstan pas dbaṅ bskur ba daṅ/ go cha daṅ/ dar dpyaṅs bciṅs pas lhag par grol bar 'gyur ro// dus thams cad du mchod pa daṅ/ bstod pa daṅ/ bsgom pa sṅon du 'gro bar byas nas bzlas par bya'o//

(2.4.2) raṅ gi sñiṅ gar zla ba'i steṅ du yi ge drug pa 'od zer gyi phreṅ ba bźin du byas pa'i khyim gyi naṅ du blta bar bya'o// sṅags ni/ oṃ ma ṇi pa dme hūṃ/ źes pa yi ge 'bum du bzlas so// de nas gñis pa daṅ gsum pas sdig pa dag par 'gyur[17] ro// mtshams med pa lṅa byed pas kyaṅ bye ba bzlas pas dṅos grub tu 'gyur ro//

---

1 P bhāḥ.
2 P haṃ.
3 D illegible; TP ni.
4 D illegible before -g.
5 D, TP wa.
6 P rmā.
7 P bha.
8 D, TP wa.
9 P haṃ.
10 P gi.
11 P om.
12 P 'phreṅ; TP phriṅ.
13 P om.
14 D, TP bstan.
15 D bdzra.
16 TP ho.
17 P om.

(3) de las ldaṅ bar 'dod na mchod yon la sogs pa phul nas/ khyad par 'phags pa'i rgyal gyis gnas par bya'o// thun mtshams bźir bzlas śiṅ dge ba'i rtsa ba mṅon par 'dod pa'i sṅos grub tu[1] bsṅo'o// nam phyed na[2] ye śes sems dpa' gśegs su gsol// la yi ge brgya pa brjod ciṅ/ lus daṅ/ ṅag daṅ/ yid bsruṅ bar byas nas ci bder gnas par bya ste/

(4) gal te nad la sogs pa źi par 'dod na/ de la ji ltar ñe bar bstan pas skar ma rgyal la sa la ma lhuṅ ba'i[3] lci bas rje btsun gyi druṅ du maṇḍal gru bźi bya ste/ mṅon par 'dod pa la yi ge drug pa daṅ sbyar nas lan brgya rtsa brgyad bzlas par bya'o// zla ba drug gis the tshom med par 'grub po źes so/

za ma tog bkod pa'i man ṅag gis[4] mdzad pa'i yi ge drug pa'i sgrub thabs rdzogs so//

---

1 P du.
2 D, TP nas.
3 TP add. ba'i.
4 P gi.

## 4.3 (T1) āryaṢaḍakṣarīmahāvidyālokeśvarabhaṭṭārakopa-deśaparamparāyātasādhanavidhiḥ

rgya gar skad du/ ṣa ḍa kṣa ra sā dha naṃ/ bod skad du/ yi ge drug pa'i sgrub thabs/

(0) 'jig rten dbaṅ phyug yi ge drug pa la phyag tshal lo//
(1) gźan la yaṅ dag phan brtson par//
yid kyi lus can rnams la dmigs//
sdug bsṅal ma lus ñer źi źiṅ//
dam pa'i bde bas rab gnas pa//
(2.1) de yi[1] sñiṅ la legs bsams la/
bsgom par bya ba'o dag pa'i 'od//
'od de spros pas lus can raṅ//
kun nas gsal bar bya ba yin//
(2.2) ṅal bsos[2] sṅags pas cho ga bźin//
rnam rtog dam pa min spaṅs la//
'od dkar lhag par 'bar ba yis[3]//
gsal por sṅags ni brjod par bya//
raṅ gi lte[4] ba'i dkyil 'khor du//
de ltar rab źugs sñiṅ gar bsdu//
'di byed pa na lus ṅag yid//
rnam gsum dag pa bsgom par bya//
de la raṅ lus legs gnas pas//
bdag ñid lus sogs dag par ro//
phyir 'phros ba'i[5] sṅags rnams kyis//
srog chags rnams la 'aṅ rnam par bsam//
(3.1) sṅags brjod pa las bźeṅs par ni//
mdun du lha gsum blta byas la//
sṅags brjod sdud pa'i rim pa yis//
re re źiṅ ni dgoṅs[6] pa daṅ//
(3.2) sna tshogs mchod pa sprul pa daṅ//
de dag dbul ba ñid kyaṅ ṅo//
de dag dag pa yoṅs rdzogs nas//
'dod pa'i don du yoṅs su bsṅo//
(3.3) de nas bzlas pa tshul bźin bya//
sṅags bzlas pa'i[7] tha mar yaṅ//
mchod sogs sṅa ma bźin byas la//

---

1 D yid.
2 D, TP sos.
3 P yi.
4 TP lta.
5 D pa'i; TP pa yi.
6 P, D, TP dgod.
7 TP pa yi.

lha rnams sñiṅ gar legs par bsdu[1]//
daṅ por tiṅ 'dzin legs 'thob pa'i//
sṅags pas dben daṅ khyim sogs su//
cho ga 'di ni thun[2] tshod bźir//
'bum phrag bzlas par bya ba yin//
spro daṅ bzlas pa kun spaṅs te//
mtsho mchis[3] sems bral[4] bya ba min//
(4.1) sdig pa sbyaṅs sogs thams cad la//
dkyil 'khor gru bźi byas la ni//
thaṅ ka la sogs mdun du bsgom//
yaṅ na rje dpon maṇḍal la//
mchod byas mchod pa byas nas kyaṅ//
cho ga 'di ni bya ba yin//
(4.2) de las lha'i sku'i gdam ṅag ni 'di yin te//
skyil kruṅ dkar źiṅ phreṅ ba daṅ//
pad bcas thal mo kha sbyor[5] ba'i//
rje lta de daṅ mthun par ni//
lha mo źen pa med par bsten//
'phags pa ser por bsam bya ste//
g'yon pas rin chen gdugs 'dzin ciṅ//
rin chen dbu rgyan phyag g'yas stoṅ//
źen pa med pas rjes su 'gro//

'phags pa yi ge drug pa rig pa chen po rje btsun[6] 'jig rten dbaṅ phyug gi gdams ṅag rgyud nas 'oṅs ba'i[7] sgrubs thabs kyi cho ga'o// dge sloṅ tshul khrims rgyal mtshan gyis bsgyur ba'o//

---

1 D, TP bsdus.
2 TP zun.
3 TP chis.
4 TP khral.
5 TP sbyar.
6 P bstu na.
7 P, D, TP pa'i.

## 4.3 (T3) āryaṢaḍakṣarīmahāvidyālokeśvarabhaṭṭārakopadeśa-paramparāyātasādhanavidhiḥ

//rgya gar skad du/ ṣa ḍa kṣa ra sā dha naṃ/ bod skad du/ yi ge drug pa'i sgrub thabs/

(0) 'jig rten dbaṅ phyug yi ge drug pa la phyag 'tshal lo//
(1) lus can gźan la yaṅ dag par//
yid kyis phan par dmigs bya ste//
sdug bsṅal ma lus ñer źi źiṅ//
dam pa'i bde la dgod par bya//
(2.1) de nas yid kyis sñiṅ ga du//
zla ba dkar po yaṅ dag bsgom//
de las 'od zer 'phros gyur pas//
raṅ lus 'od kyis gaṅ bar bsam//
(2.2) ṅal bsos sṅags pas cho ga bźin//
ṅan pa'i rnam rtog bsdus nas ni//
'od zer dkar po 'phro ba yis//
sṅags ni gsal[1] por brjod par bya//
lte ba'i dkyil 'khor la źugs nas//
ñid kyi sñiṅ gar yaṅ dag bsdu//
lus ṅag[2] yid ni dag bya'i phyir//
lan gsum du ni bsgom par bya//
de nas raṅ gi lus gnas la//
bdag gi sku[3] la sogs pa dag//
sṅags ni phyi rol 'thun gyur nas//
srog chags rnams la phog par bsam//
(3.1) blta źiṅ brjod pa'i sṅags las bskyed//
mdun du lha rnams gsum yin te//
sṅags ni brjod nas yaṅ dag bsdu//
rim pas so sor re rer dpyad[4]//
(3.2) sna tshogs mchod par[5] sprul nas ni//
de bźin de la ṅes par 'bul[6]//
yoṅs su gaṅ źiṅ de nas dag/
'dod[7] pa'i don rnams yoṅs su bsṅo//
(3.3) sṅags ni de las bzlas par bya//
cho ga'i mtha' la bzlas pa daṅ//
mchod pa la sogs sṅon bźin bya//
lha rnams thugs kar yaṅ dag bsdu//

---

1 D illegible before -sal.
2 P ṅan.
3 D, TP lus.
4 P, D dbyad.
5 D pa.
6 P dbul.
7 TP illegible after 'do- .

tiṅ 'dzin so sor dmigs la sogs//
thun mtshams dag ni bźi rnams su//
skye bos dben pa'i khyim sogs su//
sṅags pas 'bum phrag gcig tu bzlas//
rluṅ daṅ sems kyi byed pa spaṅs//
bzlas pa spro źiṅ yaṅ dag bsdu//

(4.1) sdig pa kun las[1] zad sogs la/
maṇḍal la gru bźir byas nas ni//
bris sku la sogs bkram byas la//
de yi mdun du gtso bo bsgom[2]//
dkyil 'khor mchod par[3] bya ba ni//
cho ga 'di yis mchod par bya//

(4.2) de la 'dir lha'i rnam pa'i ñe bar bstan pa ni/
dkar źiṅ skyil kruṅ bgraṅ phreṅ daṅ/
chu skyes daṅ bcas thal mo sbyor//
gtso bo lta[4] źiṅ de yi sku//
lha mo dpa' bo'i stan la rten[5]//
'phags ma ser mo bsam par bya//
g'yon na rin chen phreṅ ba bsnams//
g'yas pa'i phyag ni stoṅ pa ste//
rin po che yi cod pan daṅ//
dpa' bo'i stan daṅ ldan pa'o//

źes pa ni 'phags pa yi ge drug ma'i rigs sṅags chen mo rje btsun 'jig rten dbaṅ phyug gi man ṅag rgya cher brgyud pa'i sgrub thabs kyi cho ga'o//

---

1 D, TP nas.
2 P bsdom.
3 P pa.
4 D, TP blta.
5 P brten.

## 4.4 (T1) Ṣaḍakṣarīsādhana/ Upadeśaviśeṣasādhana

rgya gar skad du/ u pa de śa bi śe ṣa sā dha naṃ/ bod skad du/ gdams ṅag gi khyad par/

(1) yi ge drug pa'i sgrub thabs 'ga' źig la/ bcom ldan 'das ni nor bu daṅ bcas pa'i po tis mtshan pa'i padma bsnams pa'o// nor bu 'dzin pa ni po ti daṅ bral ba'i nor bu daṅ padma 'dzin pa'o// yi ge drug pa ni nor bu daṅ bral ba'i[1] po ti padma 'dzin pa'o//

(2) mchod pa'i sṅags ni/ oṃ 'jig rten dbaṅ phyug me tog bźes su gsol swāhā/ de bźin du bdug[2] spos[3] daṅ mar me źes bya ba la sogs pa dag gis go bar bya'o// lha gźan dag rnams la yaṅ des go bar bya ba'o//

(3) ye śes kyi kyil 'khor spyan 'dren pa'i sṅags ni 'di yin te/ oṃ bde ba chen po rdo rje sems dpa' jaḥ hūṃ baṃ hoḥ dpa' bo khyod a la la la la hoḥ aḥ aḥ aḥ aḥ [(4-]źes so[-4)]/

yi ge drug pa'i gdams ṅag gi khyad par rdzogs so// // [(5-]dge sloṅ[-5)] tshul khrims rgyal mtshan gyis bsgyur ba'o//

---

1 D pa'i.
2 P add. pa.
3 P om.
4 P om.
5 D, TP om.

## 4.4 (T3) Ṣaḍakṣarīsādhana/ Upadeśaviśeṣasādhana

(1) yi ge drug pa'i sgrub thabs kha cig las bcom ldan 'das nor bu daṅ bcas pa'i po tis daṅ mtshan pa daṅ/ padma bsnams pa daṅ/ nor bu 'dzin pa ni po ti daṅ bral źiṅ nor bu daṅ padma 'dzin pa'o// yi ge drug ma ni nor bu daṅ bral źiṅ po ti daṅ padma 'dzin pa'o//

(2) mchod pa'i sṅags ni/ oṃ lo ke śwa ra pu ṣpaṃ pra tī tstsha swāhā/ de bźin du dhū paṃ/ dī pa[1] źes pa la sogs pa yaṅ śes par bya'o// lha gźan rnams la yaṅ 'dis śes par bya'o//

(3) ye śes kyi dkyil 'khor 'grugs[2] pa'i sṅags 'di'o// oṃ ma hā su kha ba dzra satwa jaḥ hūṃ baṃ hoḥ su ra ta stwaṃ/ a la la la la ho/ aḥ aḥ aḥ aḥ[3] źes so//

yi ge drug pa'i sgrub thabs rdzogs so//

---

1 D, TP paṃ.
2 D, TP dgug.
3 D, TP āḥ.

## 5.1 (T3) Siṃhanādalokeśvarasādhana

(1-// seṅ ge sgra'i sgrub thabs bźugs so//-1) rgya gar skad du/ siṃ ha nā da sā dha naṃ/ bod skad du/ seṅ ge sgra'i sgrub thabs/

(0) rje btsun seṅ ge sgra la phyag 'tshal lo//
źal gcig phyag gñis sku mdog dkar//
spyan gsum seṅ ge la gnas śiṅ//
bla ma nad kun 'joms byed pa'i//
seṅ ge sgra la phyag 'tshal lo//

(1) daṅ por re źig sṅags pas/ kha bsaṅ ba la sogs pa byas te/ yid daṅ 'thun[2] pa'i gnas su gdan[3] bde ba la ñe bar 'dug ste/

(2.1.1) a[4] yig dkar po yoṅs su gyur pa las zla ba'i dkyil 'khor/ de'i steṅ du hrīḥ yig dkar po sñiṅ gar bltas la/ de'i 'od zer gyis[5] khams gsum snaṅ[6] bar byas te/ 'og min gyi gnas su soṅ ste/ seṅ ge sgra daṅ/ bla ma daṅ/ saṅs rgyas daṅ/ byaṅ chub sems dpa' thams cad gdan draṅs te/ mdun gyi nam mkha' la bźugs nas/

(2.1.2) de'i rjes su mchod pa daṅ/ sdig pa bśags pa la sogs pa bya'o// de nas tshaṅs pa'i gnas bźi bsgom[7] par byas nas/ oṃ śū nya tā dzñā na bdzra swa bhā ba[8] ātma ko 'haṃ[9] źes pa'i sṅags 'dis stoṅ pa ñid du byin gyis brlab par bya'o//

(2.2) de nas smon lam rjes su dran par byas nas paṃ yig dkar po yoṅs su gyur pa las padma/ de'i steṅ du a[10] yig dkar po yoṅs su gyur pa las zla ba'i dkyil 'khor/ de'i steṅ du āḥ yig dkar po yoṅs su gyur pa las/ seṅ ge dkar po/ de'i steṅ du aṃ yig dkar po yoṅs su gyur pa las padma dkar po/ de'i lte ba la hrīḥ yig dkar po 'od zer 'phro źiṅ 'gyed pa/ de thams cad yoṅs su gyur pa las seṅ ge sgra'i gzugs su bdag ñid blta bar bya'o// yan lag thams cad dkar źiṅ źal gcig phyag gñis pa/ spyan gsum pa ral pa'i cod pan bciṅs pa/ 'od dpag tu med pas dbu brgyan pa/ rgyal po chen po rol pa'i stabs kyis seṅ ge'i khri la bźugs pa/ stag gi pags pa'i na bza' bsnams pa/ de bźin gśegs pa lṅa 'phro źiṅ rol pa'i dpa' bo lṅa daṅ zla ba phyed pas brgyan pa/ phyag g'yon na padma dkar po'i steṅ du ral gri dkar po daṅ/ de daṅ ñe bar gnas pa'i[11] padma dkar po'i steṅ du me tog dri bzaṅ[12] sna tshogs pas yoṅs su gaṅ ba'i thod pa dkar po/ g'yas na padma dkar po'i steṅ na sprul dkar pos dkris pa'i (13-dbyu gu-13) rtse gsum pa dkar po'o//

(2.3) de lta bur gyur pa'i bcom ldan 'das bsgom par bya'o// bsgoms pas ṅal na sṅags bzlas par bya'o// de la sṅags ni 'di'o/ oṃ āḥ hrīḥ siṃ ha nā da hūṃ/ phaṭ swāhā/

---

1 D, TP om.
2 D, TP mthun.
3 P stan.
4 P oṃ.
5 P gyi.
6 TP smaṅ.
7 P bsgoms.
8 D, TP wa.
9 P haṃ.
10 P oṃ.
11 P pa.
12 P add. po.
13 P dbyug.

(3.1) cho ga 'dis sku gzugs byas te/ yaṅ na ras bris[1] byas la/ bcom ldan 'das kyi mdun du so so'i maṇḍal byas la gzuṅs lan gcig bklag par bya'o// de la gzuṅs ni 'di'o// na mo ratna tra[2] yā ya/ na ma[3] ā ryā ba lo ki te śwa rā ya/ bo dhi satwā ya/ mahā satwā ya/ ma hā kā[4] ru ṇi kā ya/ ta dya thā/ oṃ a ka ṭe/ bi ka ṭe ṇi ka ṭe/ kaṭaṃ kaṭe/ ka ro ṭe/[5] (6-bī rye-6) swāhā/ sa la ma lhuṅ ba'i lci ba la mṅon par bsṅags[7] nas maṇḍal brgyad byas la/ maṇḍal so so la lan bcu gsum gyi bar du gzuṅs[8] bklag par bya'o// maṇḍal so so'i dri ma lhag pa'i lci ba de la gzuṅs lan bdun du mṅon par bsṅags nas des[9] nad pa la byug par bya'o//

(3.2) ñi ma bdun nam/ ñi ma bcu gsum mam/ ñi (10-ma ñi-10) śu rtsa gcig gis de bźin du byas pas mtshams med pa lṅa byed pas kyaṅ 'grub par 'gyur ro/ gal te ma grub na de'i tshe ṅas mtshams med pa lṅa byas 'gyur ro/

(11-seṅ ge sgra'i sgrub thabs rdzogs so/-11)

(4) bdag gi sgrub thabs cho ga 'dis//
gaṅ źig nor daṅ dge thob ciṅ//
mgon po seṅ ge sgra daṅ ni//
'gro ba rnams ni nad med śog//

paṇḍi ta a ba dhu ti dpal ldan gñis med rdo rje źabs kyis mdzad pa'o[12]//

---

1 D, TP ris.
2 P trā.
3 P maḥ.
4 P ka.
5 P add. ka ro ṭaṃ/.
6 P bi dya; D bi dye.
7 P sṅags.
8 P om.
9 P de yis.
10 D, TP om.
11 P om.
12 P pa rdzogs so//.

## 5.2 (T1) Siṃhanādalokeśvarasādhana

(1-// seṅ ge sgra'i sgrub thabs rim pa bźugs so//-1) //rgya gar skad du/ siṃ ha nā da sā dha naṃ/ bod skad du/ seṅ ge sgra'i sgrub thabs/

(0) seṅ ge sgra la phyag 'tshal lo//

(1) daṅ por gdoṅ bkru ba la sogs pa byas nas bde ba'i stan la gnas te/

(2.1.1) rnal 'byor pas raṅ gi sñiṅ gar ñi ma'i dkyil 'khor la yi ge a bltas pas mdun du bla ma daṅ saṅs rgyas la sogs pa spyan draṅs la sdig pa bśags pa la sogs pa[2] rnams bya'o//

(2.1.2) de nas stoṅ pa ñid mṅon du byas śiṅ byin gyis kyaṅ brlabs la/ smon lam rjes su dran par bya ste/

(2.2) de las āḥ'i rnam pa yoṅs su gyur pa las yi ge hūṃ do// de yoṅs su gyur pa las zla ba'o// de'i steṅ du yi ge oṃ yoṅs su gyur pa las padma dmar po/ de'i steṅ du yi ge āḥ yoṅs su gyur pa las seṅ ge dkar po'o// de'i steṅ du yi ge hrīḥ las byuṅ ba'i rje btsun seṅ ge sgra ste/ dkar po phyag gñis pa ral pa daṅ dbu rgyan daṅ ldan pa spyan gsum pa dka'[3] thub kyi cha lugs 'dzin pa rgyal po chen (4-po rol pa'i-4) stabs su bźugs pa phyag g'yon pa na gnas pa'i padma'i/ steṅ na ral gri 'bar ba gyen du laṅs pa'o// g'yas na rtse gsum dkar po la sbrul dkar po gdeṅs ka can gyis dkyis pa'o// g'yon na[5] me tog dri źim po sna tshogs kyis yoṅs su bkaṅ ba'i thod pa dkar po/ dbu rgyan la[6] mi bskyod pa bźugs pa de bźin bśegs pa lṅa spro bar mdzad pa/ sprul pa chen po'i skur gyur pa bsgom par bya'o//

(3) bzlas pa'i sṅags ni oṃ āḥ hrīḥ siṃ ha na da hūṃ phaṭ/

di ni seṅ ge sgra'i sgrub thabs so// dge sloṅ tshul khrims rgyal mtshan gyis bsgyur ba'o//

---

1 D om.
2 D, TP om.
3 P dkar.
4 D po'i.
5 D pa, TP pa ni.
6 D and TP add. ni.

## 5.2 (T3) Siṃhanādalokeśvarasādhana

(1-// seṅ ge'i sgra'i sgrub thabs rim pa bźugs so//-1)// rgya gar skad du/ siṃ ha nā da sā dha naṃ/ bod skad du/ seṅ ge sgra'i sgrub thabs/

(0) rje btsun seṅ ge sgra la phyag 'tshal lo//

(1) rnal 'byor pas daṅ por kha bsaṅ ba la sogs pa byas nas/ stan bde ba la 'dug ste/

(2.1.1) raṅ gi sñiṅ gar ñi ma'i dkyil 'khor la āḥ[2] yig bltas nas mdun du bla ma daṅ/ saṅs rgyas la sogs pa gdan draṅs nas/ sdig pa bśags pa la sogs pa bya'o//

(2.1.2) de nas stoṅ pa ñid mṅon du byas śiṅ byin gyis brlabs nas smon lam rjes su dran par bya'o//

(2.2) de nas āḥ yig yoṅs su gyur pa las hūṃ yig/ de yoṅs su gyur pa las zla ba'i steṅ du/ oṃ yig yoṅs su gyur pa las padma dmar po/ de'i steṅ du āḥ[3] yig yoṅs su gyur pa las seṅ ge dkar po/ de'i steṅ du zla ba la hrīḥ las byuṅ ba'i rje btsun seṅ ge sgra dkar po/ ral pa'i cod pan can/ spyan gsum pa/ phyag gñis pa/ dka' thub kyi cha lugs 'dzin pa/ rgyal po chen po rol pa'i stabs kyis bźugs pa/ phyag g'yon na padma laṅs pa'i steṅ na 'bar ba'i ral gri gyen du 'phyar ba/ g'yas na sprul dkar pos dkris pa'i rtse gsum dkar po bsnams pa/ g'yon na me tog dri bzaṅ po sna tshogs pas gaṅ ba'i thod pa dkar po/ 'od dpag tu med pas dbu rgyan[4] ciṅ/ de bźin gśegs pa lṅa 'phro ba sprul pa'i sku chen po bsgom par bya'o//

(3) bzlas pa'i sṅags ni/ oṃ āḥ hrīḥ siṃ ha nā da hūṃ phaṭ ces so/

---

1 D, TP om.

2 D a.

3 P a.

4 D, TP brgyan.

## 5.3 (T1) Siṃhanādānāṃ dhāraṇī

rgya gar skad du/ siṃ ha nā da dhā ra ṇi/ bod skyad du/ seṅ ge sgra'i gzuṅs/

(0) na mo ratna tra yā ya/

(1) nama[1] ārya[2] a ba lo ki te śva ra ya/ bo dhi satwā[3] ya/ ma hā satwā ya/ ma hā ka ru ṇi kā ya/ tadyathā/ oṃ a ka ṭe bi ka ṭe ṇi ka ṭe ka ṭaṃ ka ṭe ka ro ṭe (4-ka ro ṭa-4) bīr ye swāhā/

(2.1) 'di ni bcom ldan 'das 'phags pa 'jig rten dbaṅ phyug gi mdun du nad par sṅa mor ba'i lci ba sa la ma lhuṅ bas maṇḍal brgyad bya ste/ maṇḍal re re źiṅ lan bcu[5] gsum du bzlas par bya ba'o// de nas lan bdun du ba'i lci ba lhag ma mṅon par sṅags[6] la nad pa la byug par bya ste/

(2.2) nad rnams thams cad[7] źi bar 'gyur ro// gal te mtshams med pa lṅa byas pas kyaṅ ñi ma bdun pa 'am bcu gsum pa 'am ñi ma ñi śu rtsa gcig pa la yaṅ ma grub na de'i tshe ṅa[8] ñid kyis mtshams med pa lṅa byas pa yin źiṅ/ ṅas saṅs rgyas bcom ldan 'das rnams bslus par yaṅ 'gyur ro//

seṅ ge sgra źes bya ba'i gzuṅs rdzogs so// // dge sloṅ tshul khrims rgyal mtshan gyis bsgyur ba'o//

---

1 P namaḥ.
2 P arya.
3 P satwa.
4 D, TP om.
5 D, TP om.
6 D bsṅags.
7 P add. ñe bar.
8 TP de.

## 5.3 (T3) Siṃhanādānāṃ dhāraṇī

(0) na mo ratna tra yā ya/

(1) na maḥ ā ryā ba lo ki te śwa rā ya/ bo dhi satwā ya/ mahā satwa ya/ mahā kā ru ṇi kā ya/ tadya thā/ oṃ a ka ṭe/ bi ka ṭe/ ṇi ka te/ ka ṭaṃ ka ṭe/ ka ro ṭe/ ka ro ṭaṃ/ [(1]bī rya[1)] swāhā/

(2.1) 'di rnams 'phags pa spyan ras gzigs dbaṅ phyug gi mdun du sṅar sa la ma lhuṅ ba'i lci ba blaṅs nas maṇḍal brgyad byas te/ maṇḍal so so la lan bcu gsum bzlas par bya'o// de nas lan bdun pa'i lci ba lhag ma la mṅon par bsṅags nas/ nad pa la ñe bar byug par bya'o//

(2.2) nad thams cad ñe bar źi bar 'gyur ro// gal te ñi ma bdun nam// bcu gsum mam/ ñi śu rtsa gcig tu byas na[2] mtshams med pa lṅa byas pas kyaṅ 'grub par 'gyur ro// gal te ma grub na de'i tshe ṅas mtshams med pa lṅa byas par 'gyur ro//

seṅ ge sgra'i sgrub thabs rdzogs so//

---

1 P bi dya.

2 P nas.

## 5.4 (T1) Siṃhanādalokeśvarasādhana

rgya gar skad du/ siṃ ha nā da sā dha naṃ/ bod skad du/ seṅ ge sgra'i sgrub thabs/

(1) daṅ por re źig sṅags pas bźiṅ gyi[1] gtsaṅ sbra la sogs pa byas pa bde ba'i stan la gnas te/

(2.1.1) raṅ gi sñiṅ gar zla ba'i dkyil 'khor la yi ge hrīḥ dkar po dmigs la/ de'i 'od zer gyis legs par spyan draṅs pa'i bla ma daṅ saṅs rgyas daṅ byaṅ chub sems dpa' rnam mdun du bsgom par bya ba'o//

(2.1.2) de'i rjes su mchod pa daṅ sdig pa bśags pa la sogs pa byas la/ stoṅ pa ñid legs par bsgom par bya źiṅ/ oṃ stoṅ pa ñid kyi ye śes rdo rje'i raṅ bźin gyi bdag ñid ni ṅa yin no źes bya ba 'dis byin gyis brlab par yaṅ bya ba'o//

(2.2) de nas de ma thag tu yi ge paṃ yoṅs su gyur pas padma dkar po'o// de'i steṅ du yi ge siṃ[2] yoṅs su gyur pa las seṅ ge dkar po'o// de'i rgyab tu zla ba la yi ge hrīḥ las kun nas byuṅ ba'i 'jig rten dbaṅ phyug seṅ ge sgra'i skur bdag ñid bsgom par bya ba'o// dkar po phyag gñis pa snaṅ ba mtha' yas daṅ ral pa daṅ dbu rgyan can/ spyan gsum pa dka' thub kyi cha byad 'dzin pa rgyal po chen po'i 'gyiṅ bag gis bźugs pa/ phyag g'yon na padma laṅs pa'i steṅ na ral gri laṅs pa'o// g'yas na rtse gsum dkar po la sbrul dkar po gdeṅs ka daṅ ldan pas dkris pa'o// g'yon na me tog dri źim po sna tshogs kyis yoṅs su bkaṅ ba'i thod[3] pa dkar po'o// de bźin gźegs pa lṅa 'phro bar mdzad pa/ mya ṅan las 'das pa chen po'i skur bsgom par bya ba'o//

(2.3) bzlas pa'i sṅags ni oṃ āḥ hrīḥ siṃha[4] nā da hūṃ phaṭ/

(3.1) de'i rjes thogs la ni gzuṅs yin te/ dkon mchog gsum la phyag 'tshal lo// thugs rje chen po daṅ ldan pa'i byaṅ chub sems dpa' sems dpa' chen po 'phags pa spyan ras gzigs dbaṅ phyug la phyag 'tshal lo// 'di lta ste// oṃ a ka ṭe bi ka ṭe ṇi ka ṭe ka ṭaṃ ka ṭe ka ro ṭa bī ra ye swāhā// bya ba 'di'i rim pa ni ba'i lci ba ma lhuṅ bas[5] nad par śin tu sṅa bar bcom ldan 'das kyi spyan sṅar maṇḍal brgyad bya ste/ maṇḍal re re źiṅ lan bcu gsum rjes su brjod par bya ba'o//

(3.2) ba'i lci ba'i lhag ma lan bdun du mṅon par sṅags[6] la/ nad pa[7] la ñe bar byug par bya ste/ nad rnams thams cad ñe bar źi bar byed pa[8] yin no// gal te mtshams med pa lṅa byas pa rnams kyis kyaṅ ñi ma bdun nam[9] ñi ma bcu gsum mam ñi ma ñi śu rtsa gcig na yaṅ 'di 'grub par ma gyur na ni/ de'i tshe ṅa ñid mtshams med pa lṅa byed par 'gyur ba yin no/

seṅ ge sgra'i sgrub thabs so// paṇḍi ta ratna a[10] ka ra'i źal sṅa nas/ dge sloṅ tshul khrims rgyal mtshan gyis bsgyur ba'o//

---

1 P gyis.
2 D, TP si.
3 P thob.
4 P siṅha.
5 D, TP bar.
6 D, TP bsṅags.
7 P pha.
8 P pha.
9 P nas.
10 D, TP ā.

## 5.4 (T2) Siṃhanādalokeśvarasādhana

(1-seṅ ge sgra'i sgrubs bźugs so//-1) // rgya gar skad du siṃ hā nā da sā dha naṃ/ bod skad du/ seṅ ge sgra'i sgrub pa'i thabs/

(0) 'phags pa seṅ ge[2] sgra la phyag 'tshal lo//

(1) daṅ por re źig sṅags pas gdoṅ bkru ba la sogs pa byas nas/ bde ba'i gdan la 'dug ste//

(2.1.1) rnal 'byor pas raṅ gi sñiṅ gar zla ba'i dkyil 'khor la yi ge hrīḥ bltas la/ mdun du bla ma daṅ/ saṅs rgyas daṅ/ byaṅ chub sems dpa' rnams bsgom par bya'o//

(2.1.2) de'i rjes la mchod pa daṅ sdig pa bśags pa la sogs pa byas nas stoṅ pa ñid bsgom par bya ste/ oṃ śūnyatā dzñāna bdzra swa bhā ba[3] ātma ko 'haṃ[4]/ źes brjod pas byin gyis brlabs la/

(2.2) de nas skad cig tsam[5] gyis[6] yi ge paṃ yoṅs su gyur pa las/ padma dmar po de'i steṅ du yi ge siṃ yoṅs su gyur pa las[7] seṅ ge dkar po/ de'i steṅ[8] du zla bá la hrīḥ las yaṅ dag par byuṅ ba'i rje btsun seṅ ge sgra'i sku gzugs su bsgoms[9] te[10]/ sku mdog dkar po ral pa'i thor tshugs can/ spyan gsum pa/ phyag gñis pa/ dka' thub can gyi cha byad 'dzin pa/ rgyal po rol pas[11] gnas pa'o// phyag g'yon pas ni padma bsgreṅ ba'i steṅ na ral gri 'bar bas brgyan pa'o// g'yas su sbrul[12] dkar pos dkris pa'i mduṅ rtse gsum pa'o// g'yon du dri źim po'i me tog gi tshogs kyis bkaṅ ba'i thod pa dkar po'o// sku las de bźin gśegs pa lṅa 'phro ba'i sprul pa'i gzugs su bsgoms la/

(2.3) sṅags 'di bzlas bar bya'o/ oṃ āḥ hrīḥ siṃ ha na da hūṃ phaṭ/

(3.1) sṅon du bsñen pa 'bum phrag gcig bzlas pa bya'o// de nas na mo ratna tra yā ya/ nam[13] ārya a ba lo ki te śwa rā ya bo dhi sa twā[14] ya/ ma hā satwa ya/ ma hā ka ru ṇi kā ya/ tadya thā/ oṃ a ka ṭe/ bi ka ṭe/ ni ka ṭe/ ka ṭaṃ ka ṭe[15]/ ka ro ṭa ba re swāhā/ di'i ñe bar spyod pa ni bcom ldan 'das kyi mdun du gzuṅs sṅags 'dis[16] sa la ma lhuṅ ba'i lci bas maṇḍal brgyad phul te/ maṇḍal re re źiṅ lan bcu gsum bcu gsum brjod par bya'o//

(3.2) de nas lci ba lhag ma de ñid la mṅon par sṅags te/ lus la ñe bar dbyugs na nad thams cad rab tu źi bar 'gyur ro// gal te mtshams med pa'i las byas kyaṅ ñi ma bdun nam/ bcu bźi 'am/ ñi śu rtsa gcig gis ma grub na de'i tshe bdag gis mtshams med pa lṅa byas pa yin no//

seṅ ge sgra'i sgrub thabs slob dpon tsandra go mis mdzad pa rdzogs so// // paṇḍi ta don yod rdo rje daṅ/ khams pa lo tstsha ba dge sloṅ ba ris bsgyur ba'o//

---

1 D, TP om.
2 P ge'i.
3 D, TP wa.
4 P haṃ.
5 P add. gcig.
6 P om.
7 P la.
8 P illegible.
9 P bsgom.
10 P te.
11 P pa'i.
12 P sprul.
13 P namaḥ.
14 P twa.
15 P re.
16 P 'di.

## 5.4 (T3) Siṃhanādalokeśvarasādhana

rgya gar skad du/ ā rya siṃ ha nā da sā dha naṃ/ bod skad du/ 'phags pa seṅ ge sgra'i sgrub thabs/

(0) rje btsun seṅ ge sgra la phyag 'tshal lo//

(1) daṅ por re źig sṅags pas kha bsaṅ ba la sogs pa byas nas stan bde ba la 'dug te[1]/

(2.1.1) raṅ gi sñiṅ gar zla ba'i dkyil 'khor la hrīḥ yig dkar po bltas nas/ de'i 'od zer gyis[2] mdun du bla ma daṅ/ saṅs rgyas daṅ/ byaṅ chub sems dpa' rnams gdan draṅs par bsgoms nas/

(2.1.2) de nas mchod pa daṅ/ sdig pa bśags pa la sogs pa byas nas stoṅ pa ñid bsgom par bya'o// oṃ śūnya[3] tā dzñā na bdzra swa bhā ba[4] ātma ko 'haṃ[5]/ źes pa 'dis byin gyis brlab par bya'o//

(2.2) de nas skad cig gis paṃ yig yoṅs su gyur pa las padma dmar po// de'i steṅ du siṃ yig yoṅs su gyur pa las seṅ ge dkar po'o// de'i steṅ du zla ba la hrīḥ yig las byuṅ ba'i 'jig rten dbaṅ phyug seṅ ge sgra'i skur bdag ñid bsgom par bya'o// sku mdog dkar po ral pa'i cod pan can/ 'od dpag tu med pas dbu brgyan pa/ spyan gsum pa/ phyag gñis pa/ dka' thub kyi tshul 'dzin pa'o// rgyal po chen po rol pas bźugs pa/ phyag g'yon na[6] padma laṅs pa'i steṅ du ral gri 'bar ba/ g'yas na sbrul[7] dkar pos dkris pa'i rtse gsum dkar po/ g'yon na dri źim po'i me tog sna tshogs pas bkaṅ ba'i thod pa dkar po'o/ de bźin gśegs pa lṅa 'phro źiṅ sprul pa chen po'i skur bsgom par bya'o//

(2.3) bzlas pa'i sṅags ni/ oṃ āḥ hrīḥ siṃ[8] ha nā da hūṃ phaṭ/

(3.1) de nas gzuṅs bzlas te/ na mo ratna tra yā ya/ na ma ārya ba lo ki te śwa rā ya/ bo dhi satwā ya/ mahā satwā ya/ mahā kā[9] ru ṇi kā[10] ya/ tadya thā/ oṃ a ka ṭe/ bi ka ṭe/ ṇi ka ṭe/ ka ṭaṃ ka ṭe/ ka ro ṭe/ ka ro ṭaṃ/ bī[11] dya swāhā// sṅags 'di brjod nas bcom ldan 'das kyi mdun du nam laṅs pa daṅ/ sa la ma[12] lhuṅ ba'i[13] ba'i lci ba la maṇḍal brgyad byas nas maṇḍal so so la lan bcu gsum bzlas par bya'o//

(3.2) lci ba lhag ma la lan bdun mṅon par bsṅags nas nad pa la byug par bya'o// des nad thams cad (14-ñe bar-14) źi bar 'gyur ro// ñi ma bdun nam/ ñi ma bcu gsum mam/ ñi śu rtsa gcig de bźin du byas pas mtshams med pa lṅa byed pas kyaṅ 'grub par 'gyur ro// gal te de'i tshe ma grub na ṅas mtshams med pa lṅa byas par 'gyur ro//

seṅ ge'i sgra'i sgrub thabs rdzogs so//

---

1 P ste.
2 P gyi.
3 P śūn ya.
4 D, TP wa.
5 P haṃ.
6 D, TP om.
7 P sprul.
8 P si.
9 P ka.
10 P ka.
11 P bi.
12 P om.
13 TP pa'i.
14 P om.

## 5.5 (T3) Siṃhanādalokeśvarasādhana

rgya gar skad du/ śrī siṃ ha nā da sā dha naṃ[1]/ bod skad du/ dpal ldan[2] seṅ ge sgra'i sgrub thabs/

(0) dpal ldan seṅ ge sgra la phyag 'tshal lo//
nad kun 'joms byed bla ma ste//
seṅ ge sgra la phyag 'tshal lo//
rnal 'byor bsgoms pa tsam gyis ni//
sdig pa kun las grol bar 'gyur//

(1) daṅ por re źig kha bsaṅ ba la sogs pa byas te/ gos gtsaṅ ma gon nas sa gźi gtsaṅ mar stan bde ba la ñer bar 'dug ste/

(2.1.1) raṅ gi sñiṅ gar zla ba la hrīḥ yig bsgom par bya'o// de'i 'od zer gyis de bźin gśegs pa thams cad gdan draṅs te/ mchod par[3] byas nas sdig pa bśags pa la sogs pa bya'o//

(2.1.2) de nas byams pa daṅ/ sñiṅ rje daṅ/ dga' ba daṅ/ btaṅ sñoms rnams rnam par bsgoms te/ raṅ bźin gyis dag pa'i sṅags brjod pa sṅon du 'gro bas stoṅ pa ñid bsgom pa bya'o// oṃ swa bhā ba[4] śuddhaḥ sarba dharmāḥ swa bhā ba[5] śuddho 'haṃ[6]/ oṃ śūnya[7] tā dzñāna bdzra swa bhā ba[8] ātma ko 'haṃ[9] źes so//

(2.2) de nas raṅ gi lus sgra brñan daṅ[10] 'dra bar bltas nas ra[11] yig dmar po yoṅs su gyur pa las padma dmar po 'dab ma brgyad pa'i steṅ du āḥ yig yoṅs su gyur pa las/ seṅ ge dkar po/ de'i steṅ du hrīḥ yig de'i 'od zer gyis de bźin gśegs pa rnams gdan draṅs śiṅ/ bdag ñid la bcug nas 'jig rten dbaṅ phyug seṅ ge sgra bsgom par bya'o// sku mdog dkar po spyan gsum pa/ ral pa'i cod pan gyis brgyan pa/ stag gi pags pa'i na bza' bsnams pa/ seṅ ge daṅ/ zla ba'i gdạn la rgyal po[12] rol pa'i stabs kyis bźugs pa/ zla ba'i 'od lta bu bsgom par bya'o// phyag g'yas na sbrul dkar pos[13] dkris pa'i rtse gsum dkar po'o// phyag g'yon na padma laṅs pa'i steṅ na ral gri 'bar ba'o// g'yon na me tog dri źim po sna tshogs pas gaṅ ba'i padma'i snod do// raṅ gi lus las de bźin gśegs pa lṅa 'phro bar blta'o//

(2.3) de nas raṅ gi sñiṅ ga'i sa bon gyis ye śes sems dpa' bkug ciṅ bcug nas de bźin gśegs pa rnams 'phro źiṅ bdag ñid la dbaṅ bskur nas/ 'od dpag tu med pas dbu brgyan ciṅ/ rgyas btab par bsam par bya'o//

(2.4) de nas sṅags bzlas par bya'o// lha rnams kyi gzugs[14] kyis so// de la sṅags 'di'o// oṃ āḥ hrīḥ siṃ ha nā da hūṃ phaṭ swāhā/

---

1 TP na.
2 D, TP om.
3 D, TP pa.
4 D, TP wa.
5 D, TP wa.
6 P haṃ.
7 P śūn ya.
8 D, TP wa.
9 P haṃ.
10 P daṅ.
11 D, TP raṃ.
12 P add. chen po.
13 P po.
14 D, TP gzuṅs.

(3.1) de nas mchod pa'i phyir dri bzaṅs la sogs pa'i maṇḍal[1] byas la me tog la sogs pa dbul źiṅ mchod par bya'o// yaṅ phreṅ ba'i sṅags bzlas par bya'o/ na mo ratna tra yā ya/ na maḥ āryā ba lo ki te śwa rā ya/ bo dhi satwā ya/ ma hā satwā ya/ mahā kā ru ṇi kā ya/ tadya thā/ oṃ āḥ ka ṭe/ bi ka ṭe/ ṇi ka ṭe/ kaṭaṃ kaṭe/ bī[2] dya swāhā//

(3.2) sṅags 'dis maṇḍal gyi gzugs bzuṅ nas lan ñi śu rtsa gcig bzlas nas/ nad pa la byugs na 'tsho bar 'gyur ro//

'jig rten dbaṅ phyug seṅ ge sgra'i sgrub thabs rdzogs so//

1 P add. la sogs pa.
2 P bi.

## 6 (T3) Nīlakaṇṭhāryāvalokiteśvarasādhana

[(1-]'phags pa spyan ras gzigs dbaṅ phyug mgrin pa sṅon po can gyi sgrub thabs bźugs so//[-1)] rgya gar skad du/ nī la ka ṇṭha ā[2] ryā ba lo ki te śwa ra sā dha naṃ/ bod skad du/ 'phags pa spyan ras gzigs dbaṅ phyug mgrin pa sṅon po can gyi sgrub thabs/

(0) 'phags pa spyan ras gzigs dbaṅ phyug la phyag 'tshal lo//

(1) [(3-]daṅ po re źig sgrub pa pos sṅa bar laṅs te/ stan bde ba la sems dpa'i skyil mo kruṅ gis ñe bar 'dug ste/

(2.1.1) raṅ gi sñiṅ gar dbyaṅs yig daṅ po yoṅs su gyur pa las zla ba'i dkyil 'khor gyi steṅ du hrīḥ yig ser po rnam par bsgom par bya'o//

(2.1.2) de'i 'od zer gyi tshogs kyis bsgom par bya ba'i bcom ldan 'das gdan draṅ[4] te/ de nas lha rnams bskyed ciṅ spros nas/ me tog la sogs pa rnams kyis yaṅ dag par mchod nas/ de'i mdun du sdig pa bśags pa la sogs pa byas te/ byams pa la sogs pa tshaṅs pa'i gnas bźi bsgom par bya'o//

(2.1.3) de nas phyi daṅ naṅ du bcas pa'i dṅos po rnams stoṅ pa'i raṅ bźin du rnams par bsgoms nas/ oṃ swa bhā ba śu dhāḥ sar ba dhar māḥ swa bhā ba śu dho 'haṃ źes pa'i sṅags brjod par bya'o//

(2.2) de nas nam mkha'i phyogs su dbyaṅs yig daṅ po las zla ba'i dkyil 'khor de'i steṅ du hrīḥ yig ser po'o// des de bźin du padma dmar po de las skyes par byin gyis brlabs nas/ de yoṅs su gyur pa las bcom ldan 'das sku mdog ser po zla ba phyed pa daṅ ral pa'i cod pan gyis dbul brgyan pa/ 'od dpag tu med pas spyi bo'i phyogs su ñe bar mtshan[5] pa/ padma dmar po'i steṅ du [(6-]ri dwags nag po'i pags pa la[-6)] rdo rje skyil kruṅ gis bźugs pa/ tiṅ ṅe 'dzin gyi phyag rgya'i steṅ du rin po che sna tshogs pas yoṅs su gaṅ ba'i thod pa bsnams pa/ e na ya'i[7] pags pas mchod phyir thogs byas pa/ stag gi pags pa'i na bza' bsnams pa/ rgyan med pa mgrin pa sṅon po phreṅ ba sṅon pos khyad du 'phags pa/ mgul pa'i gźogs gñis su phan tshun du nor bu daṅ bcas pa'i sbrul dag gi mjug[8] ma mṅon par bciṅs śiṅ byad par du 'phags pa'i bcom ldan 'das spyan ras gzigs la gźan sbrul nag po gñis steṅ du kha phyogs pas ñe bar mtshan pa'i bdag ñid du bsgom par bya'o//

(3) de nas sṅags bzlas par ba'o/ oṃ sphu liṃ gā ṭṭa hā sa kṣaḥ źes so//

'de ni bsam gyis mi khyab pa'i rje su 'braṅs pa'i 'phags pa spyan ras gzigs dbaṅ phyug mgrin pa sṅon po can gyi sgrub thabs rdzogs so//[-3)]

---

1 D, TP om.
2 P om.
3 P missing.
4 TP draṅs.
5 TP mtshon.
6 The rendering follows Sanskrit: kṛṣṇasāraharinacarmaṇi. D, TP ri dags nag po'i pags pa la.
7 P, D illegible before -'i.
8 P dug.

## 7.1 (T3) Sarvakāmaprasādhanahālāhalaparitoṣaṇavajrasādhana

(1-rdo rje chos kyi sgrub thabs bźugs so-1)// rgya gar skad du/ bajra darma[2] sā dha naṃ/ bod skad du/ rdo rje chos kyi sgrub thabs//

(1) rdo rje chos la phyag 'tshal lo//
hrīḥ yig ye śes rdzogs pa la[3]//
hā la hā la'i sku chen po//
źal gsum spyan yaṅ gsum pa ste//
ral pa'i cod pan gyis brgyan ciṅ//
zla ba phyed pa 'dzin pa'i lha//
dbu la thod pa'i phreṅ bas brgyan//
ral pa'i naṅ nas rgyal ba'i sku//
rgyan rnams kun gyis brgyan gyur ba//
chu skyes dkar[4] po daṅ mtshuṅs śiṅ//
sgeg pa la sogs ñams daṅ ldan//
phyag drug źal ni 'dzum pa daṅ//
stag gi pags pa'i na bzar bcas//
phyag g'yas na ni mchog sbyin daṅ//
gñis pa na ni bgraṅ 'phreṅ daṅ//
gsum pa mda' daṅ gar mdzad do//
g'yon pa na ni padmas brgyan//
gñis pa de bźin nu ma 'dzin//
gsum pa la ni de bźin gźu//
sbrul gyis yoṅs su dkris pa yis//
rtse gsum g'yas kyi phyogs su'o//
me tog dri bzaṅ[5] sna tshogs kyis//
gaṅ ba'i thod pa g'yon phyogs su//
padma dmar po'i steṅ du ni//
rol pa'i stabs kyis yaṅ dag bźugs//
rin chen ri bo'i phug mthar gnas//
rnal 'byor can gyis bsgom par bya//
cho 'phrul rnam pa sna tshogs kyis//
saṅs rgyas raṅ bźin sku spros te//
(2) rnam par mi rtog tiṅ 'dzin gyis//
zas rnams kun la loṅs spyod ciṅ//
bsgom pa'i rim pa'i sbyor ba yis/
naṅ gi gsaṅ sṅags bzlas par bya//
(3) bla na med pa'i byaṅ chub ni//
myur du thob ciṅ bde bar 'jug//

---

1 D, TP om.
2 P darmā.
3 D, TP las.
4 P dgar.
5 D, TP bzaṅs.

hā la hā la yoṅs mñes pas//
'dod pa thams cad rab tu 'grub//
rdo rje źes bya'i tiṅ ṅe 'dzin//

## 7.2 (T1) Hālāhalalokeśvarasādhana

(1-sñiṅ rje khros pa'i sgrub thabs rim pa bźugs so//-1) rgya gar skad du/ hā (2-lā ha-2) la sā dha naṃ/ bod skad du/ sñiṅ rje khros pa'i sgrub thabs/

(0) sñiṅ rje khros pa la phyag 'tshal lo//

(1) sṅar bźin du stoṅ pa ñid kyi bar du bsgoms la/

(2) sa bon gyi[3] yi ge hrīḥ yoṅs su rdzogs pa las sñiṅ rje[4] khros pa'i[5] thugs rje chen po źal gsum pa ñid yaṅ spyan gsum pa ral pa daṅ dbu rgyan daṅ ldan la ste/ daṅ po'i źal dkar ba g'yas pa sṅo ba g'yon pa dmar ba zla ba phyed pa daṅ ldan pa'i dbu la thod pas thod byas pa ral pa'i mtha' na ri dags[6] kyi pags pa rgyan thams cad kyis legs par brgyan pa śin tu dkar ba'i[7] gaṅs kyi ri mo daṅ[8] mtshuṅs par snaṅ ba sgeg pa'i ñams daṅ ldan pas śin tu mdzes pa'o// źal 'dzum pa daṅ ldan źiṅ phyag drug pa stag gi pags pa'i śam thabs mnabs pa ste/ phyag g'yas pa ni mchog sbyin pa'o// gñis pas[9] ni phreṅ ba'o// gsum pa ni mda' gar stabs[10] su bsnams pa'o/ g'yon pa mi[11] bskyod pa daṅ ldan pa'o// de bźin du gñis pas ni padma dkar po'o// gsum pas ni gźu ñid do// pus mo g'yon pa nas mdog dkar ba'i lha mos brten pa ste/ g'yon pas padma 'dzin pa phyag g'yas pas bcom ldan 'das la ched du 'khyud par mdzad pa'o// ral pa'i tshogs la me tog gis mdzes par gyur pa'o// g'yas kyi zur na sbrul gyis[12] dkris[13] pa'i mduṅ rtse gsum pa'o/ g'yon gyi zur na padma la gnas pa'i thod pa me dog dri źim po sna tshogs kyis legs par bkaṅ ba'o/ padma dmar po daṅ zla ba la g'yon bslaṅ ba'i phyed kruṅ gis bskyod par gnas pa'o[14]/ bcom ldan 'das bsgom par bya ba'o//

(3) de nas gsaṅ sṅags bzlas bar bya ste/ oṃ bdzra dharmā hrīḥ

hā (15-lā ha-15) la 'jig rten dbaṅ phyug gi sgrub thabs rdzogs so// (16-paṇḍi ta chen po'i źal sṅa nas dge sloṅ tshul khrims rgyal mtshan gyis bsgyur pa'o//-16)

---

1 D, TP om.
2 P, TP la hā.
3 P add. saṃ.
4 P rjes.
5 P pas.
6 The rendering is probably a misprint for dwags. M dags.
7 D pa; TP ba.
8 TP om.
9 D, TP pa.
10 D thabs.
11 P ni.
12 P om.
13 P mkhris.
14 M pa'i.
15 D la hā.
16 D, TP om.

## 7.2 (T2) Hālāhalalokeśvarasādhana

rgya gar skad du/ ha la ha la sā dha naṃ/ bod skyad du/ ha la ha la'i sgrub pa'i thabs/

(0) bcom ldan 'das ha la ha la la phyag 'tshal lo/

(1) sṅon du bstan pa'i cho gas stoṅ pa ñid bsgom[1] pa'i rjes su

(2) padma dmar po daṅ/ zla ba las hrīḥ yig dkar po yoṅs su gyur pa las yan lag thams cad dkar ba/ źal gsum pa/ phyag drug pa/ nag po daṅ dmar po ni g'yas daṅ g'yon gyi źal lo// źal so so la spyan gsum gsum mo// mda' daṅ/ phreṅ ba daṅ/ mchog sbyin pa ni g'yas kyi phyag gsum na'o// gźu daṅ/ padma daṅ/ nu ma bzuṅ ba ni g'yon gyi phyag gsum na'o// 'od dpag tu med pa daṅ/ rin po che daṅ/ zla phyed kyi ral pa bciṅs śiṅ/ thod pa'i phreṅ bas mtshan pa'i dbu rgyan[2] can/ rgyan bzaṅ pos brgyan pa/ stag gi[3] pags[4] pa'i śam thabs can/ sgeg pa'i rol pas mdog bzaṅ po la sogs pa'i yon tan gyi bcom ldan[5] 'das ma[6] skyil kruṅ bcas pa rnam par bsams te/ de'i g'yas phyogs su 'jigs par byed pa'i sbrul gyis dkris pa'i rtse gsum mo// g'yon phyogs su sna tshogs kyi me[7] tog gis bkaṅ ba'i thod pa'o// rol bas[8] gnon źiṅ yaṅ dag par gnas pa'i rin po che mi g'yo ba'i ri'i phug gi naṅ na[9] gnas pa'i ha la ha lar bdag ñid skad cig gis bsams la/

(3) oṃ bdzra dha rmā[10] hrīḥ źes bya ba'i sṅags bzlas pa bya'o/

ha la ha la'i sgrub pa'i thabs/ slob dpon lhan cig skyes pa'i rol pas mdzad pa rdzogs so// // paṇḍi ta don yod rdo rje daṅ/ khams pa lo tstsha ba dge sloṅ ba ris bsgyur ciṅ[11] gtan la phab pa'o[12]//

---

1 TP bsgoms.
2 P om.
3 P, M gis.
4 P, D, M dpags.
5 M add. ma in the variants.
6 D, TP om.
7 P med.
8 M pas.
9 P, D nas.
10 TP rma.
11 D źus ste; TP źus te.
12 D, TP pa.

## 7.2 (T3) Hālāhalalokeśvarasādhana

(1-'jig rten dbaṅ phyug hā la hā la'i sgrub thabs rim pa bźugs so//[1]-1) rgya gar skad du/ hā la hā la lo ke śwa ra sā dha naṃ/ bod skad du/ 'jig rten dbaṅ phyug hā la hā la'i sgrub thabs/

(0) hā la hā la la phyag 'tshal lo//
(1) sṅon ma bźin du stoṅ pa ñid kyi mthar[2] thug pa bsgoms nas/
(2) hrīḥ yig sa bon las skyes pa'i//
hā la hā la brtse chen po//
źal gsum de bźin spyan gsum pa//
ral pa'i cod pan gyis brgyan ciṅ/
daṅ po'i źal ni dkar po ste/
g'yas pa sṅon po g'yon pa dmar//
dbu la zla ba phyed pas brgyan/
thod pa rnams kyis zur phud[3] byas//
ral pa'i naṅ gnas rgyal ba daṅ//
rgyan rnams kun gyis yaṅ dag rgyan//
chu skyes dkar po'i mdog daṅ mtshuṅs//
sgeg pa'i ñams kyis śin tu mdzes//
phyag drug źal ni (4-sma ra-4) can//
stag gi pags pa'i[5] na bza' dgyes//
phyag g'yas daṅ po mchog sbyin daṅ//
gñis pa na ni bgraṅ phreṅ bsnams//
gsum pa mda' daṅ gar gyi stabs//
g'yon ba na ni de bźin gźu//
gñis par padma dkar po daṅ//
gsum pa de bźin sgyu[6] ma 'dzin[7]//
brla g'yon pa'i steṅ du lha mo sgeg mo ste[8]// g'yon pa chu skyes bsnams pa/ phyag g'yas pas bcom ldan 'das la 'khyud pa/ gźan na me tog gis mdzes par byas pa/ ral pa'i tshogs daṅ bcas pa'o// g'yas logs na sbrul gyis dkris pa'i rtse gsum/ g'yon logs na padma la gnas pa'i me tog dri źim po sna tshogs pas yoṅs su gaṅ ba'i thod pa'o// padma dmar po daṅ zla ba la rol pa'i stabs kyis bźugs pa'i bcom ldan 'das bsgom par bya'o//
(3) de nas sṅags bzlas par bya ste/ oṃ bdzra dharmā hrīḥ źes so//
'jig rten dbaṅ phyug hā la hā la'i sgrub thabs rdzogs so//

---

1 D, TP om.
2 D illegible before -thar.
3 D puḍ.
4 P rmar.
5 P pa.
6 D, TP rgyu.
7 P bźin.
8 P om.

## 7.4 (T1) Hālāhalasādhana

rgya gar skad du/ hā [(1-]lā ha[-1)] la sā dha naṃ/ bod skad du/ sñiṅ rje khros pa'i sgrub thabs/

(0) bsam pa thams cad rdzogs mdzad pa'i//
sñiṅ rje[2] khros la gus pas 'dud//
thugs rje'i bdag ñid de yi ni//
mdor bsdus sgrub thabs brjod par bya//

(1.1) daṅ por yid 'oṅ gnas su ni//
tsandan sogs kyis legs byugs la[3]//
thaṅ ka bkram sogs la bźugs pa'i//
bcom ldan mchod par bya ba yin//
me tog la sogs dbul ba'i sṅags ni/ oṃ rdo rje'i me tog hūṃ/ oṃ rdo rje'i bdug pa hūṃ/ oṃ rdo rje'i mar me hūṃ/ źes bya ba la sogs pas so/ oṃ de bźin gśegs pa rnams thams cad la bdag gis mchod pa'i sprin tshogs 'dis khyab nas nam mkha'i dbyiṅs kun tu 'phro bar hūṃ/ mchod pa thams cad dbul ba'i sṅags so//

(1.2) rab tu mchod nas de mdun du//
bde ba'i stan la gnas nas kyaṅ//
byams pa skye dgu rnams la bsgom//
brtse chen gyis ni sñiṅ[4] rje yaṅ//
sñiṅ gar zla ba'i steṅ du ni//
sṅags yig hrīḥ ni rnam bkod la//
saṅs rgyas daṅ bcas de sras rnams//
gsal bar nam mkha' gaṅ bar blta//

(1.3) hrīḥ yig 'od zer mchod pa yis//
de dag legs mchod 'khrul bral bar//
bsod nams 'phrel ba sgrub don du//
daṅ po sdig pa bśags sogs bya//
dkon mchog gsum mdun skyabs soṅ la//
chos rnams thams cad mchog bdag med//
gsal byed sñiṅ rje dri med pas//
sṅags 'di ṅes par brjod par bya//
chos thams cad raṅ bźin gyis rnam par dag pa ni bdag raṅ bźin rnam par dag pa'o źes so//
sṅags don mṅon du byed pa[5] na//
gzuṅ 'dzin dag las ṅes grol ba'i//
dṅos kun bdag ñid chen po pa//
śes pa tsam du bsgom par bya//
hrīḥ[6] yig zla ba legs gnas pa//

---

1 D, TP la hā.
2 D, TP rjes.
3 P pa.
4 D, TP rdo.
5 D, TP pas.
6 P hrī.

so so raṅ rig de ltas[1] la//
de skyes pad dkar bsgom bya ste//
lte ba'i[2] hrīḥ yig daṅ ldan pa'o//
(2.1) de las saṅs rgyas tshogs spro daṅ//
'gro ba saṅs rgyas la yaṅ dgod//
slar yaṅ de ñi la bsdus la//
phyis ni sñiṅ rje khros raṅ ñid//
rin chen ri bo'i phug rtan pa'i//
źal gsum phyag drug bźir[3] gyur pa//
padma dmar gnas zla ba la//
g'yas brkyaṅ bskyod pas legs bźugs par//
rtsa ba g'yon pa gźan gyi źal//
dkar daṅ ser sṅon po che[4]//
spyan gsum stag gi śam thabs mnabs[5]//
rgyan rnams kun ldan rab tu mdzes//
g'yas na mchog sbyin mda' daṅ phreṅ//
g'yon pa sgeg pas[6] bkur brten daṅ[7]//
pad dkar daṅ ni gźu[8] ñid kyaṅ//
'gyur ba'i phyag gi bskor bar mdzad//
thod pa g'yon na bźag pa na//
me tog sna tshogs kyis[9] rab bkaṅ//
g'yas na dug can gyis dkris pa'i//
rtse gsum de bźin padma yaṅ//
snaṅ mtha' gtsug tor dam pa ste//
thod pa yis ni thod du byas//
zla ba phyed pa daṅ ldan mthor//
ral pa dbu rgyan legs par brtsegs//
rtogs[10] pa'i dra ba rnam bsal ba'i//
saṅs rgyas 'od zer tshogs rnams 'phro//
(2.2) sñiṅ rje khros pa 'dir gyur nas//
raṅ sñiṅ mgrin[11] pa spyi[12] rnams su//
zla ba sṅo dmar dkar rim bźin//
hūṃ ā oṃ rnams bsgom par bya//

---

1 D, TP bltas.
2 D, TP ba.
3 D, TP źir.
4 D, TP daṅ.
5 P mnabs.
6 D, TP pa'i.
7 TP pa.
8 D illegible.
9 P gis.
10 D rtog.
11 P illegible between m- and -n.
12 P, TP 'gro.

de bźin (1-mgrin sñiṅ-1) bar dag tu[2]//
zla ba legs gnas hrīḥ bsgom bya//
(2.3) de nas gnas g'yo'i dṅos gyur pa//
de dag de yi gzugs su bsgom//
dam min rnam rtog las grol ba'i//
mñam par bźag[3] pas sṅags bzlas te//
oṃ (4-hā lā hā-4) la hrīḥ
myur min bul bar ma yin źiṅ//
śin tu gsal bar maṅ[5] du bzlas//
bzlas pa byas nas ci bde bar//
gśegs su gsol źiṅ legs mchod daṅ/
legs par bstod daṅ brtan byas la/
yi ge brgya pa[6] gdon par bya//
oṃ rdo rje sems dpa' dam tshig rjes su brkyaṅ du gsol// bdag rdo rje sems dpa' ñid du ñe
bar gnas pa brtan par dgoṅs//
bdag la śin tu dgyes par dgoṅs//
bdag la rgyas par mdzad du gsol//
bdag la rje su chags par mdzad du gsol//
dṅos grub thams cad bdag la legs par stsol//
bdag gi las thams cad grub par mdzod//
sems ṅes par[7] legs par mdzad du gsol//
hūṃ ha ha ha ha hoḥ bcom ldan 'das de bźin gśegs pa rnams thams cad kyi rdo rje'i raṅ
bźin las bdag la bral[8] bar mdzod// rdo rje'i ṅo bo'i dam tshig sems dpa' chen po[9] āḥ
oṃ bdag daṅ sems can kun don mdzad//
dṅos grub stsol[10] nas ji bźin gśags[11]//
saṅs rgyas yul du gśegs su gsol//
slar yaṅ 'byon par gsol ba 'debs//
'di yis legs par skul[12] byas la//
oṃ ā yig sgor ni chos rnams kun//
gdod nas[13] skye ba[14] med phyir ro//
mu źes bya ba'o//

---

1 D sñiṅ ga.
2 P du.
3 D, TP gźag.
4 D, TP ha lā ha.
5 P nan.
6 P ba.
7 D, TP pa.
8 D, TP grol.
9 D illegible.
10 P, D, TP stsal.
11 P bśags; TP gśegs.
12 D, TP bskul.
13 D and TP add. ma.
14 D om.

(3) bsam gtan legs laṅs[1] rnal 'byor pas[2]//
raṅ gi nus pa'i sbyin pa btaṅ[3]//

(4) gzugs sogs 'dod pa spyod pa na//
ma lus rtog pa gtan nas spaṅs//
bla med byaṅ chub riṅ min par//
sgrub pa po ni dam[4] pas thob//
sgrub thabs bris las bdag gis ni//
dge ba bla med thob pa gaṅ//
des ni 'jig rten ma lus pa//
myur bar sñiṅ rje[5] khro thob śog/

hā lā ha la'i sgrub thabs dge sloṅ tshul khrim rgyal mtshan gyis bsgyur ba'o//

---

1 P, D, TP blaṅs.
2 P bas.
3 D, TP gtaṅ.
4 TP da ma.
5 D, TP rje'i.

## 7.4 (T2) Hālāhalasādhana

rgya gar skad du/ hā la hā la sā dha naṃ/ bod skad du/ hā la hā la'i sgrub thabs/

(0) bcom ldan 'das hā la hā la la phyag 'tshal lo//
bsam pa thams cad rdzogs byed pa'i//
hā la hā la[1] gus phyag 'tshal//
sñiṅ rje'i bdag ñid sgrub pa'i thabs//
mdor bsdus de ni brjod par bya//

(1.1) daṅ por yid daṅ mthun pa'i gnas su tsan dan la sogs pas legs par byugs la thaṅ ka la sogs pa gnas pa bźugs su gsol te/ bcom ldan 'das la[2] mchod par bya'o// me tog la sogs pa dbul ba'i sṅags ni/ oṃ bdzra puṣpe hūṃ/ oṃ bdzra dhū pe[3] hūṃ/ oṃ bdzra dīpe hūṃ/ oṃ bdzra gandhe hūṃ/ oṃ bdzra nai be[4] dye[5] hūṃ źes bya ba la sogs pas so// oṃ sarba ta thā ga ta pū dza me gha pra sa ra sa mu tre spha ra hi maṃ ga ga na khaṃ hūṃ mchod pa thams cad dbul ba'i sṅags so//

(1.2) rab tu mchod la de'i mdun du//
bde ba'i stan la rab gnas ste/
'gro la byams pa rnam par sgom[6]//
sñiṅ rje yaṅ ni brtse[7] chen pos//
hrīḥ yig zla ba'i (8-rgyab tu-8) ni/
sṅags pas sñiṅ gar dgod par bya//
saṅs rgyas sras bcas gsal por ni//
nam mkha' gaṅ bar blta bar bya//

(1.3) hrīḥ yig 'od zer mchod pas ni//
de[9] la rab tu bskor źiṅ mchod//
sdig pa la sogs bśags par bya//
bsod nams 'phel phyir[10] bya ba ni//
mchog gsum skyabs 'gro la sogs bya//
sṅags 'di[11] dag ni brjod bya ste//
chos rnams bdag ni med pa'i mchog//
sñiṅ rje yis[12] ni gsal byed pa//

---

1 D, TP lar.
2 P om.
3 P ṣpe.
4 P, D, TP bi.
5 P dya.
6 D, TP bsgom.
7 P brtsa.
8 D steṅ du.
9 P da.
10 P źiṅ.
11 D and TP add. 'di.
12 P yi.

oṃ swa bhā ba[1] śuddhaḥ sarba dharmāḥ[2] swa bhā ba[3] śuddho 'haṃ[4]/
źes bya ba'i sṅags kyi don mṅon[5] du byas la[6]/
dṅos po daṅ bcas bdag ñid kyaṅ//
gzuṅ daṅ 'dzin pa rnam grol ba'i//
ye śe tsam du bsgom par bya//
so so raṅ gi rig pas blta//
hrīḥ yig zla ba'i steṅ gnas pa//
de skyes padma dkar po bsam//
hrīḥ yig daṅ ldan pad dkar las//
(2.1) de nas saṅs rgyas tshogs spros te//
'gro ba saṅs rgyas byas nas su//
yaṅ nì de ru gźug par bya//
de ñid gyur las hā[7] la[8] ste[9]/
źal gsum phyag drug źi ba'i chas//
rin chen mi g'yo'i ri phug brten//
padma dmar daṅ zla gnas pa'i/
rol pas gnon ciṅ yaṅ dag gnas//
dkar po ser po sṅo chen po//
rtsa ba g'yon daṅ cig śos źal//
stag gi śam thabs spyan gsum pa//
rgyan rnams kun gyis mdzes pa yi//
mchog[10] sbyin phreṅ daṅ mda' g'yas phyag//
g'yon pas 'dod pa'i nu ma 'dzin//
padma dkar po dbyug pa ni//
(11-yal ga gsum pa'i dbyug pa ste/-11)
phyag gi yal ga dag gis bsnams//
sna tshogs me tog gis bkaṅ ba'i//
g'yon par thod pa dgod pa bya//
sbrul gyis dkris pa'i rtse gsum yaṅ//
de bźin padma'i steṅ g'yas dgod//
dpag med gtsug gi nor bu byas//
thod pa'i phreṅ bas dbu la brgyan//
ral pa'i dbu brgyan cher 'dziṅs la//
zla ba phyed pa'i dum bu ldan[12]//

---

1 D, TP wa.
2 P dharmaḥ.
3 D, TP wa.
4 P haṃ.
5 P sṅon.
6 D pa.
7 P ha.
8 P lar.
9 P om.
10 P mchod.
11 P om.
12 P lṅa'o.

rtog pa'i dra ba rnam bcom pa'i//
saṅs rgyas tshogs kyi 'od zer spro//
(2.2) hā la hā la 'dir gyur nas//
raṅ sñiṅ mgrin pa spyi bor yaṅ//
hūṃ āḥ oṃ ni bsgom par bya//
zla ba la gnag dmar dkar rims[1]//
de bźin sñiṅ daṅ mgrin pa'i bar//
hrīḥ yig zla ba la gnas pa//
(2.3) de na[2] brtan daṅ g'yo dṅos kun//
de yis rnam par bsgoms par bya//
log pa'i rnam rtog spaṅs nas su/
mñam par bźag[3] pas sṅags bzlas bya//
oṃ hā la hā la hrīḥ/
naṅ gi bzlas pa śin tu gsal//
[(4-]bul ba[-4)] ma yin myur ba 'aṅ min//
ji ltar bde bas bzlas par bya//
bsdus la[5] rab tu mchod pa bya//
[(6-]yaṅ dag[-6)] bstod ciṅ brtan byas la//
yi ge brgya pa brjod par bya//
oṃ bdzra satwa sa ma ya/ ma nu pa la ya/ bdzra satwa twe[7] no pa ti ṣṭha/ dri ḍho med bha ba/ su to ṣyo me bha ba [(8-]su to ṣyo me bha ba[-8)]/ a nu rakto me bha ba/ [(9-]śu po ṣyo me bha ba//[-9)] sarba siddhi me pra yatstsha/ sarba ka rmā su tsa[10] me tsi dhaṃ śre[11] yaḥ ku ru hūṃ/ ha ha ha ha hoḥ bha ga [(12-]bān sarba ta thā ga ta[-12)] bdzra mā me muñdza[13] bdzri bha ba[14] ma hā sa ma ya satwa āḥ źes bya'o//
oṃ sems can kun gyi don mdzad bdag//
rjes su mthun pa'i dṅos grub stsol//
saṅs rgyas yul du gśegs nas kyaṅ//
slar yaṅ 'byon par mdzad du gsol//
de ltar 'di yis bskul nas ni//
sṅags 'di dag ni brjod par bya//
oṃ ā[15] kā ro mu khaṃ sarba dha rmā ṇāṃ[16] ā dya nu tpan na twā ta muḥ źes bya'o//

---

1 P rim.
2 D, TP ni.
3 D, TP gźag.
4 P bum pa.
5 D, TP pas.
6 D illegible.
7 P te.
8 D, TP om.
9 P om.
10 P om.
11 P śrī.
12 D illegible after bā-.
13 D, TP muñtsa.
14 P ga.
15 D a.
16 P rṇāṃ.

(3) rnal 'byor bsam gtan laṅs nas su//
raṅ gis ci nus sbyin pa btaṅ//

(4) ma lus rnam rtog daṅ bral bas//
gzugs sogs 'dod yon spyod byed[1] pas//
riṅ por[2] mi thogs sgrub po mchog//
bla na[3] med byaṅ chub thob par 'gyur//
sgrub thabs bris las gaṅ thob pa'i//
bdag gi[4] dge ba mchog gis ni//
de yis 'gro ba ma lus pa//
myur du hā la hā lar śog//

hā la hā la'i sgrub thabs slob dpon lhan cig skyes pa rol pas mdzad pa rdzogs so// paṇḍi ta don yod rdo rje daṅ/ lo tstsha ba dge sloṅ ba ris bsgyur ba'o//

---

1 P byad.
2 D, TP po.
3 D, TP om.
4 P ni.

## 7.4 (T3) Hālāhalasādhana

rgya gar skad du/ (1-hā lā ha-1) la śā dha naṃ/ bod skad du/ (2-hā lā ha la'i-2) sgrub thabs/

(0) bcom ldan 'das hā la hā la phyag 'tshal lo//
bsam pa thams cad yoṅs su[3] rdzogs pa'i/
hā la hā lar[4] gus phyag 'tshal//
sñiṅ rje yi ni bdag ñid can//
de'i[5] sgrub thabs mdor bsdus brjod//

(1.1) daṅ po yid du/ 'oṅ ba'i gnas su tsan dan la sogs pas legs par byugs la/ ras bris[6] la sogs pa bkram ste/ bcom ldan 'das la mchod par bya'o// me tog la sogs pa 'bul ba'i sṅags ni oṃ bdzra puṣpe hūṃ/ oṃ bdzra dhū[7] pe hūṃ/ oṃ bdzra dīpe hūṃ/ źes pa la sogs pas so// oṃ sarba ta thā ga tā pū jā[8] me gha pra sa ra sá mū[9] hi/ spha ra ṇa hi ma ga ga na kaṃ hūṃ/ mchod pa thams cad dbul ba'i sṅags[10] so//

(1.2) rab tu mchod pa[11] bya de yi mdun//
bde ba'i stan la 'dug byas nas//
'gro la byams pa rnam par bsgom//
sñiṅ rje daṅ ni brtse[12] chen po//
sṅags pas sṅiṅ gar zla ba'i steṅ//
hrīḥ yi yi ge dgod par bya//
saṅs rgyas sras bcas gsal[13] por ni//
bkug[14] nas nam mkha' gaṅ bar bsgom//

(1.3) hrīḥ yig 'od zer mchod[15] pas ni//
de la skor[16] źiṅ rab tu mchod//
sdig pa bśags pa la sogs bya//
bsod nams 'phel[17] bar bya ba'i phyir//
mkon mchog gsum mchog skyabs 'gro sogs//
sṅags 'di dag ni brjod par bya//
chos kun bdag med pa yi mchog//
'od gsal sñiṅ rje dri ma med//

---

1 P hā la hā; TP hā la hā.
2 P hā la hā la'i.
3 D, TP om.
4 P la.
5 D de yi.
6 D, TP ris.
7 P dhu.
8 D, TP ja.
9 P mu.
10 D illegible.
11 D, TP om.
12 P rtse.
13 P gsol.
14 D, TP kun.
15 P ches.
16 D bsgom; TP bskor.
17 P spel.

oṃ swa bhā ba[1] śuddhaḥ[2] sarba dharmāḥ[3] swabhā ba[4] śuddho 'haṃ[5]/
źes pa'i sṅags don mṅon[6] du bya//
dṅos po kun daṅ bdag ñid[7] bcas//
gzuṅ daṅ 'dzin las ṅes par grol//
ye śes cha tsam bsgom par bya//
so so raṅ rig[8] de bltas nas//
hrīḥ yig zla ba la gnas pa//
de skyes padma dkar po bsam//
hrīḥ yig daṅ bcas padma las//
(2.1) de las saṅ rgyas tshogs spros te//
'gro ba rnams kyaṅ saṅs rgyas bya//
slar yaṅ de la bcug gyur pas//
raṅ byuṅ hā la hā la ste/
źal gsum phyag drug źi ba'i tshul//
rin chen mi g'yo'i phug na bsten//
padma dmar daṅ zla ba la//
rol pa'i stabs kyis yaṅ dag bźugs//
dkar po ser po sṅon po che//
rtsa źal g'yon pa cig śos so//
stag gi pags pa'i na bza'[9] ldan//
rgyan rnams kun gyis śin tu mdzes//
phyag g'yas mchog spyin phreṅ ba mda'//
g'yon pas 'dod ldan nu ma 'dzin//
padma dkar daṅ gźu dag ni//
phyag gi yal ga dag gis bsnams//
sna tshogs me tog gis bkaṅ ba'i/
thod pa g'yon par dgod[10] par bya//
sbrul gyis dkris pa'i rtse gsum g'yas//
chu skyes steṅ du de bźin dgod//
gtsug gi nor bu 'od dpag med//
thod pa rnams kyis zur phud[11] byas//
ral pa'i tshogs kyi cod pan can//
dbu la zla ba phyed[12] pas brgyan//
rtog pa'i dra ba rnam bcom pa'i//

---

1 D, TP wa.
2 D śuddha.
3 P dharmā.
4 D, TP wa.
5 P haṃ.
6 P sṅon.
7 P gñid.
8 P gi.
9 D, TP bzar.
10 P dgos.
11 P phur.
12 D byed.

saṅs rgyas rnams kyi 'od zer 'phro//
(2.2) 'di yis hā la hā lar gyur//
raṅ gi sñiṅ mgrin spyi bor yaṅ//
hūṃ āḥ oṃ rnams bsgom par bya//
zla bar gnag dmar dkar po'i rim//
de bźin sñiṅ ga mgrin pa'i dbus//
hrīḥ yig zla ba la gnas pa//
(2.3) de nas brtan g'yo'i dṅos po rnams//
de yi rnam par bsgom par bya//
log pa'i rnam rtog ṅes spaṅs śiṅ//
sṅags bzlas nas ni mñam par bźag[1]
oṃ hā la ha la hrīḥ
naṅ gi bzlas pa śin tu gsal//
dal ba ma yin myur ba min//
ji ltar ba[2] bde bar gnas par bya//
bsdus nas so so'i mchod pa daṅ//
yaṅ dag bstod ciṅ brtan byas la//
yi ge brgya pa brjod par bya//
oṃ bdzra satwa sa ma ya ma nu pā la ya/ bdzra satwa twe no pa ti ṣṭha dri ḍho me bha ba/
su to ṣyo me bha ba/ su po ṣyo me bha ba/ a nu rākto[3] me bha ba/ sarba siddhi mme[4] pra
yatstsha sarba karma su tsa me tsi ttaṃ śre[5] yaḥ ku ru hūṃ/ ha ha ha ha hoḥ/ bha ga bān
sarba ta thā ga ta[6] bdzra mā me muñtsa bdzri bha ba ma hā sa ma ya satwa āḥ/
oṃ sems can kun gyi don mdzad khyod//
ji ltar rjes 'jug dṅos grub stsol[7]//
saṅs rgyas yul du gśegs nas kyaṅ//
slar yaṅ 'byon par mdzad du gsol//
'di yis yaṅ dag bskul byas nas//
sṅags 'di dag ni brjod par bya'o//
oṃ a kā ro mu khaṃ sarba dharmā ṇāṃ[8] ādya nu [(9-]tpan na twāt[-9)] muḥ źes so//
(3) rnal 'byor bdag gñid bsam gtan laṅs//
sbyin pa raṅ gis[10] ci grub btaṅ[11]//
(4) ma lus rtog pa daṅ bral bas//
gzugs sogs 'dod pa spyod byed pa//
bla med byaṅ chub thob 'gur te//
rin por mi thogs sgrub pa'i mchog//

---

1 D, TP gźag.
2 D, TP om.
3 P rāga to.
4 P me.
5 P śri.
6 P tā.
7 D stsal.
8 P naṃ.
9 P tpa nna twad.
10 P gi.
11 D, TP gtaṅ.

sgrub thabs bris pas gaṅ thob pa//
bdag gi[1] dge ba'i mchog de yis//
'gro ba rnams ni ma lus pa//
myur du hā la hā lar śog/

hā la hā la'i sgrub thabs/ slob dpon[2] lhan cig skyes pa'i rol pas mdzad pa rdzogs so//

1 P gis.
2 D spon.

## 8.1 (T1) Padmanarteśvaralokanāthasādhana

[(1-]// padma gar gyi dbaṅ phyug gi sgrub thabs rim pa bźugs so//[-1)] rgya gar skad du/ padma [(2-]na rte[-2)] śwa ra sā dha naṃ/ bod skad du/ padma gar gyi dbaṅ phyug gi sgrub thabs//

(1) sṅar brjod pa'i rim pas sna tshogs padmar zla ba la yi ge hrīḥ dmar po yoṅs su gyur pa las/ bdag ñid padma gar gyi dbaṅ phyug tu bsgom par bya ste/ sems dpa'i skyil kruṅ gis bźugs pa/ źal gcig phyag gñis pa sku mdog dmar po rgyan rnams thams cad kyis brgyan pa snaṅ ba mtha' yas dbu rgyan du byas śiṅ/ g'yon ṅos na gos dkar mos legs par 'khyud ciṅ 'khyud pa'i staṅs kyis gnas pa'o// phyag g'yon pas padma dmar po bsnam pa'o[3]/ phyag gźan g'yas pa ni gar byed pa'i staṅs kyis khab kyi phyag rgyar kha 'byed pa'o//

(2) de nas ni oṃ de bźin gśegs pa rnams thams cad kyi sku daṅ gsuṅ daṅ thugs rdo rje'i raṅ bźin gyi[4] bdag ñid ni ṅa yin no źes sṅags brjod par bya ba'o//

(3.0) de'i rjes la phyogs brgyad du lha mo brgyad rnam par bsam par bya ba'o/

(3.1) de la padma dmar po 'dab ma brgyad pa'i śar gyi 'dab ma la rnam par gzigs ma padma dkar po daṅ dmar po 'dzin pa'o//

(3.2) lha'i 'dab ma la sgrol ma ljaṅ gu śiṅ sṅon po daṅ padma 'dzin pa'o//

(3.3) nub kyi 'dab ma la rṅa ma 'khor lo ser po daṅ/ utpa la sṅon po 'dzin pa'o//

(3.4) byaṅ gi 'dab ma la khro gñer can// padma [(5-]skya bo[-5)] daṅ ser po 'dzin pa'o//

(3.5) śar gyi grwa'i[6] 'dab ma la padma'i dri ldan ma padma ser po daṅ dmar ser 'dzin pa'o//

(3.6) lho'i grwa'i 'dab ma la rdo rje padma'i dbaṅ phyug ma nam mkha'i mdog daṅ dkar ba'i padma 'dzin pa'o//

(3.7) nub kyi grwa'i 'dab ma la sna tshogs padma dkar ba daṅ dmar po 'dzin pa'o//

(3.8) byaṅ gi grwa'i 'dab ma la sna tshogs rdo rje ma kha dog sna tshogs pa sna tshogs padma 'dzin pa'o//

(3.9) de dag thams cad kyaṅ źal gcig phyag gñis ma skyil kruṅ bcas śiṅ źi ba'o// lte ba la ni bcom ldan 'das ñid do//

(4) de nas gsaṅ sṅags bzlas par bya ste/ oṃ hrīḥ padma na rte[7] śwa ra hūṃ/

padma gar gyi dbaṅ phyug ces bya ba'i 'jig rten dbaṅ phyug gi sgrub thabs so// paṇḍi ta chen po ratna a[8] ka ra'i źal sṅa nas dge sloṅ tshul khrims rgyal mtshan gyis bsgyur ba'o//

---

1 D, TP om.
2 P nir te.
3 P pa.
4 P gyis.
5 P skya'o.
6 TP gra'i.
7 P ri te.
8 D, TP ā.

## 8.1 (T2) Padmanarteśvaralokanāthasādhana

(1-// padma gar gyi dbaṅ phyug gi sgrub thabs bźugs so//-1) rgya gar skad tu/ padma (2-nar te-2) śwa ra sā dha naṃ[3]/ bod skad du/ padma gar gyi dbaṅ phyug gi sgrub pa'i thabs/

(0) bcom ldan 'das padma gar dbaṅ la phyag 'tshal lo//

(1) sṅon du bstan pa'i cho gas stoṅ pa ñid bsgoms pa'i rjes su sna tshogs padma'i steṅ du zla ba la hrīḥ yoṅs su gyur pa las padma gar gyi dbaṅ phyug ces bya ba/ 'phags pa spyan ras gzigs dbaṅ phyug sems dpa'i skyil mo kruṅ gis gnas pa/ phyag gñis pa/ źal gcig pa/ yan lag thams cad dmar po/ lha rjas kyi na bza'i rgyan gyis brgyan pa/ 'od dpag tu med pa'i cod pan can/ g'yon phyogs su gos dkar mo la mñam par 'khyud pa'i tshul gyis gnas pa'o// g'yon pa'i phyag na padma dmar po bsnams pa/ gar gyi tshul gyis khab kyi phyag rgyas padma kha 'byed pa ni phyag g'yas pas so//

(2) bdag ñid skyad cig gis bskyed la/ oṃ kā ya bā ka tsi tta[4] bdzra swa bhā ba ā tma ko 'haṃ[5]/ źes bya ba'i sṅags brjod par bya'o//

(3.0) de nas phyogs mtshams brgyad daṅ/ lha mo brgyad bsam par bya ste/

(3.1) de la 'dab ma brgyad pa'i padma'i śar gyi 'dab ma la rnam par gzigs ma/ dkar mo padma dmar po bsnams pa'o//

(3.2) lho phyogs kyi 'dab ma la sgrol ma utpa la ljaṅ gu bsnams pa'o//

(3.3) nub phyogs kyi 'dab ma la dbaṅ phyug ma ser mo utpa la sṅon po bsnams pa'o//

(3.4) byaṅ gi 'dab ma la khro gñer can dkar mo padma ser po bsnams pa'o//

(3.5) śar gyi mtshams kyi[6] 'dab ma la gnas[7] ma ser mo btsod[8] lta bu'i padma bsnams pa'o//

(3.6) lho phyogs kyi mtshams kyi 'dab ma la padma'i dbaṅ phyug nam mkha'i mdog lta bu padma dkar po bsnams pa'o//

(3.7) nub phyogs kyi mtshams kyi 'dab ma la sna tshogs padma dkar po padma nag po bsnams pa'o//

(3.8) byaṅ gi[9] phyogs kyi mtshams kyi 'dab ma la sna tshogs rdo rje ma sna tshogs kyi padma bsnams pa'o//

(3.9) 'di thams cad ni[10] skyil mo kruṅ can phyag gñis pa/ źal gcig pa ñe bar źi ba'o// ze'u[11] 'bru'i dbus su 'dod chags chen po'i raṅ bźin bcom ldan 'das 'phags pa spyan ras gzigs kyi[12] dbaṅ phyug go//

(4) oṃ hrīḥ padma na rte[13] śwa ra hūṃ/ źes bya bas[14] bzlas pa bya'o//

---

1 D, TP om.
2 P ni rte.
3 P na.
4 P ta.
5 P haṃ.
6 D and TP add. padma'i.
7 P gags.
8 P, D bcod.
9 D, TP om.
10 TP na.
11 P ze.
12 D, TP om.
13 P ra te.
14 D, TP ba.

padma gar dbaṅ gi sgrub pa'i thabs rdzogs pa'i saṅs rgyas kyis gsuṅs pa rdzogs so// // paṇḍi ta don yod rdo rje daṅ/ khams pa lo tstsha ba dge sloṅ ba ri bsgyur pa'o//

## 8.1 (T3) Padmanarteśvaralokanāthasādhana

(1-//padma gar gyi dbaṅ phyug sgrub thabs bźugs so//-1) //rgya gar skad du/ padma na rte śwa ra sā dha naṃ/ bod skad du/ padma gar gyi dbaṅ phyug gi sgrub thabs/

(0) 'phags pa spyan ras gzigs dbaṅ phyug la phyag 'tshal lo//

(1) sṅon du gsuṅs pa'i cho ga 'dis sna tshogs padma daṅ zla ba la hrīḥ yig[2] dmar po yoṅs su gyur pa las padma gar gyi dbaṅ phyug tu bdag ñid bsgom par bya ste/ sems dpa'i skyil kruṅ gis bźugs pa/ phyag gñis pa/ źal gcig pa/ sku mdog dmar po rgyan thams cad kyis brgyan pa/ 'od dpag tu med pa'i cod pan can/ g'yon phyogs su gos dkar mo daṅ sñoms par źugs śiṅ 'khyud pa'i tshul gyis bźugs pa/ phyag g'yon na padma dmar po bsnams pa/ gźan phyag g'yas pa na gar gyi tshul gyis khab kyi phyag rgyas padma kha 'byed pa'o//

(2) de nas oṃ kā ya bā ktsi tta bdzra swa bhā ba[3] ātma ko 'haṃ[4] źes pa'i sṅags brjod par 'bya'o//

(3.0) de'i rjes su phyogs mtshams brgyad du lha mo brgyad bsam par bya'o//

(3.1) de la padma dmar po 'dab ma brgyad pa'i źar gyi 'dab ma la rnam par gzigs ma dkar mo padma dmar po bsnams pa'o//

(3.2) lho'i[5] 'dab ma la sgrol ma ljaṅ gu padma ljaṅ gu bsnams pa'o//

(3.3) nub kyi 'dab ma la dbaṅ phyug ma ser mo 'khor lo daṅ/ (6-utpa la-6) bsnams pa'o//

(3.4) byaṅ gi 'dab ma la khro gñer can/ dkar po[7] padma ser po bsnams pa'o//

(3.5) śar gyi mtshams kyi 'dab ma la padma'i gnas can ser po[8] btsod[9] kyi kha dog lta bu'i padma bsnams pa'o//

(3.6) lho'i mtshams kyi 'dab ma la rdo rje padma'i dbaṅ phyug ma nam mkha'i mdog lta bu padma dkar po bsnams pa'o//

(3.7) nub kyi mtshams kyi 'dab ma la sna tshogs padma dkar po[10] padma nag po bsnams pa'o//

(3.8) byaṅ gi mtshams kyi 'dab ma la sna tshogs rdo rje ma kha dog sna tshogs padma bsnams pa'o//

(3.9) de rnams thams cad sems dpa'i skyil kruṅ can phyag gñis pa/ źal gcig pa źi ba'o// ze'u[11] 'bru'i dbus su bcom ldan 'das lta bu'o//

(4) de nas sṅags bzlas par bya'o// oṃ hrīḥ padma na rte śwa ra hūṃ/

'jig rten mgon po padma gar gyi dbaṅ phyug gi sgrub thabs rdzogs so//

---

1 D, TP om.
2 P om.
3 D, TP wa.
4 P haṃ.
5 P lha'i.
6 D, TP padma.
7 D, TP mo.
8 D, TP mo.
9 P bcod.
10 D, TP mo.
11 P ze.

## 8.3 (T1) Padmanarteśvarasādhana

rgya gar skad du/ padma na[1] rte śwa ra sā dha naṃ/ bod skad du/ padma gar gyi dbaṅ phyug gi sgrub thabs/

(1) sṅar bśad pa'i cho gas stoṅs pa ñid bsgoms pa'i rjes la sna tshogs padma la gnas pa'i zla ba'i steṅ tu yi ge hrīḥ dkar po rnam par bsams śiṅ/

(2.1) de yoṅs su gyur[2] pa las kyaṅ padma gar gyi dbaṅ phyug gi gdams ṅag rje btsun 'phags pa spyan ras gzigs/ dbaṅ phyug tu bdag ñid bsgom par bya ba ni/ źal gcig[3] phyag bco brgyad skyil kruṅ phyed pa snaṅ ba mtha' yas daṅ ral pa'i thor tshugs daṅ ldan pa/ phyag thams cad kyis sna tshogs padma bsnams pa/

(2.2) rnal 'byor ma'i tshogs kyis yoṅs su bskor ba/ g'yas daṅ g'yon gyi phyogs na sgrol ma daṅ ni nor bzaṅs daṅ khro gñer can daṅ rta mgrin gnas pa/ lha rdzas kyi rgyan daṅ na bza mṅa ba'o//

(3) de nas sṅags bzlas par bya ba yaṅ/ oṃ hrīḥ padma (4-na rte-4) śwa ra hūṃ/

(4) nad ñe bar źi bar byed pa'i phan yon chen po daṅ ldan pa ste/

padma gar gyi dbaṅ phyug gi sgrub thabs rdzogs so// //mkhas pa ratna a[5] ka ra'i źal sṅa nas tshul khrims rgyal mtshan gyis bsgyur ba'o//

---

1 P ni.
2 D illegible.
3 P cig.
4 P nir te.
5 D, TP ā.

## 8.3 (T3) Padmanarteśvarasādhana

rgya gar skad du/ padma na rte[1] śwa ra sā dha naṃ/ bod skad du/ padma gar gyi dbaṅ phyug gi sgrub thabs/

(0) padma gar gyi dbaṅ phyug la phyag 'tshal lo//

(1) sṅon du gsuṅs pa'i cho gas stoṅ pa ñid bsgoms te/ de nas sna tshogs padma la gnas pa'i zla ba'i steṅ du hrīḥ yig dkar po rnam par bsgoms te/

(2.1) de yoṅs su gyur pa las padma gar gyi dbaṅ phyug gi rigs rje btsun 'phags pa spyan ras gzigs dbaṅ phyug gi bdag ñid bsgom par bya ste/ źal gcig phyag bco brgyad pa skyil kruṅ phyed pas bźugs pa/ 'od dpag tu med pa daṅ ral pa'i thor tshugs kyis brgyan pa/ phyag thams cad kyis sna tshogs padma bsnams pa

(2.2) rnal 'byor ma'i tshogs kyis yoṅs su bskor ba'o// lho daṅ byaṅ phyogs logs na[2] gnas pa'i sgrol ma daṅ/ nor bzaṅs daṅ/ khro gñer can daṅ/ rta mgrin rnams te/ lha'i rgyan daṅ gos kyis brgyan pa'o//

(3) de nas sṅags bzlas par bya ste/ oṃ hrīḥ padma na rte śwa ra hūṃ/

(4) nad pa[3] la sogs pa ñe bar źi ba'i mthu chen po[4]

źes pa ni padma gar gyi dbaṅ phyug gi sgrub thabs rdzogs so//

---

1 P rta.

2 D illegible.

3 D, TP om.

4 P po'o.

## 9.1 (T1) Hariharihariváhanodbhavalokeśvarasādhana

(1-seṅ ge daṅ bya khyuṅ daṅ khyab 'jug la bźugs sgrub thabs rim pa bźugs so//-1) rgya gar skad du/ ha ri ha ri ha ri bā ha na[2] sā dha naṃ/ bod skad du/ seṅ ge daṅ bya khyuṅ daṅ khyab 'jug la bźugs pa'i sgrub thabs/

(1) sṅar brjod pa'i rim pa ñid kyis stoṅ pa ñid bsgoms pa'i rjes thogs la/

(2) yig ge hrīḥ dkar po yoṅs su rdzogs par gyur pa las/ seṅ ge daṅ bya khyuṅ daṅ khyab 'jug la bźugs pa las 'byuṅ ba'i bcom ldan 'das sbyan ras gzigs dbaṅ phyug tu bdag ñid bsgom par bya ste/ sku thams cad dkar ba ral pa daṅ dbu rgyan daṅ ldan pa źi ba'i cha byad can phyag g'yas pas bcom ldan 'das de bźin gśegs pa dbaṅ[3] du mdzad pa/ gñis pas phreṅ ba bsnams[4] pa gsum pas tshul ṅan par gnas pa'i 'jig rten pa rnams ston[5] par mdzad do// g'yon pas dbyug tho bsnams pa gñis pas (6-ri dwags kriṣ ṇa sā ra'i pags pa bsnams pa/-6) gsum pas ril[7] pa spyi blugs bsnams pa'o// seṅ ge daṅ bya khyuṅ daṅ khyab 'jug gi phrag pa na gnas par ro//

(3) oṃ hrīḥ hūṃ źes pa'i sṅags 'dis bzlas par bya ba'o//

seṅ ge daṅ bya khyuṅ daṅ khyab 'jug la bźugs pa las 'byuṅ ba'i sgrub thabs so// dge sloṅ tshul khrims rgyal mtshan gyis bsgyur ba'o//

---

1 D om.
2 P om.
3 P dpaṅ.
4 P illegible between bs- and -ams.
5 P stoṅ.
6 The rendering follows Sanskrit: kṛṣṇājinadharaṃ. P ri dags kri śwa'i pags pa bsnams pa/; D ri dags kriṣ ṇa sa ri'i pags pa bsnams pa/; TP ri dags kriṣ ṇa sā ri'i pags pa bsnams pa/.
7 P ral.

## 9.1 (T3) Hariharihariváhanodbhavalokeśvarasādhana

(1-ha ri ha ri ha ri la źon par gyur pa'i sgrub thabs rim pa bźugs so//-1) rgya gar skyad du/ ha ri ha ri ha ri bā[2] ha nod[3] bha[4] bā sā dha naṃ/ bod skad du/ ha ri ha ri ha ri la źon par gyur pa'i sgrub thabs/

(0) 'phags pa spyan ras gzigs dbaṅ phyug la phyag 'tshal lo//

(1) sṅon du gsuṅs pa'i cho gas stoṅ pa ñid bsgoms nas/

(2) de nas hrīḥ yig dkar po yoṅs su gyur pa las/ ha ri ha ri ha ri la źon par gyur ba'i[5] bcom ldan 'das 'phags pa spyan ras gzigs dbaṅ phyug yan lag thams cad dkar po ral pa'i cod pan can/ źi ba'i cha lugs can/ phyag g'yas pa na bcom ldan 'das de bźin gśegs pa dbaṅ por[6] mdzad pa/ gñis pa bgraṅ phreṅ bsnams pa/ gsum pas ṅan soṅ[7] na gnas pa'i 'jig rten pa la dge ba ñe bar ston pa'o/ g'yon pa na[8] dbyug pa bsnams pa'o// gñis pa na (9-ri dwags nag po'i pags pa bsnams pa/-9) gsum pa na ril pa spyi blugs bsnams[10] pa/ seṅ ge daṅ/ nam mkha' ldiṅ daṅ/ khyab 'jug gi phrag pa la yaṅ dag par bźugs[11] pa'i bdag ñid bsgom par bya'o/

(3) oṃ hrīḥ hūṃ źes pa'i sṅags bzlas par bya'o//

ha ri ha ri ha ri la źon par gyur pa'i sgrub thabs rdzogs so//

---

1 D, TP om.
2 P ba.
3 P na de.
4 D bhā.
5 TP pa'i.
6 P po.
7 P seṅ.
8 P om.
9 The rendering follows Sanskrit: kṛṣṇājinadharaṃ. P ri dags nag po'i lpag pa bsnams pa/; D, TP ri dags nag po'i pags pa bsnams pa/.
10 P bsgoms.
11 P źug.

## 9.2 (T1) Harihariharivāhanodbhavalokeśvarasādhana

rgya gar skad du/ ha ri ha ri ha ri bā ha na sā dha naṃ/ bod skad du/ seṅ ge daṅ bya khyuṅ daṅ khyab 'jug la bźugs pa'i sgrub thabs/

(1) daṅ por re źig sṅags pas bde ba'i stan la gnas te 'gro ba gdon par 'dod pa'i bsam pas sdig pa bśags pa la sogs pa'i bla na med pa'i mchod pa rnam pa bdun byas la/

(2.1) yi ge yaṃ [(1-]yoṅs su[-1)] rdzogs pa las rluṅ gi dkyil 'khor gźu'i rnam pa 'dra ba bdan sṅon pos mtshan[2] pa'o// de'i steṅ du raṃ las byuṅ ba'i me'i dkyil 'khor kha dog dmar po gru gsum na raṃ dmar pos mtshan pa'o// de'i steṅ du baṃ yig rdzogs pa las chu'i dkyil 'khor kha dog dkar po bum pa dkar pos dbus na mtshan[3] pa'o// de'i steṅ du yi ge laṃ las legs par byuṅ ba'i sa'i dkyil 'khor gru bźi pa kha dog ser po rdo rje rtse gsum pa ser pos [(4-]grwa bźir[-4)] mdzes par byas pa'o//

(2.2) de'i steṅ du suṃ yig rdzogs pas rin po che bdun gyi raṅ bźin cog brgyad daṅ ldan pa'i ri rab lhun po'o// de'i steṅ du yi ge paṃ yoṅs su gyur pa las 'dab ma sna tshogs pa'i padma'o// de'i steṅ du bdag ñid bsams la/

(2.3) oṃ hrīḥ hūṃ rnams rim pa bźin du mgo bo daṅ mgrin pa daṅ sñiṅ gar rnam par bkod do/

(2.4.1) bdag ñid kyis thog ma med pa'i dus nas bsags pa'i las kyi sgrib[5] pa rnam par 'jig par byed pa'i seṅ ge daṅ/ bya khyuṅ daṅ khyab 'jug la bźugs pa las byuṅ ba'i 'jig rten dbaṅ phyug gi sku gser bzaṅ po'i mdog 'od zer 'bar bas 'khrigs pa gźon nu'i gzugs su sṅags pas rnam par bsams par bya ba'o//

(2.4.2) phyi nas raṅ gi sñiṅ gar bsod nams daṅ ye śes rnam par dag pa zla ba'i dkyil 'khor daṅ ñi ma'i dkyil 'khor ro// de las yi ge hrīḥ las rnam par byuṅ ba'i 'od zer 'bar bas 'chad par 'gyur ba'i gzugs kyi ye śes sems dpa' spyan draṅ źiṅ sṅar bśad pa'i mchod pa rnams kyis legs par mchod la/ ye śes sems dpa' daṅ dam tshig sems dpa' gñis gcig tu byas pa las/ bcom ldan 'das seṅ ge daṅ bya khyuṅ daṅ khab 'jug la bźugs pa las 'byuṅ ba'i 'jig rten dbaṅ phyug tu bdag ñid brtan pa'i sems kyis bsgom par bya ste//

(2.4.3) sku mdog dkar ba phyag drug pa ral pa daṅ dbu brgyan daṅ ldan pa źi ba'i cha byad kyis gnas pa/ phyag g'yas pas[6] rdzogs pa'i saṅs rgyas dpaṅ du mdzad pa/ gñis pas phreṅ ba 'dzin pa/ gsum pas ṅan soṅ na gnas pa'i 'jig rten dge ba ñe bar ston par mdzad do// g'yon pas dbyug pa bsnams pa gñis pas [(7-]ri dwags kri ṣṇa'i pags pa bsnams pa/[-7)] gsum pas ril pa spyi blugs bsnams pa'i bcom ldan 'das rnam par bsams par bya'o//

(2.4.4) de la rnam par dag pa ni rluṅ daṅ me'i dkyil 'khor [(8-]gñis kyis ni seṅ[-8)] ge'o// chu'i dkyil 'khor gyis ni bya khyuṅ ṅo// sa'i dkyil 'khor daṅ ri rab lhun po gñis kyis[9] khyab 'jug[10] go//

---

1 P om.
2 P mtshon.
3 P mtshon.
4 P grub źin.
5 D dgra be.
6 P om.
7 The rendering follows Sanskrit: kṛṣṇājinadharaṃ. P ri dags kri ṣna'i pags bsnams pa/; D, TP ri dag kri ṣna'i pag pa bsnams pa/.
8 D illegible.
9 D add. ni.
10 P bjug.

źes bya ba ni rnam par dag pa'o// rtag tu bsgom par byed pa'i rnal 'byor pa ni sems can thams cad kyi don byed pa'i nus pa daṅ ldan par 'gyur ro//
skye bo rnams thams cad dga' bar 'gyur ro//
śes rab chen po daṅ ldan par 'gyur ro//
nad med pa daṅ/ ñe bar 'tshe[1] ba daṅ bral źiṅ nor gyis phyug par yaṅ 'gyur ro// dbaṅ du bya ba daṅ dug sel ba'i las la stobs chen po daṅ ldan par 'gyur ro// (2-śes rab chen po daṅ ldan par 'gyur ro// nad med pa daṅ ñe bar 'tsho ba daṅ bral źiṅ nor gyis phyug par yaṅ 'gyur ro// dbaṅ du bya ba daṅ dug sel ba'i las la stobs chen po daṅ ldan par 'gyur ro//-2)

(3) zlas[3] pa'i sṅags ni bla ma'i gdams ṅag las śes par bya'o//

seṅ ge bya khyuṅ khyab 'jug la bźugs pa las 'byuṅ ba'i 'jig rten dbaṅ phyug gi sgrub thabs so// mkhas pa (4-chen po-4) a bha ya las tshul khrims rgyal mtshan gyis bsgyur ba'o//

1 P 'tsho.
2 D, TP om.
3 P bzlas.
4 P om.

## 9.2 (T2) Hariharihariväha nodbhavalokeśvarasādhana

[(1-]ha ri ha ri ha ri la źon par gyur pa'i spyan ras gzigs dbaṅ phyug gi sgrub thabs bźugs so// [-1)] rgya gar skad du/ ha ri ha ri ha ri bā ha nod bha baṃ lo ke śwa ra sā dha naṃ/ bod skad du/ ha ri ha ri ha ri la źon par gyur pa'i spyan ras gzigs dbaṅ phyug gi sgrub pa'i thabs/

(0) 'phags pa spyan ras gzigs dbaṅ phyug la phyag 'tshal lo//

(1) daṅ po re źig sṅags pas bde ba'i gdan la 'dug ste/ 'gro ba'i don bya ba'i bsam pas sdig pa bśags pa la sogs pa bdun yoṅs su dag pa'i mchod pa byas nas/

(2.1) yaṃ las rdzogs pa'i rluṅ gi dkyil 'khor gźu'i rnam pa lta bu'i[2] mdog sṅon po ba[3] dan gyis mtshan pa'o// de'i steṅ du raṃ las byuṅ ba me'i dkyil 'khor gru gsum dmar po raṃ dmar pos mtshan pa'o// de'i steṅ du paṃ las rdzogs pa chu'i dkyil 'khor dkar po/ bum pa dkar pos dbus su mtshan pa'o// de'i steṅ du laṃ las byuṅ ba dbaṅ chen gyi dkyil 'khor gru bźi pa mdog ser po rdo rje rtse gsum pa ser pos grwa bźir gnas śiṅ mdzes pa'o//

(2.2) de'i steṅ tu suṃ las [(4-]byuṅ ba'i[-4)] rin po che sna bdun gyi raṅ bźin lcog brgyad daṅ ldan pa'i ri rab bo// de'i steṅ du paṃ yoṅ su gyur pa las sna tshogs kyi padma'o// de'i steṅ du bdag ñid bsams la/

(2.3) oṃ hrīḥ hūṃ/ rim pa bźin du spyi bo daṅ/ mgrin pa daṅ/ sñiṅ gar rnam par bkod la/

(2.4.1) bdag ñid thog ma med pa'i dus nas bsags pa'i las kyi sgrib pa spaṅs pa'i ha ri ha ri ha ri la źon par gyur pa'i spyan ras gzigs kyi sku gser gyi mdog lta bu 'od zer 'bar źiṅ 'khrigs pa gźon nu'i gzugs su sṅags pas rnam par bsam par bya'o//

(2.4.2) phyis ni raṅ gi sñiṅ gar bsod nams daṅ ye śes kyi tshogs rnams par dag pa zla ba'i dkyil 'khor daṅ ñi ma'i dkyil 'khor ro// [(5-]de la[-5)] hrīḥ las byuṅ ba'i 'od zer gyi dra bas ye śes sems dpa' bkug ste/ 'og nas 'byuṅ ba'i[6] gzugs la sṅon gyi mchod pas yaṅ dag par mchod de/ ye śes sems dpa' daṅ dam tshig sems dpa' gcig tu byas la/ bcom ldan 'das ha ri ha ri ha ri la źon par gyur pa'i spyan ras gzigs sems brtan pas bdag ñid bsgoms par bya'o//

(2.4.3) phyag drug pa mdog dkar ba ral pa'i cod pan can/ źi ba'i cha lugs can phyag g'yas pas[7] yaṅ dag par rdzogs pa'i saṅs rgyas dbaṅ po byed pa/ gñis pa na phreṅ ba bsnams pa/ gsum pa na ṅan soṅ na gnas pa'i 'jig rten la dge ba ñe bar ston pa'o// g'yon pa'i daṅ po na dbyug pa/ gñis pa na ri dwags[8] nag po'i pags pa 'dzin pa/ gsum pa na ril pa spyi blugs bsnams pa'i bcom ldan 'das[9] rnam par bsgom par bya'o//

(2.4.4) de la rnam par dag pa ni rluṅ daṅ me'i dkyil 'khor gñis ni seṅ ge'o// chu'i dkyil 'khor ni bya khyuṅ ṅo// sa'i dkyil 'khor daṅ ri rab ni khyab 'jug rnam par dag pa'o// rgyun du bsgom par byed pa'i rnal 'byor pas sems can thams cad kyi don byed pa'i nus pa daṅ ldan par 'gyur ro// [(10-]skye 'gro thams cad dga' bar 'gyur ro//[-10)] śes rab chen por 'gyur ro// nad med

---

1 D, TP om.
2 D, TP bu.
3 D ba'i.
4 P rdzogs pa'i.
5 TP om.
6 D and TP add. zla ba'i.
7 P par.
8 P dags.
9 P add. kyis.
10 P om.

par 'gyur ro// ñe bar 'tshe ba med par 'gyur ro/ raṅ ñid nor phyug par 'gyur ro// dbaṅ du byed pa daṅ dug gi las la nus pa chen por 'gyur ro//

(3) sṅags kyi bzlas pa ni gdams ṅag las śes par bya'o//

ha ri ha ri ha ri la źon par gyur pa'i 'phags pa spyan ras gzigs dbaṅ phyug gi sgrub thabs rdzogs pa'i saṅs rgyas kyis gsuṅs pa rdzogs so// // paṇḍi ta don yod rdo rje daṅ/ khams pa lo tsa ba dge sloṅ ba ris bsgyur ba'o//

## 9.2 (T3) Haribharivāhanodbhavalokeśvarasādhana

rgya gar skad du/ ha ri ha ri ha ri [(1-]bā ha nod bha[-1)] bā sā dha naṃ/ bod skad du/ ha ri ha ri ha ri la źon par gyur pa'i sgrub thabs/

(0) 'phags pa spyan ras gzigs dbaṅ phyug la phyag 'tshal lo//

(1) daṅ por re źig sṅags pas stan bde ba la 'dug ste/ 'gro ba rnams mṅon par gdon par 'dod pa'i bsam pas sdig pa bźags pa la sogs pa bla na med pa'i mchod pa [(2-]rnam pa[-2)] bdun byas nas/

(2.1) yam yig rdzogs pa las rluṅ gi skyil 'khor gźu'i rnam pa lta bu kha dog sṅon po ba dan gyis mtshan pa'o// de'i steṅ du raṃ yig las gyur pa'i me'i[3] dkyil 'khor zur gsum pa kha dog dmar po raṃ yig gis mtshan pa'o// de'i steṅ du baṃ yig rdzogs pa las chu'i dkyil 'khor zlum po kha dog dkar po dbus su bum pa dkar pos mtshan pa'o// de'i steṅ du laṃ yig las byuṅ ba'i dbaṅ chen gyi dkyil 'khor gru bźi pa kha dog ser po zur bźi por rdo rje rtse gsum gyis mdzes par byas pa'o//

(2.2) de 'i steṅ tu suṃ yig yoṅs su gyur pa las rin po che sna bdun gyi raṅ bźin lcog[4] brgyad daṅ ldan pa'i ri rab daṅ sna tshogs chu skyes so// de'i steṅ du bdag ñid bsnams te/

(2.3) oṃ hrīḥ hūṃ rim pa bźin du spyi bo daṅ/ mgrin pa daṅ/ sñiṅ ga rnams su rim par bkod nas/

(2.4.1) bdag gis thog ma med pa'i dus nas bsags pa'i las kyi sgrib pa daṅ bral nas ha ri ha ri ha ri la źon par gyur pa'i 'jig rten dbaṅ phyug gi sku gser gyi kha dog lta bu 'od zer 'bar ba 'khrig pa gźon nu'i gzugs su sṅags pas bsgoms par bya'o//

(2.4.2) phyi nas raṅ gi sñiṅ gar bsod nams daṅ[5] ye śes rnam par dag pa'i phyir zla ba'i dkyil 'khor daṅ/ ñi ma'i dkyil 'khor ro// de la hrīḥ yig las byuṅ ba'i 'od zer gyi dra bas ye śes sems dpa' bkug ste/ 'chad par 'gyur ba'i sku la sṅon du gsuṅs pa'i [(6-]yaṅ dag[-6)] mchod pas mchod par bya'o// ye śes sems dpa' daṅ dam tshig sems dpa' dag gcig tu gyur nas bcom ldan 'das ha ri ha ri ha ri la źon par gyur ba'i[7] 'jig rten dbaṅ phyug tu sems brtan pos bdag ñid bsgom par byas te/

(2.4.3) phyag drug pa[8] sku mdog dkar po ral pa'i cod pan daṅ źi ba'i cha lugs can/ phyag g'yas pas rdzogs pa'i saṅs rgyas dbaṅ por[9] mdzad pa/ gñis pa na phreṅ ba bsnams pa/ gsum pas ṅan soṅ na gnas pa'i sems can la dge ba ston par mdzad pa/ g'yon pas dbyug pa bsnams pa/ gñis pas [(10-]ri dwags nag po'i pags pa bsnams pa/[-10)] gsum pa na ril ba spyi lugs bsnams pa'i bcom ldan 'das bsgom par bya'o//

(2.4.4) de la rnam par dag pa ni rluṅ daṅ me'i dkyil 'khor dag ni seṅ ge'o// chu'i dkyil 'khor ni nam mkha ldiṅ ṅo// dbaṅ chen gyi dkyil 'khor daṅ ri rab ni 'phrog byed rnam par dag pa'o// rtag

---

1 P ba ha na de bha.
2 P om.
3 P me yi.
4 P cog.
5 P om.
6 D, TP om.
7 P pa'i.
8 P om.
9 P po.
10 The rendering follows Sanskrit: kṛṣṇājinadharaṃ. P, D, TP ri dags nag po'i pags pa bsnams pa/.

tu sgom par byed pa'i rnal 'byor pas sems can thams cad kyi[1] don byed nus par 'gyur ro// skye 'gro thams cad dga' bar 'gyur ro// śes rab chen por 'gyur ro// nad med par 'gyur ro// ñe bar 'tshe ba med par 'gyur ro// nor la sogs pa daṅ ldan par 'gyur ro// dbaṅ du byed pa daṅ dug gi las la nus pa chen po daṅ ldan par 'gyur ro//

(3) sṅags bzlas pa ni zla ma'i gdams ṅag las śes par bya'o//

ha ri ha ri ha ri la źon par gyur pa'i 'jig rten dbaṅ phyug gi sgrub thabs rdzogs pa'i saṅs rgyas kyis gsuṅs pa rdzogs so//

1 TP gyi.

## 10.1 (T1) Trailokyavaśaṅkaralokeśvarasādhana

(1-'jig rten gsum dbaṅ du byed pa'i 'jig rten dbaṅ phyug gi 'grub thabs bskoṅ bźugs so//-1) rgya gar skad du/ trai lo kya ba śyaṃ ka ra lo ke śwa ra sā dha naṃ/ bod skad du/ 'jig rten gsum dbaṅ du byed pa'i 'jig rten dbaṅ phyug gi sgrub thabs/

(1.1) daṅ por re źig yid daṅ rjes su mthun pa'i gnas su thaṅ ka dgram par bya'o/ de'i mdun du sa'i dkyil 'khor gyi[2] dbus su gur kum[3] gyis zla ba'i dkyil 'khor bya ste/ rdo rje'i ri mo hūṃ/ źes bya ba'i sṅags kyis so//

(1.2) de'i rjes la/ jaḥ hūṃ baṃ padma la bźugs su gsol hoḥ źes bya ba'i sṅags kyis spyan draṅs la maṇḍal gyi dbus su 'jig rten gsum dbaṅ du mdzad pa'i rje btsun 'jig rten dbaṅ phyug mchod pa bya ba'o/ sṅags 'di dag gis bya ba yin te/ oṃ 'jig rten gsum dbaṅ du mdzad pa'i rdo rje me tog hūṃ bźes su gsol swāhā// de nas oṃ (4-rdo rje thub pa-4) muḥ źes bya bas[5] gśegs su gsol la/

(2.1) raṅ gi sñiṅ gar yi ge oṃ dmar po rnam par bsams la de yoṅs su gyur pa las ñi ma'o// de'i steṅ du yi ge hrīḥ dmar po'o// de'i 'od zer gyis de bźin gśegs pa snaṅ ba mtha' yas legs par spyan draṅs la yaṅ dag par mchod de/ sdig pa bśags pa la sogs pa byas śiṅ 'jig rten gsum dbaṅ du bya ba'i thabs rnams kyaṅ 'od kyis raṅ gi sa bon la legs par 'jug par bya ste/

(2.2) de dag yoṅs su gyur pa las skad[6] cig gis sku thams cad dmar po chen pos dmar bar gyur ba'i[7] 'jig rten dbaṅ phyug źal gcig pa phyag gñis pa spyan gsum pa ral pa daṅ dbu rgyan daṅ ldan pa// rdo rjes mtshan pa'i źags pa daṅ lcags kyu phyag na bsnams pas gsum gyi[8] lug gñis kyi (9-źags pas bciṅ ba'i-9) steṅ na/ padma dmar po la rdo rje skyil mo[10] kruṅ gis bźugs śiṅ lha rdzas kyi rgyan daṅ na bzas rnam par brgyan par bdag ñid bsams la/

(2.3) rdzu 'phrul sna tshogs daṅ ldan pa'i saṅs rgyas daṅ byaṅ chub sems dpa' rnams daṅ/ rdo rje rnal 'byor ma daṅ lha rnams kyis kyaṅ dbaṅ bskur bar byed par rnam par bsams te/ mgo bo la snaṅ ba mtha' yas bsgom par bya'o//

(2.4) de nas sñiṅ ga'i ñi ma la hrīḥ hūṃ yāṃ źes bya ba bzlas pa'i sṅags yi ge gsum po 'di bsgoms la/ oṃ stoṅ pa ñid kyi ye śes rdo rje'i raṅ bźin gyi bdag ñid ni ṅa yin no// chos thams cad rdo rje'i bdag ñid kyi rdo rje'i bdag ñid ni ṅa yin no/ źes bya ba rdo rje'i bdag ñid kyi sṅags gñis brjod par bya ba'o// de ltar goms par byas pa la g'yo ba 'phar ba la sogs pa'i yon tan 'byuṅ bar 'gyur ro//

(2.5) de'i rjes la/ oṃ hrīḥ āḥ hūṃ 'phrog ma gnod sbyin gyi dbaṅ phyug ma swāhā/ źes bya ba 'dis chaṅ bu sbyin no// oṃ āṃ kroṃ[11] hrīṃ dpa' bo daṅ dpa' mo'i dbaṅ phyug ma'i tshogs 'khor daṅ bcas pa ma lus pa rnams a a a ba ta ra a ba ta ra phyogs bcu nas gśegs su gsol

---

1 D, TP om.
2 P gyis.
3 D, TP gum.
4 P thub pa rdo rje.
5 P bar.
6 TP sgad.
7 D pa'i.
8 D, TP po.
9 P om.
10 P om.
11 D kaṃ.

ba yaṅ/ 'jig rten skyoṅ ba rnams kyis kyaṅ gtor ma 'di gri hna gri hna hūṃ swāhā/ źes bya bas gtor ma btaṅ la/ lha'i rnal 'byor gyis rnam par rgyu bar bya ba yin no//

oṃ ḍya[1] nas 'byuṅ ba'i rim pa 'jig rten gsum dbaṅ du byed pa'i 'jig rten dbaṅ phyug gi sgrub thabs/ sa ra ha'i źal nas mdzad pa rdzogs so// // a bha ya'i źabs druṅ nas lo[2] tsha ba tshul khrims rgyal mtsan gyis bsgyur ba'o//

1 P ṭu; D ḍan.
2 P ba; D, TP pa.

## 10.1 (T3) Trailokyavaśaṅkaralokeśvarasādhana

[(1-]'jig rten gsum po dbaṅ du byed pa 'jig rten dbaṅ phyug gi sgrub thabs rim pa bźugs//[-1)] // rgya gar skyad du/ trai lo kya ba śaṃ ka ra lo ke śwa ra sā dha naṃ/ bod skad du/ 'jig rten gsum po dbaṅ du byed pa'i 'jig rten dbaṅ phyug gi sgrub thabs/

(0) 'phags pa spyan ras gzigs dbaṅ phyug phyag[2] 'tshal lo//

(1.1) daṅ po re re[3] źig yid daṅ mthun pa'i gnas su ras ris[4] bkram ste/ de'i mdun du dbaṅ chen gyi dkyil 'khor gyi dbus su gur kum[5] gyis zla ba'i dkyil 'khor bya ste/ oṃ bdzra re khe hūṃ źes pa'i sṅags 'dis so//

(1.2) de nas dzaḥ hūṃ baṃ padma stha hoḥ źes pa'i sṅags kyis maṇḍal gyi dbus su 'jig rten gsum po dbaṅ du byed pa'i rje btsun bźugs nas sṅags 'dis mchod par bya'o// oṃ trai lo kya ba śaṃ ka rā ya bdzra puṣpe hūṃ pra ti tstsha swāhā/ de nas oṃ mu ni bdzre muḥ źes pas gśegs su gsol//

(2.1) raṅ gi sñiṅ gar oṃ yig dmar po rnam par bsams te/ de yoṅs su gyur pa las ñi ma'i steṅ du hrīḥ yig dmar po de'i 'od zer gyis de bźin gśegs pa 'od dpag tu med pa gdan draṅs la yaṅ dag par mchod nas sdig pa [(6-]thams cad[-6)] bśags pa la sogs pa byas nas/ yaṅ 'jig rten gsum po dbaṅ du byed [(7-]pa 'di[-7)] 'od zer gyi rnam pas raṅ gi[8] sa bon la rab tu bźugs[9] te/

(2.2) de yoṅs su gyur pa las skad cig gis 'jig rten dbaṅ phyug yan lag thams cad chags pa chen pos dmar źiṅ źal gcig phyag gñis pa/ spyan gsum pa/ ral pa'i cod pan gyis brgyan pa/ rdo rjes mtshan pa'i źags pa daṅ/ lcag kyu phyag na bsnams pa/ padma dmar po la rdo rje skyil kruṅ gis bźugs pa/ mdzes pa'i rgyan daṅ gos rnams kyis brgyan pa'i bdag ñid rnam par bsams te/

(2.3) sa gsum po lugs gñis la gnas pa rdo rje źags pa'i steṅ na bźugs pa/ sna tshogs pa'i sprul pa 'dzin ciṅ saṅs rgyas daṅ byaṅ chub sems dpa' daṅ rdo rje rnal byor ma daṅ lha la sogs pa rnams kyis dbaṅ bskur bar bsgom źiṅ spyi bor 'od dpag tu med pa bsam par bya'o//

(2.4) de nas sñiṅ gar ñi ma la hrīḥ hūṃ yāṃ źes pa'i yi ge gsum gyi sṅags bzlas śiṅ bsgoms nas// oṃ śūnya tā dzñāna bdzra swa bhā ba ātma ko 'haṃ[10]/ oṃ bdzra ā tma ko kāḥ sarba dharmā bdzra ātma ko 'ham[11] źes pa'i rdo rje'i bdag ñid kyi sṅags gñis po brjod par bya'o// de bźin du goms pas 'dar ba daṅ g'yo ba la sogs pa'i yon tan skye bar 'gyur ro//

(2.5) de nas oṃ hrīḥ a [(12-]hāṃ hā rī ti ya kṣe śwa ri[-12)] swāhā// źes pas chaṅ bu sbyin par bya'o// oṃ āṃ kroṃ hrī sa ka la ga na bī re śwa rī ṇāṃ pa ri ka rai/ a a a ba ta ra/ a ba ta rantu da

---

1 D, TP om.
2 P om.
3 D om.
4 P bris.
5 D gum.
6 D, TP om.
7 TP pa'i.
8 P gyi.
9 D, TP źugs.
10 P ham.
11 P ham.
12 D, TP hūṃ hā ri ti ya kṣe śwa rī.

śa dig lo ka pā la i maṃ ba li (1-grihṇa grihṇa-1) hūṃ swāhā// źes pas gtor ma dbul źiṅ lha'i rnal 'byor gyis gnas par bya'o//

oṃ (2-ḍi yā-2) na rim pa'i 'jig rten gsum po dbaṅ du byed pa'i 'jig rten dbaṅ phyug gi sgrub thabs sa ra ha'i źabs kyis mdzad pa rdzogs so//

1 P grinha grinha.
2 P dya.

## 10.2 (T1) Trailokyavaśaṅkaralokeśvarasādhana

rgya gar skad du/ trai lo kya ba śyaṃ ka ra lo ke śwa ra sā dha naṃ/ bod skad du/ 'jig rten dbaṅ phyug 'jig rten gsum dbaṅ du mdzad pa'i sgrub thabs źes bya ba/

(1.1) re źig daṅ por yid kyi rjes su mthun pa'i gnas su rnal 'byor pas thaṅ ka bkram la/ de'i mdun du sa'i dkyil 'khor gyi dbus su gur gum gyis zla ba'i dkyil 'khor mdzes par bya ba'o// sṅags 'dis bya ste/ oṃ rdo rje ri mo hūṃ/

(1.2) jaḥ hūṃ baṃ padma la bźugs hoḥ// sṅags 'dis spyan draṅs la/ oṃ 'jig rten gsum dbaṅ du mdzad pa rdo rje'i me tog hūṃ bźes su gsol swāhā/ sṅags 'dis maṇḍal gyi dbus su 'jig rten gsum dbaṅ du mdzad pa'i rje btsun 'jig rten dbaṅ phyug mchod par bya'o// oṃ thub pa rdo rje muḥ 'di ni gźegs su gsol ba'i sṅags yin no//

(2.1) phyi nas ni raṅ gi sñiṅ gar yi ge oṃ bsam par bya ba'o// de yoṅs su gyur pa las ñi ma'i dkyil 'khor grub par bya'o// de'i steṅ du chags pa'i sa bon skya[1] reṅs daṅ po'i 'od zer daṅ mtshuṅs par bltas la/

(2.2) 'od zer de dag gis kyaṅ snaṅ ba mtha' yas mchod ciṅ sdig pa bśags pa la sogs pa yaṅ byas la/ slar yaṅ lus la legs par bźugs[2] par bya'o[3]//

(2.3) de dag thams cad yoṅs su gyur pa las skad cig gis sa gsum gyi lug gñis źags pas sbrel ba'i thog gi padma'i steṅ du rdo rje'i skyil mo kruṅ gis bźugs pa ste[4]/ spyan gsum rnam par phye ba[5] ral pa daṅ cod pan daṅ ldan pa rdo rje kha dog dmar pos mtshan pa'i źags pa daṅ lcags kyu bsnams pa'o//

(2.4) sprul pa sna tshogs pa mṅa' ba'i rdo rje rnal 'byor ma rnams la dbaṅ bskur bar gsol ba gdab pa'o// de bźin du byaṅ chub sems dpa' sna tshogs pa'i rgyan daṅ ldan pa rnams kyis[6] mchod par byed do// rig pa 'dzin pa daṅ khyab 'jug daṅ dbaṅ phyug daṅ tshaṅs pa daṅ rnal 'byor ma'i tshogs rnams kyis kyaṅ gar daṅ rol mo'i sgra byed ciṅ// sna tshogs pa'i 'byuṅ po'i tshogs la sogs pa rnams daṅ mi mgo'i thod pa'i phreṅ ba sna tshogs pas brgyan pa rnams kyis kyaṅ ṅo// de bźiṅ du sna tshogs pa'i gdugs daṅ rṅa yab la sogs pa yaṅ blta bar bya ba'o// de dag dmigs la dam tshig tu de bźiṅ gśegs pa snaṅ ba mtha' yas mgo bo la blta bar bya'o// 'di lta bu dag tu bdag gñid bsam par bya ba'o//

(2.5) de nas lte ba'i ltag tu ñi ma'i dkyil 'khor 'od zer gyi raṅ bźin daṅ ldan par bsams la/ de'i steṅ gi g'yon du chags pa'i sa bon no/ sñiṅ gar khro bo'i sa bon no/ dbyaṅs yig āḥ 'di rnams ni bsgom par bya ba'i sṅags so//

(2.6) de dag thams cad bsgoms śiṅ rdo rje'i bdag ñid kyi sṅags brjod pas rdo rje'i bdag ñid du bsam par bya ste/ oṃ stoṅ pa ñid kyi ye śes kyi rdo rje'i raṅ bźin gyi bdag ñid ni ṅa'o// rdo rje'i bdag ñid kyi sṅags so//

(2.7) de dag goms par gyur pa'i sbyor bas g'yo ba daṅ bskyod pa daṅ/ dbab pa byas la gñis su med pa'i ye śes bskyed[7] par bya ba'o// rnal 'byor pa de glaṅ po bźin du grags par 'gyur źiṅ

---

1 TP skye.
2 D, TP gźugs.
3 P bya ba'o.
4 P illegible.
5 TP bar.
6 P kyi.
7 D, TP bskyod.

śiṅ tu dga' ba bźin du rigs lṅa 'du bar 'gyur ro// [(1-]gal te[-1)] rigs lṅa 'du bar ma gyur na/ de'i tshe de'i lus la g'yo ba daṅ bskyod pa daṅ dbab pa la sgos pa gnas pa ma yin no// de ltar ñin re bźin rigs lṅa 'du ba des ni 'grub par 'gyur ba yin la/ grub pa thob pas kyaṅ gźan gyi lus g'yo ba daṅ/ bskyod pa daṅ gab pa byas la/ 'dod chags daṅ źe sdaṅ la sogs pa dgag par bya ste/ dper na grub pa'i gser 'gyur gyis phug pa'i zaṅs ni mdog ṅan pa daṅ bral bar 'gyur ro// de bźin du lus ñid kyaṅ 'bigs byed kyi bcud can gyis phug pas 'dod chags daṅ źe sdaṅ la sogs [(2-]pa daṅ[-2)] bral bar 'gyur ro/

(2.8) hūṃ hūṃ yī/ bzlas pa'i sṅags so// oṃ hrī āḥ gnod sbyin dbaṅ phyug ma 'phrog ma swāhā/ 'phrog ma'i sṅags so/ oṃ āṃ[3] kroṃ hrīṃ[4] dpa' bo daṅ dpa' mo dbaṅ phyug ma'i tshogs 'khor daṅ bcas pa ma lus pa rnams a a a ba ta ra a ba ta ra phyogs bcu nas gśegs su gsol źiṅ 'jig rten dbaṅ[5] ba yaṅ gtor ma 'di [(6-]grihṇa grihṇa[-6)] hūṃ swāhā/ gtor ma'i sṅags so//

sa ra ha'i źal sṅa nas mdzad pa/ o ḍḍi[7] ya nas rnams par phyuṅ ba 'jig rten [(8-]dbaṅ phyug 'jig rten[-8)] gsum dbaṅ du mdzad pa'i sgrub thabs so// mkhas pa [(9-]ratna a ka ra[-9)] las[10] dge sloṅ tshul khrims rgyal mtshan gyis bsgyur ba'o//

---

1 P illegible.
2 P pad.
3 P aṃ.
4 P hrī.
5 P skyoṅ.
6 P grihna grihna.
7 D, TP ḍi.
8 D, TP om.
9 D ratnā ā ka ra̦, TP ratna ā ka ra.
10 D, TP daṅ/.

## 10.2 (T2) Trailokyavaśaṅkaralokeśvarasādhana

[(1-]//khams gsum dbaṅ du byed pa'i spyan ras gzigs kyi sgrub pa'i thabs bźugs so// //[-1)] rgya gar skad du/ trai lo kya ba śaṃ ka ra lo ke[2] śwa ra sā dha naṃ/ bod skad du/ khams gsum dbaṅ du byed pa'i spyan ras gzigs dbaṅ phyug gi sgrub pa'i thabs/

(0) 'phags pa spyan ras gźigs dbaṅ phyug la phyag 'tshal lo//

(1.1) daṅ po re źig yid daṅ mthun pa'i gnas su rnal 'byor pas thaṅ sku bkram ste/ de'i mdun du dbaṅ chen gyi dkyil 'khor gyi dbus su gur gum[3] gyis zla ba'i dkyil 'khor [(4-]zlum po[-4)] sṅags 'dis bya'o// oṃ bdzra re khe hūṃ

(1.2) dzaḥ hūṃ baṃ hoḥ/ źes bya ba'i sṅags 'dis phab la dkyil 'khor gyi dbus su khams gsum dbaṅ du byed pa'i rje btsun spyan ras gźigs sṅags 'dis mchod par bya'o// oṃ trai lo kya ba śaṃ ka ra ya bdzra pu ṣpe hūṃ prati tstsha swāhā/ oṃ mu ne bdzra muḥ 'di ni bsdu ba'i sṅags so//

(2.1) phyis ni raṅ gi sñiṅ gar āṃ yig bsam par bya ste/ de yoṅs su gyur pa las ñi ma'i dkyil 'khor rdzogs par bya'o// de'i steṅ du nus pa'i sa bon ñi ma śar ba lta bu'i 'od bltas[5] la/

(2.2) [(6-]'di yi[-6)] 'od zer gyis 'od dpag med pa mchod nas/ sdig pa bśags pa la sogs pa byas te/ yaṅ raṅ gi lus la gźug go//

(2.3) de thams cad yoṅs su gyur pa las skad cig gis padma'i steṅ du [(7-]rdo rje[-7)] skyil mo kruṅ gis gnas pa phye ba'i spyan gsum pa ral pa'i dbu rgyan 'chaṅ ba/ mdog dmar ba rdo rjes mtshan pa'i źags pa daṅ/ lcags kyu phyag na'o//

(2.4) sa gsum gyi raṅ bźin lug gñis źags pas bciṅs pa/ de'i steṅ du bźugs pa sna tshogs pa'i sprul pa 'chaṅ źiṅ rdo rje rnal 'byor ma rnams kyis dbaṅ bskur bar ba tu spyin pa/ de bźin du byaṅ chub sems dpa' rgyan sna tshogs daṅ ldan pas mchod par byed pa/ rig pa 'dzin pa daṅ/ khyab 'jug daṅ/ bde byed daṅ/ tshaṅs pa daṅ/ sna tshogs pa'i rnal 'byor ma'i tshogs kyis gar daṅ brduṅ 'khrol la sogs pa byed pa sna tshogs kyi 'byuṅ po'i tshogs pa la sogs pas/ sna tshogs kyi mi mgo daṅ keṅ[8] rus la sogs pas brgyan pa de bźin du sna tshogs kyi gdugs daṅ rṅa yab la sogs pa blta bar bya'o// de lta bu'i dus su de bźin gśegs pa 'od dpag med pa spyi bor blta bar bya ste/ 'di lta bu'i bdag ñid bsam par bya'o/

(2.5) phyis ni lte ba'i steṅ du ñi ma'i dkyil 'khor gyi 'od kyi raṅ bźin bsams la/ de'i steṅ du g'yon phyogs su nus pa'i sa bon sñiṅ gar khro bo'i sa bon dbyaṅs yig as[9] brgyan pa źes bya ba ni bsgom pa'i sṅags so//

---

1 D, TP om.
2 P te.
3 P kum.
4 P om.
5 P ltas.
6 D, TP di'i.
7 D illegible.
8 P, TP rkeṅ.
9 P āḥ sa.

(2.6) 'di thams cad bsams nas rdo rje'i bdag ñid kyi sṅags brjod par byas la/ de'i[1] bdag ñid du bsams par bya'o/ oṃ śū nya tā[2] dzñāna bdzra swa bhā ba[3] ā tma ko 'haṃ[4]/ rdo rje'i bdag ñid kyi sṅags so//

(2.7) 'di la yaṅ goms pa'i śbyor bas 'dar ba daṅ/ g'yo bas dbab par byas la/ gñis su med pa'i yes śes [(5-]skye bar[-5)] 'gyur ro// 'di lta bu'i rnal 'byor pa ni glaṅ po che smyon pa de[6] ltar myos[7] kyi chu yis myos pa bźin du rigs lṅa loṅs spyod do// gal te rigs lṅa la mi spyod pa de'i[8] lus la 'dar ba daṅ/ g'yo ba la sogs pa 'bab pa daṅ/ gñis su med pa'i ye śes mi gnas so// de ltar rtog par byas nas rigs lṅa la loṅs[9] spyod[10] des[11] ni 'grub par 'gyur ro// grub par gyur nas gźan gyi lus la yaṅ g'yo ba daṅ/ 'dar bas dbab par byas la 'dod chags daṅ/ źe sdaṅ la sogs pa dgag par mi bya'o// de ltar grub pa'i dṅul chus phug pa'i zaṅs ma'i nag po spaṅs pa bźin du lus po ñid gñis med kyi ro yis phug na 'dod chags daṅ/ źe sdaṅ la sogs pa spoṅ bar 'gyur ro/

(2.8) hrīḥ hūṃ āḥ bzlas pa'i sṅags so// oṃ hrīḥ āḥ[12] ha ri ti ya kṣe[13] śwa ri swāhā/ 'phrog ma'i sṅags so// oṃ oṃ kroṃ hrīṃ sa ka la ga ṇa nī dā[14] bī rī[15] śwa ri ṇīṃ pa ri ka re a a a ba ta ra a ba ta ra ntu da śa dig lo ka pā la mi[16] daṃ ba liṃ grihṇa grihṇa hūṃ phaṭ swāhā/ gtor ma'i sṅags so//

khams gsum dbaṅ du byed pa'i spyan ras gzigs dbaṅ phyug gi sgrub thabs slob dpon sa ra has mdzad pa rdzogs so// // paṇḍi ta don yod rdo rje daṅ/ khams pa lo tsha ba dge sloṅ ba ris bsgyur ba'o//

---

1 P rdo rje.
2 P ta.
3 D, TP wa.
4 P haṃ.
5 D om.
6 D, TP om.
7 D and TP add. byed.
8 D and TP add. tshe de'i.
9 P om.
10 P spyad de; D add. de.
11 D add. de.
12 D, TP aḥ.
13 P kṣa.
14 D, TP de.
15 P ri.
16 P, TP i.

## 10.2 (T3) Trailokyavaśaṅkaralokeśvarasādhana

rgya gar skad du/ trai lo kya ba śam ka ra lo ke śwa ra sā dha naṃ/ bod skad du/ 'jig rten gsum po dbaṅ du byed pa'i 'jig rten dbaṅ phyug gi sgrub thabs/

(0) 'phags pa spyan ras gzigs dbaṅ phyug la phyag 'tshal lo//

(1.1) daṅ por[1] re źig rnal 'byor pas yid daṅ mthun pa'i gnas su bris pa'i sku la sogs pa bkram ste/ de'i mdun du dbaṅ chen gyi dkyil 'khor gyi dbus su gur gum gyis[2] zla ba'i dkyil 'khor bya ste/ sṅags 'dis so// oṃ bdzra re khe hūṃ/

(1.2) dzaḥ hūṃ baṃ padma stha hoḥ sṅags 'dis bźugs su gsol nas maṇḍal gyi dbus su 'jig rten gsum po dbaṅ du byed pa'i rje btsun 'jig rten dbaṅ phyug sṅags 'dis mchod par bya'o// oṃ trai lo kya ba śaṃ ka rā[3] ya bdzra pu ṣpe hūṃ pra tī tstsha swāhā/ oṃ mu ni bdzra muḥ sṅags 'dis gśegs su gsol lo//

(2.1) phyi[4] nas raṅ gi sñiṅ gar oṃ yig bsam par bya'o// de yoṅs su gyur pa las ñi ma'i dkyil 'khor bskyed la/ de'i steṅ du nus pa'i sa bon [(5-]hrīḥ dmar po[-5)] skya[6] reṅs[7] gsar[8] pa'i mdog lta bu bltas la/

(2.2) de'i 'od zer gyis 'od dpag tu med pa[9] [(10-]nam mkhar spyan draṅs nas[-10)] mchod nas sdig pa bśags pa la sogs pa byas te/ yaṅ raṅ gi lus la gźug go/

(2.3) de rnams thams cad yoṅs su gyur pa las skad cig gis padma'i steṅ du rdo rje'i[11] skyil kruṅ gis bźugs pa/ spyan gsum rgyas śiṅ ral pa'i cod pan 'chaṅ ba/ sku mdog dmar po rdo rjes mtshan pa'i źags pa daṅ/ lcags kyu phyag na bsnams pa/

(2.4) sa gsum po lugs gñis kyi[12] źags pas bciṅs pa'i steṅ du[13] na bźugs śiṅ sna tshogs pa'i sprul pa 'chaṅ ba/ rnal 'byor ma'i tshogs kyis dbaṅ bskur bar rab tu sbyin pa/ de bźin du byaṅ chub sems dpa' rgyan sna tshogs daṅ ldan pas mchod pa byed pa rig 'dzin daṅ/ khyab 'jug daṅ/ bde byed daṅ/ tshaṅs pa daṅ/ sna tshogs pa'i rnal 'byor ma'i tshogs kyis gar daṅ rol mo la sogs pa sna tshogs byed ciṅ/ 'byuṅ po la sogs pa sna tshogs pas mi mgo daṅ thod pa'i phreṅ bas brgyan pa daṅ/ de bźin du sna tshogs pa'i gdugs daṅ/ rṅa yab la sogs pa blta bar bya'o/ de lta bu'i dus su de bźin gśegs pa 'od dpag tu med pa spyi bor blta bár bya'o// de daṅ 'dra bar bdag ñid bsam par bya'o//

---

1 D po.
2 P gyi.
3 P ra.
4 P phyis.
5 P om.
6 P skye; D dkya.
7 D, TP reṅ.
8 P sar.
9 P pas.
10 P om.
11 D, TP rje.
12 D, TP om.
13 D, TP om.

(2.5) phyi nas lte ba'i steṅ du ñi ma'i dkyil 'khor la 'od zer gyi raṅ bźin du[1] bsam la/ de'i steṅ du g'yon phyogs su nus[2] pa'i[3] sa bon sñiṅ gar khro bo'i sa bon āḥ yig dbyaṅs yig gis brgyan pa źes pa ni bsgom pa'i sṅags so//

(2.6) de thams cad bsams la rdo rje'i bdag ñid kyi sṅags brjod par bya źiṅ rdo rje'i bdag ñid du bsam[4] par bya'o// oṃ śū nya tā dzñā na bdzra swa bhā ba[5] ātma ko 'haṃ[6]/ rdo rje'i bdag ñid kyi sṅags so/

(2.7) 'di la goms pa'i sbyor bas 'dar ba daṅ g'yo ba dbab par byas pas[7] gñis su med pa'i ye śes skye bar 'gyur ro// de lta bu'i rnal 'byor pa de glaṅ po che smyon pa ltar[8] myos byed kyi chus myos pa bźin du rigs lṅa la loṅs spyod do// gal te rigs lṅa la loṅs mi spyod na de'i tshe de'i lus 'dar ba daṅ g'yo ba daṅ 'bab pa la sogs pas[9] mi gnas so// de ltar ṅes pas rigs[10] lṅa la loṅs spyod par bya'o// des 'grub par 'gyur ro// grub par gyur na gźan gyi lus la yaṅ 'dar ba daṅ g'yo ba dbab par byas pas 'dod chags daṅ źe sdaṅ la sogs pa 'gag par 'gyur ro// ji ltar grub pa'i dṅul chus phug pas zaṅs ma'i nag po spaṅs pa de bźin du lus po ñid kyaṅ gñis su med pa'i ros phug nas 'dod chags daṅ źe sdaṅ la sogs pa spoṅ bar 'gyur ro//

(2.8) hrī hūṃ[11] yāṃ bzlas pa'i sṅags so// oṃ hrīḥ āḥ hā rī ti ya kṣe śwa ri swāhā/ 'phrog ma'i sṅags so// oṃ ā kroṃ hri sa ka la gā ṇā[12] bī rā bī re śva rī ṇaṃ pa ri ka raiḥ a a a ba ta ra/ a ba ta ra a ba ta ran[13] tu da śa dig lo ka pā la i daṃ ba liṃ grihṇa grihṇa hūṃ swāhā/ gtor ma'i sṅags so//

oṃ ḍi yā ṇa nas byuṅ źiṅ sa ra ha'i źabs kyis gdan draṅs pa 'jig rten gsum dbaṅ du byed pa'i 'jig rten dbaṅ phyug gi sgrub thabs rdzogs so//

---

1 TP om.
2 P nub.
3 TP ba'i.
4 P bsams.
5 D, TP wa.
6 P haṃ.
7 D nas.
8 TP om.
9 P pa.
10 P rig.
11 P hūḥ.
12 D, TP nā.
13 P ra na.

# 10.3 (T3) Trailokavaśaṅkaralokeśvarasādhana (Trailokavaśaṅkarāmnāyabhugmalokeśvarasādhana)

rgya gar skad du/ śrī trai lo kya ba śaṃ ka rā[1] rya bhugma sā dḥa naṃ/ bod skad du/ dpal 'jig rten gsum po dbaṅ du byed pa 'phags pa bhu gma[2] sgrub thabs/

(0) 'phags pa spyan ras gzigs dbaṅ phyug thugs rje chen po la phyag 'tshal lo//

(1.1) saṅs rgyas byaṅ chub sdig pa daṅ dral ba//
bde gśegs sras daṅ rgyal ba'i yab ñid daṅ//
'gro mgon 'jig rten mnan[3] rnams phyag 'tshal nas//
ṅo mtshar can gyi sgrub thabs bśad par bya//

(1.2) sñiṅ gar a yig las skyes zla ba
chu skyes zla ba yid kyi[4] mun 'joms pa yi//
hrīḥ yig 'od zer dra ba'i tshogs 'phro
chu skyes dmar po skya reṅs mdog lta bu//

(2.1) rnam thar gsum po yaṅ dag bsam źiṅ
mkhas pas gzugs ni dri med źal sogs bsaṅ//
khro las rgyal bas daṅ por gnas daṅ
bdag ñid bsruṅ ba'i[5] sbyor ba ñid byas te//
chaṅ daṅ gur kum[6] bzaṅ po'i lde[7] gus byugs//
me togs dri bzaṅs rab byed gcal du bkram//
bsam gtan gnas ni rab dgar bde ba'i stan//
mthon po la ni rab tu 'dug byas te/

(2.2) gur kum[8] tsan dan dmar pos de mdun du//
maṇḍal śin tu zlum byas legs pa byugs//
me tog dmar po so ma gcal du bkram//
raṅ gi sṅags bzlas mchod yon dam pa'i snod//

(3) de nas nam mkhar[9] rgyal sras kun bltas nas//
mkhas pas gcig tu 'gro kun skrag bcas gdon pa'i phyir//
mchod pa'i cho ga rnam maṅ raṅ gi sa bon bskyed//
de rnams blo gros ldan pas mñam gźag yid kyis[10] bya//
de nas de rnams kyi mdun du pus mo sa la btsugs śiṅ btud nas 'dug ste/ thal mo sbyar nas bdag ñid lhag par grol ba'i phyir sdig pa bśags pa la sogs pa bya ste/
skrag pas[11] sdig pa ma lus bśags bgyid ciṅ//

---

1 D, TP ra ā.
2 D gma'i.
3 TP mnon.
4 P kyis.
5 TP pa'i.
6 D, TP gum.
7 P 'de.
8 D, TP gum.
9 P mkha'.
10 P kyi.
11 P las.

ma lus sdig la[1] dga' bar mi bgyid do//
dge ba kun la rjes su yi raṅ źiṅ//
byaṅ chub mchog tu bdag gis yoṅs su bsṅo//
dpuṅ gñen dkon mchog gsum la bdag skyabs mchi//
saṅs rgyas rnams la bdag gis lus 'di 'bul//
'gro la phan bgyid byaṅ chub sñiṅ po bzuṅ//
saṅs rgyas phun tshogs gnas la yaṅ dag bsten//

(4) 'gro ba mtha' dag sdug bsṅal gyis mnar yaṅ dag blta//
sṅags pas de la brtse chen 'od zer bsgom bya ste//
bdag daṅ 'gro ba ma lus gñis med stoṅ par bsgom//
kun la phan par yaṅ ni rab tu blta bar bya/
de nas oṃ swa bhā ba śu ddhaḥ sarba dharma[2] swa bhā ba śuddho 'haṃ[3]/ oṃ śun ya tā dzñā na bdzra swa bhā ba[4] ātma ko 'haṃ[5] źes pa 'dis byin gyis brlab par bya'o//

(5.1) de nas mdun du 'od zer dra ba 'phro ba yi//
pa[6] la śa'i me tog lta bu'i hrīḥ yig bsam//
des byuṅ zla ba gaṅ ba'i gzugs bltas la//
hrīḥ yig 'od zer dra ba'i 'od kyi dbus//
de steṅ hrīḥ yig las byuṅ ñi ma ste//
'od kyis phyogs rnams kun tu snaṅ byed ciṅ//
dbus gnas hrīḥ[7] yig las byuṅ 'od zer 'bar//
mun pa mtha' dag 'joms byed yaṅ dag bsam//
de steṅ raṅ gi sa bon las skyes pa'i//
'dam skyes rnam rgyas ñi ma'i kha dog bźin//
yi ge hrīḥ yis rab mdzes dbus ma'i cha//
mkhas pas yid kyi mun 'joms rnam par bsam byas la//

(5.2) de nas raṅ gyi sa bon ma lus pa las ni//
thub dbaṅ spro daṅ de las bsdu byas nas//
sa bon gyis mtshan ñi zla'i thig les bskyed//
'gro ba'i mgon[8] du bdag ñid blta bar bya//
padma daṅ ni zla ba'i steṅ na
rol źiṅ mñam pa'i źabs kyis yaṅ dag bźugs//
'khrul pa rab bcom padma rgyas pa'i
źal mṅa' glog daṅ byu[9] ru lta bur gsal//
spyan gñis yaṅs pa utpa la sṅon po 'dra
źiṅ smin 'khyug[10] mdzes pas brgyan gyur pa//
ral pa mdzes śiṅ mu tig chun pos

1 P pa.
2 D, TP dharmaḥ.
3 P haṃ.
4 D, TP wa.
5 P haṃ.
6 D, TP pā.
7 P hrī.
8 P mṅon.
9 D, TP byi.
10 P 'khyugs.

rnam brgyan lha yi gos kyis rab mdzes pa//
'od zer dmar po 'phro ba'i sa bon las
skyes rgyal ba phun tshogs sems can don//
phyag ni g'yon pa padma dmar po
rnam par rgyas pa rnam par bsnams gyur pa//
mkhas śiṅ phyag g'yas nas ni rnam pa
kun gyi mchog ni rab tu stsol[1] bar mdzad//
rin chen rgyan gyis rab mdzes yid rab
dad pa'i 'jig rten dbaṅ phyug 'od rab gsal//
(5.3) de nas sñiṅ gar chu skyes zla ba la//
hrīḥ[2] yig 'od kyis yoṅs bskor ñe bar bsam//
sñiṅ mgrin sbyi bor zla ba'i steṅ rnams su//
hūṃ āḥ oṃ yig 'od 'bar myur du blta//
(5.4) de nas phyogs min padma yaṅ dag blta//
ban du'i kha dog phyogs bźir rab tu rgyas//
de steṅ bsil zer byed pa yoṅs rdzogs pa//
gur kum[3] lta bur rab gsal bsgom par bya//
de la raṅ sñiṅ sṅags kyi 'od zer ni//
źal nas ṅes 'thon zla ba bźi yi bdag//
gaṅ la de źugs de rnams steṅ du ni//
mun pa'i tshogs 'joms ñi ma de bźin du//
me sogs mtshams gyur ñi ma gnas pa la//
sa bon śin tu dkar nag dmar daṅ ser//
lāṃ māṃ de nas pāṃ daṅ hūṃ bźi las//
zla ba ñi ma yaṅ dag sbyor bar bsam//
(5.5) de nas zla ba'i sa bon las skyes blta//
ji ltar raṅ gi rten[4] ni gźir gyur pa//
lha mo sna tshogs rgyan daṅ na bza' mchog//
rin chen thor tshugs rab bciṅs rgyan gyis mdzes//
me ru padma zla la spyan draṅs[5] te[6]//
kun da zla 'od yid 'oṅ phyag gñis ma//
bden bral pa padma zla la mā ma kī//
brtse ldan snum bcas indra nī la'i[7] mdog/
zluṅ gi padma zla la gos dkar mo//
chu skyes dmar po ñi ma daṅ mtshuṅs bde//
dbaṅ ldan padma zla la sgrol ma ste//
gser mdog śin tu źi ba bsgom par bya//
de rnams pus mo sa la btsugs śiṅ riṅ źiṅ yaṅs pa'i spyan//

---

1 P brtsol.
2 P hrī.
3 D, TP gum.
4 P bstan.
5 D, TP ma.
6 D, TP ste.
7 P li'i.

nu ma zuṅ dag mtho źiṅ[1] mkhregs la rked pa'i dbus cha phra[2]//
gus pa daṅ bcas rol pa'i sku smad rgyas śiṅ yan lag mchog/
skra yi 'od zer 'khyil śiṅ 'dzum ldan thal mo rab tu sbyor//
(5.6) de nas sñiṅ ga'i sṅags kyi 'od zer phreṅ ba yis//
gdan draṅs mdun gyi bar snaṅ la ni bźugs par bsam//
dpal ldan ye śes 'khor lo'i cho ga bźin du ni//
raṅ gi 'khor los gdan draṅs gźug pa la sogs bya//
(5.7) de nas raṅ gi bdag ñid rjes 'jug[3] bum pa yis//
dbaṅ bskur ye śes chu yis mṅon par gaṅ bar blta//
rgyal ba'i dbaṅ bskur chu las rab tu skyes gyur pa'i//
kun[4] gyi spyi bor ṅag gi dbaṅ phyug legs par bsam//
(5.8) de nas raṅ sñiṅ sa bon 'od zer las skyes pa'i//
lha mo'i tshogs daṅ lha rnams kyis ni gaṅ[5] gyur te//
dpag tu med pa'i mchod pa sna tshogs 'phro ba yis//
raṅ gi 'khor lo yaṅ ni yoṅs su mchod par bsgom//
(5.9) de nas sñiṅ gar zla ba dmar po yoṅs rdzogs la//
'od zer dmar po'i cha śas tshogs kyis yoṅs su bskor//
śin tu dmar po'i[6] oṃ hūṃ yi ge dbus su gnas//
bdag gi sa bon las ni rab tu 'bar bar blta//
rnam par 'phro ba'i 'od zer rjes 'jug kha dog tshogs//
rgya skyegs dmar po bźin du 'jig rten snaṅ bar byed//
rdzogs pa'i saṅs rgyas rnam par dag pa'i byaṅ chub bzuṅ//
sṅags pas de la de bźin so sor bsdus[7] ba daṅ//
yaṅ dag spro daṅ bsdu ba'i cho ga yaṅ yaṅ du//
rnam par skyo ba med pa'i yid kyis de bźin bya//
de dag gis ni ṅal ba cher[8] gaṅ gi tshe//
de tshe źal 'jug 'khor lo daṅ ldan sṅags bzlas bya//
ñi ma so so'i thun mtshams la//
bsgom pa la 'bad sṅags bzlas bya//
(5.10) gal te skabs ni yod gyur na//
ji srid mṅon sum mi snaṅ bar//
thun mtshams so sor cho ga bźin//
rnam dag yig[9] gsum sṅags byin brlab//
(6.1) sṅags pas mṅon par bzlas pa bya//
'byuṅ po kun la gtor ma sbyin//
(6.2) de nas ldaṅ bar 'dod pa na//
tshigs bcad gcig pa'i smon la gdab//

---

1 P śiṅ.
2 D pra.
3 The rendering is possibly a misprint for mjug.
4 P phun.
5 TP gar.
6 P ba'i.
7 D TP bsdu.
8 D and TP add. gyur.
9 The rendering follows Skt: -akṣara-. P, D, TP yid.

yaṅ na dpal ldan klu grub źabs//
la sogs kyis mdzad mṅon 'phags kyis//
bdag gi bsod nams 'di yis ni//
'gro kun rtag tu dri med pa'i//
dpal ldan khams gsum dbaṅ byed gnas//
de bźin myur du thob par śog//
(6.3) oṃ āḥ hūṃ źes brjod sñiṅ gar//
lha mo bźi bsdu sa bon la//
(6.4) laṅs nas bya ba thams cad bya//
sna tshogs pa yi[1] don rnams daṅ//
de bźin thun mtshams gźi'i[2] dus rnams te//
'on kyaṅ khyad par cuṅ zad 'di yod de//
blo yis ye śes sems dpa' gśegs nas ni//
raṅ gi 'khor lor ma lus bsdu bya ste//
thun mtshams lhag ma don dam sems ñid ni//
yaṅ dag mṅon du byas nas sṅags pas ñal//
sṅa ma'i dus su smon lam nus pa yis//
rab tu sad nas de bźin laṅs par bya//
(7.1) gaṅ[3] gis kun tu 'jig rten mgon po bsgom//
de yis 'jigs pa che rnams rab tu źi//
ri dags[4] dbaṅ po chu daṅ thog srin po//
sbrul daṅ me daṅ dgra daṅ 'chiṅ ba rnams//
gaṅ gis[5] raṅ lus 'jig rten dbaṅ phyug rta[6]//
de las ñer 'phros nad daṅ bgegs la sogs//
dbul daṅ skal ṅan mi bdag gis 'dzin daṅ//
dus min dus su 'chi bar 'gyur ba daṅ//
gaṅ gyis thog med srid pa'i naṅ źugs nas//
lus daṅ ṅag daṅ yid kyi sdig pa rnams//
mi śes dbaṅ gis byas pa de rnams ni//
gaṅ gis 'jig rten mgon dran ñams śiṅ źi//
(7.2) gaṅ gis [7-rtag tu gus pas sgom byed na//
dag gi raṅ bźin kun śes skye bo'i dpaṅ/
sṅon ma mthoṅ ba'i sgyu rtsal tshogs rnams daṅ//
chuṅ ṅu la sogs yon tan brgyad rnams thob//
(7.3) gaṅ gis 'jig rten dbaṅ phyug sgom byed na/
zla ba drug gis rig pa 'dzin par 'gyur//
de yis zas skom stan daṅ padma'i sa//
rdzas la sogs pa mchog rnams ṅes 'byuṅ 'gyur//

---

1 P yid.
2 D, TP bźi yi.
3 P bdag.
4 The rendering is probably a misprint for dwags.
5 D, TP gi.
6 D, TP blta.
7 P missing.

(7.4) gaṅ gis sṅags ni yaṅ dag bzlas byas na//
ñes pa daṅ bcas thams cad spoṅ bar 'gyur//
yon tan thams cad yaṅ dag skye źiṅ brtan//
de phyir ṅal med sems kyis sṅags bzlas bya//

(8) dpal ldan khams gsum dbaṅ byed 'jig rten
dbaṅ phyug gi ni yon tan gsal byed pa'i//
bdag gis sgrub thabs zla ba'i 'od zer
bgyis pa'i gaṅ źig bsod nams stobs kyis ni//
de yis 'gro ba ma lus sñiṅ rje'i
gźan dbaṅ yid kyi mun pa 'joms gyur pa'i//
'gro ba thams cad dbaṅ du byed pa'i
go 'phaṅ thob ciṅ rtag tu źi gyur cig//

'jig rten gsum po dbaṅ du byed pa'i 'phags pa bhu gma'i sgrub thabs rdzogs so// slob dpon dpal ldan śū nya tā sa mā dhi ba dzra pā das mdzad pa'o//[7)]

## 11 (T1) Raktalokeśvarasādhana

rgya gar skad du/ ra kta lo ke śwa ra sā dha naṃ/ bod skad du/ 'jig rten dbaṅ phyug dmar po'i sgrub thabs źes bya ba/

(0) 'jig rten dbaṅ phyug dmar po la phyag 'tshal lo/

(1) oṃ chi ṭi chi ṭi/ bi klo li bi klo li/ che ge mo 'khor daṅ bcas pa bdag gi dbaṅ du 'gyur bar sgrubs swāhā/ sṅon du 'gro ba khri phrag bzlas la[1] phyi nas bsgrub pa brtsam par bya'o//

(2) lho daṅ byaṅ gi ṅos na lha mo sgrol ma daṅ khro gñer can daṅ bcas pa'i rje btsun 'phags pa spyan ras gzigs dbaṅ phyug sku mdog dmar po dbyug pa daṅ phreṅ ba daṅ na bza dmar po daṅ ldan pa phyag bźin źags pa daṅ lcags kyu daṅ mda' daṅ gźu bsnams pa gcig tu sgeg pa'i sñims pa me tog dmar pos/ mdzes par gyur pa'i śiṅ mya ṅan med de'i druṅ na bźugs par bdag ñid thun tshod gsum du bsam par bya ba'o//

(3) lan tshwa daṅ a hu ta'i źes bya ba brgya rtsa brgyad sbyin sreg[2] byas na skyes pa 'am bud med kyaṅ ruṅ ste/ źag bdun na dbaṅ du 'gyur ro// bdun phrag gsum gyis ni skyes bu chen po yaṅ ṅo// lan tshwa daṅ bsres pa'i spra tshil gyi chaṅ bu byas la sor bźi'i tshad kyi gzugs brñan byas te du ba med pa'i seṅ ldeṅ gi sol me la sṅags zlo yin thun tshod gsum du sreg[3] par gyur na gaṅ gi miṅ byas pa dbaṅ du 'gyur ro// rdo rje'i chus bsgos pa'i lan tshwa[4] la lan brgya rtsa brgyad du yoṅs su bsṅags[5] nas gaṅ la byin par gyur pa des zos pa tsam ñid na dbaṅ du 'oṅ ba yin no//

'jig rten dbaṅ phyug dmar po'i sgrubs thabs so// dge sloṅ tshul khrims rgyal mtshan gyis bsgyur ba'o//

---

1 P pa.
2 P bsreg.
3 P srog.
4 D tshwā.
5 P sṅags.

## 11 (T3) Raktalokeśvarasādhana

rgya gar skad du/ ra kta lo ke śwa ra sā dha naṃ/ bod skad du/ 'jig rten dbaṅ phyug dmar po'i sgrub thabs/

(0) 'phags pa spyan ras gzigs dbaṅ phyug la phyag 'tshal lo//

(1) oṃ ci ṭi ci na ṭi/ bi klo li bi klo li/ a mu kaṃ sā dha na pā ri bā ra mme ba śa mā na ya swāhā/ sṅon du bsñen pa khri bzlas nas phyi nas sgrub pa brtsam par bya'o/

(2) g'yas phyogs daṅ[1] g'yon phyogs logs su sgrol ma daṅ khro gñer can te[2] lha mo gñis bźad pa'o// rje btsun 'phags pa spyan ras gzigs dbaṅ phyug sku mdog dmar po phreṅ ba daṅ na bza' dmar pos brgyan ciṅ phyag bźi na źags pa daṅ/ lcags kyu daṅ/ gźu daṅ/ mda' bsnams pa sgeg pa'i ñams daṅ ro gcig pa'o// me tog dmar pos brgyan pa'i mya ṅan med pa'i śiṅ gi 'og tu 'dug nas bdag ñid thun mtshams gsum du bsgom par bya źiṅ

(3) tshwa[3] yis[4] yan lag byugs pa'i sbyin sreg brgya rtsa brgyad bya'o// ñi ma bdun gyi bud med dam skyes pa dbaṅ du 'gyur ro// ñi ma bdun pa gsum gyis skyes bu chen por 'gyur ro/ tshwa daṅ lhan cig chaṅ gis thum po byas nas bsgrub par bya ste/ gzugs brñan sor bźi'i tshad tsam byas nas seṅ ldeṅ gi me du ba med pa la thun mtshams gsum du bsro źiṅ sṅags bzlas pas miṅ gaṅ yin pa de dbaṅ du 'gyur ro// rdo rje'i chu'i raṅ bźin daṅ tshwa la lan brgya rtsa brgyad yoṅs su bzlas nas gaṅ la byin pa de zos pa tsam gyis dbaṅ du 'gyur ro//

'jig rten dbaṅ phyug dmar po'i sgrub thabs rdzogs so//

---

1 P om.
2 P de.
3 P tswas.
4 P om.

## 12 (T3) Lokeśvarasya vaśyādhikāravidhi

rgya gar skad du/ lo ke śva ra sya ba śyā dhi kā[1] ra bi dhiḥ[2]/ bod skad du/ 'jig rten dbaṅ phyug gi[3] lhag par dbaṅ du bya ba'i cho ga//

(0) 'phags pa spyan ras gzigs dbaṅ phyug la phyag 'tshal lo//

(1) sṅon du gsuṅs pa'i cho gas de bźin du stoṅ pa ñid du byas nas/ hrīḥ yig dmar po las skyes pa'i padma dmar po/

(2) de'i dbus su āḥ yig yoṅs su gyur pa las 'phags pa spyan ras gzigs dbaṅ phyug sku mdog dmar po ral pa'i cod dpan can/ 'od dpag tu med pa ral pa'i naṅ du bźugs pa/ phyag g'yon na padma dmar po bsnams pa phyag g'yas pas gsal bar mdzad pa/ sna tshogs pa'i rgyan daṅ gos kyis brgyan pa'i bdag ñid du bskyed la/

(3) raṅ gi sñiṅ gar hrīḥ yig las skyes pa'i padma dmar (4-po'i dab-4) ma la dbyaṅs yig bcu drug gis yoṅs su bskor ba'i gzugs dkar po 'khor bar bsam par bya'o// de nas bsgrub bya'i sñiṅ gar yaṅ sṅon ma bźin du padma bsam źiṅ raṅ gi sñiṅ gar gnas pa'i padma las raṅ gi rdo rje'i lam nas 'khor źiṅ źugs te/ oṃ bhra ma rāḥ sā dhya hri di padmā[5] mri ta mā ka[6] rṣa jaḥ[7] źes pas bsgrub bya'i rdo rje la źugs te/ de'i padma la gnas pa'i bdud rtsi 'khor źiṅ bkug nas de la slar yaṅ de'i rdo rje las 'thon te/ raṅ gi rdo rje'i lam la de bźin du źugs nas sems kyi bdud rtsis sbraṅ gi thig le 'byuṅ źiṅ de la blta bar bya'o//

(4) sṅags ni oṃ hūṃ

(5) ji srid rgyun ma chad par de srid ñi ma bdun bsgoms pas bsgrub bya rkaṅ pa dag gi rtsar lhuṅ bar 'gyur ro//

'jig rten dbaṅ byug gi lhag par dbaṅ du bya ba'i cho ga rdzogs so//

---

1 TP ka.
2 P dhi.
3 TP gis.
4 TP po 'dab.
5 P padma.
6 TP kā.
7 P, D om.

# 13 (T1) Māyājālakramāryāvalokiteśvarasādhana

(1-'phags pa spyan ras gzigs dbaṅ phyug gi sgrub thabs bskor bźugs so//-1) rgya gar skad du/ ā ryā ba lo ki te śwa ra sā dha naṃ/ bod skad du/ 'phags pa spyan ras gzigs dbaṅ phyug gi sgrub thabs/

(1) sṅar bśad pa'i 'tshul gyis stoṅ pa ñid bsgom pa'i rjes thog[2] la

(2.1) nam mkhar ra las ṅes par byuṅ ba'i ñi ma la gnas pa'i yi ge hūṃ las byuṅ ba'i sna tshogs rdo rje yoṅs su gyur pa las/ rdo rje'i ra ba daṅ rdo rje'i gur rnam par bsgom par bya ba'o// de'i dbus su śin tu 'jigs pa'i[3] dur khrod do/ de'i yaṅ dbus su padma dmar po 'dab ma brgyad pa'o//

(2.2) de'i dbus su yaṅ yi ge hrīḥ[4]/ sṅon po las yaṅ dag par byuṅ ba bcom ldan 'das 'phags pa spyan ras gzigs dbaṅ phyug ste/ sku mdog nag po g'yas brkyaṅ ba'i gnas pas ñi ma'i dkyil 'khor la bźugs pa/ źal lṅa pa spyan gsum pa phyag bcu gñis pa g'yas kyi źal gñis ni dkar ba daṅ dmar ba'o// de bźin du g'yon gyi źal gñis ni ser po daṅ ljaṅ gu'o// g'yas kyi phyag rnams na ni ḍa ma ru daṅ kha ṭwāṃ ga daṅ lcags kyu daṅ źags pa daṅ rdo rje daṅ mda' bsnams pa'o// g'yon gyi phyag rnams na ni sdigs mdzub daṅ thod pa daṅ padma dmar po daṅ/ nor bu daṅ 'khor lo daṅ gźu bsnams pa'o// źal thams cad kyaṅ mche ba rnam par gtsigs pa'o// phyag rgya drug daṅ ldan pa 'dzag[5] pa daṅ ldan pa'i mgo bo'i phreṅ bas sku la rgyan du byas pa gcer bu sku thams cad kyaṅ śin tu mdzes par bdag ñid skad cig gis rtogs par byas la/

(3) dus phyis sñiṅ gar zla ba la yi ge hrīḥ dbus su chud par/ oṃ āḥ hūṃ źes bya ba'o// mu ni ba[6] ra brdzre hūṃ dzaḥ źes bya ba'i sṅags 'di phreṅ ba byas la bzlas pa bya ba'o/ mtshams med pa lṅa byes pa rnams kyis kyaṅ 'bum bzlas na 'grub po//

sgyu 'phrul gyi dra ba'i lugs kyis 'phags pa spyan ras gzigs dbaṅ phyug gi sgrub thabs/ paṇḍi ta chen po śā ntā[7] ka ra'i źal sṅa nas dge sloṅ tshul khrims rgyal mtshan gyis bsgyur ba'o//

---

1 D, TP om.
2 D, TP thogs.
3 D, TP pa.
4 P hrī.
5 D 'dzig.
6 P pa.
7 TP nta a.

# 13 (T2) Māyājālakramāryāvalokiteśvarasādhana

(1- sgyu 'phrul dra ba'i rim pa'i spyan ras gzigs kyi sgrub thabs bźugs// -1) rgya gar skad du/ mā yā jā la kra ma[2] a ba lo ki te śwa[3] ra sā dha naṃ/ bod skad du/ sgyu 'phrul[4] dra ba'i rim pa'i spyan ras gzigs dbaṅ phyug gi sgrub pa'i thabs/

(0) 'phags pa spyan ras gzigs dbaṅ phyug la phyag 'tshal lo//

(1) sṅon du bstan pa'i cho gas stoṅ pa ñid bsgoms pa'i rjes su/

(2.1) nam mkha' la ram las byuṅ ba'i ñi ma'i dkyil 'khor la hūṃ/ de yoṅs su gyur pa las/ sna tshogs rdo rje rgya gram/ de yoṅs su gyur pa las rdo rje'i ra ba daṅ/ rdo rje'i gur yaṅ ṅo// de'i naṅ du mi bzad pa'i dur khrod rnam par bsgoms nas/ de'i dbus su padma dmar po 'dab ma brgyad pa/

(2.2) de'i dbus su hrīḥ las byuṅ ba'i bcom ldan 'das 'phags pa spyan ras gzigs dbaṅ phyug mdog nag po/ ñi ma'i dkyil 'khor la g'yon brkyaṅ ba'i źabs kyis gnas par[5] bya'o// źal lṅa pa spyan gsum pa/ phyag bcu gñis pa'o// dkar po daṅ[6] dmar po ni/ g'yas kyi źal gñis so// de bźin du ser po daṅ/ ljaṅ gu ni g'yon gyi źal gñis so// g'yas kyi phyag na rṅe'u chuṅ daṅ/ kha ṭwāṃ ga daṅ/ lcags kyu daṅ/ (7- źags pa daṅ -7)/ rdo rje daṅ/ mda' bsnams pa'o// g'yon na sdigs mdzub daṅ/ thod pa daṅ/ padma dmar po daṅ/ nor bu daṅ/ 'khor lo daṅ// gźu bsnams pa'o/ źal thams cad mche ba gtsigs pa/ phyag rgya drug daṅ ldan pa/ sku la mgo bo rlon pa'i phreṅ bas brgyan pa/ gcer bu g'yon brkyaṅ ba'i źabs kyis bźugs pa/ yan lag thams cad mdzes pa'i bdag ñid du skad cig gis rab tu brtags la/

(3) sñiṅ gar zla ba'i dbus su hrīḥ yig gnas pa'o/ oṃ āḥ hūṃ iti mu ṇi ba ra bdzre hrīḥ hūṃ[8] dzaḥ/ źes bya ba'i sṅags phreṅ ba'i rnam pa can du bzla bar bya'o// mtshams med pa rnam pa lṅa byas pa yaṅ/ 'bum phrag gcig bzlas pas 'grub par 'gyur ro/

sgyu 'phrul dra ba'i rim pa'i 'phags pa spyan ras gzigs dbaṅ phyug gi sgrub thabs/ slob dpon dgra las rnam par rgyal bas mdzad pa rdzogs so// // paṇḍi ta don yod rdo rje daṅ/ khams pa lo tstsha ba dge sloṅ ba ris bsgyur ba'o[9]// //

---

1 D, TP om.
2 P mā.
3 P swa.
4 P 'phral.
5 D, TP pa bsam.
6 P om.
7 P om.
8 P om.
9 P ciṅ źus te gtan la phab pa'o.

# 13 (T3) Māyājālakramāryāvalokiteśvarasādhana

(1-sgyu 'phrul dra ba'i rim pa'i 'phags pa spyan ras gzigs dbaṅ phyug gi sgrub thabs bźugs so//-1) rgya gar skad du/ mā yā dzā la kra (2-ma ārya a ba lo ki te-2) śwa ra sā dha naṃ/ bod skad du/ sgyu 'phrul dra ba'i rim pa'i 'phags pa spyan ras gzigs dbaṅ phyug gi sgrub thabs/

(0) 'phags pa spyan ras gzigs dbaṅ phyug la phyag 'tshal lo/

(1) sṅon du (3-gsuṅs ba'i-3) cho gas 'dir stoṅ pa ñid du bsgoms nas

(2.1) nam mkhar raṃ yig las (4-gyur pa'i-4) ñi ma/ de'i steṅ du hūṃ yig las byuṅ ba'i sna tshogs rdo rje/ de yoṅs su gyur pa las rdo rje'i ra ba daṅ rdo rje'i gur bsgoms par bya'o// de'i dbus su mi bzad pa'i dur khrod do// yaṅ de'i dbus su padma dmar po 'dab ma brgyad pa'o//

(2.2) yaṅ de'i dbus su hūṃ yig sṅon po las byuṅ ba'i bcom ldan 'das 'phags pa spyan ras gzigs dbaṅ phyug sku mdog nag po ñi ma'i dkyil khor la g'yon brkyaṅ gis bźugs pa/ źal lṅa pa/ spyan gsum pa/ phyag bcu gñis pa'o// dkar po daṅ/ dmar po ni g'yas kyi źal gñis so// de bźin du ser po daṅ/ ljoṅ gu dag ni g'yon gyi źal gñis so// g'yas kyi phyag rnams kyis ḍa ma ru daṅ/ kha ṭwāṃ ga daṅ/ lcags kyu daṅ/ źags pa daṅ/ rdo rje daṅ/ mda' rnams[5] bsnams pa/ g'yon gyi phyag rnams kyis sdigs mdzub daṅ/ thod pa daṅ/ padma dmar po daṅ/ nor bu daṅ/ 'khor lo daṅ/ gźu rnams bsnams pa/ źal thams cad mche ba gtsigs pa/ phyag rgya drug daṅ ldan pa/ mgo bo rlon pa'i phreṅ bas skul brgyan pa/ gcer bu yan lag thams cad mdzes pa'i bdag ñid du skad cig gis brtags la/

(3) sñiṅ gar zla ba'i dbus su hrīḥ yig la bskor ba'i oṃ āḥ hūṃ/ i ti mu ni ba[6] ra bdzre hrīḥ[7] hūṃ dzaḥ źes pa'i sṅags kyis phreṅ ba'i rnams par bzlas par bya'o// 'bum bzlas na mtshams med pa lṅa byas pas kyaṅ 'grub par 'gyur ro//

sgyu 'phrul dra ba'i rim pa'i 'phags pa spyan ras gzigs dbaṅ phyug gi sgrub thabs so//

1 D, TP om.
2 P mā ryā lo ke.
3 P gsuṅ pa'i.
4 D byuṅ ba'i.
5 P om.
6 P pa.
7 P hrī.

# 14 (T3) Sopacārāmāsamukhadhāraṇī

(1) nama[1] āryā ba lo ki te śwa rā ya bo dhi satwā[2] ya/ mahā satwā ya/ mahā kā ru ṇi kā ya/ tadya thā/ oṃ tsa la tsa la/ tsi li tsi li/ tsu lu tsu lu/ hū[3] lu hū[4] lu/ mu lu mu lu/ hūṃ hūṃ hūṃ hūṃ/ phaṭ phaṭ phaṭ phaṭ/ padma haste[5] swāhā/ ñi ma re re źiṅ lan lṅar thun mtshams gsum du bzlas par bya'o// boṅ bu yin yaṅ gźuṅ sum brgya 'dzin par 'gyur ro// padma'i phyag gi gzuṅs so//

(2.1) na ma āryā[6] ba lo ki te śwa rā ya bo dhi satwā ya mahā satwā ya/ ma hā kā ru ṇi kā ya/ tadya thā/ oṃ dha ra ṇa[7] dhare[8] (9-dha ra -9) dha re bha (10-dre su bha dre -10) swāhā/

(2.2) zla ba gzas bzuṅ ba'i dus sam yaṅ na ñi ma gzas bzuṅ ba'i[11] tshe ba'i rnam lṅas khrus byas te brgya rtsa brgyad bzlas nas sran ma ṣa khar bcug nas ji srid ma grol gyi bar[12] du[13] de srid tu bzlas par bya'o// 'jig rten mgon po'i bris sku mdun du byas nas mar gyi mar me rab tu sbar te/ tsan dan daṅ sa la ma lhuṅ ba'i ba'i[14] lci bas maṇḍal byas nas spyod lam gtsaṅ ma daṅ bcas pas sgrub pa pos[15] byaṅ phyogs kyi sgor gnas nas raṅ gi zla ba daṅ ñi ma la[16] blta bar mi bya'o//

sṅon du bsñen pa khri bzlas nas//
tshaṅs par spyod pas bsgrub par bya//

(2.3) ma thos pa'i[17] bstan bcos kyaṅ//
rig ciṅ loṅs spyod nus par 'gyur//
thos pa rnams ni mi brjed ciṅ//
gzuṅs[18] 'dzin stobs[19] daṅ ldan par 'gyur//
gaṅ gis spyi bor phye ma yis//
rab tu byin gyur rkaṅ pa daṅ//
thams cad de yis[20] dbaṅ du 'gyur//
ji srid ñi ma zla ba'i bar//
mkha' 'gro ma daṅ gza' daṅ ni//
dgra daṅ nad rnams skye mi 'gyur//

---

1 P, D namaḥ.
2 P satwa.
3 D hu.
4 D hu.
5 P, M ha de.
6 D, TP ārya a.
7 P, TP ṇi; M nī.
8 P dharā.
9 P om.; M dha rā.
10 P tre.
11 M om.
12 TP par.
13 D, TP om.
14 P om.
15 D po.
16 P, M om.
17 D pa yi.
18 P, M gzugs.
19 P, TP stabs.
20 D, TP yi.

byugs pas nad rnams thams cad kyaṅ//
rtag tu rab tu źi bar 'gyur//

(2.4) hrīh yig rkan[1] las byuṅ ba'i[2]//
jig rten mgon po rnam par bsgom/
phyag gñis g'yas pa mchog sbyin daṅ//
g'yon pa pad bsnams sku mdog dkar//
ral pa'i naṅ gnas 'od dpag med//
sna tshogs chu skyes zla ba la/
mgon po rdo rje skyil kruṅ bźugs//
mkhas pas cho ga bźin du bsgom//

ñe bar spyod pa daṅ bcas pa/ (3-sran ma ma ṣa'i-3) źal gyi gzuṅs rdzogs so//

1 The rendering is possibly a misprint for rkaṅ; M rkan.
2 P ba'o.
3 P sran ma ṣa'i.

# Bibliograhpy


Bhattacharyya, Benoytosh

1968a (1924) *The Indian Buddhist Iconography.* Calcutta: Firma K.L.Mukhopadhyay. (Reprint of Second Edition 1958, Revised and Enlarged with 357 Illustrations)

1968b (1925, 1928) *The Sādhanamālā.* 2Vols. Gaekwad's Oriental Series nos. 26, 41, Baroda, Oriental Institute.

Bendall, C.

1883 *Catalogue of the Buddhist Sanskrit Manuscripts in the University Library, Cambridge.* Cambridge: The University Press.

Bühnemann, Gudrun (compiled)

1994 **Sādhanaśataka and *Sādhanaśatapañcaśikā Two Buddhist Sādhana Collections in Sanskrit Manuscript.* Wiener Studien zur Tibetologie und Buddhismuskunde Heft 32, Wien: Arbeitskreis für Tibetische und Buddhistische Studien Universität Wien.

Finot, L.

1934 "Manuscrits Sanskrits de Sādhana's retrouvé en Chine." *Journal Asiatique* 225: 1-85.

Filliozat, Jean

1941 *Catalogue du Fonds Sanscrit.* Fascicule I, Paris.

Foucher, A.

1900, 1905 *Étude sur l'Iconographie Bouddhique de l'Inde.* Bibliothèque de l'École des Hautes Études Sciences Religieuses Treizième volume 2e partie, Paris: Ernst Leroux, Éditure.

Goshima, Kiyotaka and Noguchi, Keiya (compiled)

1983 *A Succinct Catalogue of the Sanskrit Manuscripts in the Posession of the Faculty of Letters, Kyoto University.* Kyoto.

Grünendahl, Reinhold

1989 *A Concordance of H. P. Śāstri's Catalogue of the Durbar Library and the Microfilms of the Nepal-German Manuscript Preservation Project.* Stuttgart: Franz Steiner Verlag Wiesbaden GMBH.

Hara Prasād Shāstri, Mahāmahopādhyāya (ed.)

1915 *A Catalogue of Palm-leaf & Selected Paper MSS belonging to the Durbar Library, Nepal.* Vol. II, Calcutta: The Baptist Mission Press.

1917 *A Descriptive Catalogue of Sanscrit Manuscripts in the Government Collection Under the Care of the Asiatic Society of Bengal.* Vol. I, Buddhist Manuscripts. Calcutta.

Koetsuka Takashi

1967 "Meiso to Zokei." *Nanto Bukkyo (Journal of the Nanto Society for Buddhist Studies)* 20: 60-79. (in Japanese)

Lokesh Chandra

1987 *Buddhist Iconography newly revised and enlarged edition.* 2 Vols. Śata-Piṭaka Series Vol. 342, New Delhi: Aditya Prakashan.

Mallmann, Marie-Thérèse de

1948 *Introduction a l'Étuede d'Avalokiteśvara.* Ministère de l'Éducation Nationale Annales du Musée Guimet Bobliothèque d'Étude - Tome Cinquante-Septième, Paris: Civilisations du Sud.

1964 *Étuede Iconographique sur Mañjuśrī*. Paris: École Française d'Éxtrême-Orient Vol. LV.

Matsunami, Seiren (ed.)

1965 *The Catalogue of the Sanskrit Manuscripts of the Tokyo University Library*. Tokyo: Suzuki Research Foundation.

Meisezahl, R.O.

1980 *Geist und Ikonographie des Vajrayāna-Buddhismus*. Beiträge Zentralasienforshung Band 2, Sankt Augstin: VGH Wissenschaftsverlag.

Mori, Masahide

1992 "The Sādhana Practice of Mahāmāyā." *The Mikkyo Zuzo (The Journal of the Buddhist Iconography)* 11: 23-43. (in Japanese)

Moriguchi, Mitsutoshi

1989 *A Catalogue of the Buddhist Tantric Manuscripts in the National Archives of Nepal and Kesar Library*. Tokyo: Sankibou Busshorin.

Nihom, M.

1992 "The Goddess with the Severed Head: a recension of Sādhanamālā 232, 234 and 238 attributed to the Siddhācārya Virūpā." *Ritual, State and History in South Asia*. A. W. Van Den Hoek, D. H. A. Kloff, M. S. Oort (ed.), Leiden/ New York/ Köln: E. J. Brill, pp.222-243.

Okuyama, Naoji

1988 " Two Problems Relating to the Development of the Buddhist Pantheon in Tibet." *Journal of Indian and Buddhist Studies* 34-2: 94-100. (in Japanese)

1998 "On Sādhanaśataka." *Journal of Indian and Buddhist Studies* 46 (2): 914-919. (in Japanese)

Petech, Luciano

1984 (1958) *Mediaeval History of Nepal*. Serie Orientale Roma Vol. LIV, Roma: Is.M.E.O.

Pūrṇaratnavajrācārya Sāhityaśāstriṇā (ed.)

1964 *Nepālarājakīya-Vīrapustakālayasthahastalikhitasamastapustakānām Saṃkṣiptasūcīpatram*. Purātattvaprakāśanamālā 18, Kāṭhmāṇḍhū: Vīrapustakālaya.

1967 *Nepālarājakīya-Vīrapustakālayasthahastalikhitasamastapustakānāṃ Bṛhatsūcīpatram*. Purātattvaprakāśanamālā 39, Kāṭhmāṇḍhū: Vīrapustakālaya.

Sakuma, Ruriko

1990a "The Sanskrit Manuscripts of the *Sādhanamālā*." *TOKAI-BUKKYO (Journal of Tokai Association of Indian and Buddhist Studies)* 35: 88-103. (in Japanese)

1990b "Iconographical Material for the Study of Tantric Buddhism in India (1): The *Sādhanas* of Siṃhanāda-Avalokiteśvara in the *Sādhanamālā*." *Bulletin of the National Museum of Ethnology* 15 (2): 511-564. (in Japanese)

1991 "On the Sādhanas of Avalokiteśvara expounded in the *Sādhanamālā*." *The Mikkyo Zuzo (The Journal of the Buddhist Iconography)* 10: 1-16. (in Japanese)

1993 "Jñānasattva and Samayasattva in the *Sādhanamālā*." *Indogaku Mikkyogaku Kenkyū: Miyasaka Yūsho Hakase Kokikinen Ronbunshū*. Kyoto: Hozokan, pp.793-807. (in Japanese)

1995 "Translation on *sādhana*s of Khasarpaṇa Lokeśvara." *Nanto Bukkyo (Journal of the Nanto Society for Buddhist Studies)* 71: 13-28. (in Japanese)

1996 "A Study of Visualization on Ṣaḍakṣarī Lokeśvara." *TOKAI-BUKKYO (Journal of Tokai Association of Indian and Buddhist Studies)* 41: 83-94. (in Japanese)

1998 "Visualization based on the Teaching of the *Kāraṇḍavyūha*: A Study of Visualization on Ṣaḍakṣarī Lokeśvara (II)." *TOKAI-BUKKYO (Journal of Tokai Association of Indian and Buddhist Studies)* 43: 103-116. (in Japanese)

1999 "An Introduction to a Study of Avalokiteśvara in India and Nepal: Expressions of generosity and appeasement on the Iconography of Trailokyavaśaṅkara Lokeśvara." *The Journal of the Nippon Buddhist Research Association* LXIV: 91-104. (in Japanese)

2000 "A Study of the Avalokiteśvaras in the *Sādhanamālā*. " D.Lit. dissertation (Nagoya University, Japan). (in Japanese) (unpublished)

2001a "Sanskrit Manuscripts of the *Sādhanamālā*." *Nagoya Studies in Indian Culture and Buddhism: Saṃbhāṣā* 21: 27-43. (a revised English edition of Sakuma[1990a])

2001b "Sādhana practice." *Iyashi to Sukui (Healing and Salvation)*. M. Tachikawa (ed.) Tamagawa University Press, pp.227-244. (in Japanese)

Sanskrit Seminar of Taisho University

1955 "Buddhist Manuscrits of the Bir Library." *Memoirs of Taisho University* 40: 55-84. (in Japanese)

Shimizu, Tadashi

1977 "Dhyāna (image) and Religious Observance in the *Sādhanamālā*." *The Journal of the Nippon Buddhist Research Association* 43: 59-72. (in Japanese)

Shimoizumi, Zengyo

1981 "On the Kyoto University Manuscript of the *Sādhanamālā*.' *Journal of Indian and Buddhist Studies* 30(1): 136-137. (in Japanese)

Takaoka, Hidenobu. (ed.)

1981 *A Microfilm Catalogue of the Buddhist Manuscripts in Nepal.* Vol.1, Nagoya: Buddhist Library.

Thomas, F. W.

1903 "Deux collections sanscrites et tibetaines de Sādhanas." *Le Museon* 4: 1-42.

Tsukamoto, Keisho/ Matsunaga, Yukei/ Isoda, Hirofumi (ed.)

1989 *A Descriptive Bibliography of the Sanskrit Buddhist Literature*, Vol.IV (The Buddhist Tantra). Kyoto: Herakuji shoten. (in Japanese)

Yamada, Ryūjo

1959 *Bongo butten no shobunken: daijobukkyoseiritsujosetsu shiryohen.* Heirakuji shoten. (in Japanese)

Yamaguchi, Shinobu

1997 "The Saptākṣaramantra of Saṃvara: Sādhanamālā 251." *Journal of Indian and Buddhist Studies* 46(1): 398-404. (in Japanese)

Yoshizaki, Kazumi

1979 "A Critical Study of the Sādhanamālā (1)." *Bulletin of the Graduate School, Toyo University Graduate Program of Liberal Arts* 16:15-31. (in Japanese)